WITHDRAWN

WITHDRAWN

Metacognition, Motivation, and Understanding

THE PSYCHOLOGY OF EDUCATION AND INSTRUCTION

A series of volumes edited by:
Robert Glaser and **Lauren Resnick**

METACOGNITION, MOTIVATION, AND UNDERSTANDING

Edited by

Franz E. Weinert
Max-Planck Institute for Psychological
Research, Munich

Rainer H. Kluwe
University of Bundeswehr, Hamburg

LAWRENCE ERLBAUM ASSOCIATES, PUBLISHERS
1987   Hillsdale, New Jersey   London

Lawrence Erlbaum Associates, Inc., Publishers
365 Broadway
Hillsdale, New Jersey 07642

Library of Congress Cataloging-in-Publication Data
Metakognition, Motivation und Lernen.
   Metacognition, motivation, and understanding.

   Translation of: Metakognition, Motivation, und Lernen.
   "Based on the Heidelberg symposium on 'The Development
of Metacognition, the Formation of Attribution Styles,
and Learning' at Heidelberg University . . . sponsored by
the German Foundation 'Volkswagenwerk,' Hannover"—Pref.
   Bibliography: p.
   1. Learning, Psychology of—Congresses.   2. Metacognition—Congresses.   3. Motivation in education—Congresses.
4. Cognition—Congresses.   I. Weinert, Franz E., 1930–
II. Kluwe, Rainer.   III. Title.

LB1065.M3813 1987   370.15   86–29223
ISBN 0-89859-569-X

Printed in the United States of America
10 9 8 7 6 5 4 3

Contents

Contributors to This Volume

ANN L. BROWN · Center for the Study of Reading, University of Illinois at Urbana-Champaign, 51 Gerty Drive, Champaign, IL 61820

JOSEPH C. CAMPIONE · Center for the Study of Reading, University of Illinois at Urbana-Champaign, 51 Gerty Drive, Champaign, IL 61820

MICHELENE T. H. CHI · Learning Research and Development Center, University of Pittsburgh, 3939 O'Hara Street, Pittsburgh, PA 15260

JOHN H. FLAVELL · Department of Psychology, Stanford University, Jordan Hall, Stanford, CA 94305

ROBERT GLASER · Learning Research and Development Center, University of Pittsburgh, 3939 O'Hara Street, Pittsburgh, PA 15260

JAMES G. GREENO · University of California, Berkeley, Berkeley, CA 94720

HEINZ HECKHAUSEN · Max-Planck-Institut für Psychologische Forschung Leopold Strasse 24, 8000 Munich 40, Germany

RAINER H. KLUWE · Universität der Bundeswehr, Abt. Allg. Psychologie, Holstenhofweg 85, 2000 Hamburg 70, Germany

JULIUS KUHL · Max-Planck Institut für Psychologische Forschung, Leopold Strasse 24, 8000 Munich 40, Germany

JAMES W. PELLEGRINO · School of Education, University of California, Santa Barbara, CA 93106

CHRISTOPHER PETERSON · University of Pennsylvania, Department of Psychology, University of Pennsylvania, 3015 Walnut Street, Philadelphia, PA 19104

MARY R. RILEY · Learning Research and Development Center, University of Pittsburgh, 3939 O'Hara Street, Pittsburgh, PA 15260

MARTIN E. P. SELIGMAN · Department of Psychology, University of Pennsylvania, 3015 Walnut Street, Philadelphia, PA 19104

FRANZ E. WEINERT · Max-Planck Institut für psychologische Forschung, Leopold Strasse 24, 8000 Munich, Germany

Preface

This volume is based on the Heidelberg Symposium on "The Development of Metacognition, the Formation of Attribution Styles, and Learning" at Heidelberg University. The Conference was sponsored by the German Foundation "Volkswagenwerk," Hannover.

During the last few years developmental research concerned with metacognition, attribution styles, and self-instruction extended rapidly. Though there are common theoretical concepts, as well as research questions, all three fields have been studied separately.

Metacognition refers to cognition about cognition, and means knowledge about one's own thinking, and cognitive activity having as its object own thinking processes. *Attribution styles* are considered to be motivational preferences with respect to explanations of own success and failure, given different types of tasks. *Self-instruction* refers to the way and the degree to which a subject initiates, plans and organizes, monitors and regulates own learning processes.

All three approaches refer to the acquisition and availability of knowledge about cognition, and of cognitive processes to monitor and regulate the stream of own thinking. This volume represents a first step to integrate these fields of developmental research with respect to their theoretical basis, and with respect to some of the results. The contributors to this volume are considered to be experts in their field.

The research reported here is important for the elaboration of theories of cognitive development. Furthermore, this work has consequences for educational strategies and related applied problems.

F. E. Weinert
R. H. Kluwe

Introduction and Overview:
Metacognition and Motivation as Determinants of Effective Learning and Understanding

F. E. Weinert
Max-Planck-Institute for Psychological Research
Munich

> *Also, if somebody knows something, then he knows that he knows it, and at the same time he knows that he knows that he knows.*
> —Spinoza, 1632–1677

Do you learn more effectively when you know how to learn? Do you learn more effectively when you are highly motivated? Although our intuitions suggest positive answers to each of these questions, everyday experiences provide counter-examples. On the one hand, we can all think of remarkable accomplishments made by people who consciously employ special techniques for learning. Examples are actors or orchestra conductors who learn vast amounts of material for performances, or mnemonists, the "memory experts," who entertain us with the size and precision of their memories. On the other hand, a group of people without such techniques—for instance children—also learn and remember large amounts of material. A general belief is that children are more effective learners than adults. For example, over half the students in an introductory psychology class believed that children's memories are better than adults' memories (Vaughan, 1977).

Contradictory examples also come to mind when we ask about the effects of motivation on learning. We can imagine a student studying for an important exam whose extreme motivation to do well actually interferes with efficient learning; however, many school children who seem less gifted than their peers learn effectively when they are keenly interested and highly motivated.

Everyday experience does not provide definitive answers to our questions about what contributes to effective learning. Can we find a clarification of the

1

effects of skill and motivation on learning at the level of scientific theory? That is, does the present psychology of learning and memory provide us with an adequate, acceptable model for analyzing learning effectiveness and the factors affecting it? A direct answer to this would have to be negative. This unsatisfactory situation is due to several reasons, among them the pragmatic fact that learning in everyday situations is variable and complex, and thus difficult to study, and the historical fact that such questions have been largely neglected in traditional learning research. However, this situation is changing. Over the last 15 years, converging ideas arising from different theoretical perspectives are being systematically developed and integrated, promising that a better understanding of intra– and inter–individual differences in learning effectiveness may now be possible.

GENERAL LAWS OF LEARNING AND INDIVIDUAL LEARNING EFFICIENCY

Regardless of the definition and the theoretical explanation of learning used, the goal of learning psychology has traditionally been to formulate general laws of learning, valid for all humans if not all higher organisms. Although Hermann Ebbinghaus (1885), the founder of modern learning research, recognized the endless individual differences in human memory, he nonetheless called for and initiated the study of general, universal laws of learning. Beginning with this research, learning was the central focus of empirical efforts, and the learner was considered as a source of error to be ignored or controlled for in the description of lawful regularities governing the average human. Earlier, Wilhelm Wundt cautioned that "there is not a single psychological law that does not admit to more exceptions than confirmations" (1886, p. 473), but this observation was not sufficient to encourage a parallel development of a psychology of individual differences in learning and memory. However, even the most strident follower of a behaviorist perspective had to admit that people differed with respect to learning effectiveness, even when external conditions were held constant. The dilemma this posed was resolved by positing empirically definable, static individual difference parameters, such as IQ, which could be inserted into general formulas to describe learning (Hull, 1945). The theoretical problems arising from such a solution were expressed clearly by Woodrow (1942):

> Now these parameters may refer to anything whatsoever, conscious, physiological, environmental, psychic, or purely imaginary. Here one is free to follow his predilections, whether for motives, excitatory or inhibitory substance, field forces, states of disequilibrium, inertia of the nervous system, abilities, or what not. (p. 4)

Despite the problems in delineating what the relevant dimensions of individual differences might be, there were some interesting early studies that emphasized individual differences in learning effectiveness. Noteworthy among these were: the psychometric classification of memory abilities (Spearman, 1927), the consideration of effects of pre-experimental learning experience on verbal learning in the lab (Plenderleith & Postman, 1957), studies on motivational and social influences on recall (Bartlett, 1932; Zeigarnik, 1927), the demonstration of a relationship between personality and learning (Eysenck, 1957; Pawlow, 1953), experiments on the importance of learning habits and study skills for success at school (Robinson, 1941), and the many studies showing developmental differences in learning and memory performance (Netschajeff, 1900; review of early studies by McGeoch & Irion, 1952). Although there are other noteworthy examples of an early psychology of individual differences, none of these findings altered the intensive search for general regularities in human learning.

The emphasis in the attempt to find regularities in learning began to change in the 1950s when a "new look" (Bugelski, 1956) in learning research occurred, a change that mirrored the new look in theories of cognition and memory. Although theories of cognition and memory were also clearly oriented toward formulating general and universal processes, individual differences assumed a new role. Differences in the learner's prior knowledge base, in available cognitive processes and in learning and memory strategies, were used to explain inter– and intra–individual performance variation in learning and memory tasks. One lasting result of this new look is that it is, at present, not clear at what level of generalization regularities in learning, forgetting, and remembering should be formulated.

Do individual learning histories result in different functional relations between the external parameters of learning situations and learning outcomes (e.g., an aptitude-treatment interaction)? Or should one hypothesize functional invariance in the relation between input and outcome (i.e., a universal learning mechanism)? More concretely, one observes learning differences when younger and older children, or experts and novices, or people differing in intelligence levels are compared. Do these differences arise because the older, more expert, or more intelligent people learn faster, more or better (e.g., they have similar, but more efficient learning mechanisms), or do they arise because of more fundamental differences in how different people learn, and if so, what are these differences?

Although these are important theoretical questions, contemporary empirical efforts are reasonably enough not focused on answering such broad issues. Rather, contemporary work is focused on the clarification of several, more specific issues concerning learning and memory. The development and effects of differences in learning competence plays a limited but noteworthy role in current explanations of differences in learning effectiveness.

COMPETENCE AND PERFORMANCE AS DETERMINANTS OF INDIVIDUAL LEARNING EFFECTIVENESS

When one reviews the history of scientific concern with individual differences in learning effectiveness, it is clear that static approaches have overshadowed dynamic ones. This is not surprising if one considers that psychological thinking in this century is deeply rooted in the "faculty psychology" of past eras. From the faculty psychology perspective, it seems self-evident that individual differences in learning and memory performance can be explained by stable capacity differences in the learner. A classic example of this viewpoint is a formula developed by Thurstone (1930) to express the amount of time required to learn nonsense syllable lists. In contrast to many learning theorists of his time, Thurstone did not consider that the time required to learn a list of items was a simple function of the number of items. Instead, he added two individual difference parameters, memory span and learning capacity. His formula is as follows:

$$T = c/k \, (n \, \sqrt{n\text{-}a} \;)$$

In this formula, T is the time required to recall a row of syllables, c and n are variables for the task conditions: c refers to the criterion for learning in the particular task and n refers to the number of items in the list. K and a are individual difference variables: k is a constant for the individual's learning capacity and a is a constant for the learner's memory span. It proved relatively easy to determine a measure for a, the memory span constant (although by 1925 Guilford and Dallenbach had compiled at least 16 memory span measures). However, it did not prove possible to find a useful measure for k, the learning capacity constant in Thurstone's formula. Despite many attempts to determine a valid measure on the basis of general intelligence or specific memory abilities, this construct could not be operationalized (McGeogh & Irion, 1952). Later attempts by developmental psychologists to explain age-dependent changes in learning and memory performance in terms of the development of general intellectual competence of general memory capacity met a similar lack of success (see Weinert, 1979). Learning performance, whether in experimental or school settings, could not be predicted on the basis of correlations with either global or specific capacities (McNemar, 1964).

Attempts to predict learning and memory performance met with more success when researchers began to move away from the psychometric classification of learning capacities and began to analyze those cognitive structures and processes that were postulated as necessary components for solving items specific to cognitive abilities. An important impetus for this line of reasoning was Glaser's (1972) conceptualization of the "new aptitudes" and his related empirical work. Glaser and Pellegrino (this volume) summarize this work:

The research carried out along these lines is predicated on the assumption that aptitude tests should be viewed as more than primarily predictors of achievement. Rather, such tests should assist in identifying the processes involved in intellectual competence, and further indicate how these processes can be influenced and utilized to benefit learning. (p. 267)

The analysis of competence in terms of rule induction allowed Glaser and Pellegrino (this volume) to identify:

Three interrelated factors . . . that appear to differentiate high and low skill individuals. One is the management of memory as this is reflected by speed of performance and the handling of demands on working memory. Secondly, individuals show differences in their knowledge of the constraints of problem-solving procedures. . . Thirdly, the structure of the declarative-conceptual knowledge base and the level of representation of this knowledge differ as a function of ability. High skill individuals employ conceptual forms of knowledge that constrain their induction of relations, whereas low skill individuals encode their knowledge at more concrete surface levels; this is manifested by their limited inferential power. (p. 285)

Greeno and Riley (this volume) studied the comprehension of mathematical problems, and provide empirical support for the theoretical distinction between problem schemata (semantic knowledge) and action schemata (procedural knowledge—plans for solving problems, knowledge about actions at different levels of generality). M. Chi (this volume) similarly differentiates domain specific knowledge, general strategies, and metacognitive knowledge as determinants of learning and memory performance. In this development there has been a general emphasis on the individual's accessible, domain-specific knowledge. Here, command over facts is ascribed less important than the availability of relevant concepts and rules. Chi (1978), for example, demonstrated that many typical age differences in memory performance can be explained by differences in the knowledge base: developmental differences in memory were equalized or even reversed when younger experts and older non-experts (novices) were compared in a specific content domain (chess). These results have since been replicated many times.

In addition to declarative knowledge, the authors of the chapters pertaining to learning psychology in this volume postulate another form of knowledge, one that is important for the discussion of planning and self-direction in problem-solving on specific tasks. This procedural knowledge allows the learner to use and manipulate his skills and knowledge through the organization of learning activities. Such process-related aspects of learning have been emphasized in the recent developmental literature. There are three frameworks that emphasize this perspective:

(1) The meaning of activity, actions, and related experiences for the ontogeny of mental abilities is emphasized in the soviet literature. For example, Rubinstein (1969) defined *competence* as "systems of generalized psychic activities, that are fixed in the individual" (p. 110). According to this theoretical viewpoint, the study of the nature and development of human abilities must take into account the demands of the socio-cultural environment, and the objectives of the individual. Integrating both these demands, this approach begins with a broad, functional analysis of actions in social context. This perspective, applied to the study of learning and memory, raises some interesting developmental questions, although as yet there have been few definitive findings (Reese, 1979; Meacham, 1983).

(2) Development during middle childhood is increasingly interpreted in terms of an increase in competence and self-regulation. Piaget's concept of biological and cognitive autoregulation is an important point of departure for this interpretation (see Piaget, 1976, 1978; Brown, this volume). According to Piaget (1971):

> What knowledge really consists of is not just the acquisition and accumulation of information, since that alone would remain inert and sightless, as it were. But knowledge organizes and regulates this information by means of autocontrol systems directed toward adaptation, in other words, toward the solving of its problems. (p. 61)

Investigations of knowledge over one's actions and over the self as actor are one example of the psychological interest in self-control systems. The assumptions underlying such studies of metacognitive development have been described by W. Mischel (1981):

> We view children as potentially sophisticated (albeit fallible) intuitive psychologists who come to know and use psychological principles for understanding social behavior, for regulating their own conduct, and for achieving increasing mastery and control over their environments. (p. 240)

In addition to the formation of self-regulatory skills, a number of other processes have been studied within the framework of motivation and personality research. These include the development of control beliefs (Bandura, 1981; Krampen, 1982), causal attributions (Heckhausen, this volume; Peterson & Seligman, this volume), and other regulatory factors connected with achievement-related actions (Heckhausen, 1982; Trudewind, 1982).

(3) Research oriented toward a micro-genetic perspective emphasizes that learning and remembering are not simply determined by available learning and memory abilities, but that one must also consider the meaning of the learning activities in the specific task situation. In this orientation, system-theoretic approaches (Carver & Scheier, 1981) and action-theoretic approaches (Hacker, Volpert, & von Cranach, 1982) play an often mixed role. The main interests are

in questions of how task perception, action goals, planning, regulation, self-evaluation, and self-correction are related to task behavior, as well as how experience is utilized in the learning process, and how the experience of success or failure is processed. This orientation focuses on how cognitions and motivations guide learning-related actions (see Kluwe, this volume; Kuhl, this volume).

METACOGNITION AND MOTIVATION AS DETERMINANTS OF INDIVIDUAL LEARNING ACTIVITY

To illustrate the phenomena that should be studied in order to analyze how metacognition and motivation may affect learning activities, imagine a student attending a lecture just before an important examination. From the beginning of the lecture, the student concentrates on comparing what is being said with what he already knows in order to find out what information he lacks. If the student perceives a gap in his knowledge, he may attempt to take notes on the relevant information, to understand it, or if possible, to memorize it. If the student has the impression that these efforts have not been successful, hectic activities or passive resignation may appear.

After the lecture the student may try to borrow notes from a fellow student, for further study. If so, we could also observe learning activities from a written text: the student skims the contents, underlines important passages, looks up or studies unclear parts, memorizes important points by silently repeating them, and finally checks whether he has successfully mastered the material. We may then observe different emotional reactions, depending on whether the student is pleased or not with the achieved results. If we could then question this imaginary student about the reasons for his various activities, he might tell us how his assessment of his own knowledge compares with his expectations about the demands of the upcoming examination, and about the difficulties he has with the material. In addition, we may learn about the student's preferred learning strategies, and his evaluation of his own situation and the possible consequences.

It seems intuitively obvious that behaviors such as those just described must have an important effect on learning effectiveness. Indeed, asking what such effects might be is the focus of many lively research efforts subsumed under the labels of *metacognition* and *achievement motivation*.

What Are "Metacognitions" and What Effects Do They Have on Learning Behavior and Learning Performance?

Psychology in general, and developmental psychology in particular, are presently awash in a "meta" flood (metacognition, metacommunication, metamemory, metalanguage, and so on). Although some believe that these constructs reflect a new and stimulating research perspective (e.g., Paris & Lindauer, 1982), others find fault with the vague and often arbitrary distinction between cognition and metacognition. Apart from this fundamental controversy, the construct of metacognition is very attractive, especially within developmental psychology, as suggested by a number of recent review articles (Brown, this volume; Cavanaugh & Perlmutter, 1982; Schneider, 1985; Wellman, 1983). At first blush, this attraction may seem paradoxical. Most developmental authors agree with Cavanaugh and Perlmutter's (1982) evaluation: "the present state of metamemory is not good" (p. 22). However, they also would agree with Cavanaugh and Perlmutter's further argument that the concept is useful, and should be retained, and with their call for an intensification of research in the area. The reasons for interest in an increase in metacognitive research are presented in several chapters in this volume: Brown; Campione; Chi; Flavell; Kluwe; Kuhl. In this volume we present only a brief introduction to the themes, findings, problems and perspectives of metacognition research.

On the surface, it seems easy to distinguish between cognition and metacognition. *Metacognitions* are second-order cognitions: thoughts about thoughts, knowledge about knowledge, or reflections about actions. However, problems arise when one attempts to apply this general definition to specific instances. These problems concern whether metacognitive knowledge must be utilized, whether it must be conscious and verbalizable, and whether it must be generalized across situations. For example, should someone who has learned from a psychology textbook that distributed practice is more effective than massed practice, but who does not apply this knowledge in actual learning situations, be granted metacognitive knowledge of learning processes? Or, consider a child who takes more time to study difficult than easy items when learning a word list (a learning strategy), but who is not aware of the easy-difficult distinction, and who is unable to describe his learning strategy. Does this child have metacognitive knowledge? Finally, consider a driver who strategically finds clever short cuts when travelling in a familiar part of town, but who becomes disoriented in unfamiliar districts. Should the driver be denied metacognitive knowledge because it is not always displayed? The problems in answering such questions highlight the criticism that the working definition of metacognition is vague and imprecise.

Similar difficulties arise when one considers a specific type of metacognition, metamemory. *Metamemory* is generally defined as: the knowledge one has about memory in general; knowledge about the peculiarities of one's own memory system; sensitivity to past experience with memorizing, storing, and retrieving different types of information in various situations; and a system of skills for planning, directing, monitoring, and evaluating one's behavior during learning and remembering. Such an omnibus definition does not easily afford a theoretically or thematically coherent research program. Indeed, the field is characterized by a variety of different lines of research that have little in common apart from the label "metamemory." Examples of this variety are studies on: declarative metaknowledge, executive processes, the relationship between domain specific knowledge and metaknowledge, predictions and evaluations about one's own achievements, and so on. The data collection procedures are similarly variable and include interviews and "thinking aloud," questionnaires and rating scales, and observations of behavioral indicators of metacognitive activity. It is not surprising that the empirical relations among such diverse measures are variable—a finding that, often noted, need not speak against the utility of the construct of metamemory.

The metamemory framework is used to provide explanations for some phenomena, and to generate practical suggestions for improving cognitive processes. For example, lack of metamemorial knowledge is used to account for the production deficiency of younger children (available and useful memory strategies were/are not used, Flavell, 1970). On the applied side, training programs for metacognitive skills have, in many cases, led to stable improvements in reading, learning, and memory achievements in both average (Pressley, Forrest-Pressley, & Elliot-Faust, in press) and below average subjects (Campione, this volume). In addition, metacognitive variables have proved to be the best predictors of memory performance differences for both children and adults (Weinert, Knopf, & Barann, 1983; Weinert, Knopf, & Körkel, 1983). Given these positive results, why then is the construct metamemory criticized? Although some of the problems, such as the diversity in research questions, procedures, and operationalization have been previously summarized, there are three points that bear additional comment:

(1) The conceptualization and operationalization of constructs like metamemory are hampered by the "consciousness" problem, a persistently unsolved issue in psychology. Although this issue is frequently omitted (or ignored) in studies of cognition, it is not possible to do so when investigating metacognition, where the measures may include introspection or verbal reports about one's own behavior, and where the relation between tacit, implicit, and explicit knowledge is important. As Brown (this volume) points out, one's position with respect to consciousness and implicit knowledge influences the collection, analysis, and interpretation of metamemory data.

(2) The relationship of memory performance and metamemory remains unclear, both theoretically and empirically. Based on a statistical meta-analysis of approximately 50 studies, Schneider (1985) concluded:

In sum, the meta-analytical findings confirmed the assumption that different patterns of correlations can be found for different classes of memory tasks and strategies, and that developmental trends are demonstrable for the memory-metamemory relationship within each paradigm. On the other hand, most of the numerical values obtained for the different relationships were surprisingly high. A mean correlation of .41 between metamemory and memory behavior-performance based on the data of several hundred subjects clearly contradicts the conclusion conveyed in most reviews of the field that only a weak link between the two variables had been found. Rather the quantitative integration of the empirical findings does indicate that metamemory is substantially related to memory behavior and performance. (p. 98)

In fact, the average relationship between memory performance and metamemory reported by Schneider does seem surprisingly high, and one should not overlook the considerable variation among the results from different studies. More surprising, however, is that many developmental psychologists seem to expect or hope for such strong relationships between memory and metamemory. For one thing, we know that task difficulty may determine whether we should expect a relation between memory and metamemory at all. On extremely difficult tasks, the use of metamemory may not lead to a solution, but may lead only to the realization that further effort will not be productive. Conversely, on easy tasks, metacognitive differences do not contribute to performance variance. It is only for tasks of medium difficulty, where strategic solutions are possible, that learning behavior and performance can be positively influenced by metamemory skills. Thus, the functional relation between metamemory and memory performance must be task– and population–specific. Because the difficulty of any task changes with general cognitive development, as well as with increasing expertise, in principle it is not possible to expect a stable and general pattern of correlations between indicators of metamemory and memory performance.

(3) *Metacognition* is often regarded as referring to general and flexible knowledge that is not domain specific. It is apparent that in research where relatively easy and content-general tasks are used (e.g., reading and learning from simple texts, memorizing and free recall of word lists, and so on), both the effects of domain-specific knowledge and the role of content-dependent strategies and metastrategies for learning will be minimized (Chi, this volume; Glaser & Pellegrino, this volume; Greeno & Riley, this volume). Although resolving the problem of the role of domain specific content in the assessment of knowledge is crucial for planning empirical studies and developing adequate models of metacognitive knowledge, the failure to do so has done little to detract from the popularity of the metacognitive research domain. However, tackling the problem is especially important for studies in the field of developmental psychology because substantial changes in knowledge, abilities, and executive skills occur that, in comparison to simple autoregulations, allow higher forms of self-regulatory, goal-adaptive actions and thoughts (Körkel, 1984).

Is There a Relationship Between Metacognition and Motivation Based on Their Effects on Learning Behavior and Learning Performance?

The distinctions between knowledge about the self and self-related beliefs, between predictions of one's future performance and related hopes and fears, and between observations of one's own behavior and related, ongoing self-evaluation are difficult to make, both in everyday experience and in psychological investigations. An attempt to integrate motivation and metacognition means one must relate theoretical concepts concerned with knowledge about the self, performance expectations and monitoring of one's own actions as perceived in the metacognition literature with concepts such as self-perception of ability, expectation of success and fear of failure, causal attributions for success and failure, and processes of self-evaluation, from the motivation research domain. These two research traditions, metacognition and motivation, have as yet been largely independent, with little common ground. Nonetheless, there is some apparent overlap in the variables the two research traditions consider and in how these variables are operationalized, as suggested in Table 1. The points of similarity in the phenomena studied, questions asked, and variables considered have not been completely ignored. To illustrate: Brown has frequently noted that close relationship between metacognition and motivation; the relationship between metacognitive judgment and causal attributions for success and failure has been studied (Fabricius & Hagen, 1984; Kurtz & Borkowski, 1984); metacognitive and motivational determinants of memory performance have been analyzed (Weinert, Knopf, & Barann, 1983); and it has been suggested that the concept of metamemory be expanded into a scientific theory of naive models of memory with motivational components (Wellman, 1983; see also Dixon & Hertzog, in press).

Although it is noteworthy to point out the similarities, it is also important to keep in mind the different perspectives of the two research traditions. For example, a central point in the analysis of metacognition is the extent to which an individual's metacognitive judgments correspond to the actual state of affairs, whether the judgments are about abilities, learning strategies, or task difficulty. In contrast, researchers studying motivation are more concerned with individual biases and subjective distortions in tasks (such as setting aspiration levels, explaining success or failure, evaluating outcomes, or assessing personal ability).

However, despite the differences in perspective, some very similar and valid predictions concerning behavior and performance have been proposed by researchers from each area (see Schneider, 1985, for metacognition; see Kuhl, 1983; Peterson & Seligman, this volume; Stipek & Weisz, 1981, for motivation). Indeed, interesting new questions arise from a consideration of the somewhat different findings from metacognitive and motivation research. For

TABLE 1.1
A Summary of Similar Variables and Their Different Functions in
Motivation and Metacognition Research

Motivation Research	*Metacognition Research*
1. Judgments of task difficulty as a function of one's own experience	
—Performance expectations	—Performance predictions
—Setting aspiration levels	—Action planning
—Effort allocations	—Choice of appropriate strategies
2. Causal attributions for success and failure	
—Self-concept of own ability	—Knowledge of own cognitive competence
—Individual attribution style	—Metacognitive judgments about the determinants of performance
—Predictions of future performance	—Predictions of future performance
3. Evaluation of action outcomes	
—Use of self-relevant evaluation criteria	—Metacognitive knowledge about task and person variables
—Subjective experience of success and failure	—Evaluation of correct and incorrect judgments
—Emotional reactions and their consequences	—Improvement of task-related metacognitive knowledge

example, during childhood the ability to process information accurately and to use metacognitive knowledge improves greatly. Yet, at the same time there is an increase in the asymmetry with which children make causal attributions for success and failure, an asymmetry that can be detrimental to self-esteem. Heckhausen (this volume) asks:

Why do a good many people seem intent on preserving the depressive image they have of self and own abilities and do not opt for more sanguine expectations, even when good opportunities are offered? (p. 178)

Perhaps it is possible to identify those people who have both good metacognitive skills and a characteristically "helpless" attributional style. If so, one could ask how such a combination affects behavior and achievement in various learning tasks, and whether attributional biases can be directly influenced by metacognitive knowledge. Another question is whether the frequently observed but unrealistically pessimistic appraisals older people make about their memories may be given a motivational explanation (Weinert, Knopf, & Barann, 1983). One could also ask whether such an underestimation of one's abilities affects learning and remembering.

These questions illustrate the importance of coordinating studies of the cognitive, metacognitive, and motivational determinants of learning behavior and performance. Additionally, as Kuhl (1982) has noted:

> To the extent that emotions are involved in actions, cumulative motivational effects must be taken into account. . . . This assertion does not exclude the special case of a purely rational or reflexively driven action, in which the actor chooses among alternative actions on the basis of specific information in the situation. However, it does suggest that the generalization of this special case to cover a general theory of human action, a generalization made in the dominant models of motivation, is not warranted. (p. 22)

METACOGNITION, MOTIVATION, AND LEARNING: PROGRESS IN THE INTEGRATION OF DIFFERENT RESEARCH PARADIGMS?

Books that include contributions from different research traditions often imply that there is thematic and theoretical convergence, although with closer examination one sees that variety and diversity predominate. An introduction to such a volume may strengthen this perception because similarities rather than differences are emphasized. Perhaps that is the case in this introductory chapter as well, although such was not the intention.

There are good reasons to establish connections between research efforts in metacognition, achievement motivation, and learning, areas that have been relatively isolated from one another. For example, if we attempt to explain individual differences in learning and memory as more than the simple consequences of stable ability differences (which proved impossible to do anyway), the questions we ask about the relation between learning activities and learning outcomes, or about the process and conditions of learning, are given a new meaning. Cognition, metacognition, procedural skills, and motivational factors are important determinants of learning activity, but they must be differentially weighted depending on task types. An integration of the different research approaches is also necessary if one wants to study and measure phenomena of learning by doing, and doing in order to learn.

The difficulties encountered in attempting to combine different research orientations should not, however, be underestimated. For instance, the use of different prototypical tasks in memory, metamemory, and motivational research leads inevitably to different conclusions regarding the relative importance of domain-specific knowledge, procedural skills, and motivational factors in predicting or explaining individual learning and performance differences. This problem is compounded by the lack of a theoretically grounded taxonomy for learning and memory tasks. Additionally, the role of motivational processes in learning has seldom been considered because there have been no systematic efforts to study how people with specific motivational characteristics behave when given different types of tasks in situations that the subjects consider to be important.

Keeping these cautions in mind, however, there is sufficient overlap in the tasks and concerns of the fields of cognition, metacognition, and motivation to urge the development of an integrated research program.

REFERENCES

Bandura, A. (1981). Self-referent thought: A developmental analysis of self efficacy. In J. H. Flavell, & C. Ross (Eds.), *Social cognitive development* (pp. 200–239.) Cambridge University Press.

Bartlett, F. C. (1932). *Remembering: A study in experimental and social psychology*. Cambridge: Cambridge University Press.

Bugelski, B. R. (1956). *The psychology of learning*. New York: Holt.

Carver, C. S., & Scheier, M. F. (1981). *Attention and self-regulation: A control-theory approach to human behavior*. New York: Springer.

Cavanaugh, J. C., & Perlmutter, M. (1982). Metamemory: A critical examination. *Child Development, 53*, 11–28.

Chi, M. T. H. (1978). Knowledge structure and memory development. In R. S. Siegler (Ed.), *Children's thinking: What develops?* (pp. 73–96). Hillsdale, NJ: Lawrence Erlbaum Associates.

Dixon, R. A., & Hertzog, C. (in press). A functional approach to memory and metamemory development in adulthood. In F. E. Weinert and M. Perlmutter (Eds.), *Memory development: Universal changes and individual differences*. Hillsdale, NJ: Lawrence Erlbaum Associates.

Ebbinghaus, H. (1885). *Über das Gedächtnis*. Leipzig: Duncker & Humblot.

Eysenck, H. J. (1957). *The dynamics of anxiety and hysteria*. London: Routledge & Kegan Paul.

Fabricius, W. V., & Hagen, J. W. (1984). *The use of causal attributions about recall performance to assess metamemory and predict memory behavior in young children*. Developmental Psychology, 20, 975–987.

Flavell, J. H. (1970). Developmental studies of mediated memory. In H. W. Reese, & L. P. Lipsitt (Eds.), *Advances in child development and behavior* (Vol. 5, pp. 181–211). New York: Academic Press.

Glaser, R. (1972). The new aptitudes. *Educational Researcher, 1*, 5–13.

Guilford, J. P., & Dallenbach, K. M. (1925). The determination of memory span by the method of constant stimuli. *American Journal of Psychology, 36*, 621–628.

Hacker, W., Volpert, W., & von Cranach, M. (Eds.). (1982). *Kognitive und motivationale Aspekte der Handlung*. Bern: Huber.

Heckhausen, H. (1982): The development of achievement. In W. W. Hartup (Ed.), *Review of Child Development Research* (Vol. 6, pp. 600–668). Chicago: The University of Chicago Press.

Hull, C. L. (1945). The place of innate individual and species differences in a natural-science theory of behavior. *Psychological Review, 52*, 55–60.

Körkel, J. 1984. *Die Entwicklung von Gedächtnis- und Metagedächtnisleistungen in Abhängigkeit von bereichsspezifischen Vorkenntnissen*. Unpublished doctoral dissertation, Heidelberg.

Krampen, G. (1982). *Differentialpsychologie der Kontrollüberzeugungen*. Göttingen: Hogrefe.

Kuhl, J. (1982). Emotion, Kognition und Motivation. I. Auf dem Weg zu einer systemorientierten Betrachtung der Emotionsgenese. Sprache und Kognition *1*, 1–27.

Kuhl, J. (1983). Leistungsmotivation: Neue Entwicklungen aus modelltheoretischer Sicht. In H. Thomae (Ed.), *Psychologie der Motive* (pp. 229–289). (Enzyklopädie der Psychologie C IV, 2) Göttingen: Hogrefe.

Kurtz, B. E., & Borkowski, F. G. (1984). Children's metacognition: Exploring relations among knowledge, process, and motivational variables. *Journal of Experimental Child Psychology, 37,* 335–354.

McGeoch, J. A., & Irion, A. L. (1952). *The psychology of human learning* (2nd ed.). New York: Longmans, Green.

McNemar, Q. (1964). Lost Our intelligence? Why? *American Psychologist, 19,* 871–882.

Meacham, J. A. (1983). *Memory functions across the life course.* Paper presented at the 7th Meeting of the ISSBD, Munich.

Mischel, W. (1981). Metacognition and the rules of delay. In. J. H. Flavell, & L. Ross (Eds.), *Social Cognitive Development* (pp. 240–271). Cambridge: Cambridge University Press.

Netschajeff, H. (1900). Experimentelle Untersuchungen über die Gedächtnisentwicklung bei Schulkindern. *Zeitschrift für Psychologie 24,* 321–351.

Paris, S. G., & Lindauer, B. K. (1982). The development of cognitive skills during childhood. In B. B. Wolman (Ed.), *Handbook of developmental psychology* (pp. 333–349). Englewood Cliffs, NJ: Prentice Hall.

Pawlow, J. P. (1953). Die Lehre von dem Typen (1935). In Pawlow, J. P., *Ausgewählte Werke,* Berlin, 235–256.

Piaget, J. (1971). *Biology and knowledge.* Chicago: University of Chicago Press.

Piaget, J. (1976). *The grasp of consciousness.* Cambridge, MA: Harvard University Press.

Piaget, J. (1978). *Success and understanding.* Cambridge, MA: Harvard University Press.

Plenderleith, M., & Postman, L. (1957). Individual differences in intentional and incidental learning. *British Journal of Psychology, 48,* 241–248.

Pressley, M., Forrest-Pressley, D., & Elliot-Faust, D. (in press). How to study strategy instructional enrichment: Illustrations from research on children's prose memory and comprehension. In F. E. Weinert, & M. Perlmutter (Eds.), *Memory development: Universal changes and individual differences.* Hillsdale, NJ: Lawrence Erlbaum Associates.

Reese, H. W. (1979). Gedächtnisentwicklung im Verlauf des Lebens: Empirische Befunde und theoretische Modelle. In L. Montada (Hrsg.), *Brennpunkte der Entwicklungspsychologie.* Stuttgart: Kohlhammer.

Robinson, F. P. (1941). *Effective study.* New York: Harper & Row.

Rubinstein, S. L. (1969). *Prinzipien und Wege der Entwicklung der Psychologie.* Berlin: Akademie Verlag.

Schneider, W. (1985). Developmental trends in the metamemory-memory behavior relationship: An integrative review. In D. L. Forrest-Pressley, G. E. McKinnon, & T. G. Waller (Eds.), *Metacognition, cognition, and human performance* (pp. 57–109). New York: Academic Press.

Spearman, C. (1927). *The abilities of man.* New York: Macmillan.

Stipek, D. J., & Weisz, J. R. (1981). Perceived personal control and academic achievement. *Review of Educational Research, 51,* 101.138.

Thurstone, L. L. (1930). The relation between learning time and length of task. *Psychological Review, 37,* 44–53.

Trudewind, C. (1982). The development of achievement motivation and individual differences. Ecological determinants. In W. W. Hartup (Ed.), *Review of Child Development Research* (Vol. 6, pp. 669–703). Chicago: The University of Chicago Press.

Vaughan, E. D. (1977). Misconceptions about psychology among introductory psychology students. *Teaching of Psychology, 4,* 138–141.

Weinert, F. E. (1979). Entwicklungsabhängigkeit des Lernens und des Gedächtnisses. In L. Montada (Ed.), *Brennpunkte der Entwicklungspsychologie* (pp. 61–76). Stuttgart: Kohlhammer.

Weinert, F. E., Knopf, M., & Barann, G. (1983). Metakognition und Motivation als Determinanten der Gedächtnisleistungen im höheren Erwachsenenalter. *Sprache & Kognition, 2*, 71–87.

Weinert, F. E., Knopf, M., & Körkel, J. (1983). Zusammenhänge zwischen Metawissen, Verhalten und Leistung bei der Lösung von Gedächtnisaufgaben durch Kinder und ältere Erwachsene. In G. Lüer (Ed.), Bericht über den 33. Kongress der Deutschen Gesellschaft für Psychologie in Mainz 1982 (Vol. 2, pp. 262–271). Göttingen: Hogrefe.

Wellman, H. M. (1983). Metamemory revisited. *Contribution to Human Development, 9*, 31–51.

Woodrow, H. (1942). The problem of general quantitative laws in psychology. *Psychological Bulletin, 39*, 1–27.

Wundt, W. (1886). Über den Begriff des Gesetzes mit Rücksicht auf die Frage der Ausnahmslosigkeit der Lautgesetze. In *Kleine Schriften* (Vol. 3). Stuttgart: Enke, 1921.

Zeigarnik, B. (1927). Das Behalten erledigter und unerledigter Handlungen. *Psychologische Forschung, 9*, 1–85.

METACOGNITION

During the last 15 years metacognition has become one of the major fields of cognitive developmental research. Research activity in metacognition began with John Flavell. His work on metamemory provided the first results on the developmental course of metamemory and raised important questions for subsequent research. Because of Flavell's efforts, a considerable amount of empirical and theoretical research dealing with metacognition can be registered. Psychological research in metacognition is concerned with two problems: The first is the availability of factual (declarative) knowledge about cognition. It is similar to other world knowledge that individuals store but focuses on general knowledge about cognitive activities and demands, as well as the features of one's own cognitive activities and capabilities. The second problem is the availability of strategies (procedural knowledge) that may be applied in order to control (monitor) and regulate cognitive activity (thinking about thinking).

Developmental research in metacognition thus far has emphasized the acquisition and application of knowledge about cognition. Central questions must be answered in order to secure the knowledge and the use of the knowledge necessary to organize and regulate the flow of own thinking. The procedural aspects of metacognition have gained more attention during testing. The chapters by Brown,

Campione, Flavell, and Kluwe provide an overview of the various research directions in the field of metacognition. Flavell, the pioneer in the field, discusses the present state of metacognition research. His analysis is based on a taxonomy of knowledge components that are important in metacognitive activity. He assumes that metacognitive knowledge has its own course of development, and introduces the interesting, although not yet precise, concept of metacognitive experiences. If these conditions exist during cognitive endeavors, they may trigger metacognitive activity. Flavell's discussion of the problems emphasizes the role of instruction in schools as one possible major source for the acquisition of metacognitive knowledge. His final evaluation of the present state of developmental research in metacognition, although connected with the hope for broader models of metacognition and for a more precise conceptualization, remains skeptical.

The chapter by Kluwe includes an approach for specifying the procedural aspects of metacognition. Within the framework of Flavell's metacognitive strategies and Brown's metacognitive skills, Kluwe focuses essentially on executive decisions. He refers to production-like rules that, given certain conditions, may be evoked during problem solving. These rules are directed at the control and regulation of the solution search. A set of hypothetical executive decisions are discussed using developmental aspects. It is assumed that during cognitive development the knowledge necessary for the formation and application of such executive rules is acquired. The availability of executive procedural knowledge allows an appropriate regulation of the own cognitive efforts to certain given demands. In addition, given changing task demands, executive decisions allow for flexible use of own thinking. Preliminary data, from a developmental study where children of different ages were required to cope with changing problem solving conditions, are presented. The significant result of this study is the awareness that 4-year-old children know when an originally selected approach to problem solving is no longer adequate, and are able to effectively regulate the own solution search. However, the relation between such regulatory activity and level of performance remains an open question.

One of the most comprehensive reviews of metacognition and related fields of research is found in the chapter by Brown. A discussion of the concept of metacognition is followed by a review of the four central issues of metacognition research: reports on own thinking; the role of executive components in information processing systems; processes of self-regulation; and processes of an individual's regulation by other persons. Similar to Kluwe, Brown's discussion connects cognitive psychological and developmental aspects. Brown emphasizes the function of success for the acquisition of self-regulatory mechanisms, and the role of parents and teachers in the formation of cognitive mechanisms that help control and regulate own thinking.

The chapter by Campione is directly connected to Brown's contribution concerning the regulation of a child's thinking by other persons. Campione provides an overview of the theoretical and empirical research concerned with the instructional aspects of metacognition. He focuses on the connection of research on metacognition with instructional applications and demonstrates that previous attempts to train and improve children's cognitive abilities have failed to include self-regulatory aspects. After considering the developmental results of metacognition research, Campione proposes a modification of training approaches. The essential feature of this approach is the consideration of the learning and thinking child in intervention studies. The cognitive resources of the child, the instruction of strategies connected with insights into the effects of a strategy, and the instruction of monitoring operations, together result in more successful training effects. Especially important are improvements in the transfer and persistence of trained strategies. This type of research demonstrates the importance of metacognitive research to instruction and education.

1 Speculations About the Nature and Development of Metacognition

John H. Flavell
Stanford University

Metacognition is usually defined as knowledge and cognition about cognitive objects, that is, about anything cognitive. However, the concept could reasonably be broadened to include anything psychological, rather than just anything cognitive. For instance, if one has knowledge or cognition about one's own or someone else's emotions or motives, it could be considered metacognitive. Any kind of monitoring might also be considered a form of metacognition; for example, attempts to monitor one's own motor activity in a motor skill situation. It is very difficult to rule out the conscious monitoring of motor acts as being something entirely different from what is ordinarily understood to be metacognition. Because some metacognitive knowledge and cognitive self-regulatory activity is not very accessible to consciousness, researchers may eventually feel compelled to include processes that are not conscious and perhaps not even accessible to consciousness as forms of metacognition or metacognitive-like phenomena.

This researcher (Flavell, 1979, 1981) tried to classify part of the domain of metacognition. The taxonomy created is not very satisfactory, but at least it helps in thinking about the domain. The key concepts in the taxonomy are *metacognitive knowledge* and *metacognitive experience*. Metacognitive knowledge refers to the part of one's acquired world knowledge that has to do with cognitive (or perhaps better, psychological) matters. As people grow up, an important part of what they learn or come to believe concerns the mind and other things psychological.

METACOGNITIVE KNOWLEDGE

Metacognitive knowledge is conceived as simply that portion of the total knowledge base that pertains to this content area. Metacognitive knowledge can be subdivided into three categories: knowledge of *person* variables; *task* variables; and *strategy* variables.

Person Variables

Knowledge of person variables refers to the kind of acquired knowledge and beliefs that concern what human beings are like as cognitive (affective, motivational, perceptual, etc.) organisms. There are three subcategories of person variables: *intraindividual; interindividual;* and *universal.* An example of an intraindividual variable is a person's belief that he or she is fairly good at dealing with verbal kinds of material, but poor at spatial tasks; therefore, it is knowledge or belief about intraindividual variation in one's own or someone else's interests, propensities, aptitudes, and the like. In the case of interindividual variables, the comparison is between, rather than within, persons. Examples might be the judgment that one is brighter than one's parents, but that the parents are more reflective and thoughtful than certain of their friends. The most interesting variables are acquired ideas about universal aspects of human cognition or psychology. It is hard to imagine a culture in which people grow up without acquiring any naive psychology; in particular, without developing any intuitions about the way the human mind works. For example, one cannot imagine anyone growing to maturity without having some kind of intuition that short term memory is fallible and of limited capacity. That is something adults know, but did not always know, about themselves; it must have been acquired in the course of childhood development. Similarly, can one imagine a culture in which a person has not acquired the concept of a mistake or error? Something is believed to be true and it turns out not to be true. You think you understand something and it turns out that you have misunderstood it or failed to understand it. Surely, adults the world over have acquired knowledge of such universal mental phenomena and make use of that knowledge in managing their lives.

Task Variables

The second subcategory is knowledge of task variables. The individual learns something about how the nature of the information encountered affects and constrains how one should deal with it. For instance, experience has taught that very difficult, very densely packed, and very low redundancy information is troublesome to process. To comprehend and to deal effectively with such information, it is necessary to proceed slowly and carefully and to process deeply and self-critically (i.e., with high comprehension monitoring activity). Other inputs are loosely packed and contain mostly familiar information. People know if they can comprehend these inputs without paying really close attention, and they are likely to process them accordingly. Thus, much is learned about the different kinds of information that are encountered and about the kind of processing that each kind of information requires or does not require. In addition, given the information, it is learned that different kinds of tasks place different kinds of information-processing demands on individuals. An example would be the knowledge that it is easier to learn the essence or gist of something, such as a story, than it is to learn it verbatim. All adults recognize that it is easier to recall the main events of a story than to recite the story word for word. Thus, one learns about the implications of various task demands for self-processing. One learns that in some cases the task demands are much more rigorous and difficult than they are in other cases, and that one must take these demands into account and act accordingly if the task goal is to be achieved.

Strategy Variables

Much is also learned about cognitive strategies or procedures for getting from here to there in order to achieve various goals (strategy variables). It has been suggested (Flavell, 1981) that one can distinguish cognitive strategies from meta-cognitive strategies. A cognitive strategy is one designed simply to get the individual to some cognitive goal or subgoal. For instance, a cognitive strategy for getting the sum of a list of numbers would obviously be to add them up. The goal is to find the sum, and in order to do so the numbers are added. In the same situation, a metacognitive strategy might be to add the numbers a second time to be sure the answer is right. If it is an income tax return or something equally important, one might even double check by adding them up a third time. The purpose of the second and third addition is somewhat different from that of the first. The purpose is no longer to reach the goal (cognitive strategy), but rather to feel absolutely confident that it has been reached (metacognitive strategy). Similarly, sometimes one reads things slowly simply to learn the content (cognitive strategy); other times one reads through things quickly to get an idea of how difficult or easy it is going to be to learn the content (metacognitive strategy). That is, one skims or scans a text in order to get some idea of how much work lies ahead. In the course of development one learns about cognitive strategies for making cognitive progress and about metacognitive strategies for monitoring the cognitive progress.

Finally, it should be emphasized that person, task, and strategy variables always interact, and that intuitions about their interaction are also acquired. For instance, I may sense that I but not my brother would do better to use strategy A rather than strategy B, because the task is of this type rather than that. Given one's particular cognitive make-up and the particular task, one develops intuitions about which strategies are better.

METACOGNITIVE EXPERIENCES

The other major conceptual entity in the taxonomy is metacognitive experiences. Metacognitive experiences are conscious experiences that are cognitive and affective. What makes them metacognitive experiences rather than experiences of another kind is that they have to do with some cognitive endeavor or enterprise, most frequently a current, ongoing one. For example, if one suddenly has the anxious feeling that one is not understanding something and wants and needs to understand it, that feeling would be a metacognitive experience. One is having a metacognitive experience whenever one has the feeling that something is hard to perceive, comprehend, remember, or solve; if there is the feeling that one is far from the cognitive goal; if the feeling exists that one is, in fact, just about to reach the cognitive goal; or if one has the sense that the material is getting easier or more difficult than it was a moment ago. Thus, a metacognitive experience can be any kind of effective or cognitive conscious experience that is pertinent to the conduct of intellectual life; often, it is pertinent to conduct in an ongoing cognitive situation or enterprise. Metacognitive experiences play a very important role in everyday cognitive lives. As one grows older one learns how to interpret and respond appropriately to these experiences. The converse implication is that young children may have such conscious experiences, but may not know how to interpret them very well; children simply may not know what these experiences mean and imply. Recent research supports this implication (Beal & Flavell, 1982; Flavell, Speer, Green & August, 1981; Singer & Flavell, 1981; see also various chapters in Dickson, 1981).

In one series of studies (Flavell et al., 1981), the young child subject hears a brief tape-recorded instruction to build a simple block structure; for example, "Take the red block and put it on top of the blue block." His task is to make a structure identical to that of the child speaker, based on her instructions. Some of the instructions are wholly unambiguous and the child can follow them without any difficulty. Other instructions are ambiguous, impossible to execute, or otherwise inadequate. For example: "Put the big block on the tray. Put the little block on top of it so you cannot see the big block." Or: "Put the red block on the tray," when there are two different red blocks to choose between. It has been found that when kindergarten children (5 or 6 years of age) hear these inadequate instructions and try to carry them out they often act puzzled or uncertain and may even say something like "Huh?" or "Which red block?" However, when they are asked if they think that their building looks exactly like that of the speaker's they are very likely to say that it does; and when they are next asked if the speaker did a good job or a bad job of telling them how to make their building exactly like hers, they are even more likely to say that she did a good job. The evidence suggests that these curious responses are not artefacts of the method of questioning used; rather, it seems that young children often do not fully understand the meaning and implications of metacognitive experiences of puzzlement and uncertainty. They may feel puzzled, but they do not know what the implication of that feeling is for the existing situation. These children cannot be sure their building matches the speaker's because the speaker did not describe it adequately enough. In conclusion, the evidence from these studies and those of other investigators suggests that young children have more trouble than older children in properly comprehending their own feelings of incomprehension, and in properly appreciating the meaning, significance, and implications of such metacognitive experiences.

QUESTIONS, PROBLEMS, AND ISSUES

The following are some of the questions, problems, and issues concerning metacognition that should be addressed. First, where does metacognition fit in psychological space? That is, what other psychological concepts does it relate to, and how does it relate to these concepts? The concepts that might be related to metacognition include: executive processes; formal operations; consciousness; social cognition; self-efficacy, self-regulation; reflective self-awareness; and the concept of psychological self or psychological subject. Also related are developing conceptions of, and about thinking, learning, and other cognitive processes—the child's emerging "theory of mind."

Another group of questions concerns the types of metacognitive acquisitions that develop and the earlier foundations or prerequisites from which they develop (the taxonomy given will probably not prove to be the best one). Similarly: What aspects of metacognition are inherent or very early acquired, and what aspects must be acquired in the course of childhood, adolescence, or even during the adult years? Some aspects of metacognition, just like some aspects of general cognition, are probably present almost from the beginning. Also, is the acquisition, use, and usefulness of some types of metacognition impeded by information-processing limitations or biases, by lack of relevant experiences in most environments, or by other factors? For example, perhaps some types of metacognition are unlikely to occur in a given cognitive domain until some amount of expertise or knowledge in that domain is acquired.

How might various types of metacognition develop? What might account for possible individual or cultural differences in what does develop? A rough distinction can be made between cognitive-developmental changes in the child that allow for metacognitive acquisitions and experiences the child might have that could assist or facilitate metacognitive development. In the case of the former, there might be three closely related but conceptually distinguishable types of changes. First, there might be cognitive-developmental changes that could lead directly to metacognitive acquisitions. For example: An increase in the capacity to plan ahead could lead, more or less directly, to a greater tendency to think about cognitive means and cognitive goals. Second, there could be changes which increase the child's cognitive readiness to profit from experiences that promote metacognitive development. Third, and closely related to the second, one can imagine cognitive-developmental changes in the child that might increase the child's opportunity to have experiences that could lead to metacognitive acquisitions. For example: Once one has developed sufficiently to start reading, one can start having the formative experiences that reading brings. These include the metacognitive experiences of conscious comprehension difficulties, misreadings, and sudden insights; thus, any experiences that can promote metacognitive growth.

Two changes in the development of the child might possibly contribute to the acquisition of metacognition. One is the developing sense of the self as an active cognitive agent and as the causal center of one's own cognitive activity. The development of such an internal locus of cognitive control could promote the monitoring and regulation of one's own cognitive enterprises. A second kind of change that should facilitate metacognitive development, an increase in planfulness, has already been mentioned. More generally, an individual that represents and interrelates past, present, and future actions and events should be in a good position to acquire metacognitive knowledge. That is, such an individual could notice and store covariations in person, task, and strategy factors. The person who can look ahead is also in a position to scan upcoming information or impending problems, and can plan in advance how processing resources should be allocated. Thus, an individual who can create conscious and explicit representations of the past, present, and the future should be in a better position to make metacognitive progress than one who does not.

There may also be a number of experiences that might assist metacognitive development; some of them may consist of direct practice in metacognitive activity. Metacognition, like everything else, undoubtedly improves with practice. Other kinds of experiences, although not themselves metacognitive activities, may simply be heuristic or propaedeutic to metacognitive development. Therefore, one way to become better at metacognition is to practice it; another way may be to practice other things which are not metacognitive themselves but which indirectly promote metacognitive activity.

One class of these experiences may be supplied by parents (Wertsch, 1978). Parents may unintentionally model metacognitive activity for their young children. They may also deliberately demonstrate and teach it, helping the child to regulate and monitor his or her actions. Similarly, teachers in schools may sometimes model, as well as teach and encourage, metacognitive activity. Schallert and Kleiman (1979) describe some of the things they have observed teachers doing to help the child regulate and monitor own cognition. They indicate how teachers provide the kind of assistance, not provided in textbooks, to help the child wend his or her way through a cognitive endeavor.

There are a variety of other school experiences that may assist the growth of metacognitive skills, including reading, which was mentioned earlier. A piece of text is very different from an oral communicative interchange between people; the text has little communicative context (Donaldson, 1978; Olson, 1972). The child has to treat a written passage as a cognitive object and attempt to figure out what can be concluded or infered from it alone, without the additional expressive and situational clues to meaning normally present in an oral communication situation. In the course of learning to read, the child gets practice in scrutinizing messages in isolation from context, and thus in evaluating the possible intended meanings and implications (a form of metacognition). Writing also affords practice and experience in metacognition. It allows one to critically inspect one's own thoughts. It also encourages the individual to imagine the thoughts of others. For example, to think about whether they will understand or believe what one is trying to convey in one's writing. Of course, learning to be a skillful speaker and critical listener also involves considerable practice and skill in cognitive monitoring. Similarly, learning mathematics provides opportunities for monitoring all sorts of activities. This was shown earlier, in the example of checking one's addition by adding the column a second time.

Good schools should be hotbeds of metacognitive development, for the banal-sounding reason that so much self-conscious learning goes on in them. In school, children have repeated opportunities to monitor and regulate their cognition, as they gradually pass from novice status to semi-expert status in microdomain after microdomain. They have innumerable metacognitive experiences and innumerable opportunities to acquire person, task, and strategy metacognitive knowledge.

There are still other interesting questions involving metacognition. What is the particular usefulness and adaptiveness of metacognition? How and why has metacognition evolved? Metacognition is especially useful for a particular kind of organism, one that has the following properties. First, the organism should obviously tend to think a lot; by definition, an abundance of metacognition presupposes an abundance of cognition. Second, the organism's thinking should be fallible and error-prone, and thus in need of careful monitoring and regulation. Third, the organism should want to communicate, explain, and justify its thinking to other organisms as well as to itself; these activities clearly require metacognition. Fourth, in order to survive and prosper, the organism should need to plan ahead and critically evaluate alternative plans. Fifth, if it has to make weighty, carefully considered decisions, the organism will require metacognitive skills. Finally, it should have a need or proclivity for inferring and explaining psychological events in itself and others, a penchant for engaging in those meta-cognitive acts termed social cognition. Needless to say, human beings are organisms with just these properties.

An important future endeavor is to try to create detailed process models for various aspects of metacognition. Process models will have to address questions such as: How is the information about cognitive processes that is needed to monitor and regulate these processes obtained? What cues are observed? One cue that might be used is the speed of processing, especially the processing of sudden changes in speed. When you are reading along and suddenly find yourself reading more slowly, the slowdown in processing may function as a cue that the material is getting difficult, or that something is puzzling, etc. Similarly, individuals may become aware that they have just read a sentence for the second time, and that awareness may serve as a metacognitive signal that the material is difficult, or that attention has wandered, etc. There is also the question of how monitoring information gets translated into self-regulatory metacognition.

The final question is: When are we most likely to have metacognitive experiences? First, they are obviously apt to occur whenever the situation explicitly demands or elicits them. For example, someone is asked to justify a conclusion, or defend a claim. Second, metacognitive experiences may be more apt to occur when the cognitive situation is something between completely novel and completely familiar. In this broad range, one knows enough to be puzzled and to formulate questions, but not enough that the processing is wholly automatic and effortlessly accurate. Third, metacognitive experiences are likely to occur in situations where it is important to make correct inferences, judgments, and decisions. If it really matters whether or not one's judgments and decisions are correct, one is apt to monitor them very carefully. Fourth metacognitive antennae are likely to go up whenever one's cognitive enterprise seems to be in any sort of trouble. There is nothing like the sudden awareness of self-contradiction or some other mental cul-de-sac to cause critical analysis of one's own thinking. And finally, one is more likely to have metacognitive experiences (useful ones, at least) when attentional and mnemonic resources are not wholly preempted by more urgent subjective experiences, such as pain, anxiety, or depression.

What will the future bring to the area of metacognition? During the next few years more careful and critical examinations of metacognition and related concepts will probably occur. Undoubtedly, the concept itself will be further refined, clarified, and differentiated. Some methodological advances, better ways to measure and assess metacognitive experiences and knowledge than is presently available, should also develop. Finally, deeper insights into the entire concept are needed. A number of psychologists have the abiding intuition that metacognition is an extremely important topic, eminently worthy of further theoretical and experimental investigation. However, none of us has yet come up with deeply insightful, detailed proposals about what metacognition is, how it operates, and how it develops. Perhaps the future will bring such proposals.

ACKNOWLEDGMENTS

I thank Ellen Markman and the members of a seminar on metacognitive development she and I co-taught for their contributions to the questions and issues raised in the latter half of this chapter.

REFERENCES

Beal, C. R., & Flavell, J. H. (1982). The effects of increasing the salience of message ambiguities on kindergartners' evaluations of communicative success. *Developmental Psychology, 18,* 43–48.

Dickson, W. P. (Ed.). (1981). *Children's oral communication skills.* New York: Academic Press.

Donaldson, M. (1978). *Children's minds.* New York: Norton.

Flavell, J. H. (1979). Metacognition and cognitive monitoring: A new area of cognitive-developmental inquiry. *American Psychologist, 34,* 906–911.

Flavell, J. H. (1981). Cognitive monitoring. In W. P. Dickson (Ed.), *Children's oral communication skills* (pp. 35–60). New York: Academic Press.

Flavell, J. H., Speer, J. R., Green, F. L., & August, D. L. (1981). The development of comprehension monitoring and knowledge about communication. *Monographs of the Society for Research in Child Development, 46*(5, Serial No. 192).

Olson, D. R. (1972). Language use for communicating, instructing, and thinking. In R. O. Freedle & J. B. Carroll (Eds.), *Language comprehension and the acquisition of knowledge* (pp. 139–167). Washington, DC: Winston.

Schallert, D. L., & Kleiman, G. M. (1979). Some reasons why the teacher is easier to understand than the textbook. *Reading Education Report Series,* University of Illinois, Center for the Study of Reading.

Singer, J. B., & Flavell, J. H. (1981). Development of knowledge about communication: Children's evaluations of explicitly ambiguous messages. *Child Development, 52,* 1211–1215.

Wertsch, J. W. (1978). Adult–child interaction and the roots of metacognition. *Quarterly Newsletter of the Institute for Comparative Human Development, 1,* 15–18.

2 Executive Decisions and Regulation of Problem Solving Behavior

Rainer H. Kluwe
University of Bundeswehr, Hamburg

It is well known that Flavell and his co-workers (1970, 1971) initiated research on metacognition. Since that time "metas," (e.g., metalistening, metacommunication, metapersuasion, metacomponents, and the like) have proliferated in the literature.

The concept of metacognition relates to a child's declarative knowledge about cognition, for example the own cognitive activities and abilities, and to procedural knowledge, processes directed at the control and regulation of one's own thinking, or "cognition about cognition" (see Kluwe, 1981, 1982). The available developmental results suggest that younger children lack knowledge about cognition; in addition, they are less engaged in monitoring the course of own thinking.

Flavell and Wellman (1977) published a taxonomy of the development of metacognitive knowledge. This classification of knowledge was the first step toward a more systematic view of metacognition and provided a starting point for subsequent research. Metacognition refers mainly to memory functions. The immense body of research, especially in developmental psychology, published under the heading of metacognition, relates mainly to "metacognitive knowledge." That is, it refers to the acquisition of knowledge, the amount of knowledge, and the assumptions and opinions about the states and activities of the human mind. Such knowledge may refer to the human cognitive system in general, as well as to an individual's own cognitive system. There is considerable evidence for the development of metacognitive knowledge (Kreutzer, Leonard & Flavell, 1975), but there are still many open questions. Researchers do not know enough about how individuals acquire knowledge about their own

31

cognitive system or about the usefulness of such knowledge (Thornquist & Wimmer, 1977; Wimmer & Thornquist, 1979).

Flavell (1981) offers a model of "cognitive monitoring," which is considered to be the first approach connecting cognitive and metacognitive activity. Of central interest is the notion of metacognitive strategies that may be applied in order to monitor cognitive progress. Another line of research, resulting in equally important contributions to the field, is the one offered by Brown (1978; Brown & DeLoache, 1978). The work of Brown and her group has placed increasing emphasis on the development of "metacognitive skills." According to Brown, metacognitive skills entail the operation of specific mental processes by which individuals organizes and monitors their own thinking. It is plausible to focus on the procedural aspects of metacognition, if one examines metacognition less from the aspect of factual knowledge, but rather as one component of cognitive activity.

Metacognition has also been receiving increased attention in cognitive psychology (e.g., Sternberg, 1979). There is no doubt that metacognition has a long history in cognitive psychology, especially in connection with assumptions concerning the function of the executive component in information processing systems (Neisser, 1967; Reitman, 1965). As a result, it is possible to use the models proposed by cognitive psychologists to discuss developmental data on metacognition.

This chapter first outlines metacognitive activity by describing executive processes, taking into account current results in developmental research and aspects of cognitive performance. Second, the preliminary results from an experimental study, that deals with children's regulation of their own problem-solving behavior under changing conditions are reported.

THE ROLE OF EXECUTIVE DECISIONS

Brown argues that cognitive activities, such as checking, monitoring, planning, and prediction (Brown, 1978; Brown & DeLoache, 1978), contribute to cognitive performance of the type investigated by developmental psychologists, and that they are subject to developmental changes. Brown and DeLoache even claim that these processes, referred to as metacognitive skills, are the "basic characteristics of efficient thought, [and] that they are transsituational" (p. 15). Similar cognitive activities are addressed, using the "imperatives" proposed by Flavell (1976) in his discussion of the improvement of children's problem-solving capacities.

Brown (1978) assigns metacognitive skills to the component of an information processing system that is designed as an executive; the central processor, or the monitoring system. She argues (Campione & Brown, 1978) that the different forms of executive decision making are at the core of intelligent problem solving, and that "variations in the efficiency of the executive" may be associated with differences in intelligence (p. 21). The attribution of metacognitive skills to the executive component of information processing systems, is important in establishing the link between cognitive developmental research and cognitive psychology. The following discussion concerns executive decisions and processes; the term metacognition is not used.

Executive functions as described by Neisser (1967) have not been studied extensively in cognitive psychology (see Ueckert, 1980). One reason for this might be that research on problem solving was first aimed at the elaboration of a general model of human problem solving processes. However, there is some progress, which allows one to ask for procedural variants of problem solving processes and for the hypothetical mechanisms producing such variants. Simon (1975) provided the first thorough analysis of the differences between problem-solving processes.

Studying the procedural attributes of different problem-solving processes is important because some understanding of the flexibility of thinking processes with respect to varying situational demands is gained. The central question concerns the intraindividual variability in problem-solving processes. The executive requirements for simulation programs, considered to be models of human problem solving processes, have so far been limited. There are no changing situational demands similar to those human beings encounter in everyday situations. Attributes of situational demands that determine the organization and the course of problem solving processes have been described by Dörner (1974). These attributes not only indicate the diversity of demands a person has to cope with; at the same time, make plausible the assumption that there is something like a central regulatory component in information processing systems, an executive.

Another aspect of the situation is that of interindividual differences in problem solving (Simon, 1975). Recent research on differences between successful and poor problem solvers (Dörner, Kreuzig, & Stäudel, 1978; Lüer, Putz-Osterloh & Hesse, 1979), research on successful and poor learners (Thorndyke & Stasz, 1980), and analyses of differences between novices and experts in problem solving (Simon & Simon, 1978) indicate that more research on executive decisions in problem solving and learning is needed. In addition, there is some evidence that an improvement of executive decision making would presumably effect an improvement of cognitive performance. Preliminary insight gained from the research cited and from other investigations (e.g., Sternberg, 1979) indicates that individual differences in executive functions might contribute to individual differences in intellectual performance. The work of Reither (1979), Hesse (1979), and Dörner (1978/1984) on self-reflection and problem solving, might be considered a move in the direction of the empirical testing of this assumption. The effects on performance of the simple instruction, to reflect on one's own problem-solving activity, as it was used in these studies, are indeed impressive.

In addition to the aspects discussed, there are two other phenomena that underscore the relevance of the conception of executive decisions and the importance of the study of their development. First, developmental studies have shown that the individual's repertory of cognitive strategies increases during the course of intellectual development. If this is the case, the developing information processing system will increasingly need the ability to decide among alternative procedures and to evaluate selected approaches; that is, the growing child has to acquire the ability to make flexible and selective use of its own growing cognitive knowledge. Second, effortful cognitive processes, unlike automated processes (see Hasher & Zacks, 1979), may vary in the efficiency of their organization and execution. It is assumed that such effortful processes grant flexibility in problem solving. However, this implies that cognitive activity exists, which not only can be regulated, but which must be monitored and regulated in order to ensure its efficiency.

The resulting picture of human thinking, therefore, is not one of an always predetermined sequence and mode of information processing. Instead, the individual may: decide about cognitive processes; interrupt, accelerate, slow down own thinking directed towards certain goals; increase the intensity of own thinking; or deliberately maintain or continue the specific course of thinking. It is, therefore, assumed that executive decisions contribute to age-related variations and to intra- and interindividual differences in thinking. Presumably, executive decisions are necessary in order to efficiently apply the growing repertory of cognitive operations and to organize and execute effortful processes efficiently. Finally, in order to maintain cognitive activity, which is subject to emotionally and motivationally determined variation, the human information processing system needs executive decision.

A SET OF EXECUTIVE DECISIONS

Executive decisions deal with the course and the organization of own mental activity, and therefore, are part of procedural knowledge. Following is a framework for executive decisions. Executive decisions are considered to be procedural knowledge directed at the flow of own thinking. With regard to the declarative component, it is assumed that cognitive knowledge is available. Cognitive knowledge refers to stored facts, assumptions, and beliefs about thinking in general and about features of own cognitive endeavors (see Kluwe, 1982; Kluwe & Friedrichsen, 1985). Executive decisions are based, in part, on the availability of cognitive knowledge. This discussion is concerned with executive decisions only (for a more complete description see Kluwe & Friedrichsen, 1985).

Executive decisions aim at the acquisition of information about own ongoing cognitive activity and about the present state of own cognitive endeavor, as well as the transformation or maintenance of one's own cognitive activity and states. Hypothetical executive decisions have three features: (a) they determine how to solve a problem, but do not actually solve it, rather they guide the selection, organization, and termination of cognitive operations; (b) they are considered to be applied, especially to avoid costs, for example, in case of risky states or failure; and (c) in the course of solution search, they are not always necessary. Certain conditions that lead to the activation of executive processes, must be satisfied.

Executive decisions may be conceived of as condition-action-connections (see also Chi, Chapter 1, this volume). Conditions correspond to internal representations of states during problem solving, such as the amount of solution effort invested, duration of search, type of problem, distance to goal, etc. Actions would correspond to cognitive operations directed at the control and regulation of the solution process. Executive decisions may then be considered as stored rules for the control and regulation of cognitive activities during problem solving. An example of a rule could be "If very long solution time (condition), then check efficiency of own approach," or "then check distance to goal" (action). The action part may correspond to a subprogram that, once called up, achieves the acquisition of information about features of the previous activity and of the present state. Another possible action component would be to activate operations, in order to estimate the effort that still has to be invested; this would be a control decision.

Regulatory decisions can be described in the same way. For example "if no progress (condition), then increase resources for solution search" (action). Again, this action will correspond to a subprogram that, if activated, would achieve the goal, for example, by selection of other strategies. It is evident that the input for the activation of a regulatory decision may be the output of the action component for a control decision.

Executive decisions are activated when certain states during problem solving match with stored declarative (cognitive knowledge). A certain state during the solution search must first be registered; that is, it must be encoded as relevant for the efficiency, the progress or the success of own approach. Thus, there has to be declarative knowledge available concerning: the approximate duration of learning and solution processes; the features of promising approaches; etc. The availability of cognitive knowledge is necessary in order for a subject to become aware of searching too long for a solution, searching without a plan, etc. Furthermore, this knowledge component must be connected with subsequent actions, that guarantee appropriate control or regulation. It also requires knowledge about how to perform, control, or regulate; that is, how to evaluate the own search, how to speed up, etc. Both knowledge components that constitute rules for executive decisions are acquired during cognitive development. It is assumed that experience in problem solving is a major determinant of this development; and that the connections between conditions, that is, identified states and appropriate actions for control and regulation, have to be acquired.

Consequently the concept of metacognition is not needed. The declarative part, referred to as cognitive knowledge is not different from other factual knowledge; the procedural component corresponds to rules that can be classified as executive decision, because they are directed at the control and regulation of the solution effort.

The following two sets of executive decisions are hypothetical; however, they have some plausibility. Important guidelines have been obtained from the work of Brown (1978), Flavell (1979), and Sternberg (1979). It has been important to find that Selz, as early as 1913 and 1922, described processes that are highly comparable to what in this discussion has been termed executive decisions. Selz distinguished between processes that prepare for a solution, and those that accompany a solution. Among others Selz (1922) mentioned the processes of pondering and reflection, and emphasized the evaluative selection of strategies (p. 597, ff.). Following is a discussion of these cognitive activities.

Executive Control

Executive decisions directed at controlling or monitoring the own ongoing cognitive activities generate information about the activity and about the present cognitive state. Presumably, this may initiate the activation of what Flavell (1979) has termed metacognitive strategies; he assumes that metacognitive strategies are invoked to monitor cognitive progress (p. 909). The four executive activities discussed serve monitoring purposes: classification; checking; evaluation; and anticipation.

Classification. *Classification* of own cognitive activity provides information about the status, type, or mode of cognitive activity, and provides an answer to the question: "What am I doing here?" It is assumed that the accuracy of classification depends, in part, on the availability of an inventory of concepts that enable a person to talk about cognition and to look at own cognitive enterprises. Thus, if someone has knowledge about the problem types available, then he or she should be better able to identify the perceived cognitive requirements as a certain type of problem, that is, to classify it. It is further assumed that in order to classify cognitive activity a "protocol," a may be more or less precise trace of its own cognitive activity is necessary. To our knowledge, this problem has not yet been studied (see Reed & Johnson, 1978; Dörner, 1984; Kluwe, 1980).

Kreutzer et al. (1975) report that even young children use such concepts as forgetting and remembering. Lompscher (1972) instructed children to understand and use the cognitive concepts of abstraction, comparison, and classification. However, none of the available results indicate a connection between the availability of cognitive knowledge, in the sense of a general inventory of cognitive concepts, and the improvement of monitoring one's own cognitive activity.

Checking.   Checking-steps taken during the process of problem solving provide information about the state of the cognitive system and the state of cognitive activity. Classification, as mentioned earlier, provides information about *what* is done, in order to find the solution to a problem. Checking is directed at the *how* of one's own cognitive activity, that is, goals, its organization, progress, success, and the results. In thinking-aloud protocols checking-steps might take the form of statements. For example: "I can remember most of the text." "My planning is pretty detailed and careful." "I still have a pretty long way to go before I get there." "There's something I do not understand here."

One of the first studies concerned with checking one's own cognitive activity was done by Flavell, Friedrichs, and Hoyt (1970). They found that with respect to certain content, even 8 to 10-year-old children could quite accurately check their recall readiness. Surprisingly, half of the nursery school children also responded accurately and appeared able to adequately check their own recall readiness. On the basis of the analysis of the children's memorization process, Flavell et al. concluded that information concerning one's own memory, in this case recall readiness, and, over a period time, the strategic deployment of various types of memorization activities "appear to be more closely intertwined than we had suspected" (p. 338). This might be responsible for the higher level of recall that is especially evident from the memorization procedure of 10-year-old children.

For adults Perlmutter (1978) reports considerable correlation between checking of own memorization, indicated by the assessment of recall readiness, and memory performance, indicated by the recall performance. However, the causal connection between the two variables, memory monitoring and memory performance, has not yet been shown.

In a comprehensive study of children between 4 to 10 years of age, Kelly, Scholnick, Travers, and Johnson (1976) did not obtain age differences with respect to memory monitoring. Furthermore, they could not detect relations between checking (as indicated by estimations of recall readiness), study strategy, and recall performance. This result is in contrast to the findings and assumptions formulated by Flavell et al. (1970). The study by Kelly and his coworkers also points to a problem that was first discussed by Masur, McIntyre, and Flavell (1973). In this study younger children, (6-year-olds) check their own cognitive state, which can be inferred from the distinction they are able to make between those items they are actually able to recall and those items they are not yet able recall. However, their strategic procedure, according to the viewpoint of the experimenter, does not match the actual information available concerning the cognitive state. The children do not focus their memorization activity on the difficult items; instead, they memorize all items. It is assumed that younger children usually do not use the available information about already learned and about not yet learned items; as a result the memorization strategy they employ will not be regulated (see Bisanz, Vesonder, & Voss 1978; Brown 1978). However, as shown by the study of Masur et al., the phenomenon seems to be more complex. It is possible to provide 6-year-old children with a more appropriate strategy; a strategy that takes into account the available information about reproduceable and nonreproduceable items. However, the more appropriate strategy does not improve recall performance. The result of this study, as well as results reported by Kelly et al., suggest a more complicated relation between the information acquired through checking, the subsequent use of the information, and the resultant cognitive performance. According to the studies mentioned, one can assume that for older children, 8–10 years of age, there might be a closer interrelation between cognitive strategy, checking activity, information acquired from checking, and the resultant performance. Only the Kelly et al. study, in which no age dependent variation was obtained, contradicts this assumption. Nevertheless, it is not clear why younger children, despite having information about the state of their own memorization activity, maintain a strategy, which from the standpoint of the adult experimenter, is judged as less efficient, and does not correspond to what they know.

The principal usefulness of checking activities is shown by another group of studies. Brown and Barclay (1976) were the first to induce monitoring activities directed at the children's own cognitive activities. They trained children of different age groups to use mnemonic strategies that incorporated self-testing elements. Training in these strategies (rehearsal, anticipation) improved memory performance and memory monitoring, indicated by more accurate estimations of recall readiness. An interesting result is that one year following the training, older children maintained the strategies. They were even able to transfer the use of these strategies to new situational demands, and outperform untrained children (Brown, Campione & Barclay 1979).

The importance of checking is also confirmed in a recent study by Ringel & Springer (1980). As in Brown and Barclay's (1976) experiment, the checking was an independent variable. The authors could show that strategic training alone was less effective in improving recall performance than was strategic training combined with feedback from the effect of training on own performance. Third graders who received training did transfer the use of the strategy to new task demands; this may be attributed to their awareness of the benefits of the strategy, which were explained by the experimenter. The authors assume that the children themselves started checking and monitoring the effects of the strategy on their own performance. Fifth graders, however, did not gain from this type of combined training; their performance improved even without explicitly provided monitoring of own performance. However, both studies do show that it is possible to enhance performance by training and by inducing checking steps directed at one's own cognitive endeavour.

Evaluation.   *Evaluation* of one's own cognitive states and activities provides information about their quality. Evaluation goes beyond checking, because, in order to judge the course and the state of own thinking, criteria are applied. Evaluations made in the course of thinking may be found in thinking-aloud protocols. For instance, there are statements such as, "My plan is not good enough to rule out any risks." or "This solution has been great work." Evaluation of own thinking is a complicated activity. As yet, little is known about the criteria a person uses to evaluate the own cognitive activity. When is a selected direction rejected because it is inefficient? When does an individual judge a state to be uncontrollable during problem solving? When is a problem rejected as too difficult?

Apparently, when an individual decides about the termination of solution activities, effort and ability play an important role—for instance, when there is no real progress. Presumably, the decision about progress during problem solving takes into account past solution efforts, beliefs about one's own cognitive abilities and estimations of the effort that has to be invested (see Heckhausen, 1982, for developmental aspects; Kluwe, 1980). This researcher is not aware of any studies that concern the criteria that may be used to evaluate cognitive efforts. Such criteria form the basis for judgments, such as systematic, chaotic, clumsy, or elegant approach. As a result, when monitoring and regulation of thinking are studied the criteria according to which monitoring and regulation are performed must be considered. Simon (1975) has provided an important analysis of different problem-solving strategies. He gives an evaluation of the strategies that might be useful in solving the "Tower of Hanoi" problem; the criteria used by Simon include memory load and transferability. The question is whether these criteria may also be regarded as subjective, that is, as criteria that individuals will take into account when deciding on a particular strategy. What a priori is considered to be an efficient strategy for a problem solution may not necessarily be the best strategy for the subject studied; this is especially true for children (see Richman & Gholson, 1978; Sternberg & Weil, 1980).

Usually, monitoring studies implicitly assume that the subjects do make evaluations. This is true for experimental studies referring to recall readiness, as well as for the developmental experiments concerning memory (Butterfield & Belmont, 1977). These studies deal mainly with evaluation of one's own cognitive activity on the basis of internal criteria; for example, the efficiency of one's own enterprise.

Presumably, beliefs about one's own cognitive ability and cognitive effort constitute, in part, evaluation of one's own cognitive state. Ruble, Parsons and

Ross (1976) report that young children, 4–6 years, estimate the own invested effort differently from older children 8–9 years. This, in turn, might affect the evaluation of the efficiency of cognitive activity. Only children older than 8 years take into account social norms when evaluating their own cognitive performance (Ruble, Boggiano, Feldman, & Lobe, 1980). However, not much is known about how beliefs concerning own cognitive abilities, already invested effort and effort still to be invested, and social norms combine when own cognitive activity is evaluated. Nicholls (1978) elaborated on a developmental sequence: Children between the ages of 9 and 10 are able to distinguish between their own ability and effort and the outcome. The development of this distinction goes along with the acquisition of a more realistic self-concept, referring to the cognitive features of an individual (Kluwe, 1980). This means that the beliefs about one's own cognitive equipment become more precise and appropriate; it might also support a more realistic evaluation of own cognitive enterprises during cognitive development. However, the question concerning about what children younger than 8 or 9 years do is still unanswered; Do they evaluate their own cognitive activity? If they do, as is assumed, then what criteria do they use?

Prediction.   Prediction of cognitive states and cognitive activities provides information about: the possible alternative options for problem solving; the possible sequence of solution steps; and the possible outcomes. Zimmer's (1976) concepts of "anticipation of methods," and "anticipation of goal states" refers to similar phenomena. Prediction will presumably take the form of verbalization, such as: "If I decide to work on this problem, all those technical details may be hard to overcome; I'll have to get someone to help me out with them." or "In the next three weeks or so, it should be possible to learn those three chapters on cognitive psychology for the exam."

Prediction, an important component in problem-solving processes, is assumed to be a function of problem-solving experience in different domains of reality. Prediction is especially necessary in complex problem situations where the effects of own solution actions may expand and result in uncertain side effects. In a similar way, prediction is needed in particularly important or risky situations, in order to avoid "costs."

The developmental picture is determined essentially by results that concern the prediction of one's own memory span. The method used requires children in different age groups to memorize a set of items; the children are told to memorize the items for later recall. They are then asked to tell the experimenter how many of the items they believe they will be able to recall. In such investigations, (Brown, 1978: Chi, 1978) no age differences are obtained beyond third grade (age 8–9 years). However, Kelly et al. (1976) did not find any age differences even for younger children; their study covered kindergarteners through fourth graders; the same is true of the results reported by Justice and Bray (1979). According to the findings of Brown (1978), due to the inconsistency in the children's response, it is necessary to take into account methodological questions. There is the possibility that because of their predictions of their memory span, children may erroneously be classified as realistic. Two other factors may influence children's predictions with respect to their own cognitive activity: (a) according to Justice and Bray (1979), one has to assume that the accuracy of predicting the own memory state depends on task variables, such as context of the task, and the connection of the task to a desired goal; (b) Chi (1978) shows that when children predict their own memory span, their declarative knowledge is an important determinant of accuracy. The conclusions that younger children in general show a deficit with regard to the prediction of own cognitive states and activities are not justified by these findings. There are situations in which younger children are able to make accurate predictions. Worden and Sladewski-Awig (1979) reported age differences (Kindergarteners, Second, Fourth, and Sixth graders) in a study of span prediction. The authors inquired into the reason for these differences, and their analysis ruled out the possibility of a faulty checking process for the kindergarteners. According to the authors, overestimation of memory span in this age group is attributable to the use of a rather liberal response criterion. A criterion shift towards a more conservative estimate that is the result of experience with such tasks might provide a more accurate picture; it would also be in accord with the finding that meaningful contexts enhance the accuracy of memory span predictions.

For adults, results appear to contradict the assumed importance of the development of executive control during childhood. Lachman, Lachman, and Thronesbery (1979) and Perlmutter (1978) did not find any age differences for adults and aged subjects with respect to metamemory. Studies concerned with prediction of cognitive states and activities, other than memory span tasks, are not available. However, in this context, one study reported by Parsons and Ruble (1977) can be cited. The authors report that preschoolers required to predict the possible outcome of own problem solving in terms of success or failure do not use the information about the outcome of own prior problem solving endeavors.

The four hypothetical processes aiming at control of the own cognitive activity are not independent of one another. In order to extrapolate the possible course of the own thinking process, evaluation requires checking; checking requires classification; and prediction requires checking. According to certain criteria, control activities have as a result the decision to regulate the own cognitive activity. This is discussed in the next section.

Executive Regulation

Executive regulation refers to decisions about the organization, effort, amount, course, and direction of one's own cognitive activity. Regulatory decisions do not necessarily imply a modification of the cognitive activity, they may also result in the maintenance and continuation of a particular cognitive enterprise. To date, regulatory decisions have been largely ignored in developmental literature. Here four hypothetical processes of regulation are discussed: regulation of processing capacity, regulation of what is processed, regulation of processing intensity, and regulation of the speed of information processing.

Regulation of Processing Capacity. Regulation of processing capacity refers to two related decisions: (a) the decision about the total amount of capacity a person is willing to invest in order to accomplish certain cognitive demands; and (b) the decision about the allocation of information processing capacity for mental operations. Information processing capacity refers to a nonspecific resource for cognitive activity. The number of resources may vary and ultimately may affect the outcome of mental operations (see Hasher & Zacks, 1979, for the concept of effortful processing).

The first type of decision deals with the total amount of effort a person invests in a problem-solving situation. The distinction between resource-limited and data-limited information processing, made by Norman and Bobrow (1975), is relevant. It relates to the question that might occur to someone involved in the process of problem solving: Does increasing effort also increase the chances of success? The second type of decision is closely related to selective attention. It is assumed that human information processing capacity is limited. Consequently, for many task demands, the problem solver has a choice as to which elements of the situation or of the information attended to, should be processed. This, in turn, means that the capacity limits need selective attention and call for executive decisions concerning the regulation of information processing capacity. The question of allocation of capacity has been studied in connection with performance differences associated with incidental versus intentional learning. The variation of capacity for processing affects the efficiency of effortful strategies; therefore, such tasks should be studied in the context of development. Depending on the age of the subjects, variations in capacity allocation may be associated with performance differences.

Crane and Ross (1967) showed that older children are less likely to focus on task-irrelevant information. Their findings were replicated by Kemler, Shepp, and Foote (1976). Five- and 7-year-old children process more task-irrelevant information than do 10-year-old children; however, some of the results are contradictory. Howard and Goldin (1979) report that even kindergardeners are able to regulate the allocation of their resources; that is, they are able to focus attention on only the relevant aspects of the situation. Contrary to earlier studies, the authors tried to maximize performance by explicitly directing the children's attention to the relevant situational features. Without this type of guidance, efficient allocation of the resources seems to develop rather late in cognitive growth. Recently, Hale and Alderman (1978) found that extending the exposure time in a learning paradigm increases the incidental as well as the intentional scores for 9-year-old children, but not for the 12-year-old children. As children grow older, they regulate the allocation of resources so that task-relevant elements acquire more attention than irrelevant elements. In all cases concerning the allocation of resources, the inferred differences go along with performance differences.

A final, somewhat puzzling, result is reported by Markman (1979). In a study on comprehension monitoring, Markman found that even 12-year-old children did not detect inconsistencies in the text although they claimed that they understood the text. Several interventions to improve children's comprehension monitoring were unsuccessful. Finally, Markman warned the children that there was a problem in each of the texts and that they should read carefully. Now the 12-year-old, but not the 9-year-old children, aware that there was a problem they would have to detect, were able to apply the necessary control processes. This relatively simple intervention conceivably could increase the children's overall processing capacity. Presumably, the allocation of capacity could also be increased so that the children would focus attention on particular parts of the text. Given these results, it can be assumed that the ability for deliberate regulation of one's own processing capacity is acquired rather late in cognitive development, probably not before the age of 10 or 11 years.

Regulation of What is Processed.   If one reads through thinking-aloud protocols, one finds that it is not self-evident at what point or segment the individual begins to search for a solution to a problem or what is the starting point selected. In protocols dealing with the problem of solving logical theorems, subjects decide whether: to work on the left side or the right side; to start working on "p" or "q." For example, in cryptarithmetic protocols subjects, decide first, to find the value for the letter E, etc. Such assumptions are implicit in the type of model concerning balance scale problems elaborated by Siegler (1976). According to Siegler's model, children process weight and distance in a certain sequence. Developmental studies concerned with this type of regulatory decision, the deliberate selection of what is processed, are not available. However, one study with adult subjects illustrates the problem. Thorndyke and Stasz (1980) report the differences between good and poor learners. They found that good learners deliberately regulate, from a complex domain, what they intend to memorize and what is subsequently to be memorized. Compared to poor learners, good learners are more involved in deciding what segment of the material should be worked on and, after successful storage of this segment, how to proceed (they were required to memorize a map). In their learning processes, poor learners adopt a rather unsystematic sampling procedure, and in some cases do not adequately focus attention on the selected segments for memorization. The same holds true for performance differences in the Raven, "Progressive Matrices" intelligence test (Lüer et al., 1979). Apparently, poor performance goes along with insufficient regulation of the own solution search; as a result, the subjects do not systematically select and analyze the segments of the task.

Regulation of Processing Intensity.   This form of executive decisions is assumed to comprise three different decisions. First, is the regulation of the frequency with which a cognitive operation or process is applied to specific segments of the problem situation. An example would be the number of comparisons made between two objects; increasing the frequency of comparisons between the two objects would also increase the reliability of the final similarity judgment. Another example would be the repeated reading of an instruction outlining the important construction steps, in order to avoid irreversible mistakes. Second is the regulation of time allotted to the execution of a cognitive operation. For example, if two objects are compared, the regulation of time allotted would refer to the time spent comparing objects. This in turn could result in a longer examination of the attributes of one object, and also in an extension of the set of attributes which constitute the final judgment; once again, the judgment might then be more reliable. Third is the regulation of the solution search by strategy shift and by modification of the perspective. The following two possibilities are considered: the solution search is not terminated when a strategic effort is revealed as being unsuccessful, that is, it did not lead to the desired goal state; rather, the solution search might be continued by shifting to an alternative strategy (see, for example, the alternative steps in case of failure described by Dörner, 1976; see also Kluwe, 1979, 1980). Work on a given problem might also be continued on the basis of some other internal representation of the problem. In other words, applying a different perspective, which entails different encoding of the problem, may bring about a new starting point for subsequent steps in the solution attempt. Therefore, when confronted with failure, a subject may substitute another strategy for the originally selected approach, for example by trial and error. Dörner (1976), in his work on problem solving, explicitly refers to the shift of heuristics as one possibility in overcoming problem solving barriers.

All three decisions directed at the regulation of processing intensity have one aspect in common: they affect the degree of persistence of processing. Each one determines to what degree the own cognitive endeavor will be exhaustive. Several findings from empirical studies show that younger children process information less exhaustively than do older children. Sternberg and Rifkin (1979), in a study of the development of analogical reasoning, found that children aged 8–10 years prefer self-terminating operations, operations that need not to be executed the maximum number of times. They offer one possible explanation for this result, the memory load associated with exhaustive processing (e.g., exhaustive encoding of an input). It is interesting to note that according to Sternberg and Rifkin's model, the less exhaustive processing characteristic of younger children can be connected with their lower performance; that is, with the higher error rate in analogical reasoning.

Similar differences may also have been responsible for the results reported by Ceci and Howe (1978). They found that in a recall task, 10-year-old children switch from one mode of memory to another in order to improve recall of the learned material. This is not the case with 7-year-old children. Perhaps, in order to reproduce as many items as possible, the younger children do not exhaustively scan the stored categories. In an earlier study, Kobasigawa (1974) observed that 6- to 8-year-old children, when compared with 1-year olds, do not sufficiently scan the categories of the memorized items for recall. Ceci and Howe report that 10-year-old children, when compared to 7-year-old children do not terminate their search for items, but instead continue memory search by applying another organization of the material. They also report that the 10-year-old children switch from a thematic to a taxonomic organization when instructed to recall memorized material. The switching from one mode of search to another is related to higher levels of recall. Examples demonstrating a connection between the regulation of intensity and preceding executive control of the own approach, are hard to find. Karmiloff-Smith (1978) reported that children between 7 and 11 years of age deliberately modify a coding system they themselves had worked out, in order to retrace a longer way of getting around a town. It should be pointed out that the children modified the coding system even though it had actually worked. From continuous evaluation of the efficiency of the earlier representational system it may be inferred that the children did not terminate the coding activity, but instead, continued the activity.

Rogoff, Newcombe, and Kagan (1974) provide another example. Their results indicate that when given corresponding task demands, only 8-year-old children increase the intensity of memorization. Only these children extended the time for memorizing pictures to be recalled later as a function of the time-interval between memorization and future recall. Rogoff et al. conclude that the ability to control and regulate the own mnemonic activity according to the task demands emerges around 6–7 years of age.

In conclusion, it may be assumed that, in general, younger children tend to process information less intensively, that is, less exhaustively, than older children. The relationship between these findings and Sternberg and Rifkin's assumption, mentioned earlier, that exhaustive processing is related to a higher memory load, must still be explored.

The Regulation of Speed of Information Processing.   Presumably, intensity regulation, in those cases where more intensive processing is necessary, results in more time-consuming activities. Given the same amount of information in a problem situation, deliberate regulation of the speed of processing might be reached through executive decisions. These decisions concern the completeness of the cognitive procedures to be used: Adding certain cognitive operations might decrease processing speed; skipping some processing steps might increase processing speed. The existence of only one small scale study in which subjects were instructed to regulate the speed of processing, is known; Barstis and Ford (1977) changed the problem solving conditions for the "Matching Familiar

Figures Test.'' Instruction emphasized either accuracy or speed of processing. On the whole, 8-year-old children were better able to increase speed than the kindergarteners, [who experienced a higher rate of error as speed increased]. There are many situations in which children, especially in school, are required to deal with a task within a certain time limit; therefore further study of this problem is necessary. The general hypotheses is that during early childhood a somewhat stereotyped pace of information processing is typical. It is assumed that in the process of cognitive development it is easier for children to first slow down processing, rather than to speed it up. Studies concerning this problem should investigate not only whether children can regulate the speed of information processing but also how it can be accomplished by children of different ages.

REMARKS ON THE DEVELOPMENT OF EXECUTIVE CONTROL AND REGULATION AND COGNITIVE PERFORMANCE

Executive Control

According to Piaget (1928), children younger than 7 years of age are unable to classify and check the features of their own thinking. The hypothetically assumed precondition of control, namely the storage of a record of own cognitive activity, is assumed to be satisfied only in later years, probably around 11 years of age. Piaget believes that children under 7 years of age are unable to retrace the steps taken in solving a problem because they are unable to keep a record of their own successive attempts. He postulates three stages for the evolution of children's introspection that occur between 7 and 10 years of age. From 7 years of age onwards we will find ''thinking about thinking'' (p. 146). Piaget considers ''The shock of our thought coming into contact with that of others'' (p. 146) to be an important source for the development of the ability to retrace and evaluate the own thinking. Until the age of 7, however, the child's attention is in no way directed towards thought as a medium interposed between the world and himself.

Yet, the research results discussed show that there are children younger than 7 who engage in control and regulation. It is remarkable that in this context Piaget suggests that social communication between the child and his parents, relatives, or other persons in his environment is an essential developmental determinant of this ability. Recent research by Wertsch (1979) deals with this phenomenon within the framework of the development of metacognition.

A few aspects of the possible relation between cognitive performance and the control of one's own thinking have already been discussed. The following discussion includes some results from experiments with adult subjects. There are individual differences in cognitive performance that apparently are connected to differences in executive control. These a posteriori differences may be examined more thoroughly in follow-up investigations where the influence of executive control can be studied more systematically.

Owings, Petersen, Bransford, Morris, and Stein (1980) compared the learning activity of successful and unsuccessful fifth grade learners. They report that successful learners spontaneously monitored as they read and studied a text. Thorndyke and Stasz (1980), in their study of learning processes of adult subjects, found that good learners check and evaluate their study progress and approach more often and more accurately than poor learners. The subjects' task was to memorize the contents of a map. Dörner et al. (1978), based on their investigation of the problem-solving behavior of adult subjects confronted by complex systems, reported that good problem solvers devote part of their solution activity to classification, checking, and evaluation of what they did and what they plan to do. These observations were based mostly on statements made by the subjects in thinking-aloud protocols. In another experiment subjects were asked only to reflect on their own approach when solving a problem (Dörner, 1984). The effects of this type of instruction on cognitive performance were not unequivocal. For instance, Hesse (1979) reported improvements in the performance of subjects solving tasks from the Raven Progressive Matrices intelligence test. However, compared with the control groups, this group's performance also was inferior on the easy tasks of this intelligence test. Reither's (1979) subjects, after working on switch light problems, were instructed to reflect on their own solution search. Given a new problem, they needed fewer steps in their search for a solution, without needing more time for the solution search, than was needed by the control group.

These results suggest a causal relation between the mode and amount of executive control and level of cognitive performance. Similar studies of developmental aspects could be undertaken; however, this would require a more careful examination of the a posteriori differences, such as in the study by Brown and Barclay (1976). The question is: Is it possible to induce other types of executive decisions in the same elegant way as was done in the Brown and Barclay's (1976) study on self-checking and monitoring of one's own memory performance?

In the study of the level of performance, one must consider that the effects of executive control on performance may not be obvious. Steps directed at control might affect performance in a way that cannot be captured by the usual success-failure distinction. One example of the possible effect of executive control, which requires careful analysis, is the ease with which cognitive strategies are transferred to new task demands. Other criteria for determining the level of cognitive performance might be the degree of organization of the subjects' approaches, the ease of solution search, memory load, frequency of corrections, persistence in case of failure, and flexibility of the approach, given changing situational demands. One problem that exists is that the extension of the criterion set for evaluating cognitive performance might reflect the effects of executive control. A second problem has been revealed in the results of Kelly et al. (1976); that is, that the relation between control of own cognitive activity and the subsequent use of the acquired information is not clear. Kelly et al. assume that there may only be a loose relationship between cognitive activity and the information acquired through control. Regardless of the strength of the hypothetical relationship, no available knowledge exists concerning the rules that govern the application of such information. It is not clear when control is activated during solution search; however, it is usually assumed that unexpected difficulties trigger cognitive operations directed at the checking and evaluation of own cognitive efforts. Yet, the behavior of good problem solvers and good learners, who are inclined to control the own approach even in the absence of difficulties, contradicts this assumption. The characteristics of the information acquired through executive control are unknown. The regulatory decisions described may follow control steps as a consequence of their results and may be the link between cognitive activity, control, and performance.

Executive Regulation

It is assumed that regulatory decisions are preceded by control activity; however, regulatory decisions need not lead to regulatory activity. In light of the issues discussed previously, it is reasonable to assume that older children (beyond third grade) are more likely than younger children to use information acquired through monitoring. However, it is, precipitous to postulate a developmental sequence from executive control alone to executive control that is connected with appropriate regulation. This sequence might be suggested by the developmental picture sometimes presented, of the successively emerging use of information acquired through control. However, it is possible that younger children regulate their cognitive activity according to criteria other than those being explored here. The relativity of criteria with regard to the appropriateness of strategies is exemplified in Sternberg and Weil's (1980) experiment, which studied the relative efficiency of strategies.

The following points are of importance to the question of what develops,

1. The ability to regulate one's own cognitive activity on the basis of information about one's own ongoing effort is developed. For example, being aware, that one's own approach is too risky, presumably, requires a decision about increasing the intensity and decreasing the speed of processing.

2. The ability to transform a regulatory decision into the appropriate cognitive operation is developed. For example, if the solution search is too risky, an appropriate implementation of the regulatory decision to decrease speed might be to include a planning phase before continuing. A child may become aware that proceeding planfully, step by step, is the best way to avoid "costs"; but the child may not know how to do this.

3. It is not assumed that during cognitive development children acquire explicit knowledge about criteria for efficient thinking. Instead, their flow of thinking, organized and directed by executive decisions, indicates implicit knowledge about efficient thinking (see Greeno and Riley, Chapter 10, this volume, for the concept of implicit understanding). Greeno and Riley's cognitive procedures match principles that might be formulated in a general theory about thinking; however, the children themselves cannot verbalize these principles. Based on this viewpoint, it is necessary to focus on the features of children's and adults' cognitive procedures.

CHILDREN'S REGULATION OF PROBLEM SOLVING AS A FUNCTION OF REVERSIBILITY VERSUS IRREVERSIBILITY OF ACTIONS

Experiment

The following is a preliminary report of the results of a developmental experiment. The goal of the experiment was to create task demands that allow inferences about children's executive regulation in problem solving. In the experiment regulatory activity is treated as a dependent variable. The purpose was to determine if changing the problem solving conditions, that is, changing from reversibility to irreversibility of actions, would cause children of different ages to increase the intensity and to decrease the speed of their solution approach. On the basis of the assumptions previously outlined, one would expect increments for the time and frequency with which solution operations are applied under irreversible conditions; one would also expect the application of new operations, which would not have necessary under reversible conditions. Finally, it was also to be determined if age differences influence the ways the assumed regulatory activity is implemented. In this context it was expected that performance differences would be associated with regulatory differences.

The subjects of the experiment were 57 children, grouped by age (4, 5, 6, and 7 years). The tasks used were puzzles, which can be applied across a wide age range; they are the type of problem in which the activities engaged in during solution search can be easily traced (for criteria for selecting tasks see Brown & DeLoache, 1978). Each of the children solved five puzzles; puzzles 1 through 3 under reversible conditions, puzzles 4 and 5 under irreversible conditions. Provision was made for the irreversibility of action for puzzles 4 and 5. Instead of using a piece of white cardboard, which had been the working surface for reversible conditions, the children were given a cardboard that was completely covered with a strong, colorless adhesive layer. Once a piece of the puzzle was placed on the working surface, it became fixed and could not be removed.

After the third reversible puzzle was accomplished each child was told that because all the pieces would fall down, the completed puzzle could not, after all, be hung on the wall like a picture. This was demonstrated to the children. Then each child was shown the cardboard with the adhesive and was encouraged to put his or her hand on the surface of the cardboard. The only information the children were given, regarding the irreversible condition, was that once the pieces of the puzzle had been put onto the cardboard, they could not be removed. Although this information was given twice, the child was not told to be particularly careful or to pay more attention.

The collected data are based on the registration of eye-fixations and of problem-solving operations. The recorded data includes:

Code   1: looking at the target picture.
Code   2: looking at the pieces of the puzzle.
Code   3: looking at the cardboard working surface.
Code 22: sorting the pieces of the puzzle.
Code 23: comparing one piece of the puzzle with the partial solution on the working surface.
Code 44: holding a selected piece close to a fixed piece on the adhesive surface without attaching it to the surface.
Code   6: model-building, that is, putting two or more pieces together next to the working surface.

Some of the preliminary results that refer to the regulation of the intensity of the solution search are reported in what follows. The analysis focusses on the transition from reversible (puzzle 3) to irreversible (puzzle 4) conditions. Only the data that refer to the interval between the end of the instruction (providing the target picture) and putting the first two parts of the solution onto the surface are considered. Thus, for each child, the segment of the problem-solving process under reversible conditions was compared with the segment under irreversible conditions. The preliminary restriction of the analysis with respect to this segment of the solution search assumes that during this interval relevant regulatory activities are especially necessary. The general hypothesis was that 7-year-old children, when compared to all younger children, would significantly increase the frequency and the time of eye-fixations and of certain solution operations.

The following six regulatory activities were subject to further analysis:

+ h: increasing the relative frequency of solution actions and/or eye fixations.
+ t: increasing the average time of actions and/or eye-fixations;
− h: decreasing the relative frequency of actions and/or eye-fixations.
− t: decreasing the average time of actions and/or eye fixations.
add: adding new operations.
sub: skipping operations.

According to our discussion of processing intensity, an increase of intensity should be indicated by +h, +t, and add-regulations.

Results

As a result of changing the task demands from reversibility to irreversibility of actions, all the children showed a high degree of regulatory activity.

1. Overall changes (+, −, add, sub) were more likely to occur than was the maintenance of the initial approach.

2. Overall increments of relative frequency and time (+ h, + t), as well as adding of new operations (add), predominated (Fig. 2.1a).

3. The regulatory activity extended over the range of encoded solution actions and eye-fixations. Changes involved primarily eye-fixations (Code 1, 2, 23, 3; see Fig. 2.1b).

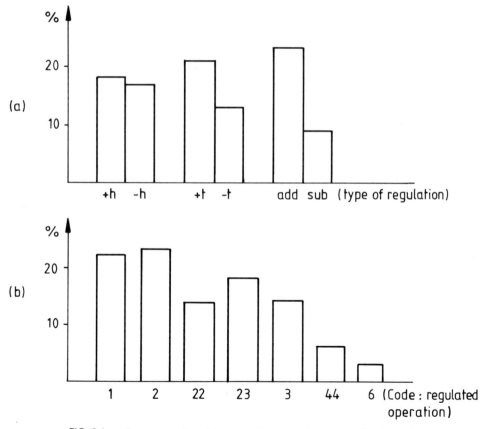

FIG. 2.1a.   Percentage of regulatory activities.   b: Percentage of actions subject to regulation.

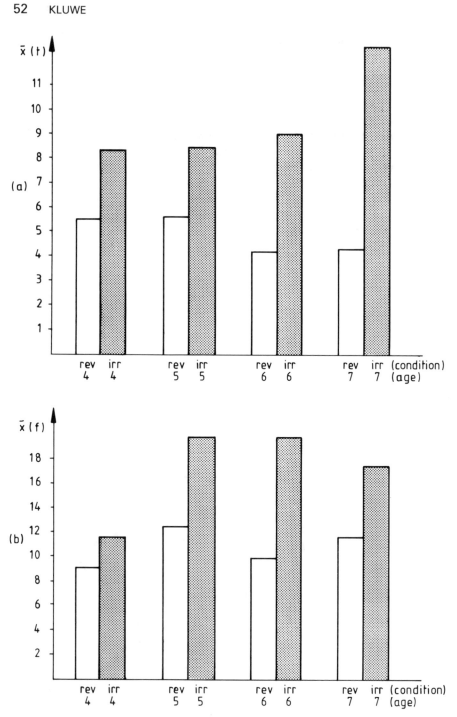

FIG 2.2.

4. The analysis of the total time used and the analysis of the total number of solution actions performed until the second part of the puzzle was placed on the working surface resulted in the following picture:

The total time of solution activities is increased significantly under irreversible conditions ($F = 14.07$; $df = 1,53$; $p \leq .01$; Fig. 2.2a). The total number of solution actions performed until the second part of the puzzle was placed on the working surface is also increased significantly under irreversible conditions ($F = 21.70$; $df = 1,53$; $p \leq .01$; Fig. 2.2b).

5. Some solution actions were systematically related to certain regulatory activities. First, the relative frequency of applying operation Code 23 (comparing one piece of the puzzle with the partial solution) increased under irreversible conditions. The difference between reversible and irreversible conditions with regard to this variable is statistically significant ($F = 16.55$; $df = 1,53$; $p \leq .01$; Fig. 2.3a). However, no comparable effects were found for the other registered operations. Contrary to what was expected, the subjects did not look more frequently at the target picture or at the pieces of the puzzles. Second, the average time for operation Code 1 (looking at the target picture) and for Code 23 (comparing one piece of the puzzle with the partial solution) also increased significantly under irreversible conditions. (F (Code 1) $= 4.14$; $df = 1;53$; $p \leq .05$; F (Code 23) $= 35.34$; $df = 1,53$; $p \leq .01$; see Fig. 2.3b, c).

Third, the adding of new operations (add), which as previously indicated was a dominant regulatory activity, focused on specific activities (25% for Code 23, 22% for Code 44, 16% for Code 22). The significant deviation from equal distribution shows that under irreversible conditions, primarily three operations were included in the solution search: Code 23 (comparing one piece of the puzzle with the partial solution); Code 22 (sorting the pieces of the puzzle next to the working surface); and Code 44 (holding a piece of the puzzle close to the adhesive without attaching it to the surface). These operations, added to the repertoire of already applied operations, provide for a more thorough, detailed analysis of the puzzle material. Later it is seen that age differences were found for this type of regulatory activity.

Fourth, the analysis also included the relation between the time spent for a certain operation and the total time spent on solution search, until the first two parts of the puzzle were fixed. The analysis of the relative amount of time for operations yielded statistically significant effects for operation Codes 1, 2, and 23. The results indicate that, compared to the total solution time, the proportion of time for the activities Code 1 and Code 2 decreased; however, the proportion

---

FIG. 2.2.   Effect of the condition reversibility vs. irreversibility on a: the average of total time t for solution actions ($\bar{x}$ (t) in min/10): ($F = 14.07$; $df = 1,53$; $p \leq .01$).   b: the average of total number of solution activities f ($F = 21.70$; $df = 1,53$; $P \leq .01$). (Averages per age group and condition).

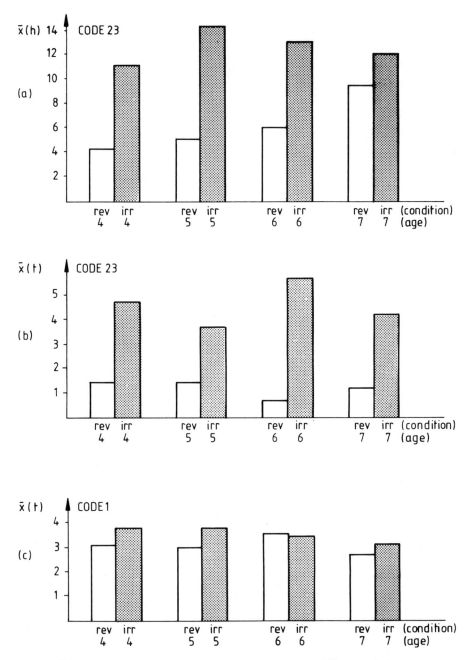

FIG. 2.3. Effect of the condition reversibility vs. irreversibility on a: Relative frequency h of operation Code 23 ($F = 16.55$; $df = 1,53$; $p \le .01$). b: Average time $(\bar{x})t$ for operation code 23 ($F = 35.34$; $df = 1,53$; $p \le .01$). c: Average time $(\bar{x})t$ for operation code 1 ($F = 4.14$; $df = 1,53$; $p \le .05$). (Averages per age group and condition; time $(\bar{x})t$ in min/10).

of time for Code 23 increased (F [Code 1] = 9.73; df = 1,53; $p \leq .01$; F [Code 2] = 5.64; df = 1,53; $p \leq .05$; F [Code 23] = 24.61; df = 1,53; $p \leq .01$).

The solution operation Code 1 (looking at the target picture) showed an increment in the average time t, discussed earlier; however, the proportion of time invested for this activity, compared to the total time, decreased. Presumably, this was due to the extension of the application of operation Code 23, as well as to the addition of new solution operations (add) under irreversible conditions.

In sum the results concerning the regulation of solution activities indicate the following: Under irreversible problem solving conditions new operations are added to the solution procedure; in general the extension of the solution activity aims at a more thorough analysis of the pieces of the puzzle (Codes 22, 23, and 44; see Duncker, 1966/1935, and the concept of "material analysis"). However, regardless of age, under irreversible conditions the average time spent for "looking at the target picture" (Code 1) is increased. In addition, before it is put down on the surface (Code 23), a selected piece of the puzzle is looked at more frequently and for a longer period of time. For some solution actions (Code 1 and Code 2) the relative amount of time is decreased.

The findings 1 to 5 indicate that, as a result of changing specific features of the task demands, it is possible to obtain certain types of regulation. The regulatory decisions are only directed at a few solution operations. Accordingly, this deliberate regulatory activity aims at increasing the intensity of the own solution search by: increasing the relative frequency of operations, increasing the average time for operations by adding new operations, and, decreasing the speed of problem solving. Therefore, it appears that regulatory activity is performed to reduce the risk of failure associated with irreversible problem solving conditions. This conclusion is referred to when the relation between regulatory decisions and cognitive performance is discussed.

6. Age differences affect type of regulation. There are certain preferences for regulatory activities, within age groups, described earlier; these include increasing the average time for solution operations and adding new operations. However, this preferential pattern is true only for children 4, 5, and 6 years of age. At the age of 7 children do not have such clearly focused preferences with regard to the type of regulation (chi-square (4) = 23.42; chi-square (5) = 16.81; chi-square (6) 27.28; chi-square (7) = 1.16; df = 5).

It must be pointed out that when the situational demands are changed from reversible to irreversible conditions, the children of all age groups show quite similar solving behavior. The average number as well as the average time of solution operations is increased for all age groups. There were no age differences in the operation Codes 1, 2, 22, and 23, considering the changes of time and number. However, important age differences existed in the operation Codes 22, 44, and 6: Code 22 (Sorting of the pieces of the puzzles) is applied under irreversible conditions significantly more often by older children (6–7 years of

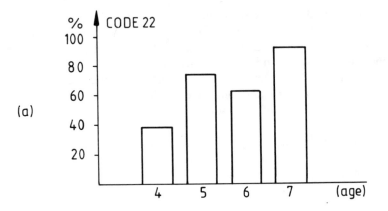

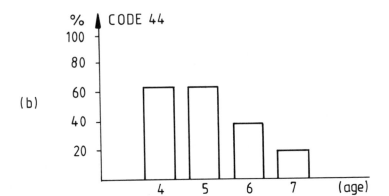

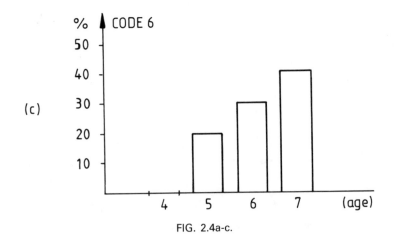

FIG. 2.4a-c.

age, chi-square = 9.81; df = 3; p ≤ .025; see Fig. 2.4a). The effect is due to the fact that only a few 4-year-old children apply this operation for a better analysis of the pieces under irreversible conditions; however, especially, the 7-year-old children do use this operation. It can be assumed that the sorting of pieces leads to decisions about the sequence of fixing pieces on the working surface. There is no such age effect for the reversible condition. Code 44 (holding one piece of the puzzle close to the surface without attaching it) is used under irreversible conditions more often by 4- and 5-year-old children (chi-square = 9.85; df = 3; p ≤ .05). There is no comparable age difference under reversible conditions (see Fig. 2.4b). Under irreversible conditions Code 6 (model-building, i.e., putting pieces together next to the working surface), significantly more older children put two or more pieces of the puzzle together before attaching them to the surface (chi-square = 8.21; df = 3; p ≤ .05; see Fig. 2.4c).

Both actions, Code 44 and Code 6, are added to the repertoire of solution activities under irreversible conditions. In the case of Code 6, which may also be used under reversible conditions, older children add this operation significantly more often under irreversible conditions (chi-square = 10.97; df = 3; p ≤ .02). The opposite is true for Code 44: younger children include this operation significantly more often in their repertoire under irreversible conditions (chi-square = 12.32; df = 3; p ≤ .01; see Fig. 2.5). In sum, age differences have the following effect: Older children extend their solution search by adding the operations that help to get a more thorough analysis of the material (Code 22, 23, 6). In contrast, younger children under irreversible conditions add Code 44, significantly more often, to their repertoire.

7. Cognitive performance and regulatory activities differences between successful and unsuccessful children apply to all age groups, and do not necessarily correspond to what is expected. One may assume that successful and unsuccessful problem solvers of different age groups have different regulatory patterns. The following differences emerge: Successful as well as unsuccessful children increase the average number of solution operations (F [Condition × success] = .23; df = 1;55; p ≤ .25). The same is true of the total time until putting the second piece on the surface; there is no interaction (F [condition × success] = .22; df = 1,55; p ≤ .25). Therefore, according to the analyses, it must be stated that successful and unsuccessful children are doing about the same. However, the open question is: Why does one group fail and the other succeed? There was only one regulatory operation where the difference resulted:

FIG. 2.4a.   Percentage of children in different age groups who sort pieces of the puzzle under irreversible conditions (Code 22). b: Percentage of children in different age groups that hold one piece close to the pieces on the working surface without attaching it (Code 44). c: Percentage of children in different age groups that put two or more pieces together next to the working surface (Code 6; model-building).

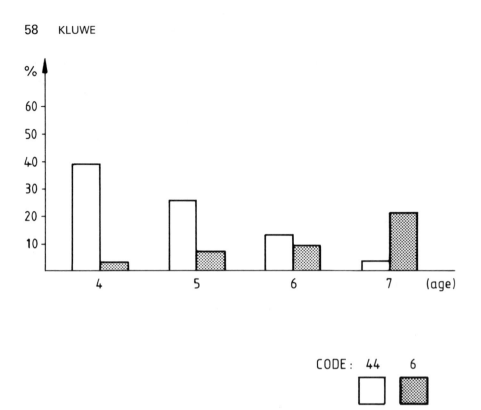

FIG. 2.5: Percentage of children in different age groups that add model-building (Code 6) and comparison of pieces with attached pieces (Code 44) under irreversible conditions.

Under irreversible conditions unsuccessful children reduce the proportion of time spent analyzing the target picture (Code 1; F [unsuccessful] $= 7.48$; $df = 1,27$; $p \leq .05$); however, this is not the case with successful children. The activities of unsuccessful children are shown in Fig. 2.6a–c. For all analyzed variables no remarkable relations with cognitive performance were found.

The interpretation offered must be kept as hypothetical. It is not permissable to say that under irreversible conditions, the mere increment of the total time for solution search and of the total number of solution operations guarantees a successful approach. Rather, it is necessary to find patterns of specific regulatory activity that correspond to levels of cognitive performance. Presumably, the conception of increasing intensity of problem solving activity under irreversible conditions, as disussed, is too simple; beyond the mere increment of time, number of operations, and adding of operations, it is necessary to expect more complex regulatory patterns.

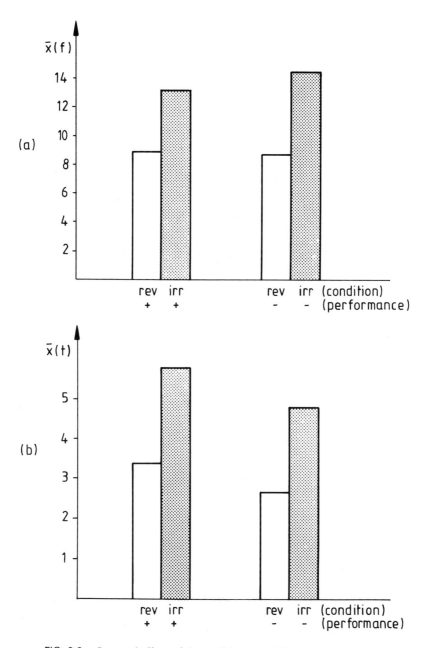

FIG. 2.6. Separated effects of the condition reversibility vs. irreversibility for successful and unsuccessful children: a: Average number of solution activities ($\bar{x}$)f: (F (condition x success) = .23; df = 1,55; $p \geq$ .25). b: Average time for solution activity $\bar{x}(t)$: (F (condition x success) = .22; df = 1,55; $p \geq$ .25). c: Unsuccessful children's average proportion of time for the analysis of the target picture: (F (Code 1) = 7.48; df = 1,27; $p \leq$ .05).

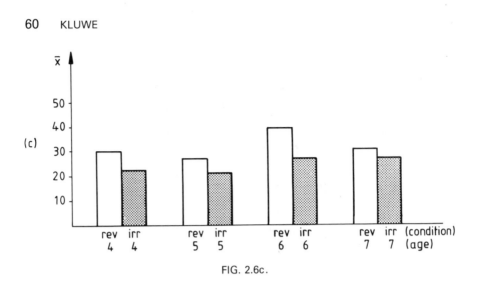

FIG. 2.6c.

Discussion

The resulting picture has been surprising. Under changing task demands, 4–5-year-old children, were not expected to engage in regulatory activity to the extent they actually did. Remember, the children were not instructed to be particularly careful or attentive when working with the adhesive surface under irreversible conditions. Because no age differences were obtained, with respect to the frequency of puzzle solutions, it may be assumed that each age group, in order to cope with the changing task demands, has its own pattern of regulatory activities. There is still no clear picture of how such regulatory patterns are constituted and structured. Further analysis is also needed to account for the factors responsible for determining performance differences; this also requires a more accurate description of performance differences. For instance, with regard to the features of the solution outcome, the groups of unsuccessful children could be divided into two subgroups; and the features of the process of solution, such as planfulness, could be given some consideration.

During the sessions, something that might most aptly be described as "persistence" of regulatory activity, was observed. The impression was repeatedly given that under irreversible conditions the children tended to fall back on a careless way of operating. Possibly, this is an additional important feature of the regulation of thinking under changing problem solving conditions.

The study of problem solving under reversible and irreversible conditions clearly revealed the effects of different regulatory decisions; differences for age and performance were infrequent. On the whole, under irreversible conditions young children appear to apply almost as many activities as older children; the same is true for the time variable. The higher frequency in the use of analytical operations (Code 22) and of model-building (Code 6) is most striking for the 7-year-old children. Only a few of the younger children, especially the 4-year-olds, use these operations. Instead, younger children in the comparison of fixed pieces with selected pieces (Code 44), show a higher frequency. However, under irreversible conditions, through their regulatory activity, younger and older children appear to create a condition in which the trial-and-error mode of operation, practiced under reversible conditions, can be used again. For younger children this is done by adding the operation Code 44 (comparing a selected piece with a fixed piece by holding the former close above the surface without attaching it to the adhesive). For the older children the same effect is achieved by building models (Code 6), that is, putting pieces together next to the surface; and by more frequent sorting of the pieces near the working surface (Code 22). Contrary to expectation, successful problem solving is not necessarily connected with more frequent visual analysis of the target, of the pieces of the puzzle, or of the working surface. The increase of time and frequency of solution activities alone is not a sufficient predictor of performance. It is assumed that one must search for certain patterns of regulatory activities that are associated with success or failure. The final question is: How can the solution behavior of children who on completing the puzzle successfully, proudly say: "Isn't that something; I have done a good job and yet I did not even once look at the picture here" (it happened twice), be analyzed.

The analysis of the available data does not justify Piaget's (1969/1928) conclusion "childish reasoning before the age of 7–8 . . . resembles a physical action during which one arm-movement will bring about another arm-movement . . ." (p. 212).

ACKNOWLEDGMENTS

Research reported here has been done as part of a research project supported by a grant from the Foundation Volkswagenwerk, Hannover, West Germany. Thanks is due to Kerstin Modrow, Traute Vaihinger, and Heidi Windeit for their contributions to the completion of this manuscript.

REFERENCES

Barstis, S., & Ford, L. H. (1977). Reflection-impulsivity, conversation, and the development of ability to control cognitive tempo. *Child Development, 48,* 953–959.

Bisanz, G. L., Vesonder, G. T., & Voss, J. F. (1978). Knowledge of one's own responding and the relation of such knowledge to learning. *Journal of Experimental Child Psychology, 25,* 116–128.

Brown, A. (1978). Knowing when, where, and how to remember: A problem of metacognition. In R. Glaser (Ed.), *Advances in instructional psychology* (Vol. 1, pp. 77–165). Hillsdale, NJ: Lawrence Erlbaum Associates.

Brown, A., & Barclay, C. R. (1976). The effects of training specific mnemonics on the metamnemonic efficiency of retarded children. *Child Development, 47,* 71–80.

Brown, A., Campione, J. C., & Barclay, C. R. (1979). Training self-checking routines for estimating test readiness: generalization from list learning to prose recall. *Child Development, 50,* 501–512.

Brown, A., & DeLoache, J. S. (1978). Skills, plans, and self-regulation. In R. S. Siegler (Ed.), *Children's thinking: What develops?* (pp. 3–35). Hillsdale, NJ: Lawrence Erlbaum Associates.

Butterfield, E. C., & Belmont, J. M. (1977). Assessing and improving the executive cognitive functions of mentally retarded people. In J. Bailer & M. Sternlicht (Eds.), *Psychological issues in mental retardation.* Chicago: Aldine.

Campione, J. C., & Brown, A. (1978). *Toward a theory of intelligence: contributions from research with retarded children.* Paper presented at the meeting of the American Educational Research Association, Toronto, Canada.

Ceci, S. J., & Howe, M. (1978). Age-related differences in free recall as a function of retrieval flexibility. *Journal of Experimental Child Psychology, 26,* 432–442.

Chi, M. T. H. (1978). Knowledge structures and memory development. In R. S. Siegler (Ed.), *Children's thinking: What develops?*, (pp. 73–96). Hillsdale, NJ: Lawrence Erlbaum Associates.

Crane, N. L., & Ross, L. E. (1967). A developmental study of attention to cue redundancy following discrimination learning. *Journal of Experimental Child Psychology, 5,* 1–15.

Dörner, D. (1974). *Die kognitive Organisation beim Problemlösen.* Bern: Huber.

Dörner, D. (1976). *Problemlösen als Informationsverarbeitung.* Stuttgart: Kohlhammer.

Dörner, D. (1984). Self-reflection and problem-solving. In F. Klix (Ed.) *Human and artificial intelligence* (pp. 101–107). Amsterdam: North-Holland, (Originally published 1978.)

Dörner, D., Kreuzig, H. W., & Stäudel, Th. (1978). *Lohhausen.* 2. Bericht, DFG-Projekt "Systemdenken." Universität Gießen.

Duncker, K. (1966). *Zur Psychologie des produktiven Denkens.* Berlin: Springer, (first published 1935).

Flavell, J. H. (1971). First discussant's comments: What is memory development the development of? *Human Development, 14,* 272–278.

Flavell, J. (1976). Metacognitive aspects of problem solving. In L. Resnick (Ed.), *The nature of intelligence* (pp. 231–235). New York: Wiley.

Flavell, J. (1979). Metacognition and cognitive monitoring: A new area of cognitive-developmental inquiry. *American Psychologist, 34,* 906–911.

Flavell, J. H. (1981). Cognitive monitoring. In W. P. Dickson (Ed.) *Children's oral communication skills* (pp. 35–60). New York: Academic Press.

Flavell, J., Friedrichs, A. G., & Hoyt, J. D. (1970). Developmental changes in memorization processes. *Cognitive Psychology, 1,* 324–340.

Flavell, J., & Wellman, H. (1977). Metamemory. In R. V. Kail, Jr. & J. W. Hagen (Eds.), *Perspectives on the development of memory and cognition* (pp. 3–33). Hillsdale, NJ: Lawrence Erlbaum Associates.

Hale, G. A., & Alderman, L. B. (1978). Children's selective attention with variation in amount of stimulus exposure. *Journal of Experimental Child Psychology, 26,* 320–327.

Hasher, L., & Zacks, R. T. (1979). Automatic and effortful processes in memory. *Journal of Experimental Psychology: General, 108,* 356–388.

Heckhausen, H. (1982). The development of achievement motivation. In W. W. Hartup (Ed.), *Review of Child Development Research* (Vol. 6, pp. 600–668). Chicago: University of Chicago Press.

Hesse, F. W. (1979). *Trainingsinduzierte Veränderungen in der heuristischen Struktur und ihr Einfluß auf das Problemlösen.* Unveröffentl. Dissertation, Technische Hochschule Aachen.

Howard, D., & Goldin, S. (1979). Selective processing in encoding and memory: An analysis of resource allocation by Kindergarten children. *Journal of Experimental Child Psychology, 27,* 87–95.

Justice, E., & Bray, N. (1979). *The effects of context and feedback on metamemory in young children.* Paper presented at the biennal meeting of the Society for Research in Child Development, San Francisco.

Karmiloff-Smith, A. (1978). *Micro- and macro-developmental changes in language acquisition and other representational systems.* Paper presented at meeting on Units of Analysis in the Study of Conceptual Development and Language Development, University of Ghent.

Kelly, M., Scholnick, E., Travers, S., & Johnson, J. W. (1976). Relations among memory, memory appraisal, and memory strategies. *Child Development, 47,* 648–659.

Kemler, D. G., Shepp, B., & Foote, K. (1976). The sources of developmental differences in children's incidental processing during discrimination trials. *Journal of Experimental Child Psychology 21,* 226–240.

Kluwe, R. (1979). *Wissen und Denken.* Stuttgart: Kohlhammer.

Kluwe, R. H. (1980). Metakognition: Komponenten einer theorie zur kontrolle und steuerung eigenen denkens. Unveröffentl manuskript, Universität München.

Kluwe, R. H. (1981). Metakognition (Positionsreferat). In W. Michaelis (Hrsg.), *Bericht über den 32. Kongreß der Deutschen Gesellschaft für Psychologie in Zürich 1980* (pp. 246–258). Göttingen: Hogrefe.

Kluwe, R. H. (1982). Cognitive knowledge and executive control: Metacognition. In D. Griffin (Ed.), *Human mind—animal mind* (pp. 201–224). New York: Springer.

Kluwe, R. H., & Friedrichsen, G. (1985). Mechanisms of control and regulation in problem solving. In J. Kuhl & J. Beckmann (Eds.) *Action Control* (pp. 183–218). Berlin: Springer.

Kobasigawa, A. (1974). *Utilization of retrieval cues by children in recall.* Child Development, *45,* 127–134.

Kreutzer, M. A., Leonard, C., & Flavell, J. (1975). An interview study of children knowledge about memory. *Monographs of the Society for Research in Child Development, 40* (1, Serial No. 159).

Lachman, J., Lachman, R., & Thronesbery, C. (1979). Metamemory through the adult life span. *Developmental Psychology, 15,* 543–551.

Lompscher, J. (1972). *Theoretische und experimentelle Untersuchungen zur Entwicklung geistiger Fähigkeiten.* Berlin: Volk und Wissen.

Lüer, G., Putz-Osterloh, W., & Hesse, F. W. (1979). *Abschlußbericht über das Projekt "Systemdenken".* Technische Hochschule Aachen.

Markman, E. (1979). Realizing that you don't understand: Elementary school children's awareness of inconsistencies. *Child Development, 50,* 643–655.

Masur, E. F., McIntyre, C. F., & Flavell, J. H. (1973). Developmental changes in apportionment of study time among items in a multitrial free recall task. *Journal of Experimental Child Psychology, 15,* 237–246.

Neisser, U. (1967). *Cognitive Psychology.* New York: Appleton.

Nicholls, J. G. (1978). The development of the concepts of effort, and ability, perception of academic achievement, and the understanding that difficult tasks require more ability. *Child Development, 49,* 800–814.

Norman, D., & Bobrow, D. (1975). *On data-limited and resource-limited processes.* Cognitive Psychology, *7,* 44–64.

Owings, R., Petersen, G., Bransford, J., Morris, D., & Stein, B. (1980). Spontaneous monitoring and regulation of learning: a comparison of successful and less successful fifth graders. *Journal of Educational Psychology, 72,* 250–256.

Parsons, J., & Ruble, D. N. (1977). The development of achievement-related expectancies. *Child Development, 48,* 1075–1079.

Perlmutter, M. (1978). What is memory aging the aging of? *Developmental Psychology, 14,* 330–345.

Piaget, J. (1969). *Judgment and reasoning in the child.* London: Routledge & Kegan Paul. (Original work published 1928.)

Reed, S. K., & Johnson, J. A. (1978). Memory for problem solutions. In G. Bower (Ed.) *The psychology of learning and motivation* (pp. 161–201). New York: Academic Press.

Reither, F. (1979). *Über die Selbstreflektion beim Problemlösen.* Unveröffentl. Dissertation, Universität Gießen.

Reitman, W. (1965). *Cognition and thought.* New York: Wiley.

Richman, S., & Gholson, B. (1978). Strategy modeling, age, and information processing efficiency. *Journal of Experimental Child Psychology, 26,* 58–70.

Ringel, B. A., & Springer, C. J. (1980). On knowing how well one is remembering: The persistence of strategy use during transfer. *Journal of Experimental Child Psychology, 29,* 322–333.

Rogoff, B., Newcombe, N., & Kagan, J. (1974). Planfulness and recognition memory. *Child Development, 45,* 972–977.

Ruble, D. N., Parsons, J. E., & Ross, J. (1976). Self-evaluative responses of children in an achievement setting. *Child Development, 47,* 990–997.

Ruble, D., Boggiano, A., Feldman, N., & Loebl, J. (1980). Developmental analysis of the role of social comparison in self-evaluation. *Developmental Psychology, 16,* 105–115.

Schneider, W., & Shiffrin, R. M. (1977). Controlled and automatic human information processing: 1. Detection, search, and attention. *Psychological Review, 84,* 1–66.

Selz, O. (1922). Zur Psychologie des produktiven Denkens und des Irrtums. Bonn: Cohen.

Selz, O. (1913). *Über die Gesetze des geordneten Denkverlaufs: 1. Teil.* Stuttgart: Speemann.

Siegler, R. S. (1976). Three aspects of cognitive development. *Cognitive Psychology, 8,* 481–520.

Simon, H. A. (1975). The functional equivalence of problem solving skills. *Cognitive Psychology, 7,* 268–288.

Simon, D. P., & Simon, H. A. (1978). Individual differences in solving physic problems. In R. S. Siegler (Ed.), *Children's thinking: What develops?* (pp. 325–348). Hillsdale, NJ: Lawrence Erlbaum Associates.

Sternberg, R. (1979). The nature of mental abilities. *American Psychologist, 34,* 214–230.

Sternberg, R., & Rifkin, B. (1979). The development of analogical reasoning processes. *Journal Experimental Child Psychology, 27,* 195–232.

Sternberg, R., & Weil, E. (1980). An aptitude × treatment interaction in linear syllogistic reasoning. *Journal of Educational Psychology, 72,* 226–239.

Thorndyke, P., & Stasz, C. (1980). Individual differences in procedures for knowledge acquisition from maps. *Cognitive Psychology, 12,* 137–175.

Thornquist, K., & Wimmer, H. (1977). Meta-gedächtnis als Bedingung der gedächtnisentwicklung. *Zeitschrift für Entwicklungspsychologie und Pädagogische Psychologie, 9,* 252–264.

Ueckert, H. (1980). *The cognitive executive: From artificial intelligence toward a psychological theory of consciousness.* Paper presented at the International Congress of Psychology, Leipzig.

Wertsch, J. (1979). *The social origins of metacognition.* Paper presented at the meeting of the Society for Research in Child Development, San Francisco.

Wimmer, H., & Thornquist, K. (1979). *The relation of metamemory to mnemonic performance in memory development: metamemory is always necessary but never sufficient.* Unpublished manuscript, University of Salzburg.

Worden, P., & Sladewski-Awig, L. (1979). *Children's mnemonic judgments and metamemory.* Paper presented at the meeting of the Society for Research in Child Development, San Francisco.

Zimmer, J. (1976). Erscheinungsformen und ausprägung der vorausschau im denken von vorschulkindern. In J. Lompscher (Hrsg.), *Verlaufsqualitäten der geistigen Tätigkeit* (pp. 126–184). Berlin: Volk und Wissen.

3 Metacognition, Executive Control, Self-Regulation, and Other More Mysterious Mechanisms

Ann Brown
University of Illinois

WHAT IS METACOGNITION?

In this chapter, the historical roots and current status of the fashionable but complex, and often poorly understood, concept of metacognition and other topics with which it shares a family resemblance are described. Metacognition refers to understanding of knowledge, an understanding that can be reflected in either effective use or overt description of the knowledge in question. Various forms of metacognition have appeared in the literature, some of these instantiations are puzzling and mysterious. For example, Marshall and Morton, (1978, p. 226) refer to the mechanism that permits the detection and correction of errors in speech production as an EMMA, or "even more mysterious apparatus," that could be an "optional extra." This researcher argues that far from being an optional extra, the processes that have recently earned the title metacognitive are central to learning and development. Although metacognitive concepts may appear mysterious, what is at issue is the concept of degree of understanding. Thus, a learner can be said to understand a particular cognitive activity if he or she can use it appropriately and discuss its use. Understanding admits of degrees, because learners can often use knowledge effectively without being able to explain how this can be so. Individuals, with severe learning problems in a domain, can neither apply nor discuss a piece of knowledge or a rule they have acquired.

An attempt is made to demystify the concept(s) and to illustrate why it is not an optional extra, or an epiphenomenon (Brown, 1978). The varied forms of behavior that have been subsumed under the heading, metacognition, are described. Then, the historical roots of metacognition are traced through four somewhat separate strands of inquiry: (a) verbal reports as cognitive processes;

(b) executive control within an information processing framework; (c) self-regulation, metaprocedural reorganization, and reflected abstraction from the Piagetian school of developmental psychology, and (d) other-regulation, a Vygotskian notion. Finally, the current status of the concept metacognition is considered and the importance of the concept for understanding mechanisms of change is emphasized.

The term "metamemory" was introduced into the literature by John Flavell (1971), who was also responsible for the first modern study of metamemorial processes in children (Flavell, Friedrichs, & Hoyt, 1970). The term metacognition came into vogue sometime around 1975. The term has been problematic from its inception, denounced as fuzzy and faddish, and even unnecessary (Marshall & Morton, 1978). It is true that metacognitive-like concepts are fraught with some of the most difficult and enduring epistomological problems of psychology. However, this researcher argues that metacognitive-like entities lie at the very roots of the learning process; and, concomitant with the revival of interest in things metacognitive, is an exciting revival of interest in mechanisms of change and development.

Metacognition refers loosely to one's knowledge and control of own cognitive system. Two primary problems with the term are: it is often difficult to distinguish between what is meta and what is cognitive; and there are many different historical roots from which this area of inquiry developed. The confusion that follows the use of a single term for a multifaceted problem is the inevitable outcome of mixing metaphors. Some attempt is made to explicate the confusion by making the metaphors somewhat more explicit.

Consider first the interchangeability of cognitive and metacognitive functions. An area where this problem is particularly acute is the currently popular domain of metacognition and reading, writing, and studying. The following quote Flavell (1976): "Asking yourself questions about the chapter might function either to improve your knowledge (a cognitive function) or to monitor it (a metacognitive function)," demonstrates the interchangeability of cognitive and metacognitive functions. A particular activity can be seen as the strategy itself (looking for main points), its monitoring function (a metacognitive activity), and a reflection of the knowledge (also metacognitive) that it is an appropriate strategy to employ in a given situation. Recent reviews of the literature by Baker and Brown (1981), have been justly criticized on the grounds that they have encouraged the practice of dubbing as metacognitive any strategic action engaged in while reading.

Metacognitive reading skills include the following activities, previously dignified with the title of mere strategies: establishing the purpose for reading; modifications in reading due to variations in purpose; identifying important ideas; activating prior knowledge; evaluation of the text for clarity, completeness, and consistency; compensation for failures to understand; and assessing one's level of comprehension (Baker & Brown, 1981). Which of these activities should be deemed metacognitive, or, more subtly, which components of these complex activities are meta, is not clear.

It is clear that these strategic reading activities were recognized well before the emergence of the term metacognition. Since the turn of the century educational psychologists (e.g., Dewey, 1910; Huey, 1908, 1968; Thorndike, 1917) were quite aware that studying and reading involve the type of activities now called metacognitive. For example, consider Dewey's system of inducing reflective reading. The aim was to induce "active monitoring," "critical evaluation," and deliberate "seeking after meanings and relationships." According to Dewey (1910), learning was "learning to think" and reading was thinking stimulated by texts: "Thinking (or reading) is inquiring, investigating, turning over, probing or delving into, so as to find something new, or to see what is already known in a new light—in short it is questioning" (p. 265).

Another early advocate of "metacognitive" processes of reading was Thorndike (1917):

> Understanding a paragraph is like solving a math problem. It consists of selecting the right elements of the situation and putting them together in the right relations, and also with the right amount of weight or influence or force for each. The mind is assailed as it were by every word in the paragraph. It must select, repress, soften, emphasize, correlate, and organize, all under the influence of the right mental set or purpose or demand. (p. 329)

Thus, there is considerable historical agreement that reading and learning from texts involve metacognitive skills. The early paradigms are hauntingly familiar. For example, Baldwin (1909) introduced the now popular (Myers & Paris, 1978) reading skills questionnaire, in which he asked 12 to 18-year-olds to describe their study habits; and Thorndike (1917) invented the error-detection paradigm now extensively studied (Markman, 1977, 1979; Stein & Trabasso, 1982). Thorndike asked sixth graders to read texts and then answer questions on what they had read. He found that sixth graders were surprisingly passive readers who, as they read, did not appear to spontaneously monitor their understanding. Although they often said they understood, it was obvious they did not. Baldwin and Thorndike were clearly able to describe these activities without once resorting to the term metacognition.

A second source of confusion concerning the wide spread use of the term metacognition is that, within the modern psychological literature, it has been used to refer to two distinct areas of research: knowledge about cognition and regulation of cognition. The two forms of metacognition are indeed closely related, each feeding on the other recursively; attempts to separate them lead to oversimplification. However, they are readily distinguishable, and they do have different historical roots.

Knowledge about cognition refers to the stable, statable, often fallible, and often late developing information that human thinkers have about their own cognitive processes; traditionally, this has been referred to as *knowing that* (Broudy, 1977). Knowledge about cognition is relatively stable. One would expect that knowledge of pertinent facts about a domain that it is fallible, severely limited for short-term verbatim retention, etc., for example, memory, would be a permanent part of one's naive theory on the topic. This form of knowledge is often statable; one can reflect on the cognitive processes involved and discuss them with others. Unfortunately, because the learner is credited with knowledge only if he or she can state it, this statability criterion is circular in most empirical studies. Of course, this form of knowledge is often fallible; the child, or adult for that matter, can perfectly "know" certain facts about cognition that are not true; naive psychology is not always empirically supportable. Finally, this type of knowledge is usually assumed to be late developing; it requires that learners step back and consider their own cognitive processes as objects of thought and reflection. For Piaget, reflected abstraction requires hypothesis testing and evaluation, and the ability to imagine possible worlds and their outcomes; therefore, it demands formal operational thought (Piaget, 1976). For others, earlier signs of emergence are possible; however, reflection is rarely attributed to the very young child or novice, regardless of how precocious they might be (Brown & DeLoache, 1978).

The second cluster of activities that is dubbed metacognitive in the developmental literature, consists of the activities used to regulate and oversee learning. These processes include planning activities (predicting outcomes, scheduling strategies, and various forms of vicarious trial and error, etc). Prior to undertaking a problem, monitoring activities (monitoring, testing, revising, and re-scheduling one's strategies for learning) during learning; and checking outcomes (evaluating the outcome of any strategic actions against criteria of efficiency and effectiveness). It has been assumed that these activities are relatively unstable, not necessarily statable, and relatively age independent (i.e., task and situation dependent). These skills are not necessarily stable; although they are ubiquitously employed by adults, on simple problems. Young children monitor and regulate their own activities. Indeed, a case can be made that all active learning involves self-regulation. These activities are often not statable; knowing how to do something does not necessarily mean that the activities can be brought to the level of conscious awareness and reported on to others.

Although knowledge and regulation of cognition are incestuously related, the two forms of activity have different roots and different attendant problems. The tension generated by the use of the same term, metacognition, for the two types of behavior is illustrated by the fact that the leading proponents in the field tend to answer questions about the nature of metacognition with: "It depends." Is metacognition late developing? It depends on the type of process referred to. Is metacognition conscious: It depends. . . .

Tension has bedevilled the area since the original use of the "meta" terms. Flavell (1971) in his initial papers on the topic, referred to both types of metamemory. In the landmark paper, where the first experimental studies were introduced (Flavell, Friedrichs, & Hoyt, 1970), two tasks were featured: span-estimation and recall-readiness. Span-estimation is a "knowledge-of" task where children are asked to estimate their own memory span; recall-readiness is a "regulation-of" situation where children are observed as they select, revise, orchestrate, and evaluate strategies for learning.

In order to make explicit the epistomological problems that surround things metacognitive, and to illustrate the dangers of mixed metaphors, four separate stands of inquiry, where the current issues of metacognition were introduced and originally disputed, are considered.

ROOTS OF METACOGNITION

The four historically separate, but obviously interlinked, problems in psychology that pertain to issues of metacognition are discussed. First, the enduring questions concerning the status of verbal reports as data (Ericsson & Simon, 1980): Can people have conscious access to their own cognitive processes? Can they report on these processes with verisimilitude? How does the act of reporting influence the processes that are the subject of the report? Second, is the issue of executive mechanisms within an information processing model of human and machine intelligence. Who or what is responsible for regulation of cognition? With what knowledge or form of knowledge must an executive be imbued? How do processing models deal with the issue of the infinite regress problem of homunculi within homunculi; how do they deal with the problems of consciousness, intention, and purpose? Third, are the issues of self-regulation and conceptual reorganization during learning and development that have always featured in Genevan developmental psychology. Self-regulation and conceptual reorganization have played a major role in Piaget's (1976, 1978) modern writings and those of his co-workers, notably Karmiloff-Smith (1979a, 1979b); Karmiloff-Smith & Inhelder (1974–75); Inhelder, Sinclair, & Bovet (1974). Fourth is the topic of other-regulation, which is central to Vygotsky's (1978) theory of development.

Verbal Reports as Data

Nature of the Problem. Central to the controversy surrounding the ability to provide verbal reports of one's own cognitive processes is the issue of reflective access (Brown, 1982a; Brown & Campione, 1981; Pylyshyn, 1978), conscious access (Rozin, 1976; Gardner, 1978), or reflected abstraction (Piaget, 1976). It refers to the essentially human ability to step back and consider one's own cognitive operations as objects of thought; to reflect on one's own thinking. The concept of cognizing about cognition, like most reasonable ideas, has a history dating back to Plato and Aristotle. Spearman (1923) points out:

> Such a cognizing of cognition itself was already announced by Plato. Aristotle likewise posited a separate power whereby, over and above actually seeing and hearing, the psyche becomes aware of doing so. Later authors, as Strato, Galen, Alexander of Aphrodisias, and in particular Plotinus, amplified the doctrine, designating the processes of cognizing one's own cognition by several specific names. Much later, especial stress was laid on this power of 'reflection', as it was now called by Locke. (p. 52–53)

Few people have been able to resist the temptation to play on words. Consider this example from Spinoza: ". . . He who knows something knows at the same time that he knows it and he knows as well that he knows what he knows" (cited in Weinert, this volume).

Special interest in children's knowledge of their own knowledge was evidenced by John Locke, who distinguished two primary sources of ideas: sensation and *reflection*. Reflection referred to the "perception of the state of our own minds," or "the notice which the mind takes of its own operations." Neither children nor the uneducated were thought to be given to bouts of reflection. According to Locke (1690/1924), primitive minds do not indulge in self-reflection.

> Hence we see the reason why it is late before most children get ideas of the operations of their own minds; and some have not any very clear or perfect ideas of the greatest part of them all their lives. Because, though they (ideas) pass there continually, yet, like floating visions they make not deep impressions enough to leave in the mind clear, distinct, lasting ideas, *till the understanding turns inwards upon itself, reflects on its own operations, and makes them the object of its own contemplation.* (p. 46)

In the late nineteenth and early twentieth centuries, an interest in self-reflection was retained as a central topic of debate in the emergent fields of psychology. Concern with verbal reports as data distinguished the Wurzburg school of thought and was vigorously contested by Wundt (for a review see Mandler & Mandler, 1964; Humphrey, 1963). For example, Buhler's (1907) protocols of verbal reports during problem solving have a delightfully contemporary ring. Buhler asked his experienced subjects (actually his professional colleagues, including Kulpe and Durr) to talk aloud about their thought processes as they attempted to answer complex questions: "Was the theorem of Pythagoras known in the Middle Ages?" "Can you get to Berlin from here in seven hours?" "Can the atomic theory of physics ever be proven untrue by any scientific discovery?" The verbal protocols revealed reasoning on the basis of incomplete knowledge that is essentially similar to contemporary work (Collins, 1977; Norman, 1973).

Indeed, many of the thorny problems of awareness, consciousness, and intro- spective reports, etc. were thoroughly aired by the Wurtzburgers in their battle with Wundt, who may have been the father of psychology but was certainly not the father of this form of metacognition! However, differing viewpoints exist (see Gleitman, in press).

Current interest in knowledge of cognition comes from many sources. A recurring theme is the distinction between *multiple* and *reflective access* that occurs in several areas of psychology; including cognitive ethology, machine intelligence, human intelligence, and developmental psychology (for further treatment see Brown, 1982a; Brown & Campione, 1981). Rozin's influential paper on the evolution of intelligence has been especially important in making the problem of access paramount. Rozin distinguishes between adaptive spe- cializations related to intelligence, which originated to satisfy specific problems of survival, and widely accessible cognitive programs. Because the adaptive specializations, common in the animal world, evolved as solutions to specific problems, they were originally tightly wired to a narrow set of situations that called for their evolution; in lower organisms they remained tightly constrained components of the system. In the course of evolution, cognitive programs be- come more accessible to other units of the system and therefore, may be used flexibly in a variety of situations. This flexibility is the hallmark of higher intelligence, reaching its zenith at the level of *conscious access* and control, which affords wide applicability over a broad range of mental functioning.

There are two main points to Rozin's accessibility theory; first, is the notion of welding (Brown, 1974, 1978; Shif, 1969). Intelligence components can be strictly welded to constrained domains (i.e., skills available in one situation are not readily used in others, even though they are appropriate). According to Rozin (1976), young children's programs are *"not yet usable in all situations, avail- able to consciousness, or statable."* (Development is) "the process of gradually extending and connecting together isolated skills with a possible *ultimate exten- sion into consciousness"* (p. 262). The second part of each of the preceding statements refers to Rozin's second major point, conscious access. Even if skills are widely applicable, rather than tightly welded, they need not be conscious and statable. Conscious access to the routines available to the system is the highest form of mature human intelligence.

A similar distinction between multiple and reflective access is made by Pylyshyn (1978). *Multiple access* refers to the ability to use knowledge flexibly; because it can be systemically varied to fit a wide range of conditions, knowl- edge is informationally plastic. *Reflective access* refers to the ability to "mention as well as use" the components of the system. Similarly, Gardner (1978) cites as hallmarks of human intelligence: (a) generative, inventive, and experimental use of knowledge, rather than preprogrammed activities (multiple access); and (b) the ability to reflect on one's own activity (reflective access). Piaget, in his most recent work, notably in *The Grasp of Consciousness* (1976) and *Success*

and Understanding (1978) also denotes reflected abstractions, "Conscious products of reflexive abstraction," as the keystone of formal operations.

The concepts of multiple and reflective access are key issues in the field of
metacognition and in developmental psychology. Original interest in the topic
was spurred by the persistent finding of a production deficiency in young children's learning (Reese, 1962; Flavell, 1970), which is a classic problem of
access. Children who know perfectly well how to use a strategy or have the
relevant prior knowledge, often fail to access it on appropriate occasions. Indeed, American and Soviet psychologists have suggested that one of the primary
problems with young learners is that they tend to acquire information that is
"welded" to the form and context in which it was acquired (Brown, 1974; Shif,
1969). Reflective access was also pinpointed as a problem for the young and, in
particular for the retarded learner. On the basis of the relative *absence* of these
qualities in slow learners, Brown, Campione, and their colleagues, diagnosed
multiple and reflective access as underlying mechanisms of intelligent behavior
(Brown, 1974, 1978; Brown & Campione, 1978, 1981; Campione & Brown,
1977). The twin concepts of flexibility and reflection are important issues that
have wide implications for theories of learning and development.

In short, several theorists from quite disparate schools agree that the most
stringent criteria of understanding involve the availability of knowledge to consciousness and reflection; thus permitting verbal reports. However, there are
problems associated with verbal reports as data (Ericsson & Simon, 1980); these
problems are well illustrated in developmental psychology (Brown, 1978; Flavell
& Wellman, 1977; Wellman, 1983). First, there is the obvious problem of asking
children to reliably inform on the content of their own conscious processes. As
Piaget and others have pointed out, children are as likely to distort and modify
their observations of their thought processes as they are their observations of the
world around them. Eyewitness testimony is fallible for the objects and events of
the internal world, as well as for the external world. This problem has been
referred to elsewhere as the problem of externalizing mental events (Brown,
1978, 1980). What a child says he or she has done or will do is not necessarily
related to his or her performance. Reliance on verbal responses and justification
is risky when the participant is a child, and is not without its problems when
adults are the informants (Ericsson & Simon, 1980; Nisbett & Wilson, 1977;
Smith & Miller, 1978; White, 1980).

Second, is the equally thorny problem of what relationship to expect between
what an informant knows and what he or she does. Studies with children, which
have been mostly correlational, have yielded only moderate correlations; for
example, between performance on a restricted class of memory tasks and children's statable knowledge of (sometimes different) class of memory phenomena
(Cavanaugh & Borkowski, 1979; Justice & Bray, 1979; Kendall, Borkowski, &
Cavanaugh, 1980). However, in some recent studies (Perlmutter, 1978; Wimmer

& Tornquist, 1978) a clearer relationship was found to exist. In most of these studies there is a less than compelling rationale as to why one would expect a link between the particular form of metamemory probed and actual performance (Wellman, 1983). Similarly, as Flavell (chapter 1, this volume) points out, in any one particular task, there are many reasons why there should not be a close link between metamemorial knowledge and memory performance. What is needed is a theory as to when one may expect to find a relationship between a subject's verbal reports and actions, and exactly what that relationship would be. The beginnings of such a theory have been posited by Ericsson and Simon (1980) and is readily adaptable to the developmental literature.

However, one must first distinguish between the many forms of contexts that the child is asked to comment on. Many forms of knowledge about cognitive things can be assumed to be stable, others are transient and are elicited only in certain situations. Stable forms of knowledge are the kinds of information learners may possess about themselves as learners and about the learning context. I have argued elsewhere that practiced learners come to know a great deal about the learning situations (Brown, 1982b; Brown, Bransford, Ferrara & Campione, 1983). They know certain stable characteristics about themselves as learners; they know the demands of certain classes of problems, and they are aware of the necessity of tailoring their learning activities so that they will be finely in tune with specific criterial tasks. These are the types of knowledge that Flavell and his colleagues (Flavell, 1980, 1981; Flavell & Wellman, 1977) have classified as person, task, and strategy variables. Learners possess naive theories of what it takes to learn certain types of materials, in order to meet certain criterial task demands. They also know a lot about their repertoire of the available strategies needed to accomplish certain ends. That young children are less informed about stable characteristics of learning is amply documented (Kreutzer, Leonard, & Flavell, 1975; Myers & Paris, 1978; for reviews see Baker & Brown, 1981, in press; Cavanaugh & Perlmutter, 1980; Flavell & Wellman, 1977; Wellman, 1983). This lack of stable, statable, knowledge is due to children's relative lack of experience in learning situations that occur repeatedly in school; it reflects their novice status as deliberate learners.

Stable forms of knowledge are the forms of metacognition that are purportedly tapped by questionnaire studies or clinical interviews. However, verbal reports are often taken in situations where the knowledge being assessed may be transient, is elicited in the face of a particular task or context, or is elicited during the actual performance of a task. Supposedly, young children are judged to be incapable of the split mental focus that is required for simultaneously solving problems and commenting on the process. Therefore, protocol analyses of performers actually solving problems have been restricted to adult or adolescent subjects. Instead, developmental psychologists have typically asked children to report retrospectively on what they have just done, with all the attendant problems associated with constructing past events (Piaget, 1976). A more common and more problematic procedure is to ask children to describe how they would behave in certain hypothetical situations.

Ericsson and Simon (1980) have criticized the practice of asking adult subjects to imagine possible worlds and how they might act in them. For example, Nisbett and Wilson (1977) asked their subjects how they would react to a story if some passages had been omitted. Similarly, Reed and Johnson (1977) asked adults how they would solve a problem if it were presented to them again, a procedure often employed in the developmental studies of memory-metamemory linkage. Later that the ability to construct possible worlds (Johnson-Laird, 1980) and operate in these worlds with facility, is a late developing skill that shares many of the "child-as-scientist" features of Piaget's formal operational period.

It is necessary to distinguish between reports on stable forms of knowledge and reports on states occurring during problem solving. It is also necessary to distinguish between: (a) *predictive verbalizations* about possible performance before the event; (b) *concurrent verbalizations* during the actual performance; and (c) *retrospective verbalization* after the event has transpired. It is also necessary to be more precise, in order to determine if the information being sought concerns specific information or very general information. Questions of the form, "How do you perform these tasks?" implicitly request very general information and leave open to the informant the creative task of constructing generality by drawing on a variety of specific prior experiences, including general knowledge of what one ought to do in such tasks.

An illustration of the demand characteristics of general inquiries was provided by Sternberg, Ketron and Powell (1982). They analyzed the systematic strategies used by adult subjects solving analogy problems and then, for a variety of theoretical reasons, trained the subjects to adopt an alternative strategy. After training, performance was again assessed to determine if the subjects had adopted the new strategy. Sternberg et al. considered the subjects' latencies and error patterns, previously found to be highly diagnostic of the particular strategy employed, and the subjects' verbal reports of the processes they were using. Sternberg et al. (p. 160) report: ". . . Subjects' descriptions were highly consistent with the strategies subjects were trained to use, but not consistent with the strategies subjects actually did use . . ." This researcher does not necessarily agree with their comment that this discrepancy indicates the subjects' lack of awareness of what they were doing. The subjects may very well know what they are doing, but they may also realize that it is different from what the experimenter told them to do. If this situation exists, college-age subjects may well respond to the demand characteristics of the situation and tell the experimenter that they are conforming. Under such circumstances it is clear why verbal reports may bear very little relation to the actual cognitive processes used in the task. Although the example given might be extreme, the tendency to construct general theories about what one ought to do is encouraged by the probe for general procedures.

Ericsson and Simon (1980) point out that in areas of applied psychology, where verbal questioning of subjects is important and has a long history, subjects are rarely asked for their general theories or impressions. Rather, Flanagan (1954) and others use what is referred to as the critical incident technique; informants are only asked to report about very specific incidents. For example, combat pilots would be asked to describe a particular, actually experienced incident, and then to answer questions on how they thought or felt during that specific event.

An adequate theory of the relation of verbal reports to actual performance must include some a priori predictions of when verbal reports influence performance and when they do not. The current state of the theory concerning the verbal reports and performance link is summarized in Flavell's morality argument. Flavell and Wellman (1977) point out that there are many reasons why there may not be a direct link between, for example, memory and metamemory.

> Suppose a person judges that categorized stimuli are easier to recall than noncategorized ones. Would he inevitably use categorization as a storage strategy, given obviously categorizable stimuli? Not at all. He may know about categorization but think that something else might be better yet in this situation. He may think the list easy enough to use simple inspection for storage. He may have enough knowledge to judge that categorization would be a good strategy, if asked about it, but not enough to think to utilize such a strategy on his own. Lastly, there are undoubted gaps between metamemory and memory behavior attributable to Original Sin. Moral action does not always accord with moral beliefs, and similarly, we do not always try to retrieve information or prepare for future retrieval in what we believe to be the most effective ways.

This is undoubtedly true, there are many reasons to explain a lack of a close correspondence between what one knows and what one does; however, Original Sin lacks something as an explanatory construct. Future research could concentrate on the specific circumstances which would result in a metacognitive-cognitive link. Under what circumstances would one predict a positive or a negative relationship between verbal reports and performances? Under what circumstances, if any, would no relationship be predicted. (Wellman, 1983)?

Ericsson and Simon (1980), for example predict that asking the learner to provide concurrent verbal reports as he or she solves a problem, will, depending on the *function* of the verbal reports in the ongoing learning process, have a neutral, positive, or negative effect. Under circumstances where the subject is asked to describe information that is already available (i.e., in STM), the effect will be *neutral*. If the subject is asked to report on information that is available, but not in verbal or propositional form, the translation process may slow down performance but will not otherwise interfere. Several examples of this form of experiment are quoted by Ericsson and Simon. One example is a discrimination learning study by Karph (1973). Subjects were divided into think aloud and control groups. They were asked to learn a discrimination between compound stimuli varying in form, size, color, shape of border, texture of line under the form, etc. The correct solution to each problem involved one of the dimensions. The stimuli were visual; therefore, the translation to a verbal hypothesis should have been relatively easy; these hypotheses, for example, "It's the black one," were available to the subjects at the time of solution. Subjects were equated for performance on a pretest. The think aloud subjects verbalized their hypotheses during the second session and returned to silent problem solving on the third session, or posttest. No differences in accuracy between the experimental and control groups were found at any stage of the experiment; however, under instructions to think aloud, the experimental group was significantly slower.

The relation between "thinking aloud" and problem solving can sometimes be beneficial. This is particularly true if the type of verbalization that is required is a statement of a rule or a reason for an action. Ericsson and Simon (1980) quote many examples where, on a standard laboratory puzzle, such as the Tower of Hanoi, instructions to state a rule significantly accelerate the learning process. For example, Gagné and Smith (1962) had subjects state a reason for each move they made. The simple "state a reason" procedure significantly improved both learning and transfer performance. Gagné and Smith (p. 17) concluded, rather vaguely, that instructions to verbalize the reasons for moves "forced subjects to think, induced more deliberate planning," etc. The study was criticized on the grounds that the verbalization group had extra learning time. However, follow-up studies found that instructions to state the reasons for moves covertly were equally as effective as overt statements, and that learning time was not a confounding factor (Wilder & Harvey, 1971); Davis, Carey, Foxman, and Tarr (1968) found that the presence or absence of an audience was also insignificant. The Gagné and Smith findings are robust and suggest that forcing learners to make a rule explicit helps the learning process, as well as the transfer of the rule.

Verbal reports can often have a negative effect on the learning process. This situation occurs when the requirement for overt verbalization competes for central processing capacity with the processes that must be reported. In on-line protocols it is characteristic for verbalization to stop when the going gets difficult and to resume when the cognitive load is lessened. Similarly, verbal reports of information that is not generally available to consciousness is a disruptive procedure. For example, one reason why Piaget (1976, 1978) experienced so much difficulty getting children to describe their actions may be because the subject of those descriptions were just that, actions. Perceptual motor activities are notoriously difficult to describe, and it is indeed true that people can do a great deal that they cannot describe. Requiring an expert golfer to describe his or her swing may, in fact, ruin the experts' swing, rather than help the novice. Broadbent

(1977) suggests that one is only aware of higher level processes during the performance of perceptual-motor tasks; there is some empirical support for this position. Ruger (1910) found that adult subjects solving mechanical problems could give only limited explanations of their intermediate solution steps; Klinger (1974) found a high frequency of general control verbalization, "Let's see, where was I," "Dammit," and so forth, but very few examples of detailed step by step verbalization. Many current information processing models claim that with repeated practice many of the intermediate steps of both thought and action become automatized, and therefore, they are even less available to conscious introspection (Norman & Schallice, 1980; Schneider & Shiffrin, 1977; Shiffrin & Schneider, 1977). Asking subjects to report on internal events that are not readily available to such inspection may significantly impair the processes on which they must report.

Developmental Data.   Although the majority of developmental work on met-acognition consists of studies examining children's verbal reports on their own mental processes, there are very few empirical observations that could be used to answer the questions raised by the Ericsson and Simon taxonomy. Systematic variation of the temporal relation of reporting and the variety of cognitive activities considered has not been undertaken.

Questionnaire studies consist primarily of situations where the child must imagine scenarios and how he or she might act in them. Of the fourteen main items contained in the Kreutzer, Leonard and Flavell (1975) questionnaire, ten are completely imaginary (e.g., the child is asked to imagine how two other children might perform in a task). The remaining four items demand that the child predict how he or she might perform in an as yet unexperienced activity; however, the child is given a concrete prop to help the fantasy. For example, if the child must decide whether colored pictures are easier to remember than black and white drawings, samples of the materials are provided. Furthermore, although the authors did try to query the young respondents about specific memory tasks, the kinds of processes that the children were asked to reflect on were very general. As Ericsson and Simon (1980) point out, asking people to describe the general processes they might use in imaginary situations is the least favorable circumstance for producing verbal reports that are closely linked to the cognitive processes under discussion.

The majority of quasi-experimental studies of metacognition, where children are asked to predict how they will perform in tasks or describe how they fared, are also imperfect. Some tentative evidence indicates that children are better able to identify the items they recall, than to predict in advance how well they will do (Brown, 1978), however; the data is incidental to the main purpose of the experiments from which they were gleaned.

Similarly, if one looks hard enough, examples can be found where children who are forced to state a rule during problem solving are better able to learn and transfer (demonstrated with adults in the Gagné and Smith study; however, very little data is available. One example exists in problem solving situations requiring invention (Resnick & Glaser, 1976), Pellegrino and Schadler (1974). Children were required to "look ahead" by verbalizing a sequence of goals, a procedure that produced a dramatic increase in the number of successful inventions by grade school children. In an on going study, Crisafi and Brown (work in progress) found greater transfer across problem isomorphs of an inferential reasoning task when, after each problem, three- and four-year-old learners were required to describe the solution to Kermitt the frog so that he could also perform the task. Therefore, there is some evidence that verbalizations are helpful when they should be; however, there is considerable confusion concerning when verbalization should or should not be related to cognitive processes (Wellman, 1983). Questions cannot be addressed, or answered adequately, unless researchers are precise about the type of verbalization, the type of cognitive process, and the theoretical rationale for expecting a positive, negative, and neutral relation between verbalization and the cognitive process.

In summary, there is a desparate need in the developmental literature for systematic evaluations of children's verbal reports on their own cognitive processes when stringent attention is paid to: (a) the temporal relation between these reports and the cognition in question; (b) the nature of the cognitions under evaluation; and (c) the influence of reflection on the operations of thought. It is simplistic to ask whether or not a certain group of children have reflective access to their own cognitions without specifying exactly the conditions under which these observations are made. Ideally, one would like to see programmatic research aimed at uncovering a certain child's range of understanding within a task domain. Under what conditions is it reasonable to ask for verbal reports? Can the child make predictive, concurrent, or retrospective statements about actual or potential cognitive activity within a problem space? Do the specific restrictions on adults' verbalizations, under varying circumstances, apply to children, or do young learners experience particular difficulties, for example, in imagining possible actions in situations as yet unexperienced (Brown, 1978)? Do children have particular problems talking about general rules rather than specific activities? Can the relation of verbal reports and learning be mapped in terms of predicted neutral, positive, or negative effects (as Ericsson & Simon have attempted to do for adults)?

In short, it is necessary to progress from the current piecemeal study of certain isolated metacognitions, concerning intuitively appealing but seemingly randomly chosen cognitive tasks, to a systematic evaluation of the function of verbal reports in specific learning situations. Instead of the current tendency to consider a small range of metacognitive questions in a few, possibly atypical, tasks, microgenetic case studies are advocated. These studies would involve a small number of children talking about their cognitive activities in a variety of situations within a domain. For example, some factorial combinations of predictive, concurrent, retrospective, or imaginative reporting on general or specific rules could be undertaken. This could be done within a theory that makes prior predictions of neutral, positive, or negative effects of such activities; verbal reports would not be considered as isolated from the ongoing process of learning. By examining the conditions and contexts of learning that subjects must reflect on, the current confusion concerning the relationship of verbal reports and the cognitive operations, which are the subject of these reports, can be eliminated.

Executive Control

Nature of the Problem.   The second historical root of things metacognitive is the notion of executive control taken from the information processing models of cognition. The majority of information processing models attribute powerful operations to a central processor, interpretor, supervisor, or executive system capable of performing an intelligent evaluation of its own operations. Brown (1978) maintains:

> Some form of self-awareness or explicit knowledge of its own workings is critical for any efficient problem-solving system (Becker, 1975; Bobrow, 1975; Bobrow & Norman, 1975). The basic requirements of such an executive demonstrate the complexity of the issue. It must include the ability to (a) predict the system's capacity limitations; (b) be aware of its repertoire of heuristic routines and their appropriate domain of utility; (c) identify and characterize the problem at hand; (d) plan and schedule appropriate problem-solving strategies; (e) monitor and supervise the effectiveness of those routines it calls into service; and (f) dynamically evaluate these operations in the face of success or failure so that termination of activities can be strategically timed. (p. 152)

Thus, very complex operations are attributed to something within the system, a problem of attribution that is, to say the least, theoretically problematic (Boden, 1977; Dennet, 1978).

Information-processing theories emerged in the mid-1960s along with the growing interest in computer competence and machine simulation of thought. The concurrent development of psychological models was greatly influenced by the theories and jargon of synthetic intelligence; during the past 15 years the computer metaphor has dominated theories of human cognition. By adopting the notion of a central processor or executive system imbued with very fancy powers, developmental psychologists gained a powerful analogy through which to consider the development of efficient learning. Unfortunately, along with the notion of a hierarchical cognitive system, complete with a single, god-like supervisor (Dennett, 1978; Turvey, 1977), they also adopted many of the attendant problems.

The notion of executive control was in general vogue by the early 1970s (Greeno & Bjork, 1973) and was introduced into developmental psychology

(Brown, 1974, 1975). Central within the prototypical information processing model are the concepts of executive control, implicitly or explicitly stated, and automated and controlled processes; the notions are interlinked. A description of the automated-controlled distinction and the executive systems follows.

A two-process approach to thinking, *automatic and controlled processing*, predates information-processing models. A notably lucid description of the distinction between automatic and controlled processes was provided by James (1890), who stressed the freedom from attention and effort that automatization provides: "The more details of our daily life we can hand over to the effortless custody of automatism, the more our higher powers of mind will be set free for their own proper work" (p. 130). The distinction between automatic and controlled processing, although it masquerades under different titles, is now a common feature of both the adult and developmental literatures. For example, in the adult literature are Posner and Snyder's (1974) "conscious strategies" and "automatic activation," Shiffrin's (1975) "controlled vs systemic processing," Norman and Bobrow's (1975) "resource limited" and "data limited processing," and Laberge's (1975) "automatic focusing." Obviously, 1975 was a good year for this theoretical concept. More recent theories come from Shiffrin and Schneider (1977), and Logan (1978, 1979). Developmentalists also discuss "deliberate and involuntary" (Brown, 1975), "effortful and automatic" (Hasher & Zacks, 1979), and "strategic versus automatic" (Naus & Halasz, 1978) processing.

Automatic processing is a fast, parallel process, not limited by short-term memory, that requires little subject effort, and demands little direct subject control. There are two forms of automatic processing: those activities that appear to be common to all age groups and rarely demand intensive strategic effect, for example, some forms of recognition (Brown, 1975); and activities that were once effortful but because of extensive training and experience have become automatic. Controlled processing is a comparatively slow, serial process, limited by short-term memory constraints, requiring subject effort, and providing a large degree of subject control (Schneider & Shiffrin, 1977).

Consider a concrete example, skilled reading. The skilled reader can operate with a lazy, automatic processor. Cognitive activities that once were laborious and slow have, with practice, become automatized and rapid; they require little attention. The skilled reader's top-down and bottom-up (Rumelhart, 1980) processes are so fluent that he or she can proceed merrily on automatic pilot until alerted to a comprehension failure by some triggering event (Brown, 1980; Collins, Brown, Morgan & Brewer, 1977). If the process is flowing smoothly, construction of meaning is very rapid, however, when a comprehension failure is detected the reader must slow down, and allot extra processing capacity to the problem area. The reader must employ debugging devices and strategies, which take time and effort. The difference in time and effort between the normal rapid *automatic pilot* state and the laborious activity in the *debugging state* is the difference between automatic and controlled processing. Whatever the exact nature of the triggering event one reacts by slowing down the rate of processing; allocating time and effort to the task of clearing up the comprehension failure. In the process of disambiguation and clarification, the individual enters a controlled, deliberate, planful, strategic state that is quite distinct from the automatic pilot state, where one is not actively at work on debugging activities. The smooth flow of reading abruptly stops, and the debugging activities themselves occupy the lion's portion of one's limited capacity processor.

For developmental psychologists, there are many interesting questions concerning automatizations. A major notion is that a great deal of the development that occurs with increasing expertise (age) is the result of processes that were originally controlled, effortful, and laborious becoming automated (Brown, 1975; Hasher & Zacks, 1979; Naus & Halasz, 1979). A second well aired notion is that processes that do not demand strategic control are efficient, even in the young, and are less sensitive to developmental changes (Brown, 1975; Hasher & Zacks, 1978). However, in this section, the notion of who or what does the controlling, and who or what deciphers the output of the automatized system, is of particular interest.

Heterarchies, hierarchies and demons are involved in attribution. Within the information processing system, executive power, in large or small degrees, must be attributed. It is this attribution that causes the models to run into epistomological problems of long standing, problems that are particularly recalcitrant and uncomfortably metaphysical for a psychology never truly weaned from a strict radical behaviorist tradition. The major problems are the traditional ones of consciousness and who has it (i.e., homunculi in their many manifestations). The problem is nicely stated by Norman (1980) in his inaugural address to the new Cognitive Science Society:

> Consciousness is a peculiar stepchild of our discipline, agreed to be important, but little explored in research and theory. There are legitimate reasons for this relative neglect. This is a most difficult topic, one for which it is very difficult to get the hard, sensible evidence that experimental disciplines require. . . . We cannot understand (thinking) until we come to a better appreciation of the workings of the mind, of the several simultaneous trains of thought that can occur, of the differences between conscious and subconscious processing, of what it means to focus upon one train of thought to the exclusion of others. What-who- does the focussing? . . . And what does it mean to have *conscious* attention? Can there be attention that is not conscious? What—who—experiences the results of conscious attentional processes? (p. 16)

The issue of willed action, and automatic control of behavior is discussed in depth by Norman (1981), Norman and Shallice (1980), Reason (1979) and Shallice (1978).

Norman's self-conscious use of "who" or "what" immediately conjures up a spectre traditionally feared and derided by psychologists, the ghost in the machine, the homunculus. Skinner (1971) refers to this entity as the "inner man'' whose function is ''to provide an explanation which will not be explained in turn'' (p. 14). In his article, ''Behaviorism at Fifty,'' Skinner (1964) provides a typical derisive picture of such concepts:

> The little man was recently the hero of a television program called 'Gateway to the Mind.' The viewers learned, from animated cartoons, that when a man's finger is pricked, electrical impulses resembling flashes of lightning run up the afferent nerves and appear on a television screen in the brain. The little man wakes up, sees the flashing screen, reaches out, and pulls the lever. More flashes of lightning go down the nerves to the muscles, which then contract, as the finger is pulled away from the threatening stimulus. The behavior of the homunculus was, of course, not explained. An explanation would presumably require another film. And it, in turn, another. (p. 80)

Such theories are, indeed, easy to deride, but hard to replace with an alternative. As Dennet (1978) points out (see also Boden, 1972, 1977), Skinnerian outrage at such ''mentalisms'' can be reduced to the axiom, ''Don't use intentional idioms in psychology'' (p. 33). One of the liberations of current theories of cognitive science is that researchers admit that human beings are intentional, and that an adequate explanation of human behavior necessitates reference to the intention, or the meaning of the behavior to the individual who performs it; that is, the individual's understanding of what he or she is doing (Boden, 1977; Brown, 1982a; Dennett, 1978; Flores & Winograd, 1978; Norman, 1980; Shaw & Bransford, 1977).

How do information processing models deal with the inner man? Most of the original models were hierarchical, uni-directional systems with a central processor initiating and interpreting lower level actions. More recent models tend to be heterarchical systems that permit lower nodes to feed into upper level nodes so that control can be distributed throughout the system (Hayes-Roth, 1977; Hayes-Roth & Hayes-Roth, 1979; Turvey & Shaw, 1979). Heterarchical control is clearly evident in animal physiological systems (Greene, 1971; Turvey, 1977); skilled performance, theories of action (Norman, 1981; Norman & Schallice, 1980; Turvey, 1977); and human speech perception (Newell, 1980). This notion is favored by current artificial intelligence systems (Hayes-Roth & Hayes-Roth, 1979).

Several recent theorists have claimed that heterarchies are the simplest class of system able to perform processing tasks of the complexity typical of human behavior (Greene, 1971; Koestler, 1979; Turvey, 1977; Turvey, Shaw & Mace, 1978). These systems do not rid themselves of inner men making decisions; the demons do not go away. Instead, they are distributed, a democratic solution that is much favored in current information processing models (Lindsay & Norman, 1977; Norman & Schallice, 1980), which trace their historical roots to Self-ridge's (1959) original Pandemonium model. However, even within the democratic confederacies or heterarchies, there is a supervisory processor (Lindsay &

Norman, 1977), or a decision demon (Selfridge, 1959) who listens to the pandemonium produced by the lower level demons and selects the most obtrusive. Conflicts for attentional resources must occur when several subordinate processors compete for the same resources. In such systems (McDermott & Forgy, 1978; Norman & Schallice, 1980), some conflict resolution procedure must be provided.

Central to the issues of metacognition are *computer planning models* that attempt to model problem-solving behavior. Only three are discussed here: GPS (General Problem Solver, Newell & Simon, 1972); NOAH (Nets of Action Hierarchies, Sacerdoti, 1974); and the recent cognitive model of planning functions of Hayes-Roth and her associates (Goldin & Hayes-Roath, 1980, Hayes-Roth & Hayes-Roth, 1979, and Hayes-Roth & Thorndyke, 1980). These models are briefly described.

The concept of planning was first introduced to artificial intelligence by the programmers of GPS (Ernst & Newell, 1969). The main planning strategy of GPS was means-end analysis, a hierarchical planning strategy that works backwards, from a clear idea of the goal to be achieved. A program using the strategy employs various comparison procedures to identify the difference(s) between the goal and the current state. Differences are ordered by priority that is determined by general purpose heuristics and by domain-specific heuristics. The problem solver, concentrating on the most important differences first, plans to reduce them progressively until no differences remain. The simplest situation is where only one difference exists between the current and goal state, and a single operator is found that can reduce that type of difference. More typically, no operator is found that can immediately solve the difference in these cases GPS establishes subgoals. If, for example, the initial state differs from the goal in several ways, GPS eliminates the differences, in turn, passing to the next difference only when the preceding difference has been resolved. GPS is a general problem solving strategy that can be used in any domain, providing appropriate information about states and operators is available. Domain-specific heuristics can also be incorporated if needed.

GPS works well for closed problem systems (Bartlett, 1958) that have well defined goals that can be reached by fixed means. GPS is a simple state-by-state planning strategy that does not produce an overall strategic plan of the problem before the solution is started. This type of decision maker has limited flexibility in revising and evaluating plans. Sacerdoti (1974) argues, that although it is not sensible to formulate an epistomologically adequate plan before attempting problem solution, a broad outline of the plan should be scheduled first, so that the system can see what adjustments need to be made during execution. Machine programs, like humans, can not forsee all of the possible contingencies; therefore, some form of contingency planning is incorporated in NOAH.

Sacerdoti's NOAH constructs a preplan that, during execution, can be altered on a contingency basis; NOAH works by means of a successive refinement approach to planning. However, NOAH is essentially a "top-down" processor, the planner making the high level abstract plans that guide and restrict the subsequent development of low level details. Similarly, the model assumes that the initial plan is relatively complete and subject to refinement only at lower levels; therefore, NOAH is essentially a hierarchical planning model. Recently, Hayes-Roth and Hayes-Roth (1979) developed an opportunistic planning model (OPM) that departs from the top-down, hierarchical, complete preplan assumptions of prior planning models. The OPM permits planning at many different levels, and allows several tentative, incomplete plans to coexist; therefore, it is essentially a heterarchical system. The OPM has great flexibility; it can opportunistically shift among several planning levels. At any one point in the planning process, the planner's current decisions and observations afford new opportunities for plan development; these are followed up by the model. Sometimes, opportunistic decisions result in orderly top-down routes, however, just as in human thinking, often less coherent sequences are engaged in. The OPM achieves this flexibility by assuming that the planning process consists of the independent actions of many distinct cognitive specialists (demons), each able to make tentative decisions for potential incorporation within a tentative plan. As in the classic Pandemonium model (Selfridge, 1959), the specialists record these decisions in a common data structure, known as the blackboard; enabling them to interact with each other, to influence and be influenced by one another's decisions.

The blackboard is divided into five conceptual planes that correspond to different categories of decision. These include: (a) *metaplan* decisions, dealing with the general approach to the problem; (b) *plan* decisions covering what action to take; (c) *plan-abstraction* decisions, dealing with the kinds of actions that are desirable; (d) *world-knowledge* decisions, noting specific problem environments; and (e) *executive* decisions, involved with the organization of the planning process itself. Each plane on the blackboard is also potentially served at several levels of abstraction. For example, the levels of the metaplan involve problem definition, selection of an appropriate problem-solving model, policy setting, and establishment of appropriate evaluation criteria. Plan-abstraction levels involve intentions, schemes, strategies, and tactics. The four levels of the plan plane are outcomes, designs, procedures, and operations. The executive plane involves decisions of priority, focus, and scheduling. The knowledge-base plane also has several levels of decisions, but these can only be specificed in a context-specific fashion, because knowledge factors are, by definition, problem specific.

In short, the plan, plan abstraction, and world knowledge decisions determine features of the developing plan. The executive decisions determine the allocation of cognitive resources during the planning process (i.e., what kinds of decisions to generate first, what aspect of the plan to develop next, etc.). Finally, the metaplan plane contains general decisions about how to approach the planning problem. These high level decisions reflect the planner's overall understanding of the problem, the methods that he or she will apply, and the criteria against which plans will be generated, evaluated, scheduled, rescheduled, and given priority.

The OPM, of Hayes-Roth & Hayes-Roth (1979), is indeed complex; five planes and three to four levels of decisions within each plane (19 are specified in the model). Metacognitive—like functions have liberally distributed throughout the system, where demons with homunculus sounding names also proliferate (director, referee, top management, middle management, compromisor, architect, strategist, technician, schemer, inventor, goal-setter, pattern-recognizer, designer, etc.). The full details of the model are too complex to include here; however, it is important to note that the OPM is more akin to human planning than the previous, strictly top-down, single executive, models. OPM is capable of simulating human planning on realistic problems, such as planning an economical route for a series of errands. In order to capture the flexibility and opportunitistic nature of human planning, the model involves multiple levels of decisions, of varying degrees of abstraction, taking place on multiple planes. The very complexity of the model is a reflection of the multifaceted nature of the problem of executive control within an information processing model. If, as argued elsewhere (Brown, 1974, 1978), descriptions of executive control functions within systems of machine intelligence are closely parallel to descriptions of thinking per se, one should not be surprised by the complexity; that the OPM is so explicit about the planning planes should be seen as an advantage. If one could describe the types of planning engaged in by adult problem solvers, within an explicit taxonomy of planning actions, researchers would be in a better position to examine the planning procedures of children, in conjunction with developmental changes in planning functions.

In short, the details of GPS, NOAH, and OPM are not important; instead, the lesson is that with increasing sophistication, information processing, and artificial intelligence models have gained more power by paying increasing attention to the ''metacognitive'' aspects of thinking. All models crudely distinguish between preplanning and planning-in-action (Rogoff & Gardner, in press); planning and control (Hayes-Roth, 1980); preaction and trouble shooting (Norman & Schallice, 1980); and planning and monitoring (Brown, 1978). Preplanning involves the formulation of general methods of procedure, prior to the actual onset of action. During the on-going attempt to solve the problem, there is continual planning-in-action, trouble shooting, or control processing; involving monitoring, revising, and contingency planning. Both forms of planning, recursively feed back to each other. Intelligent systems, be they machine or human, are highly dependent on executive orchestration, resource allocation, and monitoring functions. Nonintelligent systems, such as the inadequate programs or humans, are assumed to be deficient in planning functions.

Developmental Data. The central place of executive functions, such as planning and monitoring, is asserted in most current models of human and machine information processing, and there is a dearth of clear data, developmental or otherwise, that support this assertion. Examples of planning or monitoring success or failure are often given as incidental reports, following a description of the main source of interest (i.e., strategy effectiveness). Very few research programs have concentrated on planning or monitoring processes per se.

In the adult literature, notable exceptions to this rule are the program on planning in problem-solving by Hayes-Roth and her associates (Goldin & Hayes-Roth, 1980; Hayes-Roth, 1980); work on expert and novice physics problem solvers (Chi, Feltovich, & Glaser, 1981; Simon & Simon, 1978); and the recent work on comprehension-monitoring while reading (Baker & Brown, 1981; in press). For example, in a recent series of studies, Goldin and Hayes-Roth (1980) examined the planning strategies of adults. The task was to schedule a series of errands in a fictious town. The subjects read a scenario that described a series of desired errands; a starting time and location; an ending time and location; and sometimes, additional constraints. Invariably, the alloted time was insufficient to perform all the errands; therefore, the planners were obliged to organize their schedule in the most economical manner and to set priorities concerning which errands to perform. The primary data consisted of the protocols of the subject's on-line descriptions of their planning processes and the actual route taken.

Good planners made many metaplan and executive decisions and exercised deliberate control over their planning processes; they also made use of world knowledge information. Good planners showed greater flexibility than poor planners; they frequently shifted the focus of their attention among the different planes of decisions (within the OPM framework) and among the different loci within the route. More of the decisions of good planners were at a high level of abstraction; they recognized the importance of global planning, in contrast to the heavy reliance on local control, or bottom-up plans, shown by the poor planners. Poor planners tended to switch back and forth between objectives in an idiosyncratic (and often chaotic) fashion. In contrast, effective planners developed a prototypic procedure for accomplishing the errands, which they maintained over several instantiations of the task.

Poor problem solvers lack spontaneity and flexibility in both preplanning and monitoring. More extreme examples of planning deficits in adults come from the clinical literature on patients with frontal-lobe syndrome. These patients, typically, omit the initial preaction component (Luria, 1966); they also experience extraordinary difficulty with error correction (Milner, 1964). Such patients have been described as simultaneously perservative and distractible, a failure in intelligent focusing attributed to damage to the supervisory attentional mechanism, or executive system (Norman & Schallice, 1980). Although pathological cases are extreme, many descriptions of young and retarded childrens' learning are very similar. This superficial similarity is intriguing and deserves attention.

The dearth of systematic research specifically concerned with children's planning behavior is quite dramatic, although, again, there are many examples in the literature where failure to plan, monitor or check are described incidentally

(Brown & DeLoache, 1978). Brown, Bransford, Ferrara and Campione (1983) discuss some of the incidental cases of very young children planning ahead for future retrieval attempts.

A good example is provided by Karmiloff-Smith (1979b) who asked children 4–9 years of age, to construct a representation of closed circuit railways, using cardboard tracks. The children were well aware that they had to (a) use all the available pieces; (b) fit the tracks together (flush); and (c) make a closed circuit, so that the train could go around and not leave the tracks. The younger children started the task immediately, constructing the circuit by simply picking up tracks as they came to hand and placing them next to each other. No preplanning, followed by systematic search for a specific shaped piece (a curve or a straight) was shown. Older children, on the other hand, spent considerable time in the preplanning phase, piling tracks into stacks, on the basis of identity, and systematically selecting from the correct pile the desired shaped (i.e., curved, straight, curved, straight, curved, straight, etc. or two straight, two curved, two straight, two curved, etc.) in order to complete the master plan.

A similar example of planning failure in young children was reported by Kluwe (chapter 2, this volume). Children from 4–7 years of age were asked to work on a series of reversible puzzles. A reversible puzzle was arranged so that the children could correct their errors. For example, the task might be to copy a model of a ship using pieces of colored paper (shapes). If a piece was placed in the wrong position it could be corrected. After completing some reversible puzzles, the children were given irreversible puzzles. The base on which the puzzle pieces had to be assembled was covered with adhesive, so that the finished construction would be permanent and could be displayed as a picture on the wall. Even the youngest children, by spending more time looking back and forth between the model and the pieces before beginning construction, showed some signs of planning for the new contingency. However, only the older children were really clever and adopted strategies, such as constructing the entire puzzle first on a safe (reversible) surface, before transferring the pieces to the irreversible surface.

Most of the developmental descriptions of planning in children come from situations that have not been generated by information processing models of children's learning. What is needed in this area is programmatic work on preplanning and planning-in-action within a framework that takes into consideration other factors of the task environment, such as task familiarity and processing load. An excellent example of such an approach is Shatz's (1978) reconceptualization of the referential communication literature, within an information processing framework. Whether or not children will plan ahead and take the listener's perspective into account depends on the other processing demands of the task.

There is surprisingly little data on children's executive control while performing a task, or the planning-in-action phase; surprising, because of the proliferation of speculation concerning the centrality of monitoring processes to effective learning. Notable exceptions are the work on children's monitoring of oral and written communications (Flavell, Speer, Green & August, 1981; Markman, 1977, 1979; Stein & Trabasso, 1982). In general, children have difficulty detecting inconsistencies in messages, unless those inconsistencies are particularly blatant or salient (for a review see Baker & Brown, 1981b).

One example of executive monitoring during learning was provided by Belmont & Butterfield (1977). Adolescent learners were observed as they devised a systematic rehearsal plan for acquiring an eight item list of words. Over a series of ten trials the strategy became firmly established. The mature pattern to emerge in older subjects was the familiar cumulative rehearsal, fast-finish pattern. The subjects rehearsed the first words in the list cumulatively, pausing at approximately position five to establish the first set in memory, then they viewed the remaining three items very rapidly before risking a test. The subject's naive memory theory agreed with the psychologists' task analysis. The first part of the list must be rehearsed repeatedly and cumulatively to ensure memorability; the last items are viewed rapidly in the hope that they will not have faded before the test occurs.

After the subjects had established their rehearsal strategy, the experimenters, without warning, presented the same list of words repeatedly for eight trials. In the face of the changing task demands, older subjects rapidly abandoned their rehearsal strategy; younger children took more time to revise their study activity. In a subsequent test, when a repeated list was presented with two changed words, the older students were again more efficient at distributing their study time appropriately (Belmont & Butterfield, 1977). A similar sensitivity to study time apportionment, during studying, has been shown by children as young as third grade for simple repetitive lists of pictures (Masur, McIntyre & Flavell, 1973). In contrast, when the task is to monitor degree of learning from texts, adequate monitoring is not displayed until well into the high school years (Brown, Smiley & Lawton, 1978; Brown & Campione, 1978). The influence of task difficulty and familiarity must be considered in any examination of the child's propensity to plan and monitor his or her own activities.

Self Regulation

Nature of the Problem.   Any active learning process involves continuous adjustments and fine-tuning of action via self-regulating processes and "other even more mysterious apparatus" (Marshall & Morton, 1978 p. 227). Psychologists interested in mechanisms of growth and change have traditionally been concerned with self-regulating processes, because a great deal of learning takes place in the absence of external agents. However, substantial contributions are also made by external agents; these are discussed in the next section. It is certainly the case that human thinkers "play" with thinking (Gardner, 1978), that is, they subject their own thought processes to examination and treat their own thinking as an object of thought. Similarly, learners regulate and refine their own actions; sometimes this is done in response to feedback concerning errors, but often it is done in the absence of such feedback. Indeed, even if the system being experimented with is perfectly adequate, active learners will improve on their original production (Karmiloff-Smith, 1979a, 1979b).

Recently, the term metacognition has been extended to encompass regulatory functions, such as error detection and correction (Brown and DeLoache, 1978; Clark, 1979); the historical roots of these concepts can be found in most of the major developmental theories. For example, Binet, a pioneer in the empirical study of cognition and intelligence, was fascinated by individual differences in his daughters' cognitive styles of self-regulation (Binet, 1890, 1903); following intensive study with both normal and retarded children, he selected *autocriticism* (Binet, 1909) as a central component of intelligence.

In this section primary consideration is given to relatively recent Genevan research on self-regulatory mechanisms in children's thinking and on the growing emphasis in developmental psycholinguistics on error correction, systemization, and metalinguistic awareness.

Piaget's Theory of Regulation.   In the latter part of his career, the transformational period (Brown, 1979; Riegel, 1975), Piaget became more and more interested in mechanisms of learning and the influence of both conscious and unconscious regulatory functions in promoting conceptual change. Space restrictions, prevent the author from describing Piaget's complex theory; instead, the reader is referred to Gelman and Baillargeon (1983). Very briefly (and probably too simplistically), Piaget (1976) distinguishes between three primary types of self-regulation: autonomous; active; and conscious regulation.

Autonomous regulation is an inherent part of any "knowing act." However small the learner and however simple the action (Bruner, 1973; Koslowski and Bruner, 1972), learners continually regulate their performance, fine-tuning, and modulating actions. *Active regulation* is more akin to trial and error, where the learner is engaged in constructing and testing "theories-in-action" (Karmiloff-Smith & Inhelder, 1974–1975). Under the guidance of a powerful theory-in-action, the learner tests a current theory via concrete actions that produce tangible results. Only when a current theory and its range of applicability are confirmed and consolidated is the learner ready to recognize that there are counterexamples that have regularity. At this point, some unifying principles for these regularities can be actively tested. Not until a much later stage can the learner mentally construct and reflect on the hypothetical situations, which would confirm or refute a current theory without the need for active regulation. *Conscious regulation* involves the mental formulation of hypotheses capable of being tested via imaginary confirmatory evidence or counterexamples.

Thus, for Piaget, self-regulation, error correction, trial-and-error, theory testing, etc., need not be conscious experiences, but may occur in the plane of action; however, the highest level of theory building and testing is conscious.

Consciousness permits mental reasoning that liberates the regulatory functions from dependence on active testing (Piaget, 1978).

In *The Grasp of Consciousness* (1976) and the companion volume, *Success and Understanding* (1978), Piaget considered degree of consciousness, when he turned his attention to the gaps that exist between succeeding in action, being capable of explaining these actions, and being capable of abstract thought that drives action sequences. According to Piaget (1976):

> Action in itself constitutes autonomous and already powerful knowledge. Even if this knowledge (just knowing how to do something) is not conscious in the sense of a conceptual understanding, it nevertheless constitutes the latter's source, since on almost every point the cognizance (consciousness) lags, and often markedly so, behind this initial knowledge, which is of remarkable efficacy despite the lack of understanding. (pp. 346–347)

To encapsulate Piaget's developmental progression: the initial stage of autonomous regulation involves unconscious adjustments and fine-tuning of motor actions; next the child becomes capable of testing out theories-in-action, via concrete trial and error. Despite the lack of conscious surveilance on the part of the learner, this active regulation can lead to successful problem-solving. Even though the learner cannot describe how they were accomplished actions can be successfully completed.

Consciousness first emerges as the child becomes capable of reflecting on his or her own actions in the presence of the actual event. According to Piaget (1976); "When the child was asked how he came to discover a specific process . . . the younger subjects merely recounted their successive actions (or at the beginning merely reproduced them with gestures and no verbalizations), the older children said for instance, I saw that . . . so I thought . . . or so I had the idea . . . and so on (p. 337). At this initial stage, reportage is tied to concrete action, but does not direct it. Because consciousness is not directly linked to conceptualization, the child's "reactions remain elementary, the subject is likely to distort conceptualizations of what he observes, instead of recording it without modification." Such distortion can be quite dramatic; for example, having witnessed an event that is contrary to a tenaciously held belief, the "subject contests the unexpected evidence of his own eyes and thinks that he sees what he predicted would happen" (Piaget, 1976, p. 340).

At the most mature level, which Piaget would prefer restricted to the stage of formal operations, the entire thinking process can be carried out on the mental plane. The learner can consciously invent, test, modify, and generalize theories and discuss these operations with others.

> Finally, at the third level (from 11 to 12 years) which is that of reflected abstraction (conscious products of reflexive abstraction) the situation is modified in that cognizance [consciousness] begins to be extended in a reflexion of the thought it-

self . . . This means that the subject has become capable of theorizing and no longer only of 'concrete', although logically structured, reasoning. The reason for this is the child's new power of elaborating operations on operations. . . . He thereby becomes capable of varying the factors in his experiments, of envisaging the various models that might explain a phenomenon, and of checking the latter through actual experimentation. (Piaget, 1976, pp. 352–353)

In brief, the developmental progression is from unconscious autonomous regulation to active regulation, in the absence of anything more than a "fleeting consciousness." The beginning of conscious reflection occurs when the child is capable of considering his or her actions and describing them to others, albeit sometimes erroneously. The mature level of reflected abstractions, however, is characterized by conscious processes, that can be carried out exclusively on the mental plane coming to direct learning. Mature learners can create imaginary worlds and theories to explain actions and reactions within them. Such theories can be confirmed or refuted via the further construction of mental tests, conflict trials, or thought experiments that extend the limits of generality of the theory. This is the essence of scientific reasoning and the end state for a Piagetian development progression of child as scientist.

Metaprocedural Reorganization and Systemization.   Piaget's colleagues, In-helder and Karmiloff-Smith, have introduced another concept relevant to the discussion of self-regulation, *metaprocedural reorganization* (Karmiloff-Smith, 1979a; Karmiloff-Smith and Inhelder, 1974–1975). The basic idea is that learning within a domain follows a predictable sequence that is characterized by internal pressure to systematize, consolidate, and generalize knowledge. Representational systems are first developed to handle pieces of the problem space adequately, however, several theories can exist side-by-side in juxtaposition, not fully integrated into a comprehensive system. Karmiloff-Smith (1979a) maintain: ". . . each time children develop an adequate tool for representing their knowledge, and once the tool functions well procedurally, then that tool is considered metaprocedurally as a problem space in its own right" (p. 92). Thus, the theory (tool) that is directing action, itself becomes an object of thought and experimentation.

Stepping-up to a Metaprocedural level appears to take place each time the child has a handle on his currently functioning system. This enables the child to treat the system, or parts thereof, as units functioning in their own right. Thus, each time a representational tool (theory) functions well procedurally, the child somehow takes it apart to analyze its implicit components and thereby the representational tool becomes part of the problem space itself. (Karmiloff-Smith, 1979a, p. 115)

The prototypic microgenetic sequence is that the child first works on developing an adequate theory for a salient aspect of the problem space. This theory is practiced and perfected until it is fully operational. During the initial period the child cannot attend to other parts of the problem space, only when the initial theory is consolidated and functioning efficiently can the child step back and consider the system as a whole. Typically, the child will develop several juxtaposed theories that are adequate for various parts of the problem space; each theory operating in isolation from the other. Once the procedures are functioning well, the next stage of development is possible, and the child "steps-up" and metaprocedurally reconsiders the problem space. Once children become aware of the discrepancies or contradictions resulting from the simultaneous existence of several different functioning units, they begin to attempt to reconcile the differences and obviate contradictions resulting from the juxtaposition (Inhelder, Sinclair and Bovet, 1974).

A concrete example might help to clarify this complicated theoretical notion. Karmiloff-Smith and Inhelder (1974–1975) asked 4 to 9-year-old children to balance rectangular wooden blocks on a narrow metal rod fixed to a larger piece of wood. Length blocks had their weight evenly distributed; the correct solution was to balance them at the geometric center. Weight blocks had the weight of each "side" varied either conspicuously (by gluing a large block to one end of the base rectangle) or inconspicuously (by inserting a hidden weight into a cavity on one end of the rectangle).

At first, the children made the blocks balance by brute trial and error, using proprioceptive information to guide their action. Behavior was purely directed at the *goal* of balancing. This ploy was obviously successful, and the child balanced each block in turn. There was no attempt to examine the properties of the objects that led to balance and no attempt to subject each block to a test of a unified theory.

This early, but unanalysed, phase, without error, was supplanted by the emergence of a strong theory-in-action. The theory was directed at uncovering the rules governing balance in the miniature world of these particular blocks. Unfortunately, it was an incomplete rule that produced errors. A common theory, developed early by the children, was to concentrate exclusively on the geometric center and attempt to balance all blocks in this fashion. This worked for unweighted blocks; however, when the theory did not result in balance (produced errors) the blocks were discarded as exceptions ("impossible to balance"). After the theory was well established and working well for length blocks, the children became discomforted by the number and regularity of errors. A new juxtaposed theory was then developed for the conspicuous weight blocks. The children compensated for the weight, obviously added to one end, and adjusted the point of balance accordingly. However, for a time, length and weight were considered independently. Length blocks were solved by the geometric center rule and conspicuous weight blocks were solved by the estimate-weight-first and then compensate rule. Inconspicuous weight problems still generated errors. The blocks looked identical to the unweighted blocks and were, therefore, subjected to the dominant geometric center rule; they were discarded as anomalies that were "impossible to balance." The children's verbal responses reflected these juxtaposed solutions, exclusively length justifications were given for unweighted blocks and weight justifications were given for conspicuously weighted blocks.

Gradually and reluctantly, the children entered the period of metaprocedural reorganization, only possible when both juxtaposed procedures were working smoothly. Now, the young theorists, made uncomfortable by the remaining exceptions to their own rules, began to seek a rule for them. In so doing, a metaprocedural reorganization was induced that resulted in a single rule for all blocks. The children abandoned the simple theories and reorganized the problem space so that a single unifying theory predominated. Now, the children paused before balancing any block, and roughly assessed the point of balance. Verbal responses reflected their consideration of both length and weight (e.g., "You have to be careful, sometimes it's just as heavy on each side and so the middle is right, and sometimes it's heavier on one side.") After inferring the probable point of balance, and only then, did the child place the block on the bar.

There are three main points to note about this example. First, there is the finding of a developmental lull, or even a seemingly retrogressive stage, when errors predominate. Initially, the children made no errors, all blocks were balanced. However, during the quest for a comprehensive theory of balance, the children generated partially adequate procedures that resulted in errors. Only when the unifying theory was discovered did the children revert to perfect performance. If errors alone formed the data base, a curvilinear developmental growth curve would be apparent (Strauss and Stavey, 1982). Actually, what is happening is that the children are analyzing the problem space to generate a theory that would account for behavior. In so doing, they made what looked like errors, but what are often tests of the existing theory (Bowerman, 1981; Karmiloff-Smith, 1979a).

The second main point is that metaprocedural reorganization, leading to a "stepping-up" in theory complexity, is only possible when the partially adequate, juxtaposed systems are well established. It is essential that the child gain control of simple theories in his or her quest for a more complex adequate theory. Karmiloff-Smith and Inhelder (1974–1975) refer to this as *creative simplification*.

> The construction of false theories or the overgeneralization of limited ones are in effect productive processes. Overgeneralization, a sometime derogatory term, can be looked upon as the *creative simplification* of a problem by ignoring some of the complicating factors (such as weight in our study). This is implicit in the young child's behavior but could be intentional in the scientist's. Overgeneralization is not just a means to simplify but also to unify; it is then not surprising that the child and the scientist often refuse counter-examples since they complicate the unification process. However, to be capable of unifying positive examples implies that one is equally capable of attempting to find a unifying principle to cover counterexam-

ples . . . [there is] a general tendency to construct a powerful, yet often inappropriate hypothesis which [learners] try to verify rather than refute. This temporarily
blinds the [learner] to counterexamples which should actually suffice to have them
reject their hypothesis immediately. (p. 209)

Progress comes only when the inadequate theory is well established and the
learner is free to attempt to extend the theory to other phenomena. In this way the
theorists, be they children or scientists, are able to discover new properties,
which in turn make it possible for new theories to be constructed.

The third main point is that metaprocedural reorganization is not solely the
response to external pressure or failure, rather it occurs spontaneously when the
child has developed well functioning procedures that are incomplete, but adequate for the task at hand. It is not failure that directs the change, but success,
success that the child wishes to extend throughout the system.

A similar U-shaped developmental pattern has been observed in children's
language acquisition (Bowerman, 1987; Karmiloff-Smith, 1979a; Nelson &
Nelson, 1979). The phenomena under consideration are ''errors'' in children's
spontaneous speech. The particular errors of interest are those that are preceeded
by a period of correct usage; hence, they are referred to as ''late errors'' (Bowerman, 1984). For example, consider the child's use of plural (s) and the past tense
(ed) morphemes. The typical developmental progression is that children produce
correct instances of the plural and past tense of both the regular (dog *s,* cat *s,* tree
s, or walk *ed,* jump *ed,* climb *ed*) and irregular (mice, feet, went, broke) forms
(Bowerman, in press). Next, the irregular pattern is replaced by an incorrect,
overgeneralization of the regular form (foots, mouses, goed and breaked).
Eventually the correct forms reappear.

The explanation for this U-shaped development is that the original correct
usage was due to the child having learned the irregular (as well as regular) forms
as individual cases. Repeated experience with the regular pattern causes the child
to recognize the systematicity involved, abstract the general rule, and apply it too
broadly to all plurals (hence, mouses) or all past tense forms (hence, goed,
breaked); errors occur, whereas, previously there had been no errors. When the
system is fully established, the child is ready to admit exception to the dominant
rule and the exceptions reappear; however, this time they are part of an integrated
theory, regarded as being exceptions to the rule, not just isolated forms.

Karmiloff-Smith's (1979a) description of French children learning to use
definite and indefinite articles is another case in point. Again, a curvilinear trend
was found: the children first used the form correctly, then incorrectly, then again
in the appropriate manner. In French the indefinite article (un or une) has a dual
function; it can either refer to nonspecific reference or act as a numeral. In
English this distinction is marked at a surface level: a man (nonspecific references); one man (numeral). At approximately 3 years of age, children appear to
be using the adult system correctly, using un in both appropriate senses. At a

somewhat later stage the child enters a phase when he or she uses two distinct forms for the two distinct meanings. For example, "une voiture," for a car, and "une de voiture," for one car. The second is ungrammatical usage; however, the child finally reverts to the correct use. At a certain point in development, the child seems to recognize that a single work in his or her repetoire, in different contexts, functions in different ways. This recognition leads him or her to temporarily create new (ungrammatical) forms that differentiate between the separate functions and conserve their separate meanings. The child at the intermediate stage needs to render tangible the distinctions in meaning by marking them externally. In the process of analyzing the system the child produces more errors. Only later will the child allow one external marker to convey many pieces of information.

Levels of Self-Regulation.   In this brief and oversimplified synopsis of latter day Genevan psychology and language acquisition data, in theoretical speculation a central place is afforded to the concept of self-regulation. There is basic agreement that self-regulatory functions are integral to learning and are central mechanisms of growth and change. Similarly, the notion of self-regulatory mechanisms has a central place in the emergent field of metacognition (Brown & Deloache, 1978).

It is agreed that there are many degrees of self-regulation and that self-regulation is essential for any "knowing act." However, it is important to note, that a sharp distinction is made in both theories of language acquisition and in Genevan psychology, a distinction that has not been made as clear in the metacognitive literature. The distinction is between conscious awareness and direction of thought, and self-correction and regulation that can proceed below the level of consciousness. For example, Karmiloff-Smith (1979a) is quite insistent that "reference is being made to spontaneous metaprocedural behavior rather than to explicit awareness" (p. 92); and, developmental psycholinguists, such as Bowerman (1981) and Clark (1979) describe error detection and correction as an implicit process. "Most of the time this is done fluently and completely unconsciously" (Bowerman, 1981). In sharp contrast is the notion of metalinguistic awareness (Gleitman, Gleitman, & Shipley, 1972), where the child is capable of consciously reflecting on his or her own language and the language of others.

Piaget is even more emphatic when he distinguishes between *success,* which means "having enough understanding of a situation to attain the requisite ends in action" and *understanding,* which means "successful mastery in thought of the same situation to the point of being able to solve the problem of the 'how' and the 'why' of the connections observed and applied in action" (Piaget 1978, p. 218). Piaget's mature stage of reflected abstraction is distinguished by the "transcendance of action by conceptualization"; understanding comes "out of the realm of successes into the realm of reason" (1978, p. 218). In a normal developmental sequence, success at an action level considerably precedes understanding, however, with reflected abstraction the "situation is reversed." Conceptual thought drives success in action.

Thus, Piaget distinguishes sharply between active regulation as part of any knowing act and conscious regulation and direction of thought. The first process is age independent; even the young learner succeeds in action by regulating, correcting, and refining his or her current theories. The second process, guided by reflected abstraction, is late developing, and indeed, for Piaget, this is the keystone of formal operational thought.

Similarly, error correction during language production is intergral to the processes of using language and is present no less in young children (Bowerman, 1981; Clark, 1979) than in adults (Fromkin, 1973; Nooteboom, 1969). In contrast, metalinguistic awareness is assumed to be late developing, and in a mature form, it is also assumed to be a product of adolescent rather than childhood thinking. The ability to step back and consider one's own thought (or language) as an object of thought and, to go further, use the subsequent conceptualization to direct and redirect one's cognitive theories, is late developing. Confused in the metacognitive literature, even lost in some versions of the concept, is the essential distinction between self-regulation during learning and mental experimentation with one's own thoughts. Whatever distinctions must be made, in order to render metacognition a more malleable concept, this one is a fine candidate for inclusion in the list.

Developmental Data.   The separation of theory and data that seemed necessary in the preceding sections is somewhat artificial in this section. In previous sections, when discussing verbal reports as data or executive control, the historical roots and current theories were gleaned from the adult literature. In this section, on self-regulation, the theories were designed to explain developmental phenomena and the data base was gathered from children. For symmetry, however, the separation is maintained; however, for brevity only one example of: (a) early error correction; (b) metaprocedural reorganization in the absence of errors; and (c) conscious direction of problem solving are included.

Consider first *error correction;* the important point is that even very young children are capable of regulating their activities via a systematic procedure of error detection and correction. In a recent study, DeLoache, Sugarman and Brown (1981) observed young children (24–42 months) as they attempted to assemble a set of nesting cups. The number of successful seriators increased with age, however, there were no age differences in the number of errors produced or the probability of correcting errors. Children in this age range did not differ in their likelihood of correcting a set of nonseriated cups; they did however differ in their strategies for correction.

The most primitive strategy, used frequently by children below 30 months, was brute force. When a large cup was placed on a smaller one, the children would press down hard on the nonfitting cup. Twisting and banging were variants of brute pressure, but the same principle held; the selected cup would fit, if only one could press hard enough. Older children also used the brute force approach, but only after an unsuccessful series of maneuvers; for them, brute force appeared to be a last resort.

A second strategy initiated by some of the younger subjects was trying an alternative. After placing two nonfitting cups together, the child removed the top cup and did one of two things, he or she either looked for an alternative base for the nonfitting cup or tried an alternative top for the original base. Both ploys involve minimal restructuring and necessitate considering the relation between only two cups at any one time. The third characteristic ploy of children below 30 months was to respond to a cup that would not fit into a partially completed set of cups by dismantling the entire set and starting again.

Older children (30–42 months) faced with a nonfitting cup engaged in strategies that involve consideration of the entire set of relations in the stack. For example, one sophisticated strategy was insertion; the children took apart the stack at a point that enabled them to insert the new cup in its correct position. The "error" is corrected without the need to dismantle work already accomplished. To do this, however, the child must be cognizant of multiple relations between the series of cups, not just the single relation between two cups at a time. A second strategy *reversal* was also shown by older children. After placing two nonfitting cups together, the child would *immediately* reverse the relation between them (5/4 immediately switched to 4/5).

These rapidly executed strategies of insertion and reversal shown by the older children were often quite dramatic in their absence in the younger group. Some young children would repeatedly assemble, for example, cup 4-1, starting with 4 as a base and then inserting 3, 2, and 1. Then they encountered the largest cup, 5, and attempted to insert it on top of the completed partial stack, pressing and twisting repeatedly. When brute force failed, they would dismantle the whole stack. Similarly, having selected 1,2,4, and 5 and then encountering 3, the younger childrens' only recourse was to begin again.

The DeLoache, Sugarman and Brown (1981) study of self-correction in young children is used as one example (see also Koslowski and Bruner, 1972) of the obvious fact that even very young children correct their errors while solving a problem. Of more interest is the demonstration that the child's error correction strategies provide a window through which the child's theories-in-action can be viewed. The very processes used to correct errors reflect the level of understanding the child has of the problem space. Similarly, developmental psycholinguists have argued that production errors, such as "slips of the tongue" are very informative, "the tongue slips into patterns" (Nooteboom, 1969). Such errors reveal a great deal about the organization of the semantic space or cognitive organization of the speaker (Bowerman, 1981).

Metaprocedural reorganization, in the absence of external pressure, feedback, or correction, is the problem solving principle examined extensively by Karmiloff-Smith. One clear example is the development and refinement of a notational system by children drawing maps of a journey (Karmiloff-Smith, 1979a). Children between 7 and 11 years were shown a roll of paper (12 meters) on which a long winding road with 20 choice points (bifurcations) was drawn. At each choice point one road led to a dead-end; the other towards the destination, which was a hospital. The child's task was to prepare to drive a patient from his house to the hospital as quickly as possible. The child was permitted a practice drive over the route; during the practice drive only one choice point is visible at any one time (as the experimeter unrolls the paper gradually). The child's preparatory task is to take notes to help remember the route, which way to turn at each of the 20 choices.

The details of the notational systems the children developed, although fascinating, are not the major concern. Instead, of interest is the systematic modification made to the systems in the course of the journey. All children initially developed an adequate form of notational systems; therefore, changes in the system were not made in response to errors, or corrective feedback. During a one hour session, 70% of the sample made systematic changes to their notational system, changes that bear a striking resemblance to modifications in language production, described earlier (Karmiloff-Smith, 1979a). Two typical changes involved progressive economy and conventionalization of marking. For example, the child might begin by writing, "I will turn to the right, I will turn to the left," and then economize to "left," "right," "left." Similarly, a child might begin by drawing a detailed depiction of a topographical landmark on the map, such as a house, and then conventionalize these marks by using a line drawing to symbolize houses or trees, etc.

However, the systematic change of most interest is progressive plurifunctionality. The child would begin by using a notational symbol, which carries all the necessary information. For example, a topographical marker might be used both to identify the particular choice point (landmark function) and to indicate the correct road (directional function), that is, a little house would be drawn on the correct fork of a bifurcation. Gradually, however, the child moves from using a form that carries all the necessary information to externally mark each piece of information with a separate symbol. It is as if once the child becomes aware of the relevant pieces of information to be conveyed, he or she needs to mark them externally in a tangible form. Finally, once the system is fully and smoothly operating, the child reverts to the economical procedure of using one form to have multiple meanings. For example, one child began by marking the choice point by drawing a topographical sign that simultaneously indicated the particular bifuration and the road to take. These functions were separated when the child indicated the direction of choice with an arrow on the correct turn of the bifurcation and, separately drew the topographical marker to indicate the particular choice point. Finally, she came to use a topographical marker which carried a plurifunctional meaning by drawing it either to the left or right of the page (e.g., to indicate left at tree or right at house).

The interesting fact about these changes is that they take place in the absence of any errors or problems that should make the child dissatisfied with the original notation, and the types of modification that occur are regular. Karmiloff-Smith (1979a) argues that the tendency toward

> . . . External explication of implicit distinctions has a dynamic psychological function. It allows the child to get a grip on the newly semanticized distinction, each piece of information thereby rendered tangible by its own external handle. . . Once the child becomes aware of the various distinctions to be indicated, he must first work at each one separately in a juxtaposed fashion . . . hence the need for separate, external markers. . . . Gradually, this tangible external marking is replaced by integration into a more abstract plurifunctional system. (p. 115)

The progress to *conscious regulation* of problem solving via thought experiments, hypothesis testing, and reflected abstraction is well illustrated in Anzai and Simon's (1979) analysis of an adult, systematically refining procedures for solving a five disc Tower of Hanoi problem. Within a single session the subject progressed through three stages. First, she was concerned with the *goal* of completing the task and therefore looked very like the young block balancers recorded by Karmiloff-Smith and Inhelder (1974–1975). In the intermediate stage she became theory driven, seeking to understand the principles behind the task, guiding herself explicitly by mentioning intermediate goals, and pausing after each goal had been reached to plan for the next goal. In this phase theories-in-action were being created and tested. In the third phase, the subject shows Piaget's "reversed order," the "transcendence of action by conceptualization," "reflection directing action." *Before* undertaking to solve the puzzle again, the subject tested her understanding by reviewing the moves of the component one, two, three, and four disc problem. In so doing, she explicitly stated the main principle of recursivity, and the essential notion of the transfer of pyramids of discs (Anzai and Simon, 1979).

The microgenetic learning route followed by this adult subject is recapitulated macrogenetically in Piaget's protocols of The Hanoi Tower. In the early stage of solution, children complete a three disc problem by trial-and-error, without being conscious of the principles. None of the younger subjects (4- to 5-year-olds) made a plan, or were able to predict how they were going to move the tower. After the fact, their justifications and explanations were noninformative. In an intermediate stage correct solutions became stable for three disc problems, there was evidence of planning ahead and the beginning of the ability to describe the procedures used during a successful attempt.

The final stage (approximately 11 years of age) was characterized by rapid and stable success on three disc problems and increasingly inferential anticipation of the rules for solving five disc problems. Having completed a four disc problem, one child asked to predict how to solve a five disc problem responded:

"Theres one more, you have to make more moves, otherwise it's the same system—you always take away the smaller one, then the middle one, then you put the small one on the middle one and you can get at the bigger one; that makes a small pyramid there, and then the way is clear to do it all again. I can start all over again; it's the same story afterward" (Piaget, 1976, p. 298).

By Piaget's Stage III, the child's understanding of the principles of recursivity and the pyramid subgoal strategy (Anzai and Simon, 1979) is not only fully articulated, but it directs the subsequent problem solving attempt. The entire procedure can be corrected, examined, and revised in thought, before it is attempted in action. In Piaget's system, this is the essence of conscious control of action, or reflected abstraction.

Other-Regulation

Nature of the Problem.   In this final section the notion of other-regulation, as it pertains to the general topic of metacognitive development, is discussed. Important as the processes of self-regulation may be, a great deal of learning occurs in the presense of, and is fostered by, the activity of others. Supportive-others, such as parents, teachers, peers, guide a novice to mastery; there seems to be a systematic regularity in how this guidance works.

A great deal of the work conducted on other-regulation has taken place within the framework of Vygotsky's (1978) theory of internalization. Vygotsky argues that all psychological processes are initially social, shared between people, particularly between child and adult; and that the basic interpersonal nature of thought is transformed through experience to an intrapersonal process. Thus, for Vygotsky, the fundamental process of development is the gradual internalization and personalization of what was originally a social activity. According to Vygotsky (1978):

> We propose that an essential feature of learning is that it creates the zone of proximal development; that is, learning awakens a variety of developmental processes that are able to operate only when the child is interacting with people in his environment and in cooperation with his peers. Once these processes are internalized, they become part of the child's independent developmental achievement. (p. 90)

Social settings, where the child interacts with experts in a problem solving domain, are settings where a great deal of learning occurs. Indeed, some would argue that the majority of learning is shaped by social processes. (Laboratory for Comparative Human Cognition, in press). A great deal of this learning involves the transfer of executive control from the expert to the child; thus, for Vygotsky, the development of cognitive control is very much a social process. Children first experience active problem solving activities in the presence of others, then gradually come to perform these functions for themselves. This process of "internalization'' is gradual: First the adult (parent, teacher, etc.) controls and guides the child's activity; gradually the adult and the child come to share the problem solving functions, with the child taking initiative and the adult correcting and guiding when the child falters; finally, the adult cedes control to the child and functions primarily as a supportive and sympathetic audience (Brown & French, 1979; Campione, Brown, Ferrara & Bryant, 1984; Laboratory of Comparative Human Cognition, in press).

The developmental progression from other-regulation to self-regulation is nicely illustrated in successful mother-child learning situations. Consider the following example from Wertsch (1978, p. 17), the mothers and their young children were given the task of copying a wooden puzzle (a truck). A completed puzzle was used as the model and the mother and child were asked to complete an identical puzzle. The mother was told to encourage the child if necessary. The following is a sample of a video-taped interaction between a mother and her 2½ year-old daughter:

1. C: Oh (glances at model, then looks at pieces pile). Oh now where's this one go? (picks up black cargo square, looks at copy, then at pieces pile).
2. M: Where does it go in this other one (the model)? (child puts black cargo square back down in pieces pile, looks at pieces pile).
3. M: Look at the other truck (model) and then you can tell (child looks at model, then glances at pieces pile).
4. C: Well (looks at copy then at model).
5. C: I look at it.
6. C: Um, this other puzzle has a black one over there (child points to black cargo square in model).
7. M: Um-hm.
8. C: A black one (looks at pieces pile).
9. M: So where do you want to put the black one on this (your) puzzle? (child picks up black cargo square from pieces pile and looks at copy).
10. C: Well, where do you put it in there? Over there? (inserts black cargo square correctly in copy).
11. M: That looks good.

In this example one can see the mother serving a vital regulatory function, guiding the problem-solving activity of her child. Good examples of the mother assuming the regulatory role are statements 2, 3, and 9, where she functions to keep the child on task and to foster goal relevant search and comparison activities. This protocol represents a midpoint between early stages of development, where the mother and child speak to each other, but the mother's utterances do not seem to be interpreted by the child as task relevant; and later stages, where the child assumes the regulatory functions, the mother functioning as a sympathetic audience.

It is argued that supportive "experts," such as mothers in Wertsch's example, master craftsmen in apprenticeship systems (Childs & Greenfield, 1980), and more experienced peers in tutoring studies (Allen, 1976), serve a major function of initially adopting the monitoring and overseeing role; these crucial regulatory activities are thereby made *overt* and *explicit.*

Ideally, teachers function as such mediators in the learning to learn process; acting as promotors of self-regulation by nurturing the emergence of personal planning, as they gradually cede their own direction. In schools, effective teachers are those who engage in continual prompts to get children to plan and monitor their own activities. Schallert and Kleiman (1979) identified four basic strategies used by successful teachers to promote critical reading. First, they attempted to tailor the information to the children's existing level of understanding. They tried to activate relevant background knowledge by having the students consider new information in light of what they already knew. Continual attempts were made to focus the students' attention on important facts, finally, because of the teachers' use of clever questioning and such Socratic ploys as invidious generalizations, counter example, reality testing, etc., students were helped to monitor their own comprehension. Thus, the expert teacher models many forms of critical thinking for the students; processes that the students must internalize as part of their own problem solving activities if they are to develop effective skills of self-regulation.

Deficiencies in such interactive learning processes have been indicted as primary sources of developmental retardation. (Brown & French, 1979; Feuerstein, 1979). Feuerstein's theory is essentially similar to Vygotsky's, for he too holds that cognitive growth is very heavily dependent on the quality of mediated learning that the child experiences. According to Feuerstein (1969): "Mediated learning is the training given to the human organism by an experienced adult who frames, selects, focuses, and feeds back an environmental experience in such a way as to create appropriate learning sets" (p. 6). These mediated learning experiences are an essential aspect of development, beginning when the parent selects significant objects for the infant to focus on and proceeding throughout development; the adult systematically shaping the child's learning experiences. It is the principal means by which children develop the cognitive operations necessary for learning independently. By interacting with an adult, who guides problem solving activities and structures learning environments, children gradually come to adopt structuring and regulatory activities of their own.

Feuerstein believes that the principal reason for the poor academic performance of many disadvantaged students is the lack of consistent mediated learning in their earlier developmental histories, because of parental apathy, ignorance, or overcommitment. Quite simply, parents in disadvantaged homes were themselves disadvantaged children and cannot be expected to teach what they do not know; large family size and the need for a working mother does not leave a great deal of time for Socratic dialogue games. In addition, these interactive styles of continually questioning and extending the limits of knowledge are typical of middle-class social interaction patterns and may be alien to some cultures (Au, 1980; Bernstein, 1971).

However, mediated learning activities are exactly what occur in schools, and the middle-class child comes well prepared to take part in these rituals. Not only does the disadvantaged child lack prior exposure, but there is some evidence that teachers give less experience in this learning mode to those who, because of their lack of prior experience, need it most. For example, recent observations of reading groups (Au, 1980; McDermott 1978) have shown that good and poor readers are not treated equally. Good readers are questioned about the meaning behind what they are reading, asked to evaluate and criticize material, etc. By contrast, poor readers primarily receive drill in pronounciation and decoding. Rarely are they given practice in qualifying and evaluating their comprehension (Au, 1980). If, as a result, their reading problems persist, such children may be singled out for special education; and again, this is likely to decrease rather than increase their exposure to the ideal mediated learning experience.

Special education classes are more likely to provide step-by-step explicit instruction for students in basic skills. Heavily programmed learning of this type may be a practical and efficient means of getting less successful students to perform better on a particular task; however, such experience is less likely to be appropriate for promoting insightful learning or the development of self-regulatory skills. Students may learn something about a particular task, but they are not likely to learn much about how to learn in general.

The development of cognitive skills proceeds normally via the gradual internalization of regulatory skills first experienced by the child in social settings (Vygotsky, 1978). Following repeated experience with experts (mothers, teachers, etc.), who criticize, evaluate, and extend the limits of their experience, students develop skills of self-regulation. If students are to learn how to learn independently, the development of a battery of such autocritical skills (Binet, 1909) is essential. If for some reason the child is deprived of a constant history of such interaction, the development of a battery of self-regulatory skills is unlikely to occur.

Developmental Data.   Only one example of the basic principle of acquiring self-regulatory skills, by first observing them in social interaction, is provided. The most frequently quoted data to support the other-regulation to self-regulation transition is Wertsch's (1978) descriptions of mother-child problem solving dyads, an excerpt was included earlier. To illustrate the generality of the process, a study from the laboratory, where much older learners are seen acquiring more complex monitoring skills (Palinscar & Brown, 1981), is used. The basic situation was an interactive tutoring dyad, where seventh graders were receiving instruction aimed at improving their reading comprehension skills. The children were referred by their teachers because, although they were able to decode at approximately grade level, they had severe comprehension problems; performing several grade levels behind their peers. Over many sessions the tutor and the child engaged in an interactive learning game that involved taking turns in leading a dialogue concerning each segment of text. Both the tutor and the child would read a text segment; then the dialogue leader would paraphrase the main idea, question any ambiguities, predict the possible questions that might be asked about that segment, and hypothesize about the content of the remaining passage segments. The dialogue leader would then ask the other a question on the segment; in the next segment the roles were reversed.

Initially, the tutor modelled these activities, however, when his or her turn came, the child had great difficulty assuming the role of dialogue leader. The tutor was forced to resort to constructing paraphrases and questions for the tutee to mimic. In this initial phase, the tutor was modelling effective comprehension monitoring strategies; the child was a relatively passive observer. In the intermediate phase, the tutee became much more capable of playing her role as dialogue leader, and by the end of 10 sessions was providing paraphrases and questions of some sophistication. For example, in the initial sessions, 19% of the questions produced by the tutees were judged as nonquestions and 36% as needing clarification. Examples of questions needing clarification are:

1. What was, who, some kings were uh, about the kings? (translated as: Why is it that kings did not always make the best judges?)

2. What were some of the people? (translated as: What kind of people can serve on a jury?)

3. What was the Manaus built for? Wait a minute, What was the Manaus built for? What certain kind of thing? Wait a minute. OK. What was the Manaus tree built for? (translated as: Why was the city of Manaus built?)

In the final sessions, only 4% of the responses were judged as uninterpretable or needing clarification.

At the beginning of the sessions, 34% of the questions were aimed at detail and only 11% at main ideas; however, by the end of the sessions, 54% of all questions probed comprehension of salient ideas. Examples of main idea questions are: "What are the three main problems with all submarines?" "Plans are being made to use nuclear power for what?" "What did these people (the Chinese) invent?" Examples of detail questions were: "What color is the guard's uniform?" "How far can flying fish leap?" "What are chopsticks made out of?"

Similar progress was made in producing paraphrases of the main ideas of the text segment. At the beginning of the sessions, only 11% of summary statements captured main ideas; at the end of the sessions, 60% of statements were so classified. The comprehension monitoring activities of the tutees certainly improved, becoming more and more like those modelled by the tutor. With repeated interactive experiences, the tutor and child mutually constructing a cohesive representation of the text, the tutees were able to employ monitoring functions for themselves.

Improvement was revealed not just in the interactive sessions but also in privately read stories, where the students were required to answer comprehension questions on their own. In the laboratory, tests of comprehension were given throughout the experiment. On the independent tests performance improved from 10 to 85% correct; in the classroom, compared with all other seventh graders in the school, the students moved from the 7th to the 40th percentile. Not only did the students learn to perform comprehension monitoring activities in interaction with their tutor, they were also able to *internalize* these procedures as part of their own cognitive processes for reading.

STATUS OF METACOGNITION AS A CONCEPT

In the preceding review, it is clear that metacognition is not only a monster of obscure parentage, but a many-headed monster at that. In this final section an attempt is made to estimate the current status of the offspring and to list some of the many problems inherent in the current use of the term.

I would like to emphasize my belief that in many ways this status report is premature. Scientific theorizing, like any other, must pass through stages. Consider as an example, the novice block balancers described earlier. Initially, they are merely goal oriented; they concentrate on getting the new theory to work. The next stage is to develop and refine subsystems so that they work fluently. Only when these subsystems are functioning efficiently can the theorist step back and consider the entire problem space and systematize or reorganize it into a cohesive whole. The recent history of theory development in the realm of metacognition can be viewed in this light. In the early 1970s, attracted by the lure of a new sounding concept, developmental psychologists engaged in demonstration studies to see how the new idea would work. These early studies were often ingenious and the wave of enthusiasm they provoked was justified.

The initial stage is now over and the current stage is, and should be, devoted to the task of developing workable theories and procedures for separate parts of the problem space. It is for this reason that the strands of inquiry that gave rise to the step-child, metacognition are examined separately. Currently a great deal of systematic work is being undertaken, hopefully, it will lead to fluently functioning subsystems that at present are merely juxtaposed, existing, and developing side-by-side; however, this is an essential stage of theory building. Later, perhaps, when the main subsystems are better understood, metaprocedural reorganization (Karmiloff-Smith, 1979a) may be possible, and a full understanding of the domain metacognition will be attained. This chapter is primarily a contribution to the ''juxtaposed procedures'' stage of development.

However, doubt remains concerning whether the domain(s) covered by meta-cognition will be tractable enough for a total systematization. If one takes the wide view, metacognition, as currently used, refers to understanding in a very broad sense; there is no simple problem space!

In a recent review, Wellman (1981), as others before have done, referred to the concept of metacognition as a fuzzy concept. Wellman, however, went on to discuss four features of the fuzzy concept.

> First, the concept encompasses an essential, central distinction. However, this distinction serves to anchor the concept not intentionally define it. Second, prototypic central instances of the concept are easily recognized. However, third, at the periphery agreement as to whether an activity is legitimately metacognitive breaks down; the definitional boundaries are truly fuzzy. Related to this, and forth, different processes all of which partake of the original distinction may be related only loosely one to another. Thus the term metacognition or metamemory serves primarily to designate a complex of associated phenomena. (pp. 3–4)

This is nicely put, and illustrates the loose confederation of topics included under the blanket term, metacognition. Of some concern, however, is whether the associated phenomena are linked closely enough to warrant the use of a single family name; that is, does it refer to family resemblances within an ill-defined, natural, or fuzzy category, or many categories? And, would it not be better, at this stage, to abandon the global term and work at the level of subordinate concepts, which are themselves fuzzy?

For clarity and communicative efficiency, a case could be made that the term metacognition should be pensioned-off, or at least severly restricted in its extensional reference. This is not because the phenomena subsumed under the term are trivial, but because they are central processes of change and development; the very theoretical ideas that this author predicts will be the main focus of developmental learning theories in the next decade. Issues of fundamental importance may be obscured by the current arguments surrounding things metacognitive; arguments that are obscured because the participants do not make it clear which head of the beast they are attacking or defending.

Wellman (1981) limits the term metacognition to knowledge, and believes that this would be an agreed on limitation. However, it is not a limitation at all, as knowledge can very easily involve all forms of information, both procedural and declarative. It is clear that may present usages of metacognition do not exclude process or factual knowledge, or anything else for that matter. One suggestion is to limit the term to one of its original uses, knowledge about cognition, where that knowledge is stable and statable (Gleitman, in press). Process terms such as planning-ahead, monitoring, resource allocation, self-questioning, self-directing, etc. would then be used alone, without the addendum, metacognition. This author has no ready solution to offer; but wishes to emphasise that there are nontrivial problems associated with the current blanket usage of the term.

This brings one back to the problems mentioned at the beginning of the chapter. At present it is difficult to answer critical questions about metacognition, such as: "Is it late developing?" "Is it general or domain specific?" "Is it conscious?" without pausing to ascertain which type of knowledge or process is in question. Although metacognition may turn out to be a fuzzy concept with indistinct boundaries, this degree of imprecision is not acceptable as a basis of scientific inquiry. By referring to the process/knowledge under discussion by its subordinate name (i.e., planning-ahead, error-correction, hypothesis-testing, etc.) many of the current controversies, but by no means all, would evaporate. At least one would know where the real problems are, and which problems are the result of communication failure.

In conclusion, some of the really interesting issues of learning and development that the concentration on metacognition has forced one to reconsider as central concerns are: conscious control over learning; learning without awareness; transfer of rule learning; relation of age and expertise to various aspects of planning; monitoring and error correcting; general rules for problem solving versus domain specific knowledge; and mechanisms of change. From this seemly random list just one, mechanisms of change, is discussed here (for a fuller review see Brown, 1979; Brown, 1982a; Brown, Bransford, Ferrara, & Campione, 1983).

One of the real advances spurred by the interest in metacognition has been a revived concern for mechanisms of change and development. This has always been the hidden agenda of developmental psychologists; however, until recently, there have been surprisingly few attempts to study change directly. Developmental studies have traditionally consisted of cross-sectional, frozen, one shot looks at age changes; the performance of groups of children, varying in age or level of expertise, is compared and contrasted. Even a great deal of longitudinal research has a surprisingly cross-sectional flavor. Both approaches provide a picture of cognition in stasis, rather than evolving, as it were, right before one's eyes. Many of the studies reviewed in this section depart from this pattern. This is because many of the studies that have been inspired by the metacognitive boom have been training studies, or have involved microgenetic analyses of children learning-by-doing on their own, or learning to develop self-regulatory skills through the intervention of supportive others.

Reverting to the microgenetic approach advocated by Vygotsky (1978) and Werner (1961) enables one not only to concentrate on qualitative descriptions of the stages of expertise, but also to consider transition phenomena and self-modification techniques underlying the progression from beginning to expert strategies. Anzai and Simon's learning-by-doing theory, and developmental microgenetic studies of young learners (Karmiloff-Smith, 1979a, 1979b; Karmiloff-Smith & Inhelder, 1974–1975; Koslowski & Bruner, 1972 for example) are some instances of the current interest in within-subject, learning-by-doing mechanisms of change that can be observed in a single subject within a short space of time.

Similarly, the current interest in attempts to understand development by engineering change via intervention has clearly been a positive outcome of interest in metacognition (Brown & Campione, 1981). Training studies in general have been a traditional tool of the developmental psychologist and are becoming of increasing importance for both practical and applied reasons (Brown, Campione & Day, 1981). Although there are many methods of intervention, the essential element in traditional studies is that the experimenter provides feedback and direction. It is the experimenter, then, who undertakes the requisite task analysis and often, it is the experimenter who maintains all of the controlling and decision making functions.

The current interest in more dynamic learning situations has seen a move away from direct instruction of the traditional kind towards the interactive processes, illustrated by the Palinscar and Brown (1981) study described earlier, and in Wertsch's (1978) examination of mother-child teaching dyads. Via the intervention of a supportive, knowledgeable other, the child is led to the limits of his or her own understanding. The teacher does not, however, tell the child what to do, he or she enters into an interaction where the child and the teacher are mutually responsible for getting the task down. As the child adopts more of the essential skills initially undertaken by the adult, the adult relinquishes control. Transference of power is gradually and *mutually agreed upon.*

Although the supportive other in the laboratory is usually an experimenter, these interactive learning experiences are intended to mimic real life learning. Mothers (Wertsch, 1978), teachers (Schallert & Kleinman, 1979) and master craftsmen (Childs & Greenfield, 1980) all function as the supportive other; the agent of change responsible for structuring the child's environment in such a way that he or she will experience a judicious mix of compatible and conflicting experiences. The importance of such interactive learning experiences for general cognitive development should not be overlooked. Many cognitive activities are initially experienced in social settings; however, in time, the results of such experiences become internalized. Initially the supportive other acts as the interrogator, leading the child to more powerful rules and generalizations. The interrogative, regulatory role, however, becomes internalized during the process of development, and children become able to fulfill some of these functions for themselves through self-regulation and self-interrogation. Mature thinkers are those who provide conflict trials for themselves, practice thought experiments, question their own basic assumptions, provide counterexamples to their own rules, etc. In short, although a great deal of thinking and learning may remain a social activity (Brown & French, 1979; Laboratory for Comparative Human Cognition, in press), through the process of internalization, mature reasoners become capable of providing the supportive other role for themselves. Under these systems of tutelage, the child learns not only how to get a particular task done independently, but also how to set about learning new problems. In other words, the child learns how to learn (Brown, 1982b; Brown, Bransford, Ferrara, & Campione, 1983).

SUMMARY

Some of the diverse historical roots of the family of concepts that are often referred to generically as metacognition have been examined. Specifically discussed are the controversies surrounding such perennial problems for psychology as: the status of verbal reports as data; executive control; consciousness and who has it; error correction and systemization in early language production and metalinguist awareness; self-regulation, metaprocedural reorganization, and reflected abstraction from Genevan psychology; and the transferrence from other-regulation to self-regulation, inspired by Vygotsky's theory of development.

The use of the blanket term metacognition for quite different theories and various levels of analyses was questioned, as was the utility of the continued use of such a catholic term. The important redirection of attention to mechanisms of change inspired by the interest in the metacognitive issues was welcomed.

ACKNOWLEDGMENTS

Preparation of this manuscript was supported in part by U.S.P.H.S. Grant HD-05951

REFERENCES

Allen, V. L. (1976). *Children as teachers: Theory and research on tutoring.* New York: Academic Press.

Anzai, Y., & Simon, H.A. (1979). The theory of learning by doing. *Psychological Review, 86,* 124–140.

Au, K. (1980). *A test of the social organizational hypothesis: Relationships between participation structures and learning to read.* Unpublished doctoral dissertation, University of Illinois.

Baker, L., & Brown, A. L. (1981). Metacognition and the reading process. In D. Pearson (Ed.), *A handbook of reading research.* New York: Plenum Press, 353–394.

Baker, L., & Brown, A. L. (1984). Cognitive monitoring in reading. In J. Flood (Ed.), *Understanding reading comprehension.* Newark, DE: International Reading Association.

Baldwin, M. J. (1909). How children study. *Archives of Psychology, 12,* 65–70.

Bartlett, F. C. (1958). *Thinking: An experimental and social study.* New York: Basic Books.

Belmont, J. M., & Butterfield, E. C. (1977). The instructional approach to developmental cognitive research. In R. V. Kail Jr. & J. W. Hagen (Eds.), *Perspectives on the development of memory and cognition.* Hillsdale, NJ: Lawrence Erlbaum Associates.

Bernstein, B. (1971). *Class codes and control* (Vol. 1). London: Routledge & Kegan Paul.

Binet, A. (1890). Perceptions d'enfants. *Revue philosophique, 30,* 582–611.

Binet, A. (1903). *L'etude experimentale de l'intelligence*. Paris: Schleicher Freres.

Binet, A. (1909). *Les idees modernes sur les infants*. Paris: Ernest Flamarion.

Boden, M. A. (1972). *Purposive explanation in psychology*. Boston, MA: Harvard University Press.

Boden, M. A. (1977). *Artificial intelligence and natural man*. Sussex, England: The Harvester Press.

Bowerman, M. (1981). Starting to talk worse: Clues to language acquisition from children's late speech errors. in S. Strauss (Ed.), *U-shaped behavioral growth*. New York: Academic Press.

Broadbent, D. E. (1977). Levels, hierarchies, and the locus of control. *Quarterly Journal of Experimental Psychology, 29*, 181–201.

Broudy, H. S. (1977). Types of knowledge and purposes of education. In R. C. Anderson, R. J. Spiro & W. E. Montague (Eds.), *Schooling and the acquisition of knowledge*. Hillsdale, NJ: Lawrence Erlbaum Associates.

Brown, A. (1974). The role of strategic behavior in retardate memory. In N. R. Ellis (Ed.), *International review of research in mental retardation* (Vol. 7). New York: Academic Press.

Brown, A. L. (1975). The development of memory: Knowing, knowing about knowing, and knowing how to know. In H. W. Reese (Ed.), *Advances in child development and behavior* (Vol. 10). New York: Academic Press.

Brown, A. L. (1978). Knowing when, where, and how to remember: A problem of metacognition. In R. Glaser (Ed.), *Advances in instructional psychology* (Vol. 1). Hillsdale, NJ: Lawrence Erlbaum Associates.

Brown, A. L. (1979). Theories of memory and the problem of development: Activity, growth, and knowledge. In L. S. Cermak & F. I. M. Craik (Eds.), *Levels of processing in human memory*. Hillsdale, NJ: Lawrence Erlbaum Associates.

Brown, A. L. (1980). Metacognitive development and reading. In R. J. Spiro, B. Bruce, & W. Brewer (Eds.), *Theoretical issues in reading comprehension*. Hillsdale, NJ: Lawrence Erlbaum Associates.

Brown, A. L. (1982a). Learning and development: The problem of compatibility, access, and induction. *Human Development, 25*, 89–115.

Brown, A. L. (1982b). Learning to learn how to read. In J. Langer & T. Smith-Burke (Eds.), *Reader meets author, bridging the gap: A psycholinguistic and social linguistic perspective*. Newark, NJ: Dell.

Brown, A. L., Bransford, J. D., Ferrara, R. A., & Campione, J. C. (1983). Learning, remembering, and understanding. In J. H. Flavell and E. M. Markman (Eds.), *Handbook of child psychology* (4th ed.). *Cognitive development* (Vol. 3, pp. 515–529). New York: Wiley.

Brown, A. L., & Campione, J. C. (1978). Permissible inferences from the outcome of training studies in cognitive development research. *Quarterly Newsletter of the Institute for Comparative Human Development, 2*, 46–53.

Brown, A. L., & Campione, J. C. (1981). Inducing flexible thinking: A problem of access. In M. Friedman, J. P. Das, & N. O'Connor (Eds.), *Intelligence and learning* (pp. 515–530). New York: Plenum Press.

Brown, A. L., Campione, J. C., & Day, J. D. (1981a). Learning to learn: On training students to learn from texts. *Educational Researcher, 10* (2), 14–21.

Brown, A. L., & DeLoache, J. S. (1978). Skills, plans, and self-regulation. In R. Siegler (Ed.), *Children's thinking: What develops?* Hillsdale, NJ: Lawrence Erlbaum Associates.

Brown, A. L., & French, L. A. (1979). The zone of potential development: Implications for intelligence testing in the year 2000. *Intelligence, 3*, 255–277.

Brown, A. L., Smiley, S. S., & Lawton, S. C. (1978). The effects of experience on the solution of suitable retrieval cues for studying texts. *Child Development, 49*, 829–835.

Bruner, J. S. (1973). Organization of early skilled action. *Child Development, 44*, 1–11.

Bühler, K. (1907). Remarques sur les problèmes de la psychologie de la pensée. *Archives de Psychologie, 6*, 376–386.

Campione, J. C., & Brown, A. L. (1977). Memory and metamemory development in educable retarded children. In R. V. Kail, Jr. & J. W. Hagen (Eds.), *Perspectives on the development of memory and cognition.* Hillsdale, NJ: Lawrence Erlbaum Associates.

Campione, J. C., Brown, A. L., Ferrara, R. A., & Bryant, N. R. (1984). The zone of proximal development: Implications for individual differences and learning. In B. Rogoff & J. V. Wertsch (Eds.), *Children's Learning in the "Zone of Proximal Development".* San Francisco: Jossey-Bass.

Cavanaugh, J. C., & Borkowski, J. G. (1979). The metamemory-memory "connection": Effects of strategy training and transfer. *Journal of General Psychology, 101,* 161–174.

Cavanaugh, J. C., & Perlmutter, M. (1980). *Metamemory: A critical examination.* Unpublished manuscript, University of Minnesota.

Chi, M. T. H. (1981). Knowledge development and memory performance learning research and development center. In M. Friedman, J. P. Das, & N. O'Connor (Eds.), *Intelligence and Learning.* New York: Plenum Press.

Chi, M. T. H., Glaser, R., & Rees, E. (1982). Expertice in problem solving. In R. Sternberg (Ed.), *Advances in the psychology of human intelligence* (Vol. 1). Hillsdale, NJ: Lawrence Erlbaum Associates.

Childs, C. P., & Greenfield, P. M. (1980). Informal modes of learning and teaching. In N. Warren (Ed.), *Advances in cross-cultural psychology* (Vol. 2). London: Academic Press.

Clark, E. V. (March, 1979). *Children's error corrections in early language production.* Paper presented at the meeting of the Society for Research in Child Development, San Francisco.

Collins, A. (1977). Processes in acquiring knowledge. In R. C. Anderson, R. J. Spiro & W. E. Montague (Eds.), *Schooling and the acquisition of knowledge.* Hillsdale, NJ: Lawrence Erlbaum Associates.

Collins, A., Brown, A. L., Morgan, J. L., & Brewer, W. F. (April, 1977). *The analysis of reading tasks and texts* (Tech. Rep. 43). Champaign: University of Illinois, Center for the Study of Reading.

Davis, J. H., Carey, M. H., Foxman, P. N., & Tarr, D. B. (1968). Verbalization in problem solving. *Journal of Personality and Social Psychology, 8,* 299–302.

DeLoache, J. S., Sugarman, S., & Brown, A. L. (1981). Self-correction strategies in early cognitive development. Paper presented at SRCD, Boston.

Dennett, D. C. (1978). *Brainstorms: Philosophical essays on mind and psychology.* Montgomery, VT: Bradford Books.

Dewey, J. (1910). *How we think.* Boston: Heath.

Ericsson, K. A., & Simon, H. A. (1980). Verbal reports as data. *Psychological Review, 87,* 215–251.

Ernst, G. W., & Newell, A. (1969). *GPS: A case study in generality and problem solving.* New York: Academic Press.

Feuerstein, R. (1969). *The instrumental enrichment Method: An outline of theory and technique.* Unpublished paper. Hadassah-Wiza- Canada Research Institute.

Feuerstein, R. (1979). *Instrumental enrichment.* Baltimore, MD: University Park Press.

Flanagan, J. C. (1954). The critical incident technique. *Psychological Bulletin, 51,* 327–358.

Flavell, J. H. (1970). Developmental studies of mediated memory. In H. W. Reese and L. P. Lipstt (Eds.), *Advances in child development and behavior* (Vol. 5). New York: Academic Press.

Flavell, J. H. (1971). First discussant's comments: What is memory development the development of? *Human Development, 14,* 272–278.

Flavell, J. H. (1976). Metacognitive aspects of problem solving. In L. Resnick (Ed.), *The nature of intelligence.* Hillsdale, NJ: Lawrence Erlbaum Associates.

Flavell, J. H. (1980). *Structures, stages, and sequences in cognitive development.* Paper presented at the Minnesota Symposium on Child Psychology, Minneapolis.

Flavell, J. H. (1981). Cognitive monitoring. In W. P. Dickson (Ed.), *Children's oral communication skills.* New York: Academic Press.

Flavell, J. H., Friedrichs, A. G. & Hoyt, J. D. (1970). Developmental changes in memorization processes. *Cognitive Psychology, 1,* 324–340.

Flavell, J. H., Speer, J. R., Green, F. L., & August, D. L. (1981). The development of comprehension monitoring and knowledge about communication. *Monographs of the Society for Research in Child Development,* (46, Whole No. 192).

Flavell, J. H., & Wellman, H. M. (1977). In R. V. Kail, Jr., & W. Hagen (Eds.), *Perspectives on the development of memory and cognition.* Hillsdale, NJ: Lawrence Erlbaum Associates.

Flores, C. F., & Winograd, T. (1978). *Understanding cognition as understanding.* Unpublished manuscript, Stanford University.

Fromkin, V. A. (Ed.). (1973). *Speech errors as linguistic evidence.* The Hague: Mouton.

Gagné, R. H., & Smith, E. C. (1962). A study of the effects of verbalization and problem solving. *Journal of Experimental Psychology, 63,* 12–18.

Gardner, H. (1978). Commentary on animal awareness papers. *Behavioral and Brain Sciences, 4,* 572.

Gelman, R., & Baillargeon, R. (1983). A review of some Piagetian concepts. In J. H. Flavell & E. M. Markman (Eds.), *Handbook of Child Development:* Vol. 1. *Cognitive Development.* New York: John Wiley.

Gleitman, H. (in press). Some trends in the study of cognition. In S. Koch & D. E. Leary (Eds.), *A century of psychology as science: Retrospectives and assessments.* New York: McGraw-Hill.

Gleitman, L. R., Gleitman, H., & Shipley, E. F. (1972). The emergence of the child as grammarian. *Cognition, 1,* 137–164.

Goldin, S. E., & Hayes-Roth, B. (1980). *Individual differences in planning processes* (Tech. Rep. N-1488-ONR). Santa Monica, CA: The Rand Corporation.

Greene, P. H. (1971). Introduction in I. M. Gelford, U. S. Garjinkel, S. V. Fourer & M. L. Tsetlin (Eds.), *Model of the structural functional organization of certain biological systems* (pp. xi–xxv). Cambridge, MA: M.I.T. Press.

Greeno, J. G., & Bjork, R. A. (1973). Mathematical learning theory and the new "mental forestry." In P. H. Mussen & M. R. Rozenzweig (Eds.), *Annual review of psychology, 24.*

Hasher, L., & Zacks, R. T. (1979). Automatic and effortful processes in memory. *Journal of Experimental Psychology, 108,* 356–388.

Hayes-Roth, B. (1977). Evolution of cognitive structure and process. *Psychological Review, 84,* 260–278.

Hayes-Roth, B., & Thorndyke, P. W. (1980). *Decision making during the planning process* (Tech. Rep. N-1213-ONR). Santa Monica, CA: The Rand Corporation.

Hayes-Roth, B., & Hayes-Roth, F. (1979). A cognitive model of planning. *Cognitive Science, 3,* 275–310.

Hayes-Roth, B. (1980). *Flexibility in executive strategies.* (Tech. Rep. N-1170-ONR). Santa Monica, CA: The Rand Corporation.

Huey, E. B. (1968). *The psychology and pedagogy of reading.* Cambridge, MA: M.I.T. Press. (Originally published, 1908).

Humphrey, G. (1963). *Thinking: An introduction to its experimental psychology.* New York: John Wiley.

Inhelder, B., Sinclair, H., & Bovet, M. (1974). *Learning and the development of cognition.* Cambridge, MA: Harvard University Press.

James, W. (1890). *Principle of psychology* (Vol. 1). New York: Holt.

Johnson-Laird, P. N. (1980). Mental models in cognitive science. *Cognitive Science, 4,* 71–115.

Justice, E. M., & Bray, N. W. (1979). *The effects of context and feedback on metamemory in young children.* Paper presented at the meeting of the society for Research in Child Development, San Francisco.

Karmiloff-Smith, A. (1979a). Micro- and macro- developmental changes in language acquisition and other representational systems. *Cognitive Science, 3,* 91–118.

Karmiloff-Smith, A. (1979b). Problem solving construction and representations of closed railway circuits. *Archives of Psychology, 47,* 37–59.

Karmiloff-Smith, A., & Inhelder, B. (1974–75). If you want to get ahead, get a theory. *Cognition, 3,* 195–212.

Karph, D. A. (1973). *Thinking aloud in human discrimination learning.* Doctoral dissertation, State University of New York at Stony Brook.

Kendall, C. R., Borkowski, J. G., & Cavanaugh, J. C. (1980). Maintenance and generalization of an interrogative strategy by EMR children. *Intelligence, 4,* 255–270.

Klinger, E. (1974). Utterances to evaluate steps and control attention distinguish operant from respondent thought while thinking out loud. *Bulletin of the Psychonomic Society, 4,* 44–45.

Koestler, A. (1979). *Janis: A summing up.* New York: Random House.

Koslowski, B., & Bruner, J. S. (1972). Learning to use a lever. *Child Development, 43,* 790–799.

Kreutzer, M. A., Leonard, S. C., & Flavell, J. H. (1975). An interview study: Children's knowledge about memory. *Monographs of the Society for Research in Child Development, 40* (1, Serial No. 159).

LaBerge, D. (1975). Acquisition of automatic processing in perceptual and associative learning. In P. M. A. Rabbitt & S. Dornic (Eds.), *Attention and performance.* New York: Academic Press.

Laboratory of Comparative Human Cognition. (in press). The zone of proximal development: Where culture and cognitive create one author. In J. Wertsch (Ed.), *Culture, Communication and Cognition: Vygotskian Perspectives.* New York: Cambridge University Press.

Lindsay, P. H., & Norman, D. A. (1977). *Human information processing* (2nd ed.). New York: Academic Press.

Locke, J. (1924). *An essay concerning human understanding.* A. L. Pringle-Pattison (Ed.). Oxford: Clarendon Press.

Logan, G. D. (1978). Attention in character classification tasks: Evidence for automaticity of component stages. *Journal of Experimental Psychology: General, 107,* 32–63.

Logan, G. D. (1979). On the use of a concurrent memory load of measure attention and automaticity. *Journal of Experimental Psychology: Human Perception and Performance, 5,* 189–207.

Luria, A. R. (1966). *Higher certical function in man.* London: Tavistock Press.

Mandler, J. M., & Mandler, G. (1964). *Thinking: From association to Gestalt.* New York: John Wiley.

Markman, E. M. (1977). Realizing that you don't understand: A preliminary investigation. *Child Development, 46,* 986–992.

Markman, E. M. (1979). Realizing that you don't understand: Elementary school children's awareness of inconsistencies. *Child Development, 50,* 643–655.

Marshall, J. C., & Morton, J. (1978). On the mechanics of EMMA. In A. Sinclair, R. J. Jarvella, & W. J. M. Levelt (Eds.), *The child's conception of language.* Berlin: Springer.

Masur, E. F., McIntyre, C. W., & Flavell, J. H. (1973). Developmental changes in apportionment of study time among items in a multitrial free recall task. *Journal of Experimental Child Psychology, 15,* 237–246.

McDermott, J., & Forgy, C. (1978). Production system conflict resolution strategies. In D. A. Waterman & F. Hayes-Roth (Eds.), *Pattern-directed influence systems.* New York: Academic Press.

McDermott, R. D. (1978). Some reasons for focusing on classrooms in reading research. In P. D. Pearson & J. Hansen (Eds.), *Reading: Disciplined inquiry in process and practice* (27th Yearbook of the National Reading Conference). Clemson, SC: National Reading Conference.

Milner, B. (1964). Some effects of frontal lobectomy in man. In J. M. Warren & K. Avert (Eds.), *The frontal granular certex and behavior.* New York: McGraw-Hill.

Myers, M., & Paris, S. (1978). Children's metacognitive knowledge about reading. *Journal of Educational Psychology, 70,* 680–690.

Naus, M. J. & Halasz, F. G. (1978). Developmental perspectives on cognitive processing. In L. S. Cermak & F. I. Craik (Eds.), *Levels of processing in human memory.* Hillsdale, NJ: Lawrence Erlbaum Associates.

Nelson, K. E. & Nelson, K. (1979). Cognitive pendulums and their linguistic realization. In K. Nelson (Ed.), *Children's Language,* New York: Gardner.

Newell, A. (1980). Production systems and human cognition. In R. A. Cole (Ed.), *Perceptive and production of fluent speech*. Hillsdale, NJ: Lawrence Erlbaum Associates.

Newell, A., & Simon, H. A. (1972). *Human problem solving*. Englewood Cliffs, NJ: Prentice-Hall.

Nisbett, R. E., & Wilson, D. (1977). Telling more than we know: Verbal reports on mental processes. *Psychological Review, 84*, 231–279.

Nooteboom, S. C. (1969). The tongue slips into patterns. In A. G. Sciarone, A. J. Van Essen & A. A. Van Raad (Eds.), *Nomen: Leyden studies in linguistics and pragmatics*. The Hague: Mouton.

Norman, D. A. (1973). Memory, knowledge, and the answering of questions. In R. L. Solso (Ed.), *Contemporary issues in cognitive psychology: The Loyola Symposium*. Washington, DC: V. H. Winston.

Norman, D. A. (1980). Twelve issues for cognitive science. *Cognitive Science, 4*, 1–32.

Norman, D. A. (1981). Categorization of action slips. *Psychological Review, 88*, 1–15.

Norman, D. A., & Bobrow, G. A. (1975). On data-limited and resource-limited processes. *Cognitive Psychology, 7*, 44–64.

Norman, D. A., & Shallice, T. (December, 1980). *Attention to action: Willed and automatic control of behavior* (CHIP Technical Report 99). LaJolla, CA: University of California.

Palinscar, A. S., & Brown, A. L. (1981). *Training comprehension-monitoring skills in an interactive learning game*. Unpublished manuscript, University of Illinois.

Pellegrino, J. W., & Schadler, M. (1974). *Maximizing performance in a problem-solving task*. Unpublished manuscript, University of Pittsburgh.

Perlmutter, M. (1978). What is memory aging the aging of? *Developmental Psychology, 14*, 330–345.

Piaget, J. (1976). *The grasp of consciousness: Action and concept in the young child*. Cambridge, MA: Harvard University Press.

Piaget, J. (1978). *Success and understanding*. Cambridge, MA: Harvard University Press.

Posner, M. I., & Snyder, C. R. R. (1974). Attention and cognitive control. In R. L. Solso (Ed.), *Information processing and cognition: The Loyola Symposium*. Potomac, MD; Hillsdale, NJ: Lawrence Erlbaum Associates.

Pylyshyn, Z. (1978). Computational models and empirical constraints. *The Behavioral and Brain Sciences, 1*, 93–99.

Reason, J. T. (1979). Actions not as planned. In G. Underwood and R. Stevens (Eds.), *Aspects of consciousness*. London: Academic Press.

Reed, S. K., & Johnson, J. A. (1977). Memory for problem solutions. In G. Bower (Ed.), *The psychology of learning and motivation* (Vol. 11). New York: Academic Press.

Reese, W. (1962). Verbal mediation as a function of age level. *Psychological Bulletin, 59*, 502–509.

Resnick, L. B. & Glaser, R. (1976). Problem solving and intelligence. In L. B. Resnick (Ed.), *The Nature of Intelligence*. Hillsdale, NJ: Lawrence Erlbaum Associates.

Riegel, K. F. (1975). Structure and transformation in modern intellectual history. In K. F. Riegel & G. C. Rosenwald (Eds.), *Structure and transformation: Developmental and historical aspects*. New York: Wiley.

Rogoff, B., & Gardner, W. P. (in press). Developing cognitive skills in social interaction. In B. Rogoff & J. Lave (Eds.), *Everyday cognition: Its development in social context*. Hillsdale, NJ: Lawrence Erlbaum Associates.

Rozin, P. (1976). The evolution of intelligence and access to the cognitive unconscious. *Progression in Psychobiology and Physiological Psychology, 6*, 245–280.

Ruger, H. A. (1910). The psychology of efficiency. *Archive of Psychology, 15*.

Rumelhart, D. E. (1980). Schemata: The building blocks of cognition. In R. J. Spiro, B. C. Bruce & W. F. Brewer (Eds.), *Theoretical issues in reading comprehension*. Hillsdale, NJ: Lawrence Erlbaum Associates.

Sacerdoti, E. D. (1974). Planning in a hierarchy of abstraction spaces. *Artificial Intelligence, 5,* 115–136.

Schallert, D. L., & Kleiman, G. M. (June, 1979). *Some reasons why the teacher is easier to understand than the text book* (Reading Education Report No. 9). Urbana: University of Illinois, Center for the Study of Reading (ERIC Document Reproduction Service No. ED 172 189)

Schallice, T. (1978). The dominant action system: An information-processing approach to consciousness. In K. Pope & J. E. Springer (Eds.), *The flow of conscious experience.* New York: Plenum Press.

Schneider, W., & Shiffrin, R. M. (1977). Controlled and automatic human information processing: 1. Direction, search, and attention. *Psychological Review, 84,* 1–66.

Selfridge, O. (1959). *Pandemonium: A paradigm for learning. Symposium on the mechanization of thought.* London: H. M. Stationery Office.

Shatz, M. (1978). On the development of communication understandings: An early strategy for interpreting and responding to messages. *Cognitive Psychology, 10,* 271–301.

Shaw, R., & Bransford, J. (1977). Approaches to the problem of knowledge. In R. Shaw & J. Bransford (Eds.), *Perceiving, acting, and knowing: Toward an ecological psychology.* Hillsdale, NJ: Lawrence Erlbaum Associates.

Shif, Z. I. (1969). Development of children in schools for mentally retarded. In M. Cole & I. Maltzman (Eds.), *A handbook of contemporary Soviet psychology.* New York: Basic Books.

Shiffrin, R. M. (1975). The locus and role of attention in memory systems. In P. M. A. Rabbitt, & S. Dornic (Eds.), *Attention and performance V.* NY: Academic Press.

Shiffrin, R. M., & Schneider, W. (1977). Controlled and automatic human information processing: 2. Perceptual learning, automatic attending, and a general theory. *Psychological Review, 84,* 127–190.

Simon, D. P., & Simon, H. A. (1978). Individual differences in solving physics problems. In R. S. Siegler (Ed.), *Children's thinking: What develops?* Hillsdale, NJ: Lawrence Erlbaum Associates.

Skinner, B. F. (1964). Behaviorism at fifty. In T. W. Wann (Ed.), *Behaviorism and phenomenology.* Chicago: University of Chicago Press.

Skinner, B. F. (1971). *Beyond freedom and dignity.* New York: Knopf.

Smith, E. R., & Miller, F. S. (1978). Limits on perception of cognitive processes. A reply to Nisbett and Wilson. *Psychological Review, 85,* 355–362.

Spearman, C. (1923). *The nature of intelligence and principle of cognition.* London: MacMillan.

Stein, N. L. & Trabasso, T. (1982). What's in a story: An approach to comprehension and instruction. In R. Glaser (Ed.), *Advances in the psychology of instruction* (Vol. 2). Hillsdale, NJ: Lawrence Erlbaum Associates.

Sternberg, R. J., Ketron, J. L., & Powell, J. S. (1982). Confidential approaches to the training of intelligence performance. In D. K. Detterman & R. J. Sternberg (Eds.), *How and how much can Intelligence be Increased.* Norwood, NJ: Ablex, (155–172).

Strauss, S., & Stavey, R. (1982). U-shaped behavioral growth: Implications for theories of development. In W. W. Hartup (Ed.), *Review of child development research* (Vol. 6). Chicago: University of Chicago Press.

Thorndike, E. L. (1917). Reading as reasoning: A study of mistakes in paragraph reading. *Journal of Educational Psychology, 8,* 323–332.

Turvey, M. T. (1977). Preliminaries to a theory of action with reference to vision. In R. Shaw & J. Bransford (Eds.), *Perceiving, acting, and knowing: Toward an ecological psychology.* Hillsdale, NJ: Lawrence Erlbaum Associates.

Turvey, M. T., & Shaw, R. (1979). The primacy of perceiving: An ecological reformulation of perception for understanding memory. In L. G. Nillson (Ed.), *Perspective of Uppsola University's 500 Anniversary.* Hillsdale, NJ: Lawrence Erlbaum Associates.

Turvey, M. T., Shaw, R. E., & Mace, W. (1978). Issues in the theory of action: Degrees of freedom, coordinative structures and coalitions. In J. Requin (Ed.), *Attention and performance VII*. Hillside, NJ: Lawrence Erlbaum Associates.

Vygotsky, L. S. (1978). *Mind in Society: The Development of Higher Psychological Processes* (M. Cole, V. John-Steiner, S. Scribner, & E. Souberman, Eds. and Trans.). Cambridge, MA: Harvard University Press.

Wellman, H. M. (1983). Metamemory revisited. In M. Chi (Ed.), *What is memory development the development of? A look after a decade* (pp. 31–51). Basel: Karger.

Werner, H. (1961). *Comparative psychology of mental development*. New York: Science Editions.

Wertsch, J. V. (1978). Adult-child interaction and the roots of metacognition. *Quarterly Newsletter of the Institute for Comparative Human Development, 1*, 15–18.

White, P. (1980). Limitations on verbal reports of internal events. A refutation of Nisbett and Wilson, and Bem. *Psychological Review, 87*, 105–112.

Wilder, L., & Harvey, D. J. (1971). Overt and covert verbalization in problem solving. *Speech Monographs, 38*, 171–176.

Wimmer, H., & Thornquist, K. (1978). *The relation of metamemory to mnemonic performance in memory development: Metamemory is always necessary but never sufficient*. Unpublished manuscript University of Salzburg, Austria.

4 Metacognitive Components of Instructional Research with Problem Learners

Joseph C. Campione
University of Illinois at Urbana-Champaign

The aim of this paper is to describe the influence that theory and research in the broad area of metacognition have had on psychoeducational research; particularly on work with slow-learning children. Any comparison of the literature 10 years ago, with the literature emerging today, makes it clear that metacognition has had a pronounced impact. It can be seen directly in a number of research efforts, and more broadly in the recent overall orientation guiding this research. On one level, specific findings, concerning the nature of individual and comparative differences in metacognitive functioning, have been borrowed directly and incorporated into instructional research; the *content* of the research changed. A related, but more general, effect can also be seen: Metacognitive work has reawakened an interest in the role of consciousness, or awareness, or understanding, in thinking and problem-solving. These topics bring with them considerable problems, nevertheless, they are intimately involved in important aspects of thinking. At first, it was difficult to see how complex forms of thinking could be inculcated without making learners aware of the operations, facts, and procedures that are the goals of instruction. However, as this fact became more apparent, the *form* of training studies changed.

In order to trace the changes in training studies, this paper is divided into three main sections: the first section deals with a description of training studies, prior to the interest in metacognition; the second section involves a brief discussion of the types of metacognitive research that emerged in the early 1970s, and influenced the instructional work; and the third section attempts a classification of a number of different types of metacognitive-instructional experiments that have been conducted, and an analysis of their effectiveness.

During the past decade, there has been an explosion of interest in ''metacognitive'' aspects of academic and social performance. Viewed in one perspective, this interest has stemmed from a concentration on the memory development research pioneered by Flavell and his colleagues (e.g., Flavell, 1971; Flavell, Friedrichs, & Hoyt, 1970; Masur, McIntyre, & Flavell, 1973). As a result, terms that sound suspiciously like metacognition and its various referents have become prominent in such diverse areas as reading and comprehension (Baker & Brown, 1981; Brown, 1980; Markman, 1981); cognitive ethology (Rozin, 1976); general cognitive development (Brown, 1982; Flavell, 1979); and intelligence, machine intelligence (e.g., Bobrow & Norman, 1975; Pylyshyn, 1978) and human intelligence (Brown, 1978; Campione & Brown, 1978; Campione, Brown, & Ferrara, 1982; Sternberg, 1980). In each case, the more advanced or successful performers are characterized as possessing more fully developed metacognitive skills than the less successful performers. Metacognitive skills are not merely factors underlying performance; frequently, they have been regarded as being of particular importance, by a number of theorists (cf. Campione, Brown & Ferrara, 1982, for a discussion of the role of metacognitive factors in theories of intelligence). Thus, despite pronounced variations in the subject populations investigated, the specific topics being addressed, and the general theoretical orientations guiding the different investigators, some agreement on the importance and centrality of metacognitive factors seems to have been reached.

The frequency with which metacognitive deficiencies have been cited as a factor in poor academic performance has led, not surprisingly many psychologists engaged in instructional research, to include metacognitive skills as part of their overall training packages. Similar instructional routines resulted from more clinical approaches to the design of curricula developed for use with slow-learning children; both at the turn of the century (Binet, 1909) and more currently (e.g., Feuerstein, 1980). The aim of this chapter is to review some of the relevant theories and resultant instructional research, summarizing the current status of these approaches. The more specific aim is to classify and illustrate some of the different types of experiments that have been done and to use the review as a means of describing the various aspects of metacognition that seem to be of particular relevance to the topic of instructional practice.

In order to do this, it is necessary to briefly review a set of experiments primarily, though not exclusively, from our laboratory. The studies reviewed typically involve students with learning problems, most frequently mildly retarded (IQ around 70) adolescents. This is the area in which the author has worked most closely, and one in which much of the metacognitively-oriented instructional work has been conducted. Some of the specific topics covered are, no doubt, a reflection of the emphasis placed on problem learners. The conclusions reached might be different if more capable students were the objects of instruction; however, in the limited space available, such a concentration seems justified.

To motivate the discussion, before proceeding to the actual research, it is necessary to address two preliminary topics. The first topic deals with the various referents of the term "metacognition"; the second deals with the status of instructional work with slow-learning children, prior to the advent of the recent interest in metacognition.

METACOGNITION AND ITS VARIOUS GUISES

The emphasis on metacognitive-like processes in recent theories is ubiquitous; however, this "agreement" should not be interpreted too strongly. Although, on a general level, there is agreement that metacognition is an important component of successful performance, there are many different kinds of knowledge and processes subsumed under that term; metacognition has been used by different authors to mean quite different things. Brown (Chapter 3, this volume) provided a detailed analysis of these variations; in this discussion, the author is much less thorough. On the most general level, the topic of metacognition includes knowledge concerning, understanding of, and access to cognition and cognitive resources. For example, Flavell (1979) has defined metacognition as "knowledge that takes as its object or regulates any aspect of any cognitive endeavor." There are two distinct referents involved in this definition: statable knowledge about the cognitive system and its contents; and the effective regulation and control of that system.

The first topic is concerned with knowledge about one's own cognitive resources. For example, mature thinkers know: that their immediate memory span is limited, that some kinds of information (e.g., organized lists of items) are easier to remember than others (disorganized lists); that some memory tasks (e.g., recognition) are easier than others (recall); and what they might do to remember a telephone number. That is, they have knowledge about "person, task, and strategy variables" (Flavell & Wellman, 1977). Some features of this knowledge, as reflected in the developmental literature, are that it is *stable* and *statable*. It is stable in that once an individual acquires some pertinent fact about cognition, he or she should continue to have that fact available; it is statable, by definition, in that the knowledge is assessed through verbal reports.

The second set of activities includes those concerned with the self-regulatory mechanisms, engaged during an ongoing attempt to learn or solve a problem. These include checking, planning, monitoring, selecting, revising, etc. (Brown, 1978, Chapter 3, this volume). These are not stable, but depend on the subject's familiarity with the task, motivation, and the like. Individuals may be capable of regulating their thought processes in one area, but not in another area. Also, these activities are not necessarily statable, because much of self-regulation must go on at a level below conscious awareness.

The distinction between the awareness of resources and the operations applied to those resources appears in various forms elsewhere in the literature (cf. Brown & Campione, 1981). For example, it is essentially the same as one embodied in Pylyshyn's (1978) discussion of reflective and multiple access. Reflective access refers to the ability to "mention as well as use" the components of the cognitive system. It implies that the organism not only has the relevant information represented in memory, but also the ability to "represent the representing relation itself"; that is, the individual possesses not only fact X but also the notion of fact X. Multiple access refers to the ability to use information flexibly. It implies that information is not delimited to a constrained set of circumstances, but rather is informationally plastic and can be "systematically varied to fit a wide range of conditions which have nothing in common other than that they allow the valid inference that, say, a certain state of affairs holds" (Pylyshyn, 1978, p. 593).

A number of writers have proposed awareness of and control of specific resources as criteria for the understanding of those resources. For example, Moore and Newell (1974) argue that learners understand some routine when they use it appropriately. Although not denying this component, Gardner (1978) and Rozin (1976) suggest that a criterion of understanding is that knowledge be available to consciousness and, perhaps, be statable. Similarly, Piaget (1978) discussed the importance to human intelligence of the concept of reflected abstraction, with the result that cognitions be made statable and available to consciousness, at which point they can be worked on and extended.

In the instructional work conducted, both types of metacognition have been incorporated. Interventions have taken the form of either providing information (statable knowledge) about, for example, the memory system or teaching the use of a number of executive functions, such as planning, overseeing, and monitoring. We are interested in, among other things, questions about the possible differential effects of the two emphases. To provide some additional background, it is worthwhile to illustrate the way in which the distinction manifested itself in the early memory development literature; work that served as the impetus for the instructional research. In fact, this can be done quite well by reference to one of the earliest papers in the area.

In a two-part experiment, Flavell et al. (1970) investigated the development of preschool through fourth grade children's ability to predict their own immediate memory span and to monitor the current state of their learning during an on going study attempt. In the span estimation procedure, subjects were given a series of trials on which they were shown a number of pictures—one on Trial 1, two on Trial 2, three on Trial 3, etc., to a maximum of 10 trials. On each trial, the experimenter showed subjects the pictures, labeled them, and then covered the pictures up. Then the subjects were asked to predict whether or not they would be able to repeat the names (n); no recall was attempted. The procedure continued until the subjects reported an inability to repeat the set, or to 10 items, the maximum tested. Each subject's span was set at the longest series of names that could be recalled. After this process was terminated, each subject's actual span for those materials was assessed.

In the second part of the experiment, subjects were given a series of three trials. On each trial they were to study a set of pictures (the number of pictures for each subject was set equal to the actual span as determined in the first phase of the experiment) for as long as they liked, until they were sure they could recall all of the pictures in order. They were told to study the items for as long as they wanted, and to ring a bell when they were sure they could repeat all the names in the correct order. At this point, recall was attempted.

The data from each phase indicated clear developmental differences. In the span estimation experiment, accuracy increased dramatically, with the mean predicted; actual span differences were 3.7, 4.4, 1.6, and .6 items for nursery school, kindergarten, second, and fourth graders, respectively. The consistent tendency was for subjects who made errors to overestimate how much they would be able to recall. For example, 60% of the nursery school and kindergarten children and 24% of the older children predicted that they would be able to recall all 10 items, the maximum tested. Turning to the recall readiness data, a clear developmental trend again emerged. Even though the task was not an exceedingly demanding one (the number of items each subject had to study and recall was equal to his or her span on this task and thus, demonstrably within the subject's capabilities), only 40% of the nursery school and kindergarten children were able to recall without error on more than one of the three trials, whereas, 95% of the older subjects were able to do so. On the other hand, 12% of the younger and 83% of the older children were consistently correct (no errors on any of the three trials). Thus, although all subjects are able to recall the total set, the younger children have a strong tendency to terminate study before they are ready to recall, that is, they do not appear adept at monitoring their current state of learning. This failure is also reflected in the study times for the various groups; older subjects spent significantly more time studying the sets than did the younger subjects.

Although there are currently many more examples in each category, the data from the initial study are sufficient to indicate that with development, children come to know more about their memory system and show an increasing tendency to oversee their cognitive activities. In addition to these developmental differences, there are strong comparative differences; children with learning problems seem to perform poorly on assessments of cognitive abilities (see Brown, 1978, for some relevant data and a review).

THE STATUS OF INSTRUCTIONAL RESEARCH

Around 1970, when metacognition work was beginning to appear, there was an increase in the amount of instructional research being conducted. In fact, the training study was beginning to emerge as one of the favorite vehicles for conducting basic research in the area of mental retardation. Why this occurred has been spelled out in considerable detail elsewhere (Belmont & Butterfield, 1977; Brown & Campione, 1978; Butterfield, 1979) and is not of concern to this discussion. Of relevance, is that it became clear that retarded children did poorly on a variety of memory and problem-solving tasks, in part because they consistently failed to produce the appropriate and necessary strategies (Brown, 1974).

In a host of studies, it was also shown that retarded children could readily be taught to employ task-specific strategies, such as rehearsal and elaboration, with the result that their performance would improve, often quite dramatically. It is also fair to say that the results tended to be of limited practical significance. This is not surprising inasmuch as the studies were done for purely theoretical reasons; they were designed to answer basic questions about the nature of intelligence-related sources of individual differences in memory performance. A prototypical situation in which a training study would be conducted is as follows: There is a specific task. Indications are that different groups of subjects perform differently on that task, and experimenters would like to know why. To deal with this question, one needs an analysis of what individuals must do to perform well on that task and some hypothesis about the specific source(s) of individual differences. As an example, consider a memory task where it is assumed that effective performance requires, among other things, the use of a rehearsal strategy. It is assumed also that retarded children, because of a failure on their part to rehearse, perform more poorly than nonretarded children. By training the retarded children to rehearse, both assumptions can be tested simultaneously. If their performance does improve significantly, it can be concluded that the original analysis of the task was correct (if rehearsal were not an important component of performance on that task, instructing individuals in its use would not lead to improved performance), and that retarded children perform poorly, at least in part, because they fail to rehearse without prompting (if they did rehearse spontaneously, training would not have been necessary). Note also that all that is required to evaluate the theoretical question is that the subjects execute the target activity. To "teach" rehearsal, the experimenter may simply model the strategy, tell the subject exactly what to do, and then continue instructing and prompting for the duration of the study (e.g., Brown, Campione, Bray, & Wilcox, 1973).

These theoretical questions can be evaluated on the basis of the subjects' immediate response to training; in the early 1970's it was typical for the research to stop at that point. The contribution of this work is obvious: it demonstrated the potential for instruction-based improvement in performance; the improvements were not trivial. In fact, given extant theories, their magnitude was frequently surprisingly large; it was this feature of the research that encouraged those interested in remediation. However, to stop the research at that point requires additional theoretical and practical questions. Strategy training, even on the training task, did not eliminate differences between retarded and nonretarded children; the implication is that there are other sources of comparative differences that remain "untreated." To advance any theory of individual differences in this domain, it is necessary to specify what those sources are; similarly, the sources must be known in order to improve on instruction. Therefore, one line of research, can address more detailed within-task analyses.

Considering the problem from a practical standpoint, demonstrations that performance on a specific task can be improved when an instructor leads a subject through a learning activity is not particularly overwhelming. Therefore, the immediate and standard questions concern the maintenance of and generalizability (Campione & Brown, 1977) of the instructed routines. Will the subject continue to execute the activity when the experimenter/instructor is absent or ceases prompting; that is, will the activity be maintained? Will the subject apply what he or she has learned to novel but related problems; that is, will the effects of training be generalized effectively? If the answers to these questions are negative, the instructional effects, although theoretically interesting, remain of dubious practical significance. A second line of inquiry would then concern between-tasks effects of training. (It may come as no surprise that both within- and between-tasks analyses led to an emphasis on metacognitive factors.)

Reports of relevant research began to appear in the mid 1970s; Campione and Brown (1977) provided an early review. At that time a brief summary of the existing situation was that retarded children: (a) did not produce the kinds of strategies necessary for efficient performance on a variety of tasks; (b) could be taught to carry out strategies, which resulted in improvements in performance, but not to the level of nonretarded comparison groups; (c) frequently abandoned the strategy when the experimenter ceased prompting its use, however, extensive training might overcome that problem; and (d) failed to apply the strategies to new problems where they would be appropriate (i.e., failed to recognize an array of problem isomorphs). In some sense, points (a) and (d) can be regarded as similar; a novel problem is presented, and the subject does not bring to bear the resources he or she has available to deal with the problem. The question, of both theoretical and practical significance, then became, Why do failures in application arise?

It was at this point that people involved in mental retardation training work became attracted to the work on metamemory. Failures to produce strategies, to carry them out most efficiently, or to transfer them widely might be due to a failure on the part of the learner to understand the significance of the instructed activities and procedures. Retarded children might not know enough about the memory system to appreciate why the strategies were necessary. Also, they might fail to monitor the effects of instructed strategy use and thus, fail to carry it out as well as might be expected. Therefore, they would derive less than the maximum benefit and/or not realize that the strategy was helpful. As a specific example, consider a child faced with the task of remembering 10 items. If he or she believes that the items can be readily remembered (overestimates his or her span), there is no reason for engaging any specific learning activity, even if one were available. Further, if the learner did not monitor performance on recall trials, he or she would not become disabused of the original notion. In addition, if instruction is provided, and if performance improves, it is reasonable to expect that the learner will continue to employ that strategy only if he or she monitors its use and notes that it has actually helped; if no such monitoring takes place, it is not surprising that transfer is limited.

METACOGNITION AND INSTRUCTIONAL ATTEMPTS

Failure to produce strategies or to transfer them might be seen as reflecting a general metacognitive deficit. The first step in evaluating this possibility was to collect some metacognitive data on retarded children to assess their competence in this domain. In a series of laboratory studies (Brown, 1978; Campione & Brown, 1977), it became clear that retarded children did experience particular problems in this area. They are not as insightful about their memories as non-retarded children of comparable age. For example, they do not appear to be aware of the severity of working memory limitations, and drastically overesti-mate their memory span (Brown, Campione, & Murphy, 1977). Also they are not as cognizant of the contents of their memory. In a study on the feeling of knowing phenomenon, Brown and Lawton (1977) found mildly retarded subjects less able to predict their ability to recognize a name they had previously been unable to recall, than nonretarded children. As a final example, retarded children do not appear to know as much as nonretarded children, about the kinds of material that are easy or hard to remember. Retarded children were asked to generate lists of items that would be easy to remember. They were given a series of key words and asked to generate items which would be easy to remember in a list, including the key items and additional items. In response to this request, the retarded children were less likely than nonretarded children (Tenney, 1975) to construct organized lists; and when they did include items from which a (tax-onomic or thematic) category, their choices were more likely to be "broad" (1 4 2 7) than "narrow" (1 2 3 4) (Brown, 1978).

Executive decision making also presented difficulty. One early demonstration of the severity of the problem for retarded children was made in the context of an attempt to teach retarded adolescents a rehearsal strategy (Butterfield, Wambold, and Belmont, 1973). In addition to providing all of the components of the strategy, the subjects were forced to provide detailed instruction in the coordina-tion and sequencing of those components. Even when each component was taught in excruciating detail, direct instruction in their management was also required. In our own work, it was found that retarded children do not tend to monitor their state of learning accurately (Brown & Barclay, 1976; Brown,

Campione & Barclay, 1979), nor do they seem to allocate study time differentially to items that have been hard or easy for them to remember (Brown & Campione, 1977).

Given the fairly impressive evidence that retarded children do experience a variety of metacognitive problems and the hypothesized relation between metacognition and transfer, it seemed obvious that training attempts should include a metacognitive component. It was also easy to rationalize the transfer failures existing in the literature; they could be regarded as attacking the symptom, but not the cause, of the problem. The typical training study, termed blind training by Brown, Campione, and Day (1981), did not in any way involve the students as active conspirators in the training process. They were induced to use a strategy, or even tricked into carrying out the desired activities; no attempt was made to impart to them any reason why those activities might be helpful. For example, the child is taught to use a cumulative rehearsal strategy by initially copying an adult but is not *explicitly* told why acting that way helps performance or that it is an activity appropriate to a certain class of memory situations. If the original problem was, due in part, to metacognitive limitations, there is nothing in the instructional interaction that would alter that state of affairs; hence the need for modified training approaches.

There was one additional reason for believing that training attempts involving general metacognitive skills would have widespread effects. One problem with the skills that were the object of training originally, was that they were specific to a very small class of situations. For learners to generalize the effects of instruction in the use of specific routines, they would have to be able to discriminate the situations in which the routine would be appropriate from those in which it would not. Adequate generalization requires both extended use in novel situations and decisions not to use the trained activity in situations where it would not be beneficial. In the case of truly general skills, this discrimination would not be necessary; the skill or routine could simply be used in a whole battery of problem solving situations, eliminating the need for a detailed analysis of the task being attempted (Brown & Campione, 1978).

This leads to one of the oldest and most discussed topics in the problem-solving area, the question of the generality/specificity of problem-solving skills. Are there truly general skills? No attempt is made to enter into that discussion; later it becomes clear that our preference (see Campione, Brown, & Ferrara, 1982) in this domain is to borrow the expanding cone metaphor proposed by Newell (1980). According to this view, there are general skills; however, their generality comes at the expense of power. General skills cannot solve problems by themselves but may provide access to the more specific and powerful skills that are necessary for problem solution. In this context, the questions are: Are (some of) the self-regulatory mechanisms general ones? If so, can they be taught alone or only in combination with the more specific skills to which they allow access?

Given these considerations, researchers have sought to incorporate theory and data from the metacognitive domain into their instructional packages. The blind training studies have been replaced or supplemented in a number of ways. One method of classifying the different approaches is in two dimensions: the kind of metacognitive supplement involved (knowledge or regulation); and the presence or absence of additional specific skills training. Reviewing some of the instructional work, Brown, Campione and Day (1981) identified a three leveled classification of training studies, the aforementioned blind studies; informed training, where the learner is given some information about him or herself, a task, or a strategy; and self-control training, in which the learner is given explicit instructions about the monitoring, checking, or evaluating of some of his or her cognitive resources. The latter two correspond to the two "types" of metacognition discussed earlier. In either case, the metacognitive component can be taught either independently (as an object in itself) or in conjunction with a specific skill or strategy. Examples of each type of study and a statement of the benefits of each approach, is discussed.

Knowledge Alone.   Retarded children do not know much about their memories. One hypothesis that might be entertained is that teaching them some facts about their memory might have a somewhat general effect on performance. One reason that retarded children might fail to produce strategies spontaneously or maintain them after (blind) training is that they do not know that the strategies are necessary; they overestimate their ability and believe they can remember the information without any undue effort. Brown, Campione, and Murphy (1977) showed retarded children with mental ages (MAs) of 6 and 8 a set of 10 pictures and asked them to predict how many of them they would be able to recall. Only about 25% of the children could be classed as "realistic" (the difference between their actual and predicted spans was no more than two items) in their predictions. The unrealistic estimators always overestimated their ability; most predicted that they could recall all 10 pictures. Given this result, training seemed appropriate.

The training consisted of a series of 10 predict-recall pairs. The subject would be shown an array of ten items and asked how many of them he or she would be able to recall (exactly as on the initial assessment). The items were then hidden and recall assessed. For half the subjects, explicit feedback was given after each pair: "You predicted that you would recall _____, and you actually recalled _____." For the remaining half, no such feedback was provided. After training, the subjects were given a series of maintenance and generalization tests.

The major findings were as follows. These subjects could be induced to become realistic, although it was not easy. For example, none of the younger (MA 6) children became realistic unless provided explicit feedback about their performance. They would predict 10 and recall 4 consistently; the fact that over the 10 trials they could never recall more than half the items did not affect their predictions. With feedback, 62% became realistic, but the effect was not a durable one; two weeks later, they reverted to overestimation. For the older children, 65% became realistic following training; however only those given explicit feedback remained realistic one year later. Thus, explicit feedback was necessary to bring about any change in the younger children and to bring about a durable change for the older ones.

One other aspect of the data from the training phase of the experiment is important to this discussion. A possibility is that the subjects who became realistic after training did not learn anything about their memory, instead, they learned a simple verbal response (e.g., to say "four," whenever they were asked a prediction question); this is very unlikely to be true. The prediction-recall series included two types of sets of items. On half the trials, the sets were categorized, and on the remaining half, they were not. All subjects actually recalled more on the categorized sets. Of the originally realistic subjects, about 75% predicted that they would recall more on the categorized, as opposed to uncategorized, sets; of the subjects who became realistic through training, almost 90% made this accurate prediction; finally, of those who remained unrealistic even following training, only 50% predicted better recall on the categorized sets, that is, their predictions were at the chance level. The result indicates that the subjects who were trained to be realistic were doing more than simply learning a single number; they came to realize that categorized lists would be easier to recall than uncategorized ones, even though that manipulation was never explicitly mentioned.

This was an encouraging beginning. The results of a number of generalization probes were quite dramatic; however, only one of the experiments is discussed here. During the initial phase of the experiment, subjects' predictions and spans were assessed by showing them a 10 item array, asking them how many they would be able to remember, and later having them attempt recall. As a transfer test, we used Flavell, Friedrichs & Hoyt's (1970) method, in which the subject was asked if he or she could remember one item, then two items, and so on. The subjects who were realistic estimators prior to training in the initial phase of the study (25% of the sample) were also realistic on this task; evidence that the same skills are being assessed. However, none of the subjects who became realistic only after training, continued to be realistic on this variant of the training task.

Teaching retarded subjects facts (at least this fact) about their memory is not very profitable. As strategies taught in isolation tend to be welded to the learning context, facts taught in isolation can suffer the same fate, a finding that is not exactly new (see Bereiter & Scardamalia's, 1980, discussion of inert knowledge).

Strategies Plus Knowledge.   In a number of studies, strategy training has been supplemented by information about the effects of that strategy. The argument is that trained subjects may abandon an instructed routine when prompting is withdrawn, because they do not realize that they performed better when using the strategy, or they do not realize that it may be helpful on more than one task. One way to deal with these problems is to simply provide subjects with that additional information; either directly or indirectly. For example, in a study with nonretarded children, Kennedy and Miller (1976) found that an instructed rehearsal strategy was more likely to be maintained in the absence of experimenter prompts if it had been made clear that the use of the strategy did result in improved performance. A similar effect with retarded children has been obtained by Kendall, Borkowski, and Cavanaugh (1980). In a similar vein, Burger, Blackman, Holmes, and Zetlin (1978) taught retarded adolescents to use an organizational strategy to facilitate recall of a list of pictures. Their students were given practice in sorting items into categories and were informed that this would help them remember. Again, the result was improved performance on the training task and increased maintenance of the activities by the students when faced with subsequent similar problems.

In these studies, the subjects were told about the effectiveness of the instructed routines. It is, of course, also possible to use less direct methods of providing information to subjects. For example, if transfer is desired, it is important that subjects be aware that a class of strategies may be applicable in a variety of situations. One approach would be to simply tell them. A more indirect approach was employed by Belmont, Butterfield, and Borkowski (1978); they resorted to training in multiple contexts. Their retarded subjects were trained to rehearse in either one or two situations. This indirect manipulation had the desired effect; the twice-trained group showed more evidence of transfer to a third (similar) rehearsal task.

To summarize, supplementing strategy training by providing additional information about their effectiveness or range of utility does lead to increased maintenance. It does seem to allow the experimenter to withdraw prompting without having the subjects abandon the trained routines, at least over short intervals. At this point, whether it is likely to lead to much generalization is unknown, for a number of reasons, it seems unlikely that it would. Recall the span estimation experiment described in the previous section. In that experiment the provision of explicit feedback was also necessary to effect either learning (for the younger subjects) or maintenance (for the older subjects); even when long-term maintenance (one year) was achieved, there was no evidence for generalization.

Why would generalization not be expected? To answer that question, another question can be asked: Why is it necessary to provide explicit feedback in the first place? A possibility is that the subjects do not monitor their own performance levels spontaneously; thus, they would not know that the strategy resulted in enhanced recall. (It is not that they *cannot* monitor when told to. For example, in the span estimation study, subjects who were not given explicit feedback could, when asked, report how many items they had just recalled.) Provision of feedback would be helpful; however, it would still not address the underlying cause of the problem. Again, the symptom (lack of awareness of performance levels) would be treated, but the underlying cause (failure to monitor performance) would not be. Alternatively stated, the necessary product would be provided, but not the processes leading to that product. As the product is, in fact, task specific and the processes are more general, it must be the latter that is of more importance; this leads to the next group of experiments.

Self-Regulation. The initial failures to obtain transfer of specific skills produced an increased interest in dealing with more general, transitutional skills. In some cases, there appeared to be an either-or approach to the specific-general issue. For example, Butterfield and Belmont (1977) argued that attempts should be made to provide direct training in executive functions rather than in specific strategies. Candidates for general executive routines include the skills discussed throughout this paper: planning, checking, monitoring, etc. In the cognitive domain, this movement received further impetus from the cognitive behavior modification programs stimulated, in part, by Meichenbaum's (1977) research. In that work, teaching general self-regulatory routines, such as continually monitoring progress through some task, questioning whether they were remaining on task has helped a variety of clinical populations. These routines are successful, and some (e.g., Belmont, Butterfield, & Ferretti, 1982) have argued that they also result in generalized effects of training.

Some problems exist with the cognitive behavior modification-cognitive skills training alliance (see Brown & Campione, 1982); the main problem is that the situations being analyzed in the two areas are quite different. From the cognitive behavior modification research, there is often good reason to believe that many of the specific skills required for efficient performance are relatively intact and that for some patients (e.g., some impulsive children), the major problem may be a failure to use those resources effectively. In that case, self-regulation instruction by itself, could be very powerful. In the cognitive domain, slow-learning children are often lacking specific skills as well as regulatory mechanisms. The result is that concentrating exclusively on regulatory mechanisms is unlikely to be of much help; whether or not self-regulation training will help depends on other factors.

As an example, consider an experiment by Brown and Campione (1977); the object was to train retarded children to allocate their study time effectively. The situation, developed by Masur, McIntyre & Flavell (1973), is an analogue of many study situations. A test is upcoming, and the student does not have sufficient time to study all the material. He or she must then decide which portions of the material have been well learned versus those which have not been learned. The strategic decision would be to spend more time studying the less known material. In the experimental situation, subjects are given a multitrial, free recall task involving N items. They study the N items and then attempt recall. Then, they are given time for further study; however, they are allowed to have only half the set available to them during that period. The question of interest concerns the items they choose for study. According to the data from Masur et al., college students and third grade children select previously unrecalled items for study; that is, they allocate more attention to the difficult (for them), unrecalled items. In contrast, first graders seem to choose randomly.

The study by Brown and Campione (1977) included two groups of retarded children, who were tested in the same situation. They saw and studied a set of 12 pictures, and then attempted recall. They were then allowed to select six pictures for further study; were told that they would have to recall all 12 pictures. During this test phase, their selections were essentially random; they showed no preferences for selecting study items they had missed earlier (subsequent tests demonstrated that they were very accurate in indicating the items they had recalled on the previous trial). During the intervention phase, the "correct executive decisions" were made for some of the subjects. The experimenter selected the six items the students would have available for further study. In one condition, she gave the students items they had missed previously; in another, she gave them a random set of six items. Thus, in one condition, the mature selection was simulated; in the other, the more primitive one.

The effect of this manipulation was different for the two groups. For the older, more academically advanced group, the subjects given previously missed items performed significantly better on the recall task than those given a random set. However, for the younger group, the treatments did not differ. Simulating the "correct" executive decision making was effective for one group, but not for the other. The proposed explanation for the difference was that selecting missed items for study was only one part of an overall plan for dealing with the task. It was presumed that subjects would have to identify missed items, select those items for study, and maintain in memory, possibly by means of rehearsal, the previously recalled items. For the older subjects, this latter step was apparently within their capabilities, and the intervention was successful; for the younger subjects, it was not, and the intervention failed. This experiment demonstrates some of the risks associated with training general skills in isolation. If some of the more specific routines are not available (or inferrable) to the learner, the training is bound to be ineffective.

Strategies Plus Regulation.   In a number of earlier studies, it became clear that even when strategies and/or their various components were taught directly to retarded or young children, they did not regulate them effectively. The Butterfield et al. (1973) experiment, cited earlier, provides one type of example. They taught their subjects a rehearsal strategy and a corresponding retrieval strategy (corresponding in the sense that the rehearsal strategy would be effective only if the appropriate retrieval plan were also used). Teaching those components separately was not sufficient to lead to optimal performance; Butterfield et al. also had to teach their subjects how to coordinate the two plans. In a number of other situations where subjects of varying cognitive maturity are taught specific strategies, there is evidence that they "execute" the strategies in accordance with instructions, but do not monitor them spontaneously. For example, Belmont and Butterfield (1971) trained retarded subjects to rehearse in a short-term memory task (the subjects saw a series of six consonants exposed sequentially and were then asked to indicate the position in which a randomly selected one had occurred). Their procedure allowed subjects to pace themselves through the list in preparation for the recall test, and thus to spend as much time as they liked studying. Rehearsal training involved having the subjects expose the first four items quickly and then pause to rehearse that set of four items; they could rehearse as long as they wanted before going on to study the final two items. In fact, they were told to pause long enough to repeat the set three times.

The retarded subjects did pause appropriately, and performance did increase, but not as much as could be expected or hoped. The presumption is that they executed the strategy in a rote fashion and did not monitor how well learning was proceeding during the pause interval. That is, they did rehearse but ceased that activity before the items were learned well enough to guarantee excellent recall. In a slightly different paradigm, a similar effect with young children has been obtained by Flavell et al. (1970). As described earlier, younger children in their recall readiness study were less likely to assess their readiness for recall than older children. Given unlimited study time, they studied for shorter periods and did not recall as well.

The recall readiness paradigm was borrowed by Brown and Barclay (1976); it seemed an excellent vehicle for investigating the combined effects of strategy training and instruction in self-regulatory activities. These authors investigated the performance of groups of mildly retarded children differing in MA (6 *vs.* 8); the recall readiness paradigm was somewhat modified. In an initial phase of the experiment, each subject's memory span for pictures was determined. In the subsequent phases of the research, subjects were given a series of trials in which they were asked to study and recall 1½ times their span—rather than just the span, as in Flavell et al. (1970). This was done to make the task more demanding for the students.

On each recall readiness trial, the subjects were told that they could spend as much time studying as they wished and that they could look at the pictures in any order and as often as they wanted. They were also told to ring a bell when they were sure they could recall all the items in left-to-right order. On a pretraining series of trials involving these supraspan lists, their performance was extremely poor. Even though they had indicated that they were ready for recall, they were able to recall only about ⅔ of the items. Only one of 27 younger children and five of 39 older children were able to recall even one list (of three) perfectly.

During the training portion of the study, children were taught strategies that could be used to facilitate their learning of the lists, along with the overseeing or monitoring of those strategies. The latter aspect of training was accomplished by employing strategies that included a self-testing component and by telling the children to monitor their own state of learning. For example, in a rehearsal condition, the subjects were told to break the list down into manageable subsets (three items) and to rehearse those subsets separately. They were also instructed to continue rehearsing the subsets until they were sure they could recall all of the items. Note that one can continue to rehearse all the items (including prior subsets) only if one can remember them well enough to produce them for rehearsal (Flavell, 1979). Thus, in this situation, rehearsal both facilitates learning and provides a check on the state of learning. Anticipation was another trained strategy that included self-testing features. The children were instructed to try to remember the name of a picture before they pressed the window exposing it. In a final condition, labeling, children served as a control group; they were told to go through the list repeatedly, labeling each item exposed. In all conditions, it was emphasized that children should engage in the instructed activity until they were sure they were ready to recall all the picture names.

The immediate effects of training were impressive. For the rehearsal and anticipation groups, recall improved significantly; one index, 13 of 18 younger subjects in these conditions had at least one trial of perfect recall, compared with 0 of 18 before instruction. Of the 26 older children given self-control training, the figures were 2 before instruction and 24 after instruction. In addition, for the older (MA 8) subjects, these effects were extremely durable; differences between the trained and control subjects were still significant on a retest given one year after training.

Also of considerable import, on a test of generalization, these trained students outperformed a number of control groups (Brown, Campione, & Barclay, 1979). On that test, the subjects were given a series of prose passages to study. As in the original experiment, they were told that they could study each passage for as long as they liked, until they were sure they would be able to recall all the important information; however, no mention was made of the earlier study. The rehearsal- and anticipation-trained students recalled more of texts and also showed some evidence of better comprehension than the did the controlled subjects.

Another relevant study (Day, 1980) compared, within one experiment, a number of the approaches outlined in this discussion. The subject population and the type of learning activity were different from the others described. The experimenter was interested in the ability of junior college students to summarize prose passages. The students were divided into two groups: "normal" students with no identified reading or writing problems (who were, however, reading at only the seventh grade level); and remedial students, who although purportedly of normal reading ability, had writing problems.

Within each of the two ability groups, there were four instructional conditions: (a) *self-management*—the students were given general encouragement to write a good summary, to capture the main ideas, to dispense with trivia and all unnecessary words, but they were not given explicit rules for achieving these ends; (b) *rules*—the students were given explicit instructions and modeling of the use of a predetermined set of rules (Brown & Day, 1980) (e.g., they were shown how to delete trivia, delete redundant information, write in superordinates for lists of items, underline topic sentences for inclusion in their summary, and invent topic sentences for paragraphs not containing them [see Day, 1980, for a more detailed discussion of the rules]); (c) *rules plus self-management*—the students were given the general self-management instructions of the first group and the rules instructions of the second group, but they were left to integrate the two sets of information for themselves; (d) *control of the rules* (strategies plus regulation in the current terminology)—involved training of the rules, as in the second group, and additional training in the control and overseeing of those rules (i.e., the students were shown how to check that they had a topic sentence for each paragraph, to check that all redundancies were deleted, etc). For the students in this condition, the integration of the rules and appropriate self-regulatory routines were explicitly modeled.

In this discussion attention is restricted to a small subset of the data, and concentration is given to the use of the most difficult rules—select topic sentence and invent topic sentence. The invent topic sentence rule is much more difficult than the selct topic sentence rule. Consider first the select data. All training conditions had some effect; however, for the less sophisticated learners, the most effective condition was the most explicit training, control of the rules. Training in rule use alone did help performance, but adding the general self-managment instruction did not provide any additional help. The poorer students did not integrate the rules and self-managment instructions for themselves; they needed explicit instruction in rule control to maximize their performance. The more sophisticated junior college students responded better to all forms of training and were able to integrate the general self-management and rule training for themselves; there was no difference between conditions 3 and 4.

A similar pattern was obtained with the very difficult invention rule. According to Brown and Day (1980), even regular college students used the rule on only 50% of the occasions where it would be appropriate. The lower ability junior college students in Day's research, only improved with the most explicit training, condition 4, and then only slightly. The higher ability junior college students showed more improvement, however, in order to achieve maximum performance levels, explicit instructions in control of the rules were required. For the easier select rule, conditions 3 and 4 were equal; with the more difficult rule, condition 4 is superior to condition 3. As the complexity of the rule being taught increases, the need for additional instruction in the monitoring of that rule also increases.

CONCLUSIONS

Although it would be useful to have more data from studies representing the different categories, some clear patterns are emerging. One pattern, which has not been emphasized in this discussion, is that the type of instruction necessary to effect meaningful change in performance varies with the maturity of the learner and the complexity of the skills being taught. This was mentioned directly in the discussion of Day's (1980) work, but only in passing elsewhere. In each of the studies from our laboratory (e.g., Brown & Barclay, 1976; Brown & Campione, 1977; Brown et al., 1977; Brown et al., 1979), instructions that produced effects with more mature (typically MA 8) retarded children were insufficient to bring about comparable results with younger (typically MA 6) subjects. In fact, in all of those studies, as in Day's, when the same intervention was applied to groups of subjects differing in ability, differences between the two groups increased. Typically, the different groups were approximately equal prior to training; following reasonable training, the more capable group was performing significantly better than their less capable counterparts. The implications of these findings for the design of instructional packages, notions of individual differences, and theories of intelligence have been discussed in some detail by Campione et al. (1982).

As illustrated by Day's data, these "between-groups" differences in response to instruction can also be captured within subjects. Although less cognitively mature learners require more complete and explicit instruction than more mature learners within a homogeneous group of learners the need for such complete instruction varies with the difficulty of the task: more complete instruction was needed to bring about use of the invent topic sentence rule than the select rule.

Ignoring these complexities, consider for example, low ability subjects and fairly complex tasks: What can one conclude from this review of intervention studies? Several features seem clear. One is that the potential effects of the varying approaches differ. On the basis of the one relevant study reviewed, it seems improbable that simply providing facts about the cognitive system is likely to be very productive. Given that low ability subjects do not have that information available to them and that a case can be made for the importance of that information, teaching such knowledge seems reasonable. Within some domains experts differ from novices, in terms of domain-specific knowledge; providing that information might be one way to narrow the expertise gap. However, the clear problem for slow learning children remains; it is the same problem that led to the metacognitive work in the first place. Availability of knowledge, either declarative or procedural, does not in itself guarantee flexible access to and use of those resources.

Providing knowledge to supplement skills training does produce some desirable effects. The most obvious one is that it can lead to maintenance of instructed routines. As we have seen, this effect can be obtained fairly easily and should not be taken too lightly. There are many situations where flexibility and creativity are not particularly necessary; where there are fairly specific routines that do need to be applied repeatedly. The contrast is between domains where there are many powerful and specific routines and ones where there may be a much more limited number, possibly only one or two. In the former case, access to and use of the particular procedures needed in a given problem is important; in the second case, the recognition conditions are much simpler. In the limiting case, where there is one routine to be used, the goal would be to guarantee that the routine is engaged; maintenance is all that is required, and the provision of explicit information about the recognition conditions and effectiveness of the instructed approaches may be all that is necessary.

It is known that low ability performers are deficient in both knowledge and the resources for controlling that knowledge; however, providing them with relevant information is not very effective. Why? One answer is that deficient knowledge is simply a symptom of the more important and pervasive problem; knowledge differences reflect processing differences. Poor learners are deficient in knowledge because of poor learning skills, in particular, the self-regulatory, executive mechanisms illustrated earlier. Providing the products of that processing (e.g., specific knowledge about the memory system) does not affect the underlying problems. It is worth noting that an asymmetry is clearly possible. For example, teaching subjects to monitor performance may well lead to the development of factual knowledge about the memory systems (e.g., span limitations and strategy effectiveness).

If this is true, more impressive differences can be expected only if the general executive processes are the subject of training. The preliminary data indicate that this is the case. Teaching (older) retarded children self-checking routines in conjunction with memory strategies leads to impressive immediate training effects, extremely durable outcomes, and evidence for generalized application of those training experiences. The differential effects of knowledge provision and regulation instruction can be seen in another way. Many of the subjects who transferred so well in the recall readiness study were the same ones who failed so dramatically in the span estimation experiment.

The general view is the same as that reached by Feuerstein (1980), among others. His Instrumental Enrichment program, which has been insightfully analyzed by Bransford, Stein, Arbitman-Smith, and Vye (in press), is essentially a program aimed at inculcating metacognitive skills. Feuerstein begins by attempting to deal with the same problem that motivated much of the metacognition/instructional work; poor academic achievers experience particular problems with transfer. His goal is to provide students with the skills of learning that allow them to deal with unfamiliar problem spaces; the general skills he focuses on are the self-regulatory and executive ones emphasized by those in the metacognitive arena (see Bransford et al., in press, and Campione et al., 1982, for further discussions).

The mention of Feuerstein's program leads into the final issue to be discussed. Presuming self-regulatory skills are to be taught, should they be taught separately or in conjunction with the more specific skills they are to control? Feuerstein's position is that those skills should be imparted as content-free activities in a setting of their own, rather than primarily in the context of specific content areas.

He also advocates the use of special materials, designed specifically as vehicles for teaching the skills. Feuerstein is certainly aware of the potential problems with this approach, namely, that the goal is to have these skills transferred to and used in traditional academic areas. His main mechanism for bringing this about is via "bridging"; the instructor points out various situations where the skills are applicable.

Feuerstein's overall argument, which includes a number of important prag-matic/social/motivational aspects, is an important one and is supported by some of the data reviewed. The first comment is straightforward; teaching general components of performance in the absence of the more powerful domain-specific skills, cannot work. Although, as argued earlier, there are certainly cases where such instruction can bring about impressive effects, it is necessary to have a detailed analysis of the domain and of the resources a learner can bring to bear on that domain, before an intelligent decision about "pure" self-regulation instruc-tion could be made. The specific example cited was that inducing some children to apportion their study time "appropriately" did not result in any improvements in performance; instruction would have to be supplemented with specific skill information to be effective.

Feuerstein's assumption, of course, is that the teaching of specific content-dependent procedures is taking place in other classroom settings. Even if this were happening, the data suggest that it might still be necessary to include explicit instruction regarding regulatory mechanisms in conjunction with some specified skills. This fact is a reflection of one of the features of this class of metacognitive skills; they are not stable. Even if the learning of regulatory mechanisms is proceeding smoothly, their use by any individual is likely to vary with task requirements. As pointed out elsewhere (e.g., Brown, Chapter 3, this volume), there are conditions where executive activities are relatively less likely to be employed. For example, the routines may compete for attentional resources with the operations they are overseeing; it might be expected that they would be most likely to be used effectively and spontaneously with simple or well-learned routines. When new, and particularly difficult, skills are being taught, it may be necessary to include self-regulation training, even for subjects who, on other occasions, have been known to engage those skills themselves (see Day, 1980).

The general conclusion is that effective performance within some domain requires knowledge about that domain, specific procedures for operating within the domain, and more general regulatory processes that are task independent; slow learners experience problems in all three areas. Presumably, the most effective teaching plan would attend to all three areas. As the data indicate, attention to only one category is unlikely to be sufficient to bring about major effects. The extent to which all three need to be treated explicitly, within any instructional package, varies with the ability and starting resources of the learner, the complexity of the target activities, and the goals of the instruction. Although no single factor is sufficient, each leads to worthwhile outcomes, and a single package incorporating all three areas would be expected to yield truly impressive results. An evaluation of that statement, however, would require an experimental approach different from that represented in the research reviewed earlier; in that work, relatively few training sessions were included. An attempt to borrow as much as is now known about metacognition and apply it seriously to the topic of instruction would require a much more extended intervention. Researchers have begun to do such experiments, and the results of these endeavors should be available in the near future.

In summary, the nature of instructional efforts with slow-learning children has changed dramatically since the emergence of interest in metacognitive skills. Rather than trying simply to impart specific skills, the programs now attempt to foster understanding of the routines by providing knowledge about the domain and the place of the skill(s) within the domain. Close attention is also paid to imparting the regulatory schemes necessary to make maximal use of resources. In these endeavors, an overriding emphasis is on making learners *aware* of themselves and of the availability and potential use of cognitive resources. These changes have been positive ones; the outcomes of current training studies are more dramatic than prior ones, and their relevance to educational issues is much clearer.

The instructional data relates to more general issues regarding the topic of metacognition. The knowledge/control distinction is powerful, enough to make it preferable to refrain from grouping the two categories together under one category; the data also indicates primacy of the control component. One suggestion is that the knowledge of the cognitive system, which develops with age and expertise, is the product of the operation of the general executive mechanisms.

ACKNOWLEDGMENTS

Preparation of this manuscript was supported in part by U.S. P.H.S. Grant HD-05951.

REFERENCES

Baker, L., & Brown, A. L. (1981). Metacognition and the reading process. In D. Pearson (Ed.), *A Handbook of reading research*. New York: Plenum Press.

Belmont, J. M., & Butterfield, E. C. (1971). Learning strategies as determinants of memory deficiencies. *Cognitive Psychology, 2*, 411–420.

Belmont, J. M., & Butterfield, E. C. (1977). The instructional approach to developmental cognitive research. In R. V. Kail & J. W. Hagen (Eds.), *Perspectives on the development of memory and cognition*. Hillsdale, NJ: Lawrence Erlbaum Associates.

Belmont, J. M., Butterfield, E. C., & Borkowski, J. G. (1978). Training retarded people to generalize memorization methods across memory tasks. In M. M. Gruneberg, P. E. Morris, & R. N. Sykes (Eds.), *Practical aspects of memory*. London: Academic Press.

Belmont, J. M., Butterfield, E. C., & Ferretti, R. P. (1982). To secure transfer of training, instruct self-management skills. In D. K. Detterman & R. J. Sternberg (Eds.), *How and how much can intelligence be increased.* Norwood, NJ: Ablex.

Bereiter, C., & Scardamalia, M. (1980). From conversation to composition: The role of instruction in the developmental process. In R. Glaser (Ed.), *Advances in Instructional Psychology* (Vol. 2). Hillsdale, NJ: Lawrence Erlbaum Associates.

Binet, A. (1909). *Les idees modernes sur les infants.* Paris: Ernest Flamarion.

Bobrow, D. G., & Norman, D. A. (1975). Some principles of memory schemata. In D. G. Bobrow & A. Collins (Eds.), *Representation and understanding: Studies in cognitive science.* New York: Academic Press.

Bransford, J. D., Stein, B. S., Arbitman-Smith, R., & Vye, N. J. (in press). Three approaches to improving thinking and learning skills. In S. Chipman, J. Segal, & R. Glaser (Eds.), *Cognitive skills and instructions.* Hillsdale, NJ: Lawrence Erlbaum Associates.

Brown, A. (1974). The role of strategic behavior in retardate memory. In N. R. Ellis (Ed.), *International review of research in mental retardation (Vol. 7).* New York: Academic Press.

Brown, A. L. (1978). Knowing when, where, and how to remember: A problem of metacognition. In R. Glaser (Ed.), *Advances in instructional psychology (Vol. 1).* Hillsdale, NJ: Lawrence Erlbaum Associates.

Brown, A. L. (1980). Metacognitive development and reading. In R. J. Sprio, B. Bruce, & W. Brewer (Eds.), *Theoretical issues in reading comprehenson.* Hillsdale, NJ: Lawrence Erlbaum Associates.

Brown, A. L. (1982). Learning and development: The problem of compatibility, access, and induction. *Human Development, 25,* 89–115.

Brown, A. L., & Barclay, C. R. (1976). The effects of training specific mnemonics on the metamnemonic efficiency of retarded children. *Child Development, 47,* 71–80.

Brown, A. L., & Campione, J. C. (1977). Training strategic study time apportionment in educable retarded children. *Intelligence, 1,* 94–107.

Brown, A. L., & Campione, J. C. (1978). Permissible inferences from the outcome of training studies in cognitive development research. *Quarterly Newsletter of the Institute for Comparative Human Development, 2,* 46–53.

Brown, A. L., & Campione, J. C. (1981). Inducing flexible thinking: A problem of access. In M. Friedman, J. D. Das & N. O'Connor (Eds.), *Intelligence and learning.* New York: Plenum Press.

Brown, A. L., & Campione, J. C. (1982). Modifying intelligence versus modifying cognitive skills: More than a semantic quibble. In D. K. Detterman, & R. J. Sternberg (Eds.), *How and how much can intelligence be increased.* Norwood, NJ: Albex.

Brown, A. L., Campione, J. C., & Barclay, C. R. (1979). Training self-checking routines for estimating test readiness: Generalization from list learning to prose recall. *Child Development, 50,* 501–512.

Brown, A. L., Campione, J. C., Bray, N. W., & Wilcox, B. L. (1973). Keeping track of changing variables: Effects of rehearsal training and rehearsal prevention in normal and retarded adolescents. *Journal of Experimental Psychology, 101,* 123–131.

Brown, A. L., Campione, J. C., & Day, J. D. (1981). Learning to learn: On training students to learn from texts. *Educational Researcher, 10,* 14–21.

Brown, A. L., Campione, J. C., & Murphy, M. D. (1977). Maintenance and generalization of trained metamnemonic awareness by educable retarded children: Span estimation. *Journal Experimental Child Psychology, 24,* 191–211.

Brown, A. L., & Day, J. D. (1980). *Strategies and knowledge for summarizing texts: The development and facilitation of expertise.* Unpublished manuscript, University of Illinois.

Brown, A. L., & Lawton, S. C. (1977). The feeling of knowing experience in educable retarded children. *Developmental Psychology, 13,* 364–370.

Burger, A. L., Blackman, L. S., Holmes, M., & Zetlin, A. (1978). Use of active sorting and retrieval strategies as a facilitator of recall, clustering, and sorting by EMR and nonretarded children. *American Journal of Mental Deficiency, 83,* 253–261.

Butterfield, E. C. (1979). *On testing process theories of intelligence.* Paper presented at NATO Conference on Intelligence and Learning, York, England, July.

Butterfield, E. C., & Belmont, J. M. (1977). Assessing and improving the cognitive functions of mentally retarded people. In I. Bailer & M. Steinlicht (Eds.), *Psychological issues in mental retardation.* Chicago: Aldine Press.

Butterfield, E. C., Wambold, C., & Belmont, J. M. (1973). On the theory and practice of improving short-term memory. *American Journal of Mental Deficiency, 77,* 654–669.

Campione, J. C., & Brown, A. L. (1977). Memory and metamemory development in educable retarded children. In R. V. Kail, Jr. & J. W. Hagen (Eds.), *Perspectives on the development of memory and cognition.* Hillsdale, NJ: Lawrence Erlbaum Associates.

Campione, J. C., & Brown, A. L. (1978). Toward a theory of intelligence: Contributions from research with retarded children. *Intelligence, 2,* 279–304.

Campione, J. C., Brown, A. L., & Ferrara, R. A. (1982). Experimental and clinical interventions of retarded individuals: Intelligence, learning, and transfer. In R. Sternberg (Ed.), *Handbook of human intelligence.* New York: Cambridge University Press.

Day, J. D. (1980). *Training summarization skills: A comparison of teaching methods.* Unpublished doctoral dissertation, University of Illinois.

Feuerstein, R. (1980). *Instrumental enrichment: An intervention program for cognitive modifiability.* Baltimore: University Park Press.

Flavell, J. H. (1971). First discussant's comments: What is memory development the development of? *Human Development, 14,* 272–278.

Flavell, J. H. (1979). *Monitoring social-cognitive enterprises: Something else that may develop in the area of social cognition.* Paper prepared for the Social Sciences Research Council Committe on Social and Affective Development During Childhood, January.

Flavell, J. H., Friedrichs, A. G., & Hoyt, J. D. (1970). Developmental changes in memorization processes. *Cognitive Psychology, 1,* 324–340.

Flavell, J. E., & Wellman, H. M. (1977). Metamemory. In R. V. Kail & W. Hagen (Eds.), *Perspectives on the development of memory and cognition.* Hillsdale, NJ: Lawrence Erlbaum Associates.

Gardner, E. (1978). Commentary on animal awareness papers. *Behavioral and Brain Sciences, 4,* 572.

Kendall, C. R., Borkowski, J. G., & Cavanaugh, J. C. (1980). Maintenance and generalization of an interrogative strategy by EMR children. *Intelligence, 4,* 255–270.

Kennedy, B. A., & Miller, D. J. (1976). Persistent use of verbal rehearsal as a function of information about its value. *Child Development, 47,* 566–569.

Markman, E. M. (1981). Comprehension monitoring. In W. P. Dickson (Ed.), *Children's or communication skills.* New York: Academic Press.

Masur, E. F., McIntyre, C. W., & Flavell, J. H. (1973). Developmental changes in apportionment of study time among items in a multitrial free recall task. *Journal of Experimental Child Psychology, 15,* 237–246.

Meichenbaum, D. (1977). *Cognitive behavior modification: An integrative approach.* New York: Plenum Press.

Moore, J., & Newell, A. (1974). How can Merlin understand? In L. W. Gregg (Ed.), *Knowledge and cognition.* Hillsdale, NJ: Lawrence Erlbaum Associates.

Newell, A. (1980). Production systems and human cognition. In R. A. Cole (Ed.), *Perception and production of fluent speech.* Hillsdale, NJ: Lawrence Erlbaum Associates.

Piaget, J. (1978). *Success and understanding.* Cambridge, MA: Harvard University Press.

Pylyshyn, Z. (1978). Computational models and empirical constraints. *The Behavioral and Brain Sciences, 1,* 93–99.

Rozin, P. (1976). The evolution of intelligence and access to the cognitive unconscious. *Progression in Psychobiology and Physiological Psychology, 6,* 245–280.

Sternberg, R. J. (1980). Sketch of a componential subtheory of human intelligence. *The Behavioral and Brain Sciences, 3,* 573–584.

Tenney, Y. J. (1975). The child's conception of organization and recall. *Journal of Experimental Child Psychology, 19,* 100–114.

II
MOTIVATION AND ATTRIBUTION STYLE

For many years, the analysis of achievement-related behaviors has been an important part of the psychology of motivation. Through investigations of the influence of dispositional factors such as hope-for-success and fear-of-failure on subjective experience, activities and performance in different task situations, the prevalence of inter-individual differences in causal attributions for success and failure was first noted. Such causal attributions have figured prominently in many of the new, cognitive models of motivation, and are also central to the learned helplessness model developed by Abramson, Seligman, and others. In this model, cumulative experiences of being unable to control situations or to influence outcomes by goal-directed actions are postulated to result in behavioral deficits and performance decrements. The impact of fear-of-failure and learned helplessness on learning activities and performance has been demonstrated in both experimental and school settings. The phenomena of learned helplessness and issues related to causal attributions for success and failure are central to the following three chapters.

Heinz Heckhausen examines individual differences in causal attributions for achievement outcomes. He describes stable intra-individual asymmetries in attribution patterns that are different for individuals who are motivated to achieve success or to avoid failure. Heckhausen distinguishes a "positive attribution pattern (PAP) from a "depressive attribution pattern" (DAP), and discusses how these patterns affect behavior and how they emerge.

Christopher Peterson and Martin Seligman focus on the relationship between a helpless attribution style and depression. Following a review of the original learned helplessness model, they analyze the role played by relatively stable attribution styles, and discuss how such attribution styles are assessed in children and adults. Peterson and Seligman then present and discuss empirical findings that speak to the relation between attribution style and depressive symptoms. They give particular attention to the question of how a depressive attribution style might develop.

Julius Kuhl proposes an alternative explanation for the phenomena of helplessness, drawing on achievement motivation theory and data. The central idea behind Kuhl's model concerns action control. Kuhl postulates that action control is determined both by dispositional differences that bias an individual toward an action or state orientation, and by situational variables such as the extent to which an outcome can be controlled by one's own actions. Kuhl presents empirical findings consistent with the model of action control, and concludes with a discussion of how this model may be applied to learning and performance problems encountered in school settings.

5 Causal Attribution Patterns for Achievement Outcomes: Individual Differences, Possible Types and Their Origins

Heinz Heckhausen
Max-Planck-Institute for Psychological Research
Munich

Given the same achievement outcomes, why will one person remain confident of success and another fearful of failure—why, in the face of the same failure will one person increase or renew efforts, and another soon become helpless and give up on the task? Typical answers are that each has a different "achievement motive." The former, to use the concepts of some research traditions, is "achievement-oriented," "nondepressive," and "internally controlled," the latter, "helpless," "depressive," and "externally controlled." Within each tradition, measures have been developed to assess some dispositional difference that covaries with some aspects of achievement behavior.

To better understand differences in achievement behavior in seemingly identical situations, one should be better able to answer two questions. The first relates to motivation: In given situations, what specific determinants of personality, other than the summary constructs, will give rise to different achievement behaviors? The second question relates to development: What are the antecedents of diverging determinants of personality in the earlier stages of the life cycle?

To the developmentalist, the question is a difficult one; the further one reaches back into the past, the more difficult is it to isolate the ontogenetic factors. Each developmental stage has a specific environmental impact; therefore, it is difficult for the developmentalist to know what specific stage to search for personality determinants. The search for a developmental explanation cannot be more specific than the determinants of personality being sought allow. The genesis of a dispositional factor as summary as the achievement motive can, with regard to the ontogenetically relevant age spans and their environmental determinants, at best be summarily accounted for only. The explanation is even more difficult because the time gap between the present and past skips long periods of development (and their accompanying psychological implications), and also because it entails attempts to reconstruct the past on the basis of current reports. For these reasons, the inconclusiveness of the findings seems to be an inevitable predicament of the usual socialization research, it also seems to be the plight of attempts to clarify the emergence of individual differences in achievement motivation.

To be sure, relationships have been found between achievement motivation and such diverging variables, such as "a democratic family climate," "love-oriented child-rearing techniques," and "child-centered independence training" (see Heckhausen, 1972). However, from the developmentalist's point of view, such relationships are trivial for two reasons: First, it is still not known at which specific age spans the variables discussed actually generate individual differences, until what age they do not as yet have this effect, and from what age on they no longer have it. Second, these determinants are too unspecific to account for the motivational differences to be accounted for because they covary with differences in other dispositional factors, such as development of conscientiousness, I.Q., and social competence.

In what follows, I attempt to avoid the aforementioned drawbacks of developmental accountability. Hence, summary constructs are not used to explain individual differences in achievement behavior. Instead, a more specific personality variable is singled out. In light of current results of achievement motivation research, three specific personality variables are suggested the valence of incentives for success or failure, personal standards of excellence (level of aspiration), and attribution patterns (see Heckhausen, 1980a).

This discussion is concerned only with attribution patterns, primarily because they are personality variables uncovered (in some studies under the term of "attribution styles") by investigators working within diverse research traditions. Attribution theory has achieved a remarkable overlap between explanatory constructs and research results.

The first section examines the *intraindividual* asymmetry of attribution patterns for success or failure and the assumed underlying motivations. This is followed by an overview of various lines of research that have brought to light an *interindividual* disparity in attribution patterns, which may produce high or low self-evaluation. Finally, a number of possible attribution patterns are specified in terms of their potential to explain success and failure according to a personal bias.

Depending on the weighting given to the causal factors, the effects of any of the attribution patterns are apt to heighten or lower self-evaluation. Accordingly each of them is analyzed to determine the level of cognitive development that must be presupposed in each case to specify the earliest level of development from which a biased attribution can be expected. The earliest level of development serves as a referent for generating assumptions concerning environmental factors that might have produced individual differences in the various attribution patterns.

My procedure is entirely hypothetical, even though it does comprehend the few research findings in this field. The intention is not to extrapolate prematurely across the few results; rather, it is designed to stimulate a systematic search for missing data.

INTRAINDIVIDUAL ASYMMETRY OF ATTRIBUTION PATTERNS

Among the individual differences in attribution patterns, a general bias is perhaps, above all, the most salient one. People tend to explain their own success or failure by asymmetric attribution patterns, even for tasks of identical difficulty. One tends to attribute success to oneself, and failure to external factors for which one is not responsible (e.g. Luginbuhl, Crowe, & Kahan, 1975). On the other hand, in explaining the achievements of others, subjects tend to be more impartial (Snyder, Stephen, & Rosenfeld, 1976). In relation to own success and failure, asymmetric attribution patterns evidently have a motivational basis; they serve to enhance one's sense of self-esteem. Miller and Ross (1975) have questioned this assumption and attribute the asymmetry to nonmotivational factors in information processing—for instance, that success, rather than failure, is intended and expected, and that accordingly, one tends to ascribe the achievement outcome to oneself. Recent empirical evidence, however, has confirmed the motivational nature of a general, self-serving bias in the attribution asymmetry (see Bradley, 1978; Miller, 1976; Stevens & Jones, 1976).

If one keeps in mind the many causes that may facilitate or inhibit a successful achievement outcome and that none of these causes can be objectified, the latitude for subjective arrangements of an attribution pattern is enormous. Further, considering the extent to which various skills and abilities (intellectual abilities in particular) are valued in our culture, and taking into account that most people want to see themselves and want to be regarded by others as competent in some respect, it is not surprising that in most cases the scope for subjective assessment of abilities is used in ways that attribute success to one's own abilities, rather than to other facilitating factors, such as ease of task, the effort expended, or good luck. By the same token, failure is ascribed less to one's own lack of abilities than to other adverse circumstances, such as insufficient efforts, too difficult a task, or bad luck. To be sure, such self-esteem enhancing propensities may be unrealistic; they may even be generated by self-deception. Nevertheless, those self-concepts will foster the motivation to expend more effort instead of giving up after experiencing failure, and in the final analysis will facilitate the further development of one's abilities. In this sense, a somewhat overoptimistic assessment of oneself, or even a kind of self-conceit, may be a characteristic that has survival value—possibly human evolution would not have taken place at all in its absence.

Against the background of the general aspiration to make one's own abilities appear in the most favorable light, attribution patterns involving self-criticism or that detract from self-esteem appear to be exceptional. Yet this type of attribution pattern has attracted attention in a number of research studies, not only in individual cases, but for whole groups of subjects selected according to very different diagnostic procedures. The selection criteria included such divergent personality traits as a perception of external control (Rotter, 1966), "help-lessness" (Diener & Dweck, 1978), "depression" (Beck, Ward, Mendelsohn, Mock & Erbaugh, 1961), "failure motivation" (Heckhausen, 1963; Schmalt, 1976), "low self-concept" (various questionaires), and, yes, even in the female gender of the subjects (e.g., Deaux & Farris, 1977).

One may ask why whole groups of persons should disparge their own effec-tiveness, abilities, and competence in their own eyes and in the eyes of others, even when there is no compelling reason—when the same achievement out-comes could have been attributed so that subjects can retain a much higher sense of self-esteem without diminishing attributional plausibility. The question, then is, whether such persons have acquired a negative self-image to which they intend to adhere, even after having had more positive experiences (see Fitch, 1970). Recent findings are surprising, they show the degree to which individuals will hold to a preconceived notion even though it has been disproved by the facts (Ross & Lepper, 1980). Can this phenomenon be explained by the assumption that an attribution pattern acquired in an earlier developmental phase is subse-quently transformed into a mode of information processing that already distorts perception at a pre-attentive level? Does this become an attribution pattern inca-pable of self-correction? Even though the individual has had positive experiences that contradict the negative self image, does this attribution pattern become "immune" to modification (see Heckhausen, 1975)? Or, on the contrary, does attribution that reduces self-esteem constitute a cognitive process motivated by the intention to avoid longer exposure to achievement situations and the self-evaluation entailed? So far, no conclusive statement can be made as to which of these explanations might be correct. One cannot dispose of investigation tech-niques that would make it possible to balance the effect of automatized sub-routines of information processing against currently motivated distortions of judgment.

Nonetheless, there are two reasons that favor the assumption that even this type of self-esteem-reducing attribution pattern should be held to be a motivated process. The first reason is simply that its counterpart, self-esteem-enhancing attribution, is undoubtedly a motivated attribution pattern. Therefore, without cogent reasons, self-esteem-reducing attribution should not be regarded as being exceptional. This argument has gained validity with investigations showing that when a particular situational context provides grounds for a modest self-image (e.g., when performance is being assessed by a team of experts), the same subjects will promptly switch from a self-esteem-enhancing attribution to its opposite. In such situations, a "counterdefensive" attribution may be observed: Subjects do not feel primarily responsible for their successes, but for their failures (Arkin, Appelman & Burger, 1980; Schlenker, 1975; Wortman, Constanzo & Witt, 1973). Even more convincing is the motivational nature of what has been termed the "self handicap." Self-handicap is a strategy of self-representation by which individuals set up in advance difficulties in their solution attempts (sometimes even at the risk of preprogramming their own failure), so that subsequent to the event they need not call their own capacity into question (Berglas & Jones, 1978). Obviously, if one is successful, with this strategy one's own abilities will appear even more impressive. The self-handicap, a precautionary attribution strategy, can be observed when it takes the form of the academic ritual, often used in the *captatio benevolentiae* turns of phrase in introductions to lectures.

Also in support of the argument that attribution pattern asymmetry is motivationally based is that the "self-esteem reducing" label itself appears to be an overstatement of what is actually at issue. In most cases, it is not possible to determine the extent to which either of these attribution patterns involves an attributional error—there are no objective criteria for "realistic" attribution. Thus, one can contrast these two attribution patterns only in their complementary relationship. It is possible that the problem group—the depressive, the failure motivated, and the like—are merely less prone to adopt a self-esteem-enhancing attribution pattern than are the "normal" groups that for this reason they make attributions that are realistic and self-critical rather than "self-esteem" reducing. Indicators of this possibility have been found.

One way to assess propensity to attributional errors is to make an intraindividual comparison of success and failure attributions, that is, to determine the asymmetry of attribution. For instance, Meyer (1973) found that failure-motivated subjects, after experiencing unexpectedly low or unexpectedly high achievement outcomes, modified their attributions concerning ability, effort, and chance only very little, success-motivated subjects were prone to tap all the possibilities provided by self-esteem-enhancing settings. Success-motivated subjects ascribed unexpectedly high performance outcomes to their own ability and unexpectedly low outcomes to (low) effort and to chance. Alloy and Abramson (1979), on the basis of stringent objectivity criteria, demonstrated that depressives were able to draw a surprisingly accurate distinction between the efficacy (contingency) of their own undertakings and chance events; nondepressive subjects appeared to overestimate their ability to exert control when the outcome aimed at was either frequently obtained as a result of chance or had been made valuable. Correspondingly, they underrated their control when the outcome was not valuable. Alloy's and Abramson's conclusion was that depressives are "sadder but wiser." Perhaps the same is true for other "problem groups"—the failure-motivated, the externally-controlled, the helpless, subjects with a low self-concept.

It may appear paradoxical that of all people it should be these problem groups who attain a more realistic self-evaluation. But is a realistic self-evaluation "normal" and helpful? Is not a certain measure of self-esteem-enhancing self-deception "normal," or at least necessary, for one to cope with the problems of life? Is such self-deception not essential to prevent one from giving up hope too soon in the pursuance of the many goals that are not easily attained? Does self-deception not enable one actually to achieve more than could be expected when starting an undertaking?

Moreover, the findings concerning those problem groups, have not in all cases indicated that they deviate from the general (self-esteem-enhancing) attribution asymmetry (e.g. Schneider, 1977). An attribution pattern deviating from the self-esteem-enhancing mode appears to be used more often subsequent to failure than subsequent to success (e.g. Fitch, 1970; Halisch, 1983; Jopt & Ermshaus, 1977). Only one success or failure may not elicit variations in attribution patterns. Halisch (1983) found that only after repeated experiences of failure do failure-motivated subjects ascribe such failure to their own lack of ability.

INTERINDIVIDUAL CONTRAST IN ATTRIBUTION PATTERNS: CONVERGENCE OF RESEARCH DOMAINS

This section reviews the various areas of research in which findings have highlighted an interindividual contrast, that is, in which different groups of respondents used an attribution pattern that deviated from general self-esteem-enhancing attribution.

Internal versus External Reinforcement Control

The personality construct postulated by Rotter (1954, 1966) is a precursor of attribution theory but it has not adequately been clarified in terms of its importance for attribution theory itself. For Rotter, internal versus external reinforcement control meant individual differences in the belief that one's own action and its results can generate desired ends. Rotter's construct involves the "instrumentality," or "contingency," between one's own activity (and its results) and its contingent consequences mediated by others. However, this research line has never clearly and consistently kept separate the result of an action and the consequences of an action (see Heckhausen, 1980a). In light of the distinctions now current in attribution theory, Rotter's usage of the expression "external" refers to noncontingent (external) causal factors, such as chance or the arbitrariness of reinforcers. "Internal" on the other hand, refers to factors relating to personal efficacy, such as ability in relation to task difficulty. The suitable experimental conditions were made operative by means of chance versus skill-dependent tasks. The experiments, however, involve attribution of action outcomes and not, as the construct postulates, attribution of action consequences. Even in a questionnaire on expectancy of control these two different attributions are confounded. The content of the questions used shows a high dispersion around very different areas of activity and life spheres; this weakens the validity of Rotter's trait construct (see Zuckerman & Gerbasi, 1977).

Distinguished in terms of this approach, the individual dispositions can best be designated as a sense of high versus low self-efficacy. The belief in external control, sensed as a feeling of low self-efficacy, thus appears to characterize the type of persons who, in accounting for their achievement outcomes only rarely use self-esteem-enhancing attribution patterns, (or even conversely, self-esteem-reducing attributions). There are findings that confirm this hypothesis. External control subjects, compared with internal control subjects, tend to attribute their success less to ability/skills and their failure less to chance, especially when their solution attempts are associated with a high expectancy of success (Gilmor & Minton, 1974; Lefcourt, Hogg, Struthers & Holmes, 1975).

There are, however, also research findings that relate to the specific attributional dimension inherent in Rotter's construct that is, the contingency of action consequences (reinforcement). Contingency attribution plays a decisive part in the experimental paradigm of helplessness research. In a training task, subjects initially receive negative or positive feedback during their solution attempts, for one group of subjects this instantiates objective noncontingency, for the other group, contingency. In a subsequent task, either similar or different, the experimenters scrutinize the extent to which noncontingency during the training task has impaired performance in the test task (i.e., to what extent noncontingency actually induced "helplessness"). To put it another way: Subsequent to the prior experience of loss of control or of being confronted with noncontrollable factors, it is assumed that the noncontingent group will exhibit greater helplessness in its solution attempts for the following controllable (contingent) task. This occurs because the previously acquired sense of loss of control is transferred to the new situation. Accordingly, external control subjects are more likely than internal control subjects to perceive noncontingent feedback as a noncontrollable factor and in the test phase will therefore, become more markedly helpless in a more generalized way.

Hiroto (1974) has provided evidence of the validity of this assumption in tasks investigating avoidance learning (escaping an aversive tone by moving hands in a "finger shuttle box"). In a similar test task, external control subjects learned more slowly than did internal control subjects or those in the control group, who had had no prior experience or training. It was also possible to induce an approximately equivalent helplessness effect when the noncontingency of the outcome was pointed out to the subjects in an instruction period preceding the test. However, "externals" appear to use not only attribution patterns, that more markedly, induce helplessness, but also those that make helplessness more generalized. After their subjects had terminated a concept-formation task such as the training task, Cohen, Rothbart, and Phillips (1976) administered two test tasks in another room. One of the test tasks consisted of tracing the lines of a diagram, without tracing any line twice and without lifting the pencil from the figure; the diagram-tracing task posed an intellectual problem, as did the training task of concept-formation. The second test task was a pure speed task (Stroop-test). Both internal and external noncontingent subjects performed more poorly on the more similar diagram-tracing task, with the externals suffering a stronger impairment (as measured by less persistence at the insolvable task). At the less similar speed task, only externals showed helplessness effects; they were slower.

Depression

The latest findings indicating that the helplessness effect will generalize across situations and time in externally controlled subjects call attention to an attributional dimension that has long been neglected. That is the dimension of globality (in contrast to specifity) (although the phenomenon itself was already incorporated by Kelley, 1967, in his conceptual schema as "entity.") Restating the original helplessness theory, Abramson, Seligman & Teasdale (1978) made use of the globality dimension in their reformulations of attribution theory (see also Miller & Norman, 1979; Roth, 1980; Peterson & Seligman this volume). Given aversive outcomes (failure), inhibitory causal factors in self-esteem-reducing attribution patterns are more global than in the event of success. Failure on a specific task is much more readily ascribed to a general lack of ability and, in the end, to lack of intelligence. To explain how reactive depression comes about, Miller & Norman (1979) have focused on the self-esteem-reducing attribution pattern and have given the following concise description:

> Due to some combination of situational cues and repeated exposure to noncontingent and nondesired outcomes, the individual's attributions of these outcomes changes from external, variable, and specific causes to internal, stable, and general causes. This change results in a change in future expectancies, performances, and mood. Thus, in new situations, the individual expects noncontingency and failure, and when these congruent outcomes occur, they are attributed to internal, stable, and general causes, whereas discrepant outcomes of success and contingency are attributed to external, variable, and specific causes and do not influence future expectancies, performance, or mood. The individual is then depressed and tends to disregard outcomes of success and contingency while overgeneralizing failure and noncontingent outcomes. Thus, response initiation declines, a greater number of failure and noncontingent outcomes do occur, and the vicious circle of depression has begun. (p. 113/114)

The original helplessness theory was simple: If specific outcomes proved uncontrollable, they would produce an expectation of one's own inefficacy; in recurrent or similar situations this expectation would generate cognitive, emotional, and affective "deficits" (cf. Seligman, 1975). However, what might have seemed from the cognitivist perspective, a daring construction when this theoretical framework to explain the findings of research conducted with infrahumans—namely, that the fatal effects of the expectation that outcomes would prove uncontrollable—proved to be even more flimsy relative to the effects of failure-related cognitions when humans were the research subjects. Unlike dogs for instance, humans displayed neither motivational deficits nor, in many cases, cognitive deficits, in the test task situation. Moreover, frequently humans exhibited an improvement rather than a decrement in performance (see, for example, Hanusa & Schult, 1977). Even "success," when it is noncontingent and is thus experienced as puzzling and enigmatic, can be perceived as a failure (Griffith, 1977). The motivational effect of the cumulative experience of failure depends on the causal attributions made, in particular on whether the scale of causal attributions tips more toward one's own lack of ability than toward task difficulty (see discussion in Heckhausen, 1980a, p. 510f). Helplessness theory, developed from investigations conducted with animals, had conceived the helplessness phenomenon to be a general fact of experimental psychology. Theory construction, however, was soon confronted by phenomena belonging to differential psychology.

Depending on experimentally induced attributions (e.g. Tennen & Eller, 1977), on personal attribution patterns, or possibly on related differences of state orientation versus action orientation (see Kuhl 1981; and this volume), only some of the subjects were observed to display helplessness. Internal versus external location of stable causes play a key role in generating feelings of helplessness. When in the training-task subjects ascribed failure to their own inability, rather than to high task difficulty, helplessness was generalized to the test task (Frankel & Snyder, 1978; Klein, Fencil-Morse, & Seligman, 1976; Tennen & Eller, 1977). Frankel and Snyder introduced the tasks as being either easy or difficult; Tennen and Eller manipulated them as involving either increasing or decreasing levels of difficulty. When, in one way or another, an attribution of very high task difficulty was suggested, the effect was not helplessness but improved performance (a performance effect that in the Tennen and Eller investigations outmatched even that of the "contingent" and control groups). Obviously, these test results must be interpreted in terms of attribution theory: A very high task difficulty attenuates the threatening inference that failure implies lack of ability, even when considerable effort has been expanded.

Following the noncontingent series of failures, susceptibility to helplessness was also shown more by subjects with higher scores of depression than by nondepressives, high-depression scorers exhibited more depressive symptoms, less self-confidence and lower expectancies of success. No differences were found for the noncontingent success series (Hammen & Krantz, 1976; Wener & Rehm, 1975). In addition to negative affect changes and lowered self-esteem (Blaney, 1977) was the characteristic asymmetry of attribution patterns (Rizley, 1978): Successes were ascribed to low level of task difficulty (external, stable, specific), and failures to one's own low ability (internal, stable, global).

The original concept that the experience of loss of control was a sufficient, although not a necessary, condition for reactive depressions (Miller & Seligman, 1975; Seligman, 1975) was afflicted by the paradox in depression: How can depressives blame themselves for outcomes they believe are uncontrollable (Abramson & Sackeim, 1977)? This paradox can be resolved if it is assumed that in addition to the expectancy of uncontrollability, depressives tend to ascribe negative outcomes to internal, stable, and global causes. To be sure, such an attribution pattern in itself does not make up depression, but it is a risk factor, that could cause depression when adverse or aversive events occur and accumulate. On the other hand, even uncontrollable outcomes, whether actually or only presumably uncontrollable, do not in themselves make people helpless or depressive. Such events must also have an aversive function, so the action sequences that comprise high positive incentive values experienced so far appear to be irretrievably lost. In cases where the attribution pattern itself was already negative and experience of aversive effects had accumulated, the incentive-disengagement-cycle (Klinger, 1975), will then no longer make possible the upswing that usually follows temporary phases of depressive reaction.

This assumption has found support in the data presented by Seligman and his associates (see Peterson & Seligman, this volume). In this study substantive progress was made in the recording of attribution patterns. Instead of measuring predetermined causal factors, Seligman, Abramson, Semmel, and von Baeyer (1979) developed a scale for measuring attributional style based on their Attributional Style Questionnaire (ASQ). Subjects were given instructions for filling out the attributional style scale. They were presented with a selection of "good" and "bad" outcomes, which included success and failure in achievement situations. The subjects were asked to try to imagine themselves in the situations specified, and to pick the one major cause if this event happened to them. The subjects were then instructed to rate each cause (on a 7 point scale) for degree of internality, stability, and globality. These attributional dimensions, separately or together but separated into good and bad outcomes, are the characteristic values for individual attribution patterns. They are relatively stable over time and fairly independent. The "insidous" attributional style (internal, stable, and global attribution for bad outcomes) correlated with depression for children, students, and clinical patients. In the latter two groups (depressed students and patients), good outcomes were explained by means of the converse attribution pattern (even if to a lesser extent), that is, by external, variable, and specific causes. The children, aged 9 to 10, had mothers for whom depression and insiduous attributional style were prominent; the results correlated with each other.

Peterson and Seligman (this volume) had also collected data showing that as a risk factor the insiduous attributional style is a necessary, but not a sufficient, condition for depression. In their study the negative event was the unsatisfactory outcome of a midterm test. In cases where insiduous attributional style and unsatisfactory test outcome coincided, depression symptoms (recorded on the basis of questionaires) were displayed one week following and four weeks following the test. Separately, neither of these two factors gave rise to depressive symptoms. A longitudinal study with the same children also demonstrated this temporal sequence, and thereby the direction of causation. The insiduous attribution style proved to be the better predictor of phases of depression than, conversely, depressive states did for attributional style. There appear, therefore, to be many factors indicating that a self-esteem-reducing attribution pattern predisposes individuals to encounter difficulty in getting out of depressive phases following a bad event.

Learned Helplessness in Schoolchildren

Dweck observed that after only a few failures, schoolchildren labeled as subject to "learned helplessness," rapidly lost the self-efficacy they usually displayed in solving tasks. As Dweck and Repucci (1973) found the children were no longer able to solve tasks they had demonstrably been able to solve previously. For some of their fifth-grade subjects. The helpless students, for whom failure resulted in decrement of performance and reduced persistence, also attracted attention by the peculiar pattern of answers they gave in the Intellectual Achievement Responsibility (IAR) scale administered to them (Crandall, Katkovsky & Crandall, 1965). Compared with their classmates who did not let themselves be thrown off balance by failure, the subjects had a greater tendency to ascribe their success to high effort and their failure to poor effort.

In a 25 day behavior change program for children characterized by "expectation of failure and deterioration of performance in the face of failure," (12 out of 750, 10- to 13-year olds), Dweck (1975) demonstrated the decisive role of effort attributions. After failing on a number of somewhat more difficult tasks, the children were urged to ascribe failure to a lack of effort. In this way it was possible to fully overcome the decrement in efficacy that had followed failure, although while the comparative treatment program that comprised solely success-only treatments showed no improvement.

In another study, Diener and Dweck (1978) traced the cognitive processes displayed by helpless and mastery-oriented children following failure. On the basis of the IAR Scale, fifth graders were divided into helpless and mastery-oriented groups. Those children who, in determining their failure, tended to neglect the role of effort were placed in the helpless group. All the children were asked to begin thinking out loud as they performed the task. The verbalization procedure revealed a striking difference: helpless children tended to dwell excessively on their failures, and attributed them primarily to lack of ability: mastery-oriented children made very few attributions, but instead engaged in solution-directed behavior to improve their performance. A first failure appeared to make the problem more interesting for the mastery-oriented children and spurred them on to search for new problem-solving strategies. Making attributions meant letting attention wander from the criterial task demands on which one must focus in such cognitive action. These findings are consistent with the distinction made between state orientation and action orientation (Kuhl, 1981), and with the task-irrelevant cognitions observed during an oral examination in subjects for whom a failure-oriented motivational state was dominant (Heckhausen, 1982).

Achievement Motives

Individual differences in attributions were also first uncovered in achievement motivation research using Crandall et al.'s (1965) IAR Scale. In correlation studies both Weiner and Kukla (1970) and Weiner and Potepan (1970) found that on the success-related items of the questionnaire, success-oriented subjects (with a resultant high achievement-motivation) checked off internal causal factors, primarily ability, more frequently than did the failure-oriented subjects. In a series of experimental studies, in particular those undertaken by Meyer (1973), after prior success or failure had been induced, subjects were asked to scale directly ability, effort, task difficulty, and good or bad luck (see also Halisch, 1983; Jopt & Ermshaus, 1977; Krug, 1972; Schmalt, 1976). Although the findings from these series are not always identical or unambiguous, they consistently show motive-linked attribution patterns that were apt to lower self-evaluation for subjects with a dominant failure-oriented motivation. This was especially true when the failure-oriented achievement-motive was rooted in a self-concept implying lack of ability rather than in fears of the social consequences of failure (Schmalt, 1976).

In spite of the more recent work in helplessness research, investigation of attribution patterns in achievement motivation research still leaves much to be done. Thus, the direct scaling of the four factors mentioned earlier, does not tell the investigator to what extent individual subjects have logically located one or another factor into the dimensional structure of internality or stability; furthermore, the dimension of globality is not represented. Nonetheless, the results obtained are sufficiently consistent to be summarized in terms of specific criteria, as done elsewhere (Heckhausen, 1980a). Accordingly:

In the case of success, the locus dimension is decisive. Success-motivated *Ss* attribute success primarily to internal factors, especially to high ability; failure-motivated *Ss* lay stress upon external factors, especially good luck, and sometimes low task difficulty. In the case of failure, the stability dimension is decisive. For success-motivated *Ss,* failure is attributable more to controllable or modifiable factors, particularly to lack of effort, sometimes to bad luck. Conversely, failure-motivated *Ss* tend to take their failure for granted and do not believe that this can be modified because they attribute failure to lack of own ability or in some cases to great task difficulty. Thus, while the success-motivated represent the image of the usual self-esteem enhancing attribution asymmetry, failure-motivated subjects tend toward an attribution pattern which does little to encourage them following the experience of success, which discourages them following failure and which thus has a self-esteem-reducing effect. (p. 524)

In light of these observations and findings, the achievement motive was conceived as a self-evaluation system (Heckhausen, 1975, 1978). On the basis of these different attribution patterns, information about otherwise identical achievement outcomes is processed into different self-evaluations and success expectancies. In this way, the attribution pattern of failure-motivated individuals, even after the experience of a series of successes, will hardly make them feel happier or more self-confident, whereas, even after repeated failures, success-motivated individuals will not give up hope. The instrumentality of the motive-linked attribution pattern for self-evaluation and success expectancy has become to the major point of attack for interventions intended to change the achievement motive from fear of failure into hope of success. A direct form of such intervention was applied by Dweck (1975) in the training program referred to earlier. Krug and Hanel (1976) trained a motive-arousing attribution pattern by means of model learning, self-observation, self-reports, and verbalizing thoughts. In postexperimental tests they were able to demonstrate motivational and attributional shifts in the direction, desired. The most successful procedures used to improve the achievement motive have aimed intervention at the three sensitive phases within the process of self-evaluation: more realistic goal setting, a motive-arousing attribution pattern, and the resultant positive self-evaluation (see Heckhausen & Krug, 1982).

Self-concept

The assumption seems justified that precisely those persons with low self-esteem or a self-concept of low ability will succumb to the self-esteem-enhancing asymmetry in their success and failure attributions. It appears, however, rather than increasing self-regard those individuals prefer to maintain their negative self-appraisal. Fitch (1970) found that to a greater (although not significant) degree than persons with high self-esteem, subjects with low self-esteem ascribed their failures to internal factors, particularly to lack of ability; they ascribed success to good luck rather than to ability. Hence, they allocate attributions along the stability dimension in such a way that success does not increase success expectancy to an extent inconsistent with self-esteem, and failure confirms failure expectancy consistent with self-esteem.

Ames (1978) found a similar effect with fifth-grade children. The children were randomly assigned first to outcome and then to reward structure (competitive and noncompetitive conditions). The children were tested in same-sex pairs, working simultaneously but independently on sets of achievement-related puzzles. Low self-concept children tended to ascribe their success less to high ability than did high self-concept children. This difference in ability attributions was particularly marked under competitive conditions. Until the fifth grade, the traditional instruction model (i.e., same amount of instruction time for all children in the grade) seems to have flooded each child with such an abundance of social comparison that a self-concept based on scholastic achievement appears to be inescapable.

Nicholls (1976) investigated the attribution patterns of the self-concept grounded in scholastic attainment. Again, the typical asymmetries of success and failure attribution were evident. Remarkable, however, was that children low in self-esteem did not attribute their success outcomes to high expenditure of effort, but rather to good luck and to teacher's assistance. It is not surprising, therefore, that even success does not give rise to satisfaction with oneself and that effort seems to be as ineffective with success as it is with failure. Nicholls (1979) found a general age trend of an increasing covariation between attribution and scholastic attainment for 6- to 12-year olds. Twelve-year-old children with high academic attainment ascribed their success to high ability and their failure to bad luck; on the other hand, poorer performers attributed their success to effort expended and good luck, and their failure to low ability.

Sex Differences

The attribution pattern a number of investigators have found for female subjects is rather discouraging. In comparison to boys, girls ascribed success less to high ability and failure less to low ability than to lack of effort or bad luck (Dweck & Repucci, 1973; Feather & Simon, 1975; Nicholls, 1975, 1978). Accordingly, the girls' self-evaluations were less positive, their effort expenditure and persistence dropped off, and performance deteriorated. This is consistent with the typical sex differences found for success expectancy when girls are confronted with new tasks. Crandall (1969), in an investigation of 7 to 12-year-olds, found that girls had lower success expectancies than boys; a study by Dweck and Gilliard (1975) is consistent with these findings. During a failure series, subjects were asked to report their expectancies of success, either after each trial or prior to the last trial only. Boys showed higher persistence when they had made their expectancy statements prior to the trial; conversely, girls were more persistent when they did not have to make expectancy statements. If one assumes that stating expectancies in the face of failure activates the personal attribution pattern, then the opposite findings for persistence in both sexes are easily accounted for.

According to Dweck and Bush (1976), at first, it may be surprising that girls are more inclined than boys, to adopt an attribution pattern that renders them helpless: As a rule teachers regard girls as more hardworking and capable of higher performance than boys (at least in the lower grades), girls receive more approval than boys. They have resolved this seeming paradox by analyzing teachers' feedback in class. For boys, feedback refers to motivational deficits, such as inattentive and disruptive behavior; for girls it refers almost exclusively to achievement deficits. Hence, in the classroom boys experience more attributions to motivation and girls more attributions to ability. Therefore, it is an unfortunate side effect of the more adapted behavior of girls that mediates a more unfavorable attribution pattern for failures in mixed classes.

Obviously, prejudice concerning sex-typical differences in ability also plays a part in generating differential attribution patterns. In a study entitled ''What's skill for the male is luck for the female,'' Deaux and Emswiller (1974), had observer subjects attribute to ability or good luck successful male and female performance on a visual discrimination task. Some of the objects to be discriminated were household articles belonging to the ''female'' work environment); others were tools (belonging to the ''male'' work environment). For both sexes, the observer subjects ascribed the causes of success in discriminating the ''female objects'' to ability. The equally successful discrimination of the ''male items'' was attributed to ability for the males and to good luck for the females. Similar sex-related attributional differences for equally successful performance have been reported when males and females judge their own performances (Deaux & Farris, 1977).

Summary

Taken together, the findings show a convergence, which is more remarkable in view of the fact that the investigations stem from divergent theoretical traditions comprise various tasks, differently manipulate success and failure, employ different causal factors, and use different techniques of assessment. In the final analysis, the only element these studies have in common is that they are concerned with mental tasks, the success or failure of which enables inferences of intellectual ability. In all investigations, some subgroups with specific personality traits tend to draw these inferences in a way that obscures the image of their own abilities, calls it into doubt, and does not enhance self-esteem. Personality characteristics linked with a negative attribution of ability cover a wide range of phenomena: external control; depression; helplessness; fear-of-failure motive; low self-concept, even being a female. The unfavorable effects of such an attribution pattern have been amply demonstrated. Obviously negative attribution is the determining mediator between success and failure on one hand and between self-evaluative affects, success expectancy, persistence, and other achievement outcomes on the other.

Within success and failure conditions favorable and unfavorable attribution patterns are opposite. However, between success and failure conditions these patterns are asymmetric. In the case of success, the opposition is primarily between internal and external locus; in the case of failure, opposition is between variable and stable causes. If one considers the findings, the data is revealing. For instance, given success, an unfavorable attribution pattern is shown if the individual does not make the obvious inference of high ability and attaches no importance to high effort expenditure. Instead, he or she judges external factors, such as good luck, support from others or (apparently less often) ease of task to be the causes. Hence, in this case the preferred causes are pervasively external and variable, rather than stable. Finally, they appear to be specific rather than global (although there are scarcely any investigations into this last dimension. Accordingly, success is something meted out to you, not something you can take the credit for.

A favorable attribution pattern ascribes success to one's own high ability. High effort (as in the case of unfavorable attribution patterns) is hardly ever perceived as a cause, probably because the inversely proportional compensation of effort and ability would diminish the role of the latter. Primarily, all those external causes, such as task ease, good luck or help from others, which might jeopardize an attribution of success to own ability, are regarded as irrelevant. In contrast to the unfavorable attribution pattern, the preferred causes are internal, and they are stable and, presumably, global rather than specific. The contrary nature of the two attribution patterns for success is centered on the question of whether or not success is ascribed to internal and, at the same time, stable causes, and to global rather than specific causes. The decisive causal dimension for success attribution is locus of control (internal versus external).

For failure, if the individual tends to make the obvious inference of lack of ability, the attribution pattern will be unfavorable; all other attributional alternatives that might weaken this inference are avoided. This applies especially to insufficient effort associated with ascriptions to internal factors; as well as to high level of task difficulty associated with external factors. The depressing and helplessness-inducing consequences are still increased by the global nature of the internal and stable causes of deficiency. A favorable attribution pattern attributes failure to a still insufficient expenditure of effort, particularly if the task is perceived as difficult. In that event, the inversely proportional compensation of effort and ability is brought into play so that failure does not elicit rash conclusions implying lack of ability. Instead of, or in addition to, lack of effort, variable causes, including external ones such as bad luck, are invoked. Variable causes are preferred; stable causes—lack of ability, as well as task difficulty—

are excluded. The preferred variable causes are more likely to be specific ones. Hence, the failure experience can be perceived as something that is not inevitable and that can be overcome in the future.

The contrast between the two attribution patterns for failure consists in the stability dimension; global, stable causes are set against specific, variable causes. In both the favorable and unfavorable attribution patterns, high task difficulty plays no differential role among the stable causes. The contrast is the sharpest within the dimension of internal locus of control: lack of ability versus lack of effort. In the first case, the prospects for success are negligible and increasing effort expenditure is hardly worthwhile; in any case, the pay-off will be low. In the second case everything remains open and there is no need to doubt one's own abilities; one could accomplish if one wanted to accomplish.

POSSIBLE TYPES OF ATTRIBUTION PATTERNS AND THEIR EMERGENCE

The summary given presents a somewhat idealized picture of the opposing attribution patterns for success and failure. The findings of a considerable number of investigations have not pinpointed the contrast expected with regard to all the relevant causes. Nonetheless, in order to infer, a maximally favorable or unfavorable image of one's own abilities, these findings have been assembled to overall patterns that employ all possible attributions for success or failure. The two opposite tendencies will henceforth be called "Positive Attribution Pattern" (PAP) and "Depressive Attribution Pattern" (DAP). Obviously, PAP and DAP will not in all cases incorporate all the elements and relations outlined earlier, nor will they always satisfy the requirements of a psychological logic.

In the case of PAP, failure is attributed either to insufficient effort or to bad luck, depending on the situational factors; insufficient effort seems the more likely inference for high task difficulty, and bad luck for moderate task difficulty. Nor will PAP and DAP always be applied only to situational demands. Both PAP and DAP may involve individual differences, that so far attribution research seems to have overlooked. Above all, both patterns may take different forms within a developmental progression before they assume the configuration outlined earlier. In what follows, the various forms taken by PAP and DAP are purely hypothetical constructions. The author's only interest is in the question of what hypothetically an individual should do in order to make own abilities (competence) appear either in a favorable or an unfavorable light. Concerning the various types of PAP and DAP analyzed, conjectures are made as to the stage of development or age at which these emerge and about possible antecedents of individual developmental differences.

Type 1: Task Difficulty and Ability as Multiple Sufficient Causes for Success and Failure

The simplest way to explain success and failure is by means of a causal schema with only one covariation dimension, that is, with a single external or internal causal factor: task difficulty or ability. Low task difficulty and high ability are facilitating factors; high task difficulty and low ability are, inhibitory factors. Covariation with task difficulty alone seems to have a developmental primacy (Heckhausen, 1982; 1983). Given successful outcomes, the task must have been easy, given unsuccessful outcomes, the task must have been difficult. Alternatively, the same covariation is applied to ability: given success, ability is high; given failure, ability is low. When ability is discussed here it should be kept in mind that in general ability cannot be conceived as a stable disposition prior to age ten. For younger children, the concept of ability is still coupled with momentary intensity of effort; therefore, for them, ability is an intraindividual variable dimension, derived primarily from the perceived degree of effort expended (see Heckhausen, 1983).

The two factors are mutually related—the more difficult the task, the more ability is needed for a successful outcome. Conceivably the simplest combination of two causal factors into one attribution pattern is the multiple sufficient causal schema (Kelley, 1972). The schema presents three logically equivalent combinations of causal factors that differ from each other in their psychological meaning. Thus, given success: (a) the two facilitating factors (low difficulty and high ability) need not coincide, but success attribution may be made; if only one facilitating factor is present, either (b) low difficulty associated with low ability, or (c) high ability associated with high level of difficulty. Conversely, given failure, even one inhibitory factor will suffice to explain the outcome. Again there are three conditions: (a) two of the inhibitory factors (high task difficulty, low ability), however, only one inhibitory factor need be present, either (b) high level of task difficulty, even though it is associated with high ability; or (c) low ability associated with low difficulty. Such a schema of *multiple sufficient causes for failure* is equivalent to a schema of *multiple necessary causes for success*. This means that the outcome will be success only if the task is easy (not too difficult) and ability is high.

The multiple sufficient causal schema is an ideal basis for PAP and DAP. Logically equivalent alternatives of explanation differ in their psychological meaning. Regardless of whether one intends to explain success or failure, the causal factors can be combined so that in all cases, either high ability (PAP) or low ability (DAP), is corroborated, or at least not called into question. Of the alternatives previously indicated, the preference for "high ability-high task difficulty" always connotes PAP, and the combination "low ability-low difficulty" connotes DAP. Figure 5.1 contains the particular causal combinations.

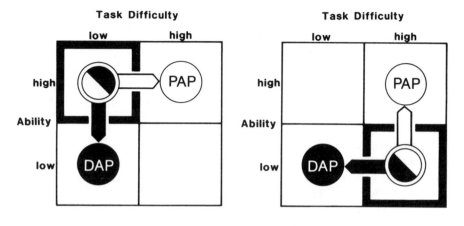

a) after success   b) after failure

FIG. 5.1.   Schema of multiple sufficient causes and preferred PAP and DAP combinations of ability and task-difficulty attributions. According to the schema of multiple sufficient causes a facilitating cause is sufficient for the occurrence of success (high ability or low task difficulty), and an inhibitory cause for the occurrence of failure (low ability or high task difficulty). See framed quadrants. A positive attribution pattern (PAP) is able to augment or at least to maintain a self-image of high-level ability. It first picks a self-serving cause—i.e., high ability after success, and high task difficulty after failure—and adds the other cause in a countereffective direction: high task difficulty in case of success (underlining or even augmenting high ability), and high ability in case of failure (high ability need not to be excluded when level of task difficulty was very high). A depressive attribution pattern (DAP) is able to maintain or even to further depreciate a self-image of low-level ability. It first picks a self-depreciative cause—i.e., low task difficulty after success, and low ability after failure—and adds the other cause in a countereffective direction: low ability in case of success (low ability need not be excluded when task difficulty is low) and low task difficulty in case of failure (underlining or even further discounting low ability).

Type 2: Direct Compensation of the one Causal Factor (internal or external) by the Complementary Causal Factor

Insofar as it is ability ascription that discounts the opposite effect of high task difficulty, two combinations within the multiple sufficient causal schema stand out. These combinations are PAP for success outcomes (high ability has mastered high level of difficulty) and DAP for failure outcomes (low ability was unable to master low difficulty). Furthermore, processes of augmentation or discounting of one's own ability may set in after having overestimated or underestimated the level of difficulty. The augmentation and discounting of one's own ability is rooted not only in the causal schema of multiple sufficient causes, but also in a causal schema that involves direct compensation of one causal factor (facilitating or inhibitory) by another causal factor (inhibitory or facilitating). Hence, the greater the master difficulty, the higher the ability; the lower the unmastered difficulty, the lower the ability. Accordingly, PAP should tend to overestimate task difficulty after success as well as after failure. For example, the more extreme the level of difficulty appears to be, the less failure will dampen the belief in one's own high ability. On the other hand, DAP should tend to underestimate task difficulty after success as well as after failure. For example, the lower the difficulty appears to be, the less success would alter the belief in one's own low ability (see Fig. 5.1).

The relief afforded by the PAP combination for failure, when the level of difficulty is very high has been demonstrated by a number of helplessness experiments, some of which have already been referred to (Frankel & Snyder, 1978; Klein et al., 1976; Snyder, Smoller, Strenta & Frankel, 1981; Tennen & Eller, 1977). In these studies, after the difficulty of the training task had been underscored, the test task elicited no helplessness effects. When difficulty is held to be high, even failure does not call one's own ability into question.

For this particular PAP combination, Frankel and Snyder (1978) and Snyder et al. (1981) introduced the term of "Egotism". They have confronted helplessness theory with egotism as an alternative explanation. "Egotism" brings to mind the "self-handicap" strategy (Berglas & Jones, 1978) discussed earlier. In a highly effective, although self-deceiving way, personal ability could eventually be augmented or discounted if after successful or unsuccessful outcomes, task difficulty is either overrated (PAP) or underrated (DAP). To overestimate task difficulty after the outcome makes success appear the more splendid, and failure can be more readily excused; to underrate task difficulty lessens the value of success and makes failure even more disheartening. No systematic investigations have yet been undertaken of augmenting and discounting ability attributions through over or underestimating task difficulty.

Emergence of Type 1 and Type 2 of PAP and DAP.   Shultz and Butkowsky (1977) found that children as young as 5 years of age mastered the schema of multiple sufficient causes, when in addition to the information about success or failure the cause given was either ability or difficulty (difficulty even in the form of consensus information: "Larry is solving a puzzle that four other children cannot solve"). Correspondingly, when success occurred, in spite of an inhibitory factor (hard task or lack of ability), most of the children inferred the other cause as facility (high competence, easy task). The findings of a study by Falbo (1975) with 5-year-old children of high and low IQ reveal attribution patterns of the first type in terms of PAP and DAP. Children of higher IQ preferred to explain failure in terms of task difficulty; whereas, children of low

IQ preferred low ability. The two IQ groups came from different family back-grounds: high-IQ subjects from middle-class homes; low-IQ subjects from fami-lies receiving welfare benefits. In explaining their success (in terms of PAP); the former used their (high) ability much more often, in explaining their failures (in terms of DAP), the latter used their (low) ability more often.

These findings suggest that as early as toward the end of preschool age one can expect to find not only cognitive prerequisites for the multiple sufficient causes schema, but also individual developmental differences in terms of PAP and DAP of the first type.

It seems that the prerequisites for the first appearance of the second type of DAP and PAP, that is the augmenting of ability after success at a difficult task and the discounting of ability after failure at an easy task, are hardly attained later than the prerequisites for the first type patterns. The causal schema of direct compensation underlying PAP and DAP of the second type seems to be derived from an integration of the schema of simple covariation (of a facilitory cause with an effect) and from the schema for multiple sufficient causes. Simple covariation of the facilitory causes of ability or effort with the outcome has been observed as early as by age 4 (see, overview in Heckhausen, 1983); and, as reported earlier children as young as 5 years of age were found to dispose of the multiple sufficient causes schema. Kun (1977) found direct compensation be-tween ability (or effort) and difficulty among 5-year-olds, although the compen-satory relationship was more evident in children in the higher grades (third and fifth grades), and initially was inferred more frequently after success than after failure. Similarly, Karniol and Ross (1976) found augmentation and discounting in motivation attributions of 4-year-olds (on first sight this cannot be equated with outcome attributions).

In light of the studies available, the assumption that there are substantial age lags in the acquisition of the developmental prerequisites for PAP and DAP of the first and second type does not seem justified. Individual differences may still emerge prior to school entry, at this age, the developmental primacy of difficult attributon is gradually disappearing. Experience of one's own competence is clearly evident and comprises an as yet diffuse concept of ability, still not independent from the effort concept. In the first few years of school attendance, both the ability and effort concepts are subject to the coupling schema ("halo schema" Kun, 1977; Surber, 1980; Tweer, 1976; overview, Heckhausen, 1983). Because only differences in degree of effort but not of ability, can be seen in oneself and in others, ability is derived from the perceived degrees of effort expended (and not the reverse, that is, effort from ability), until the inverse-compensatory causal schema for ability and effort is mastered. This means that children from 3–4 years to 7–9 years experience themselves as having higher ability (competence) in the performance of a task, the more effort they have exerted to accomplish it. As long as the focus is only on effort expenditure, this may protect the young child against the depressing effects of failure. Rholes,

Blackwell, Jordan and Walters (1980) in a repeated failure series, tried in vain to induce "helplessness" in children from 5 to 9 years. Neither the performance nor the persistence of the subjects deteriorated. The authors were able to induce helplessness in only 10 to 11-year-olds who had already overcome the coupling schema and had mastered the inverse-compensatory schema. The coupling schema was most clearly in evidence among the 5 to 6-year-olds. Even after repeated failure, this age group did not rate their ability as less high than a comparison group that had consistently experienced success.

Because the child infers his own ability from the amount of effort he has expended, one may conclude that the more opportunity to work on demanding tasks a preschool age child (about 3 to 6 years) has and the more the covariation between effort expenditure and outcome is a part of this experience, the more the child will perceive himself as competent. Accordingly, he will, after both success and failure, prefer PAP combinations of sufficient multiple causes, that is, high ability and high level of difficulty not only after success but also after failure. In contrast, DAP combinations will presumably be preferred by children who were either overtaxed or undertaxed by the demands made upon their competence in the preschool period. This is because, in either case, trying hard is a rather rare experience that offers little opportunity to infer high ability. When children's competence is undertaxed, task demands are met too quickly and too easily; when competence is overtaxed, children will stop trying too soon and cannot perceive a connection between degree of expended effort and attained outcome.

One must consider not only the beginning but also the phasing out of the critical developmental span for PAP and DAP of the first and second types. After a child enters school, cognitive developmental steps and new experiences increasingly undermine the emergence and maintenance of both attribution patterns. Cognitively, the coupling schema is replaced by the schema of an inverse compensatory relation between effort and ability. More effort, associated with the same outcome no longer leads to attribution of higher but rather to of lower ability. At the same time, the children are increasingly able to grade task difficulty, without respect to their own success or failure, on the basis of social comparison information (consensus) concerning the performance distribution within the class. This marks a change: a preconceived ability attribution made within the schema of multiple sufficient causes gives way to self-ratings based more firmly on reality, a development that takes place at age 9 to 10 (Nicholls, 1978).

This is not to imply that with the progression of development, DAP and PAP are ultimately undermined and finally discarded completely. Rather, it is more probable that, as a result of developmental progression, PAP and DAP are transformed into attribution patterns of a higher order, within which the essential characteristics that mark PAP and DAP are retained in forms commensurate with the attained level of development. The schema of inversely proportional compensation for effort and ability makes this possible (see Attribution Patterns: Type 4, later).

Origin of Individual Differences.   As mentioned, PAP will be fostered by developmental environments in which 3 to 6-year-olds find opportunities and incentives for coping with demanding tasks, to set goals for themselves that do not overtax or undertax their developing competencies, to learn to be independent, and to experience, through a variety of activities, the association between effort and outcome. DAP would be facilitated by the inverse conditions, especially by demands that overtax or undertax the developing levels of children's competencies and that block covariation of effort and persistence with action outcomes; therefore, the child will infer from the coupling schema, that his ability is low. To what extent the constellation of the developmental environment will tip the scales in favor of PAP or DAP will be determined substantially by parental (particularly maternal) child-rearing patterns. The differences in family background associated with PAP and DAP among 5-year-olds point, even if somewhat ambiguously, in this direction (Falbo, 1975).

More illuminating are the many studies of motive origin that concern the presumed influence of independence training on the formation of the achievement motive (see overview in Heckhausen, 1980a). If one holds success and failure motivation to be equivalent to PAP and DAP, then, in keeping with the findings on the influence of independence training, the following child rearing patterns should foster PAP: Expectations of independence and ability to achieve are commensurate to the child's attained level of development, are child centered, and do not overtax the child. Freedom and opportunities for probing one's developing competencies are available and are made accessible.

DAP will be facilitated by parents who do not particularly value their child's successful performance or who are not particularly sensitive to the developmental adequacy of their demands and consequently expect too much or too little from the child; freedom and opportunities for self-initiated development are heavily restricted or are not made acessible. When a child's competencies are overtaxed, repeated failure combined with negative parental reactions will produce a depressing image of one's own competence. Moreover, such children, when confronted with difficulties, will precipitately give up trying, so that covariation of effort and outcome cannot be experienced. The same deficiency will occur if the child is permanently undertaxed by the demands made on him. Even if the parents were constantly to praise the child for easily attained "successes," the effort-based inference of a high competence is denied the child. To be sure, the child is able to some degree to compensate for such parent-mediated deficits, provided freedom and opportunities for probing developing competencies are somehow accessible.

However, when children can themselves choose the levels of difficulty of their activities, under their parents' control or within the freedom and opportunities for development afforded outside the home, the question is: To what extent have they been encouraged or discouraged in a preferred level of difficulty that make demands on their attained competence (ability *and* effort, or persistence)? As shown in Fig. 5.1, the PAP combination comprises high levels of difficulty whereas the DAP combination entails low levels of difficulty. The child's preference for either of these attribution patterns may simply be due to a difference in the parental reaction pattern to success and failure. The decisive point is whether parental reactions are determined only by the outcome itself (success or failure) or whether consideration is also given to level of task difficulty that has been overcome and hence also to effort expended.

A reaction pattern that fosters preference of high levels of difficulty (PAP) does not tally with simple reinforcement theory, always praises success and makes light of failure. Rather, success should be praised only when the child has had to try hard and has mastered a difficult task; failure should be criticized only if the child has given up too soon, that is, has failed at a task that was no longer too difficult. Such a reaction pattern enables the child to experience that action outcomes are primarily competence-related, and that success and failure are attributable less to task difficulty than to one's own endeavors. The child will prefer more demanding tasks, not only because he or she has learned that only for difficult tasks will success be evaluated positively and failure not be negatively assessed, but because accomplishing a more demanding task offers a stronger sense of one's own competence. According to the schema of multiple sufficient causes, this becomes more apparent because success at a more demanding task is in all cases attributable to high competence, but failure is not necessarily attributable to lack of competence. This gives precisely the PAP combination shown in Fig. 5.1: high task difficulty and high ability.

Conversely, DAP would be facilitated if the parents reinforced their child only according to task outcome, not taking into account the level of task difficulty the child has overcome (a practice indicative of the parents' lack of sensitivity for their child's level of development). In this case, the parental reactions do not covary with the effort expenditure indicative of competence, but rather with the level of difficulty experienced. Easy tasks will bring success and ensure praise, even if the child has made no effort and consequently has not experienced a sense of personal competence. On the other hand, difficult tasks regardless of how hard the child has tried, elicit expectations of failure and blame. That is why that child prefers easily mastered tasks. Failure is always attributable to lack of competence, but success is not necessarily attributable to attained competence. This is the DAP combination: low difficulty and low ability.

The conclusion to be drawn from the diverging difficulty preferences of the children and the reinforcement patterns practiced by their parents is that DAP children not only encounter more success, but also manage to get disproportionately more praise from their parents than do PAP children. This inflation of praise for too easily attained successes neither is associated with the experience of competence based in real effort, nor does it allow this kind of inference.

Conclusions Concerning the Formation of Aspiration Level. When preschoolers in task choice studies were asked to choose between visually represented degrees of difficulty of a task they had already practiced, they preferred to resume on the difficulty level already mastered. However, when it was not a matter of choice between tasks but rather of setting a goal along a uniform continuum of achievement, the children preferred goals that went beyond what had already been attained. This contradiction between the two experimental paradigms of level-of-aspiration setting can easily be resolved if one considers that in each case a different type of covariance information is offered; information that makes salient the causal factor either of difficulty or of ability. (Heckhausen, 1982). In the case of task choice, distinctiveness information was provided (Kelley, 1967) along with its level of difficulty (what can be solved and what cannot); in the case of goal setting consistency information was provided along with its level of ability (what one has done and what one has not yet been able to do). A study repeated a few months later showed that the initial relatedness between each of the experimental paradigms and one of the two dimensions of covariance had become less close. In task choice, more children than previously preferred unsolved tasks, and in goal setting fewer children chose an unrealistic level of aspiration (Heckhausen, 1980b).

The two contrasting developmental transitions should be associated with PAP and DAP. In task choice, PAP children should show preference for unsolved tasks earlier than DAP children because by exerting effort they have learned to overcome difficult tasks and are more confident of their ability than are DAP children. For goal setting, however, the reverse should apply: PAP children should tend less, or later, than DAP children to lower the initially attempted high level of task difficulty to the attained level or below it. Both conclusions remain to be confirmed by experimental investigations:

Type 3: Discounting Success and Augmenting Failure by Attribution to External, Task-Irrelevant Causes

Success at very difficult tasks and failure in very easy tasks are unexpected events. They contradict one's idea of what one can do (the assessed relation of one's own ability to task difficulty). After unexpected success, the emergent cognitive dissonance can be reduced either by augmenting one's own ability or by discounting task difficulty. Correspondingly, after unexpected failure, one can either augment task difficulty or discount one's own ability. Whether one is able to resist the temptation offered by the first alternative, to increase self-esteem, or accepts the sobering realization of the second alternative, one will be acting in conformity with the two attribution patterns already discussed—PAP and DAP, Type 2.

To attain dissonance reduction in this way may, however, seem too irrational to be feasible. This will be the case particularly when consistency information has been given that makes the unexpected event appear to be an exception. The apparently inexplicable residue of other causes is then explained by attribution to chance or to good or bad luck. Thus, it has been shown that the more a successful outcome contrasts with previous outcomes the more success is attributed to luck (Meyer & Plöger, 1979). On the contrary depending on the circumstances, other variable causes for which one cannot be held responsible may be inferred, especially psychophysiological states (such as fatigue) and support by or hindrance from others.

Accordingly, PAP and DAP strategies can be juxtaposed as follows. After unexpected success, PAP rather than DAP will tempt actors to augment their own ability—they will draw less on luck or on the help of others to explain the event. When PAP is dominant, unexpected failure is played down by drawing on bad luck, on being in bad form, or on hindrance by others, so that one will not have to discount one's own ability. As a precautionary step, again in conformity with PAP, self-handicaps may be arranged to facilitate augmenting success and discounting failure following the achievement outcome (Berglas & Jones, 1978).

First Appearance and Development of Individual Differences.   There are as yet no studies concerned with the development of attribution factors of "good luck" or "bad luck" or support or hindrance from others. One of the cognitive prerequisites for attributions of good luck or bad luck elicited by an unexpected outcome is the ability of the child to form expectancies in which the preceding feedback has been sufficiently integrated. To do this, the child must be capable not only of sorting consistency information, but also of conceptualizing ability and difficulty as stable factors. Before the first years of grade school, the concept of ability is not clearly separated from fluctuating effort, expectancies until then remain elastic (see Heckhausen, 1982). Only from about the age of 8 to 9 years (for girls generally somewhat earlier) does prior success and failure systematically affect success predictions for boys (Crandall, 1969; McMahan, 1973; Parsons & Ruble, 1977).

The formation of Type 3 attribution patterns, at least with respect to employing good luck or bad luck attributions in terms of PAP or DAP, can not be expected to start before the age of 8 to 9. The developmental factors that produce individual differences in the use of good luck or bad luck attribution are not yet known. But we may assume that once exceptional achievement outcomes have been experienced as an unexpected event or as an event that needs to be explained (because it is inconsistent with their stable concept of ability), and once they are able to employ the concept of chance, children elaborate their so far developed PAP and DAP strategies (Type 1 and Type 2) by employing luck and bad luck attributions.

The situation is different for the factors of social support or hindrance. From babyhood onward children have assimilated many-sided experiences in relation to both these factors. Thus, the refusal of offered support is observable already in the "wanting-to-do-it-oneself" attitude that emerges in the second year of life (see Heckhausen, 1983). DAP is facilitated not only when (as is the case for attribution pattern Type 1) children's independence is not respected but also when support is needlessly obstructed simply because the parents—or later the teacher—is not willing to acknowledge the child's incomplete or imperfect achievement outcomes. Findings from a study by Nicholls (1976) are indicative of the teachers' influence in this respect. As reported earlier, 11-year-old students with a low self-concept in terms of scholastic attainment, attributed their success in the classroom to luck and to support from their teacher.

Type 4: Compensatory Causal Schemata for Ability and Effort

In Type 1 and Type 3 attribution patterns the allocation of causes is arranged among internal and external factors. However, for attribution pattern Type 4, allocation of causes is based on the facilitative internal causes of ability and effort. Within the causal schema of graded effects (Kelley, 1972, 1973) attained outcomes are a direct function of both factors. On the other hand, the same outcomes can result from entirely different inverse proportions of ability and effort. Lower ability can be compensated by greater effort, less effort by higher ability (effort compensation and ability compensation, respectively).

Again, the possible proportions of the two causal factors are also logically equivalent in the Type 4 attribution pattern. They are not equivalents in psychological terms; ability attributions generate more subsequent affect (self-evaluation), create more actionguiding cognitions (success expectancies), and lead to more subsequent activities (persistence, effort, expenditure, task-choice, seeking feedback, etc.). Although in evaluation by others, the attribution of responsibility and the reinforcement given depend on the attribution to effort, this does not hold for self-evaluation. Here, ability attribution generates more affect and has greater impact on action.

After success and failure, in order to make own ability appear greater, the PAP strategy is to minimize the effect ascribed to effort. An extreme DAP strategy would consist in the reverse procedure. In order to make one's own ability appear the lower, the effect ascribed to effort will be maximized. Because the two factors can largely compensate for each other only after success, after failure, the compensation schema is combined with the schema of multiple necessary causes. To avoid failure, a certain minimum of either effort or ability would have been required, even if the other factor was maximally strong. Within this combination of schemata, failure is regarded as a less frequent, more extreme event, as a rule, then, multiple necessary causes, rather than multiple sufficient causes, may be assumed.

To what event an inverse relationship (i.e., compensation between ability and effort) actually is employed will depend on the perceived level of task difficulty. Success at a very difficult task and failure at a very easy task are infrequent (unexpected) events. In both cases the respective presence or absence of internal factors appears to be a multiple necessary schema, rather than one for which only one of the two factors could provide a sufficient explanation.

Accordingly, to deal with such extreme effects, the scope for inverse-compensatory arrangements is also narrowed down. This curtailment facilitates the PAP and DAP strategy in explaining failure: Too little effort has been expended to render one's own high ability perceivable (PAP); when own ability is so low, even great effort makes no difference (DAP). The opportunities for compensation have the widest scope in the broad field of intermediate difficulty. If one is successful at tasks of intermediate difficulty, lack of effort makes own ability appear more decisive as the causal factor; failure still does not cast doubt on one's own ability.

First Appearance.   A basic prerequisite for Type 4 attribution patterns is mastery of the compensatory causal schema for effort and ability. To test this assumption, an effect and one of the two internal factors were given, and the other factor was to be inferred (Kun, 1977; Surber, 1980). In a paired comparison of two actors with the same outcome, but with differential weighting of the given factor, the subject was to determine the actor for which the factor to be inferred was stronger (Surber, 1980; Tweer, 1976; see overview in Heckhausen, 1983). Compensation for a given degree of ability by effort to be inferred (effort compensation) precedes the development of compensation for a given degree of effort by ability that is to be inferred (ability compensation). Depending on the kind of task and on memory load of how the information was presented, effort compensation was used by some children as young as 5 years of age and by others as old as 10. The majority of the children simply equated the degree of effort with level of outcome (centered covariation). Ability compensation appeared with an age lag of about one year between the ages of 6 to 11, after which the majority of the respective age group no longer simply inferred degree of ability from degree of effort expenditure nor equated the two (coupling or "halo" schema).

The earlier appearance of effort compensation is easy to understand. One takes into account that children can experience effort, which, in contrast to ability, is subject to volitional control—a factor that varies for each individual. Children learn early that some initially nonattained goals can be reached by the expenditure of additional effort (persistence). Later ability compensation appears, the question arises whether PAP and DAP Type 4 presuppose only effort compensation. This question makes explicit the difference between the presentation of a task within an experimental setting and self-attribution in an everyday context. In the latter case, neither effort nor ability is given as a known factor, but both must be inferred and varied in opposite directions. We may assume that not only ability compensation but even a higher order ability—for reversible operations—is required; this is not the case for experimental tests that provide the memory aids of fixed levels of outcome and one known factor. Consequently, the inverse compensatory relation between ability and effort seems to be mastered later than experimental studies have indicated—probably not earlier than around the age of 10.

Use of the inverse compensatory relation between ability and effort is but one of the cognitive prerequisites for the appearance of Type 4 PAP and DAP. Also essential for their appearance is that a clear differentiation be made between the concept of ability and the concept of effort and that ability as a personal characteristic be conceived of as a stable trait. As long as the concept of ability is only a stable trait, not an individual attribute of the self-concept, the ability concept is a requirement only for the mastery of the compensatory causal schema in dealing with both ability and effort (which itself is a cognitive prerequisite for Type 4 attribution patterns). Very few studies have been undertaken to tell from what age onward ability is not only conceptualized as a stable factor but also perceived as a self-concept of the level of one's ability. In cross-sectional studies, Nicholls (1975) investigated accurate perception of children's own reading attainment relative to all others in the class. Only from the age of 9 to 10 did the children also assign to themselves the lower ranks in the distribution of reading performance, and only between the age of 10 to 13 years did perception of their own attainment correlate significantly with teacher ratings.

Like the first developmental prerequisite for Type 4 attribution patterns (mastery of the compensatory schema), the second prerequisite (stable concept of ability and individual self-concept of ability) indicates that only after the age of 9 to 10 will the first individual differences in terms of PAP and DAP Type 4 emerge.

The elementary school classroom, where children are constantly exposed to social comparisons with their peers, appears to be the best training ground for acquisition of these two cognitive prerequisites. In another study, Nicholls (1979) examined age differences in relationship of attainment and perception of their own attainment with attributions by having children consider occasions when they performed well or poorly in reading. His subjects were 2nd, 4th, 6th, and 8th graders. The self-ratings of the 8–12 year-olds correlated increasingly with the teacher ratings of attainment. The emergence of individual differences in self-perceived attainment seem to appear first in this age group. Only the 12-year-olds' (but not among the 10-year-olds) self-concepts of reading ability were correlated with attribution patterns in terms of PAP and DAP Type 4. Nicholl's findings confirm the assumption that individual differences in Type 4 attribution patterns develop only after the age of 10.

Finally, there is yet a third developmental prerequisite: Self-attribution of ability must begin to generate relatively more affect than effort attribution. In other words, a self-concept of high ability becomes the guiding principle for the formation of PAP, a selfconcept of low ability, for DAP. In the first case, positive self-evaluation results; the self-evaluation engendered in the second case is by now a depressing one, unlike the earlier years, when low ability still produced a positive self-evaluation, because on the basis of the coupling schema, high effort still made it possible to infer high ability. In a study with 10- to 13-year-old students that examined the influence that of self-evaluation on causal attribution, only for failure-motivated subjects did effort attribution still generate more affect than ability attribution, an attributional affect characteristic for evaluation by others (Heckhausen, 1978).

Considering all three cognitive prerequisites discussed we can say that Type 4 attribution patterns may be expected to emerge at the age of 11 to 12 years. It is worth mentioning that in her helplessness studies Dweck chose her subjects from this age group.

Origin of Individual Differences.   One determinant for the development of Type 4 PAP and DAP is the traditional way school instruction is organized: a setting in which same-age classmates are constantly confronted by social comparison of achievement. Because the teachers' rating of their students in their everyday interaction with them is oriented primarily toward a social (and not an individual) reference norm (e.g., Rheinberg, 1980), good students almost exclusively experience success, bad students failure. Consequently, for high achievers success becomes an event that can only be explained by a *stable*-internal cause (ability) and not by a variable-internal cause (effort). This history of outcomes and their causal attribution prepares the ground for PAP. The situation is reversed for low academic achievers. For them it is failure that is the habitual and recurrent event to be explained only by a stable cause—lack of ability. Their rare successes must stem from a variable cause—great effort, if not good luck. The study (Nicholls, 1979) reported earlier underscores this influence of school instruction on the genesis of individual differences. The differential pattern of teacher feedback that boys and girls typically receive seems to make girls more susceptible to DAP, discussed earlier (e.g., Dweck & Bush, 1976).

To be sure, it would be overestimating the influence of school, if in addition to showing differences in ability, schoolchildren did not earlier, in the preschool period, differ from each other in attribution patterns of a simpler type. Thus, PAP Types 1, 2 and 3 predipose children to a positive self-perception and achievement behavior by the time they start school and thus favor positive academic attainments. DAP Types 1, 2, and 3 mark out a more negative development. Thus, with cognitive development, the more simple attribution patterns are transformed into more complex ones—a process in the course of which earlier attribution patterns are supplemented by those assimilated later. Within this process the weight given to the causal dimension shifts from internal versus external causal attribution to stable versus variable attribution. The details of this process and how it operates are not yet known. Longitudinal studies are needed.

Type 5 PAP and DAP: Specific versus Global Ability

As reported earlier, Abramson et al. (1978) maintain that the dimension of globality plays a crucial role for the transfer of induced helplessness to other task activities. The more that failure on a specific task is attributed to lack of global ability (e.g., to "lack of intelligence"), the sooner the individual concerned will give up. Peterson and Seligman (this volume) have highlighted the impact of the globality dimension (besides internality and stability) for depression and its aggravation following a midterm examination.

   If after success and failure the causal factor of ability is placed at the opposite endpoints of the globality dimension, a fifth and final type of attribution pattern can be distinguished. In the case of PAP, given that success is ascribed to a global (general) ability, and failure, possibly, to a highly specific lack of ability, this fifth type of attribution pattern serves to maintain a self-concept of high ability. For DAP, the "insidious attribution style," the situation is reversed: success is ascribed to a highly specific partial competence; failure, to global lack of ability. Unfortunately it is not yet known to what extent and under what conditions attribution patterns of Type 5 appear as isolated, specific attributions. Recent research efforts on helplessness start only from the total strategies of "attributional styles." The patterns "internal, stable, global" and "external, variable, specific" alternatively for good and bad events, are placed in opposition to each other. These attribution patterns also circumscribe the four Types of PAP and DAP already examined, namely, Types 1, 2, and 3 in which internal and external causes are played off against one another within the locus dimension, and Type 4, in which the inversely related proportions of the internal causal factors are reallocated along the continuum of the stability dimension.

   We are still in the dark about three questions: First, we still know nothing about the frequency of use of the total strategy (i.e., comprising all five substrategies), nor do we know anything about the possible combinations between the five attribution patterns, which might be provided by samples from age groups past the age of 10 or by subjects chosen by other sampling criteria. If the episodes to be evaluated were tailored to fit the purpose, the closed- and open-ended questionnaire format developed by Seligman et al. (1979) might yield data on the basis of which it would be possible to construct an empirically well-founded typology of attribution patterns and of their frequency. The findings published so far only report mean scores of, and intercorrelations between, single causality dimensions (e.g., Peterson & Seligman, this volume). They do not bring us any closer to answering this question.

Second, if all the cognitive prerequisites are given, it can be assumed that as more personality characteristics deviate toward psychopathological states—from slight depressive symptoms to severe depression—a growing number of the five different types of DAP will come to be combined into the total strategy, which employs each of the logically inferrable attributions within a specific self-esteemreducing pattern. Possibly there are diagnostic patterns for differentiating between particular personality traits (e.g., for type and degree of failure-oriented achievement motives) or for the degree of risk when certain bad events occur.

There is much to be said for such a differential diagnostic approach. Each type of attribution pattern focuses mainly on one of the three causal dimensions, and each of the three dimensions generates specific effects. The dimension of locus is decisive for self-evaluation; stability, for success expectancy and therefore, for persistency of actions; and the globality dimension determines the extent to which experiences of success or failure are transferred to other tasks and domains of activity. For the last point, Peterson and Seligman (this volume) have provided interesting evidence. As indicated by lower performance scores, "global" subjects, not "specific" subjects, tended to show deficits on both the similar and dissimilar test tasks.

Finally, the attribution patterns examined were ordered in their developmental sequence. The first two types appear as early as in the preschool age; Type 3, at elementary school age; and Type 4, after elementary school age. At what age Type 5 first appears is an open question, as is the developmental sequence of the decisive causal dimensions. Within attribution patterns Type 1 and 2, the possibility of direct compensation is employed for stable factors along the locus dimension. To enable subsequent explanations of unexpected outcomes, Type 3 adds external-variable causal factors. Type 4 shifts attributions to the stability dimension of internal factors and their inverse compensatory relation. When and how globality is brought into play as an additional causal dimension and how it relates to the other two dimensions are as yet not known; nor has any research been done to answer these questions. It may be that globality combines with stability rather than with the locus dimension. Stable causal factors tend to be global, and variable factors tend to be specific, regardless of whether they may be internal or external.

This is supported by evidence (Peterson & Seligman, this volume, Table 4) concerning the intercorrelations between the three dimensions for children in 3rd through 6th grades. For bad events, globality correlated with stability, but not with locus (internality). Accordingly, the global causes attributed to bad events could be both internal (e.g., low intelligence) and external (e.g., all task demands were too high), but only the first of these alternatives could be subsumed under DAP, Types 1 and 2. For good events, globality correlated with internality, which could be in accord with PAP. To show more accurately how the patterns underlying these attributional tendencies are related to each other, the causal factors but not the causality dimensions ranked in a double classification (according to stability and internality) would have to be correlated with globality versus specificity. Moreover, the correlations reported are rather low. This was to be expected because they relate to a sample in which subgroups representing PAP and DAP attributional tendencies (whose magnitude is as yet unknown) may be mixed to an unknown degree. It would be of great import to determine the causal factor of ability in terms of the degree of its globality.

First Appearance and Development of Individual Differences. Nothing is known about the emergence and development of the globality dimension or about how it is used for causal attributions. One can only speculate about whether the emergent concept of ability will, in the course of development, be attributed more to global or to specific causal factors, or whether it will be differentiated into global-specific levels of an hierarchical order. Most likely, the latter is the case. Such differentiation at least would furnish optimal cognitive prerequisites for PAP and DAP Type 5 combinations of attribution patterns.

Similarly, the development of individual differences in terms of PAP and DAP Type 5 remains a puzzle. As mentioned earlier, Peterson and Seligman found that depressive children in 3rd through 6th grades were apt to be found in families in which the mother (but not the father) was also depressed and that DAP for bad events (internal, stable, global) correlated for mothers and their children. Unfortunately, no separate correlations for the dimension of globality were reported. At what developmental stage in the first ten years of her child's life a mother becomes "depressive," or "depressogenous," (i.e., she fosters DAP in her child) and how she does this, are questions to be answered by future research. However, the influence of school, especially elementary school, should also be taken into account. It is very likely that experience at school leads poor students to believe that their lack of ability, and the level of difficulty of the demands learning makes on them, are attributable to global rather than to specific factors.

CONCLUDING REMARKS

I have demarcated five different attribution patterns, each of which, after success or failure, enables favorable (PAP) or unfavorable (DAP) inferences about one's own ability. Each of the five types of attribution patterns specified makes different demands on cognitive development. The age at which these attribution patterns appear for the first time varies and extends over a long period, ranging from the preschool period into the second decade. By specifying the "critical" age periods for the appearance of each type of attribution pattern, assumptions could be made about the developmental factors that foster the emergence of individual differences in terms of PAP and DAP. However, it is still open to question at what age, based on the concept of global competence, PAP and DAP Type 5 first appears, and when individual differences emerge.

The taxonomy of attribution patterns presented here has been elaborated from a functional perspective. That is: After success or failure, in what different ways can the image of own ability be seen in a favorable or an unfavorable light? This taxonomy need not be used only for descriptive classification. We have attempted to enanchor the particular types of attribution patterns in their developmental progression. Because differential relations between these types and certain personality variables may be expected, the taxonomy can become a useful instrument for empirical research. This is true is for the emergence of the particular attribution patterns, the combinations between different types in their developmental progression, the differential effects generated by them.

The analysis raised a number of questions that require further clarification. The first question relates to the developmental sequence of the patterns of PAP and DAP. In other words, does acquisition of PAP and DAP Type 1 predetermine the successive order in which subsequent attribution patterns are acquired? That is, will acquisition of Type 1 PAP and DAP lead to the acquisition of the later types, so that PAP and DAP become progressively more radical? Or alternatively, will the progression of these attribution patterns produce various contellations of their elements, so that total strategies that verge on the psychopathological (at least in the case of DAP) will be developed only in exceptional cases in the second decade? On the other hand, is the answer perhaps that individuals do not, in fact, acquire any sharply defined attribution patterns but, instead, only come to develop a strong or weak tendency toward either PAP or DAP, a tendency which in given situations leads them to make use of that type of the five attributions patterns specified (or of combinations between them) which seems the most appropriate?

These questions can be answered only by longitudinal studies combined with experimental variations of conditions. Such variations should not be confined only to success and failure. It would in addition be possible to reduce the attribution scope for particular causal factors. For such a purpose, the three covariation dimensions of Kelley's (1967) cube would be a suitable instrument. Entity information can narrow the causal factors down to globality or specificity; consensus information (which will be integrated only by older children; [e.g. Heckhausen, 1982]), can reduce task difficulty only to high or low degree; consistency information can imply only high or low ability or luck. This method, if developed, would show whether or not I will have to rethink my admittedly, rash tendency to consider the particular types of attribution patterns, once they have developed, as personality-specific characteristics. Instead, more credit given to situation-specific effects.

There is an additional important issue; namely, the different consequences of each type of attribution pattern. These consequences have been examined primarily in terms of self-evaluation, a self-serving versus a self-derogative bias in looking at one's competence. No doubt, in view of its behavioral effects, this is a central aspect but depending on the causality dimension in which they are based, the various types of attribution patterns, also generate specific effects. The more weight is given to internal causes, the greater the affect on self-esteem; the more weight is given to stable causes, the more constant the ensuing success expectancy and the longer will action tendencies (or nonaction tendencies) determined by it persist. Finally, the more weight given to global causes, the more their effects will be generalized across various subsequent task demands and task situations.

Concerning the various attribution patterns, the following points should be considered. The two types of PAP and DAP that emerge earliest set ability and effort within a preconceived relationship of direct compensation. The decisive dimension for this is locus of control its effects self-evaluation in terms of PAP or DAP. As both these causal factors are stable, success expectancy is also determined and stablized. In the case of PAP, success expectancy is positive, increasing the intensity and persistence of efforts; in the case of DAP, it is negative, lowering effort and persistence. PAP and DAP Type 3 make it possible to play down unexpected or undesired outcomes by attributions to luck, so that self-evaluation and success expectancy need not be modified. PAP and DAP Type 4 play their inverse-compensatory arrangements between stable ability and variable effort. As a result if high ability is inferred after success and low effort is inferred after failure (PAP), success expectations can be increased or maintained. On the other hand, if high expenditure of effort is the inference made following success and low ability the inference made following failure (DAP) expectations can be retained unmodified or be reduced. These are both internal factors; although ability generates more affects than does effort, Type 4 also serves to immunize ability-related self-esteem against negative feedback. Finally, PAP and DAP Type 5 will produce either a wider generalization of attributions to other situations and task demands or will limit such generalization. This will have an equal effect on behavior influenced by self-esteem and by success expectancy (as well as on expectancy-related action parameters, such as persistence).

Making the variety of effects of attribution patterns explicit may ultimately make its payoff in the design of individualized intervention programs for motive change (e.g., Krug & Heckhausen, 1982).

The types of effects outlined make it clear that in this context the consequences of self-evaluation are crucial, and that these consequences are the unifying thread winding its way through all types of attribution patterns and their motivating effects. However, it is also conceivable that, at least in some cases, in order to manipulate one's own expenditure of effort and persistence, especially within attribution patterns Type 3 and 4, the prime factor is a volitional arrangement of success expectancies. A certain degree of self-manipulated success expectancy, rather than self-evaluation, may play a central role in attribution biasis, this is because a given activity may be motivated by incentives of the anticipated other consequences, such as evaluation by other persons, extrinsic side effects, or superordinate goals (Heckhausen, 1977).

Finally, this discussion of the possible determinants of attribution patterns returns to the question asked at the beginning: Why do a good many people seem intent on preserving the depressive image they have of self and own abilities and do not opt for more sanguine expectations, even when good opportunities are offered? In my examination of the various types of attribution patterns, I made the assumption that DAP drifts into self-derogative frames of mind with much the same bias and lack of realism that PAP does. Perhaps I have become a victim of the aesthetics of symmetric constructions. Possibly, as Alloy and Abramson (1979) have put it, in reality, DAP people are "sadder but wiser"; and possibly, in spite of a proneness for DAP, more than PAP people, who keep so cheerful and successful by looking at the world through rose-coloured glasses, they still retain a capacity for self-criticism and for realism. This again is a question that future research will have to clarify.

POSTSCRIPT

Since writing this, Kratz (1985), in her doctoral dissertation, examined early positive and depressive attribution patterns. She compared first-graders (median 6:11) with third-graders (median 9:1) because it had proved difficult to isolate consistent attribution patterns in preschoolers.

After they had first received success and later failure feedback on the task (identifying missing parts of pictures), the children were first asked to give free attributional causes for these respective outcomes. In neither case did they experience any difficulty in coming up with plausible causes. The 7-year-olds explained success predominantly with internal causes, and failure with internal as well as external causes. The 9-year-olds demonstrated the self-serving attribution asymmetry well known among adults. They predominantly attributed success to high level of ability and failure to high task difficulty. However, in a forced-choice situation, forcing a decision between attribution to difficulty vs. ability, task difficulty was the preferred cause for both success and failure.

An attempt was then made to seek out individual differences related to PAP and DAP. After the children had stated what they thought was the main cause for the outcome, they were asked about the importance of the factor they had not named. After two success trials and two failure trials most of the children in both age groups responded in terms of a multiple necessary causal scheme, i.e. the second factor also contributed to the respective outcome, be it success or failure.

We refer to this as the "normal attribution pattern" (NAP). The remaining children were labeled DAP or PAP children, if they displayed the respective response pattern on at least two of the four trials, and their responses in the remaining trials related to multiple necessary causes. Whereas among the 7-year-olds only 24% were PAP children and only 12% were DAP children, the ratio for the 9-year-olds was reversed, 34% DAP vs. 17% PAP children. This suggests that the school experience had brought about a developmental change in favor of a depressive attribution pattern.

With the aid of further correlates, involving a different task (Matching Familiar Figures, Kagan et al., 1964), it was also possible to establish the characteristics of both subgroups' attribution patterns apart from NAP. In order to first insure that children were able to understand normatively defined differences in task difficulty, they were shown a row of the same digit, representing the age of children one year older, and some of these digits were crossed out to indicate that these children had failed the task. The success vs. failure ratio of this reference group could thus be varied. All 7-year-olds already possessed this capacity. If the children were presented with normatively defined, differing levels of difficulty, PAP children believed that they could solve more difficult problems than DAP children, with NAP children falling in between. In other words, PAP children had a self-concept of higher competence than DAP children. There was a corresponding difference between the two groups in their confidence of success on a task that they had been told was of intermediate difficulty for children who were one year older. PAP children believed that they could solve problems at this demanding difficulty level. But that was not true for the DAP children. They already anticipated failure and capitulated when they were told that 70% of the one-year-older reference group had succeeded on the task.

Kratz also obtained scales for the three causes (a) difficulty, (b) ability, and (c) effort. The children were asked to mark one of five levels represented as circles with increasing radii. Among the 7-year-olds there was no significant difference between the PAP and DAP children (an indication of the expected differences appeared only in the ability scaling). In contrast, among the 9-year-olds, the PAP children assessed their ability after success higher than the DAP children (again the NAP children fell in between).

Noteworthy is the stability of the DAP children's self-concept of low ability in both age groups (*self-concept of ability* being defined as confidence to succeed at a task of normatively defined difficulty, as described previously). Whereas PAP and NAP children assessed their ability as higher after success than after failure, the DAP children scaled their ability no higher after success than after failure. This high stability of the ability concept was clearly not due to a more advanced developmental stage of the DAP children's causal schemata of ability or effort compensation. This was established with a physical effort task in which nearly all the children were not yet able to comprehend that insufficient effort would be compensated by a higher ability (ability compensation) and lower ability by greater effort (effort compensation). This forces one to conclude that a self-depreciating attribution pattern is present prior to the development of a mature ability concept—for example, that lack of ability can be compensated by increased effort. However, even the PAP children were not arrogant in the assessment of their ability. They did not believe that they could solve a task at which 70% of the one-year-older reference group had supposedly failed.

Moreover, it was not possible to attribute either the self-concept of lack of ability or DAP to a lower stage of cognitive development. A test battery for assessing level of cognitive operations in the Piagetian sense, did not differentiate between DAP and PAP children.

Finally, an attempt was made to determine whether these children use the Type 2 of PAP and DAP, i.e., whether they augment (PAP) or discount (DAP) the difficulty of a task after success or failure, respectively. For this purpose, children were asked to assess the difficulties of various tasks in the context of normative cues (contrasting representations of two groups of children who were or were not able to solve the particular version of a task). Subsequently, the experimenter suggested that the child work on the intermediate difficulty task. Each child experienced a success and a failure series. After each series the child was asked to indicate the difficulty of the tasks for 10 same-aged children by indicating the proportion of children who passed and failed on the task. (They were given a set of cards each showing the same face on both sides. One of the faces was crossed out to indicate failure.) Although the children's judgment of the reference group's lesser or greater difficulty depended on their own experience of success and failure, respectively, there was no general augmenting or discounting the difficulty in line with PAP and DAP of Type 2. However, experimental short-comings cannot be ruled out completely.

Overall, it can be stated that individual differences in attribution patterns of the first type of PAP and DAP were already found among early grade-schoolers at ages 7 and 9. The more frequent occurrence among PAP in first-graders reverses in favor of DAP among third-graders. Compared with DAP, PAP was associated with a higher self-evaluation of ability after solving a problem and with greater expectation of success prior to tackling another problem. DAP children had a more stable self concept of (lower) ability than PAP children, which remained largely independent of antecedent success or failure. There was no difference in the cognitive developmental stage of the two groups of children. It was not possible to demonstrate an augmentation of task difficulty after success or failure, among the PAP children.

REFERENCES

Abramson, L. Y., & Sackeim, H. A. (1977). A paradox in depression: Uncontrollability and self-blame. *Psychological Bulletin, 84,* 839–851.
Abramson, L. Y., Seligman, M. E. P., & Teasdale, J. D. (1978). Learned helplessness in humans: Critique and reformulation. *Journal of Abnormal Psychology, 87,* 49–74.

Alloy, L. B., & Abramson, L. Y. (1979). Judgment of contingency in depressed and nondepressed students: Sadder but wiser? *Journal of Experimental Psychology: General, 108,* 441–485.

Ames, C. (1978). Children's achievement attributions and self-reinforcement: Effects of self-concept and competitive reward structure. *Journal of Educational Psychology, 70,* 345–355.

Arkin, R. M., Appelman, A. J., & Burger, J. M. (1980). Social anxiety, self-presentation, and the self-serving bias in causal attribution. *Journal of Personality and Social Psychology, 38,* 23–35.

Beck, A. T., Ward, C. H., Mendelson, M., Mock, J., & Erbaugh, J. (1961). An inventory for measuring depression. *Archives of General Psychiatry, 4,* 561–571.

Berglas, S., & Jones, E. E. (1978). Drug choice as an internalization strategy in response to noncontingent success. *Journal of Personality and Social Psychology, 36,* 405–417.

Blaney, P. H. (1977). Contemporary theories of depression: Critique and comparison. *Journal of Abnormal Psychology, 86,* 203–223.

Bradley, G. W. (1978). Self-cerving biasis in the attribution process: A reexamination of the fact or fiction question. *Journal of Personality and Social Psychology, 36,* 56–71.

Cohen, S., Rothbart, M., & Phillips, S. (1976). Locus of control and the generality of learned helplessness in humans. *Journal of Personality and Social Psychology, 34,* 1049–1056.

Crandall, V. C. (1969). Sex differences in expectancy of intellectual and academic reinforcement. In C. P. Smith (Ed.), *Achievement-related motives in children.* New York: Russell Sage.

Crandall, V. C., Katkovsky, W., & Crandall, V. J. (1965). Children's beliefs in their own control of reinforcements in intellectual-academic achievement situations. *Child Development, 36,* 91–109.

Deaux, K., & Emswiller, T. (1974). Explanations of successful performance on sex-linked tasks: What's skill for the male is luck for the female. *Journal of Personality and Social Psychology, 29,* 80–85.

Deaux, K., & Farris, E. (1977). Attributing causes for one's performance: The effects of sex, norms, and outcome. *Journal of Research in Personality, 11,* 59–72.

Diener, C. I., & Dweck, C. S. (1978). An analysis of learned helplessness: Continuous changes in performance, strategy, and achievement cognitions following failure. *Journal of Personality and Social Psychology, 36,* 451–462.

Dweck, C. S. (1975). The role of expectations and attributions in the alleviation of learned helplessness. *Journal of Personality and Social Psychology, 31,* 674–685.

Dweck, C. S., & Bush, E. S. (1976). Sex differences in learned helplessness: 1. Differential debilitation with peer and adult evaluators. *Developmental Psychology, 12,* 147–156.

Dweck, C. S., & Gilliard, D. (1975).Expectancy statements as determinants of reactions to failure: Sex differences in persistence and expectancy change. *Journal of Personality and Social Psychology, 32,* 1077–1084.

Dweck, C. S., & Repucci, N. D. (1973). Learned helplessness and reinforcement responsibility in children. *Journal of Personality and Social Psychology, 25,* 109–116.

Falbo, T. (1975). Achievement attributions of kindergarteners. *Development Psychology, 11,* 529–530.

Feather, N. T., & Simon, J. G. (1975). Reactions to male and female success and failure in sex-linked occupations: Impressions of personality, causal attributions, and perceived likelihood of different consequences. *Journal of Personality and Social Psychology, 31,* 20–31.

Fitch, G. (1970). Effects of self-esteem, perceived performance, and choice on causal attributions. *Journal of Personality and Social Psychology, 16,* 311–315.

Frankel, A., & Snyder, M. L. (1978). Poor performance following unsolvable problems: Learned helplessness or egotism? *Journal of Personality and Social Psychology, 36,* 1415–1423.

Gilmor, T. M., & Minton, H. L (1974). Internal versus external attribution of task performance as a function of locus of control, initial confidence and success - failure outcome. *Journal of Personality, 42,* 159–174.

Griffith, M. (1977). Effects of noncontingent success and failure on mood and performance. *Journal of Personality, 45,* 442–457.

Halisch, F. (1983). *Vorbildeinfluß und Motivationsprozesse.* Psychologisches Institut der Ruhr-Universität Bochum.

Hammen, C. L., & Krantz, S. (1976). Effects of success and failure on depressive cognitions. *Journal of Abnormal Psychology, 85,* 577–586.

Hanusa, B. H., & Schulz, R. (1977). Attributional mediators of learned helplessness. *Journal of Personality and Social Psychology, 35,* 602–611.

Heckhausen, H. (1963). *Hoffnung und Furcht in der Leistungsmotivation.* Meisenheim: Hain.

Heckhausen, H. (1972). Die Interaktion der Sozialisationsvariablen in der Genese des Leistungsmotivs. In C. F. Graumann (Ed.), *Handbuch der Psychologie* (Vol. 7/2, pp. 955–1019). Göttingen: Hogrefe.

Heckhausen, H. (1975). Fear of failure as a self-reinforcing motive system. In I. G. Sarason & C. Spielberger (Eds.), *Stress and anxiety* (Vol. 2, pp. 117–128). Washington, DC: Hemisphere.

Heckhausen, H. (1977). Achievement motivation and its constructs: A cognitive model. *Motivation and Emotion, 1,* 283–329.

Heckhausen, H. (1978). Selbstbewertung nach erwartungswidrigem Leistungsverlauf: Einfluß von Motiv, Kausalattribution und Zielsetzung. *Zeitschrift für Entwicklungspsychologie und Pädagogische Psychologie, 10,* 191–216.

Heckhausen, H. (1980a). *Motivation und Handeln.* Berlin: Springer.

Heckhausen, H. (1980b). *Preschoolers' risk-taking: A paradox resolved?* Unpublished Manuscript. Psychologisches Institut der Ruhr-Universität Bochum.

Heckhausen, H. (1981). Task-irrelevant cognitions during an exam: Incidence and effects. In H. W. Krohne & L. Laux (Eds.), *Achievement, stress, and anxiety.* Washington, DC: Hemisphere.

Heckhausen, H. (1982). The development of achievement motivation. In W. W. Hartup (Ed.), *Review of Child Development Research* (Vol. 6, pp. 600–668). Chicago: University of Chicago Press.

Heckhausen, H. (1983). Entwicklungsschritte in der Kausalattribution von Handlungsergebnissen. In D. Görlitz (Ed.), *Kindliche Erklärungsmuster.* Entwicklungspsychologische Beiträge zur Attributionsforschung (Vol. 1, pp. 49–85). Weinheim: Beltz, 1983.

Heckhausen, H., & Krug, S. (1982). Motive modification. In A. J. Stewart (Ed.), *Motivation and Society.* San Francisco, CA: Jossey Bass.

Hiroto, D. S. (1974). Locus of control and learned helplessness. *Journal of Experimental Psychology, 102,* 187–193.

Jopt, U.-J., & Ermshaus, W. (1977). Wie generalisiert ist das Selbstkonzept eigener Fähigkeit? Eine motivationspsychologische Untersuchung zur Aufgabenabhängigkeit der Fähigkeitswahrnehmung. *Zeitschrift für experimentelle und angewandte Psychologie, 24,* 578–601.

Kagan, J., Rosman, B. L., Day, D., Albert, J., & Phillips, W. (1964). Information processing in the child: Significance of analytic and reflective attitudes, *Psychological Monographs, 78,* (1, Whole No. 578).

Karniol, R., & Ross, M. (1976). The development of causal attributions in social perception. *Journal of Personality and Social Psychology, 34,* 455–464.

Kelley, H. H. (1967). Attribution theory in social psychology. In D. Levine (Ed.), *Nebraska Symposium on Motivation* (pp. 192–238). Lincoln: University of Nebraska Press.

Kelley, H. H. (1972). *Causal schemata and the attribution process.* New York: General Learning Press.

Kelley, H. H. (1973). The process of causal attribution. *American Psychologist, 28,* 107–128.

Klein, D. C., Fencil-Morse, E., & Seligman, M. E. P. (1976). Learned helplessness, depression, and the attribution of failure. *Journal of Personality and Social Psychology, 33,* 508–516.

Klinger, E. (1975). Consequences of commitment to and disengagement from incentives. *Psychological Review, 82,* 1–25.

Kratz, H. (1985). Kausalattributionen und Attributionsmuster für eigene Handlungsergebnisse im Grundschulalter. Dissertation, Fakultät für Psychologie, Ruhr-Universität Bochum.

Krug, B. (1972). *Mißerfolgsattribuierung und deren Auswirkungen auf Erwartungs- und Leistungänderungen sowie auf Persistenz.* Unpublished manuscript, Psychologisches Institut der Ruhr-Universität Bochum.

Krug, S., & Hanel, J. (1976). Motivänderung: Erprobung eines theoriegeleiteten Trainingsprogrammes. *Zeitschrift für Entwicklungspsychologie und Pädagogische Psychologie, 8,* 274–286.

Krug, S., & Heckhausen, H. (1982). Motivförderung in der Schule. In F. Rheinberg (Ed.), *Bezugsnormen zur Schulleistungsbewertung: Analyse und Intervention: Jahrbuch 1982 für Empirische Erziehungswissenschaft* (pp. 65–114). Düsseldorf: Schwann.

Kuhl, J. (1981). Motivational and functional helplessness: The moderating effect of state versus action orientation. *Journal of Personality and Social Psychology, 40,* 155–170.

Kun, A. (1977). Development of the magnitude-covariation and compensation schemata in ability and effort attributions of performance. *Child Development, 48,* 862–873.

Lefcourt, H. M., Hogg, E., Struthers, S., & Holmes, C. (1975). Causal attributions as a function of locus of control, initial confidence, and performance outcomes. *Journal of Personality and Social Psychology, 32,* 391–397.

Luginbuhl, J. E. R., Crowe, D. H., & Dahan, J. P. (1975). Causal attribution for success and failure. *Journal of Personality and Social Psychology, 31,* 86–93.

McMahan, I. D. (1973). Relationships between causal attributions and expectancy of success. *Journal of Personality and Social Psychology, 28,* 108–114.

Meyer, W.-U. (1973). *Leistungsmotiv und Ursachenerklärung von Erfolg und Mißerfolg.* Stuttgart: Klett.

Meyer, W.-U., & Plöger, F.-O. (1979). Scheinbar paradoxe Wirkungen von Lob und Tadel auf die wahrgenommene eigene Begabung. In H. Filipp (Ed.), *Selbstkonzept-Forschung: Probleme, Befunde und Perspektiven* (Pp. 221–235). Stuttgart: Klett-Cotta.

Miller, D. T. (1976). Ego involvement and attribution for success and failure. Journal of Personality and Social Pscyhology, 34, 901–906.

Miller, D. T., & Ross, M. (1975). Self-serving biases in the attribution of causality: Fact or fiction? *Psychological Bulletin, 82,* 213–225.

Miller, I. W. III, & Norman, W.H. (1979). Learned helplessness in humans: A review and attribution-theory model. *Psychological Bulletin, 86,* 93–118.

Miller, W. R., & Seligman, M. E. P. (1975). Depression and learned helplessness in man. *Journal of Abnormal Psychology, 84,* 228–238.

Nicholls, J. G. (1975). Causal attributions and other achievement-related cognitions: Effects of task outcome, attainment value, and sex. *Journal of Personality and Social Psychology, 31,* 379–389.

Nicholls, J. G. (1976). Effort is virtuous, but it's better to have ability: Evaluative responses to perceptions of effort and ability. *Journal in Personality Research, 10,* 306–315.

Nicholls, J. G. (1978). The development of the concepts of effort and ability, perception of academic attainment, and the understanding that difficult tasks require more ability. *Child Development, 49,* 800–814.

Nicholls, J. G. (1979). Development of perception of own attainment and causal attributions for success and failure in reading. *Journal of Educational Psychology, 71,* 94–99.

Parsons, J. E., & Ruble, D. N. (1977). The development of achievement-related expectancies. *Child Development, 48,* 1075–1079.

Rheinberg, F. (1980). *Leistungsbewertung und Lernmotivation.* Göttingen: Hogrefe.

Rholes, W. S., Blackwell, J., Jordan, C., & Walters, C. (1980). A developmental study of learned helplessness. *Developmental Psychology, 16,* 616–624.

Rizley, R. (1978). Depression and distortion in the attribution of causality. *Journal of Abnormal Psychology, 87,* 32–48.

Ross, L., & Lepper, M. R. (1980). The perseverance of beliefs: Empirical and normative considerations. In R. A. Shweder & D. Fiske (Eds.), *New directions for methodology of behavioral science: Fallible judgment in behavioral research.* San Francisco: Jossey-Bass.

Roth, S. (1980). A revised model of learned helplessness in humans. *Journal of Personality, 48,* 103–133.

Rotter, J. B. (1954). *Social learning and clinical psychology.* Englewood Cliffs, NJ: Prentice-Hall.

Rotter, J. B. (1966). Generalized expectancies for internal versus external control of reinforcement. *Psychological monographs, 80,* (1, Whole No. 609), 1–28.

Schlenker, B. R. (1975). Self-presentation: Managing the impression of consistency when reality interferes with self-enhancement. *Journal of Personality and Social Psychology, 32,* 1030–037.

Schmalt, H.-D. (1976). *Leistungsmotivation und kognitive Zwischenprozesse im Erleben von Erfolg und Mißerfolg.* Unpublished manuscript, Psychologisches Institut der Ruhr-Universität Bochum.

Schneider, K. (1977). Leistungsmotive, Kausalerklärungen für Erfolg und Mißerfolg und erlebte Affekte nach Erfolg und Mißerfolg. *Zeitschrift für Experimentelle und Angewandte Psychologie, 24,* 613–637.

Seligman, M. E. P. (1975). *Helplessness: On depression, development, and death.* San Francisco: Freeman.

Seligman, M. E. P., Abramson, L. Y., Semmel, A., & von Baeyer, C. (1979). Depressive attributional style. *Journal of Abnormal Psychology, 88,* 242–247.

Shultz, T. R., & Butkowsky, I. (1977). Young children's use of the scheme for multiple sufficient causes in the attribution of real and hypothetical behavior. *Child Development, 48,* 464–469.

Snyder, M. L., Smoller, B., Strenta, A., & Frankel, A. (1981). A comparison of egotism, negativity, and learned helplessness as explanations for poor performance after unsolvable problems. *Journal of Personality and Social Psychology, 40,* 24–30.

Snyder, M. L., Stephan, W. G., & Rosenfield, D. (1976). Egotism and attribution. *Journal of Personality and Social Psychology, 33,* 435–441.

Stevens, L., & Jones, E. E. (1976). Defensive attribution and the Kelley cube. *Journal of Personality and Social Psychology, 34,* 809–820.

Surber, C. F. (1980). The development of reversible operations in judgments of ability, effort, and performance. *Child Development, 51,* 1018–1029.

Tennen, H., & Eller, S. J. (1977). Attributional components of learned helplessness and facilitation. *Journal of Personality and Social Psychology, 35,* 265–271.

Tweer, R. (1976). *Das ökonomieprinzip in der anstrengungskalkulation: Eine entwicklungspsychologische untersuchung.* Unpublished manuscript, Psychologisches Institut der Ruhr-Universität Bochum.

Weiner, B., & Kukla, A. (1970). An attributional analysis of achievement motivation. *Journal of Personality and Social Psychology, 15,* 1–20.

Weiner, B., & Potepan, P. A. (1970). Personality characteristics and affective reactions toward exams of superior and failing college students. *Journal of Educational Psychology, 61,* 144–151.

Wener, A. E., & Rehm, L. P. (1975). Depressive affect: A test of behavioral hypotheses. *Journal of Abnormal Psychology, 84,* 221–227.

Wortman, C. B., Costanzo, P. R., & Witt, T. R. (1973). Effect of anticipated performance on the attributions of causality to self and others. *Journal of Personality and Social Psychology, 27,* 372–381.

Zuckerman, M., & Gerbasi, K. C. (1977). Belief in internal control or belief in a just world: The use and misuse of the I-E scale in prediction of attitudes and behavior. *Journal of Personality, 45,* 356–378.

6 Helplessness and Attributional Style in Depression

Christopher Peterson
Virginia Polytechnic Institute and State University

Martin E. P. Seligman
University of Pennsylvania

According to the reformulation of learned helplessness theory, a habitual insidious attributional style is a risk factor for depression. The thinking leading up to the reformulation is discussed and some recent research in support of it is described. Finally, some potential points of departure for subsequent investigations of attributional style and depression are outlined.

HELPLESSNESS AND ATTRIBUTIONAL STYLE IN DEPRESSION

The learned helplessness model has recently been reformulated along attributional lines (Abramson, Seligman, & Teasdale, 1978; see also Miller & Norman, 1979; and Roth, 1980). According to this reformulation, uncontrollable negative events do not automatically lead to pervasive deficits in learning, motivation, and emotion. Instead, the individual's causal attributions, concerning the uncontrollable events, govern the breadth and duration of these events, and the esteem related nature of the deficits. Only in the case of certain attributions will widespread helpless and depression result from uncontrollable events.

The reformulation was prompted by a growing number of laboratory studies. These studies demonstrated that helplessness effects were not invariably produced following uncontrollable events, and that the magnitude of helplessness effects, when they did occur, varied with factors not mentioned in the original theory. The original helplessness theory accorded importance only to uncontrollability (see Abramson, et al., 1978, and Miller & Seligman, 1980, for reviews of these studies). The reformulated model proposes that attributions subsume the most important variables neglected by the original learned help-lessness theory. The reformulation encompasses individual differences in attribu-tional style; attributional style has been conceived as a risk factor for depression (Seligman, Abramson, Semmel, & von Baeyer, 1979). The purpose of this chapter is to review some of the new empirical studies generated by the refor-mulation and, in light of these findings, to assess the reasonableness of the reformulated model.

ORIGINAL HELPLESSNESS THEORY

A brief statement of the original helplessness theory, before its reformulation, is presented (see also Alloy & Seligman, 1979; Maier & Jackson, 1979; Maier & Seligman, 1976; Maier, Seligman & Solomon, 1969; Seligman, 1975; Seligman, Maier, & Solomon, 1971). Overmier and Seligman (1967) and Seligman and Maier (1967) observed that dogs given inescapable electric shock in a Pavlovian hammock showed marked difficulty in escaping shock in a shuttlebox, 24 hours later; indeed, two thirds of the animals tested failed to learn the response. This failure to learn a response, readily acquired by dogs who had not experienced previous shock, was accompanied by other surprising behavior. The helpless dogs were extremely passive, sitting and enduring the shock without moving. The occasional escape responses they did make were not reliably acquired, and some dogs who escaped once or twice never escaped again.

It was proposed that the behavior of the animals resulted from their learning, in the Pavlovian hammock, that their responses and outcomes (i.e., shocks) were independent of each other, and that nothing they did mattered. This learning was represented as an expectation of helplessness, generalized to the new situation. This expectation constituted the basic explanation of the phenomenon. The ex-planation, along with the phenomenon, was dubbed "learned helplessness."

The expectation of helplessness was said to produce several deficits: (a) the animals were less likely to initiate responses, and hence, they did not sample the fact that they had control in the new situation (motivational deficit); (b) if they did respond, the animals were less likely to perceive that responses and outcomes were related and hence, were slower to learn what to do in the new situation (associative or cognitive deficit); (c) the animals also seemed to show blunted affect (emotional deficit). New work by Maier and Jackson (1979) suggests that helplessness involves an analgesic effect as well as an associative deficit; thus, the helpless animals were less motivated to escape an aversive event because it did not hurt them as much as it hurt nonhelpless animals.

A number of experiments (see Maier & Seligman, 1976) strongly suggest that it is the uncontrollability of the aversive event and not its traumatizing properties that are responsible for the various helplessness effects. Central to these demonstrations is the *triadic design*. In the correctly done helplessness experiment, three groups are used: one group (the *escapable* group) is exposed to controllable events, such as electric shocks terminable by some response; a second (the *inescapable* group), is yoked to the first group: given the identical pattern of physical events; crucially different, however, the offsets of the events are independent of all responses; a third group (the *no-pretreatment control*) gets no programmed events, controllable or uncontrollable. All three groups are later tested on a task that involves the learning of some new response. Helplessness is demonstrated when the inescapable group has more trouble than the escapable and control groups. Learned helplessness theory for animals has been attacked by theorists inclined to explain the phenomenon in peripheral or chemical terms; many of the studies conducted by learned helplessness proponents have been attempts to defend the cognitive account against these reinterpretations (for a review of this controversy, see Maier & Jackson, 1979; Maier & Seligman, 1976, and Seligman, Weiss, Weinraub, & Schulman, 1980).

The checkered success of learned helplessness theory (as applied to animals) in maintaining its cognitive emphasis attracted the attention of psychologists interested in helplessness in people. Human experimental psychology was beginning its cognitive revolution, when dog helplessness was first described (Neisser, 1967). The learned helplessness theory was seen as an instance of this perspective, which held that overt behavior was best understood by taking into account thoughts, beliefs, and strategies. If a cognitive account of the behavior of dogs (and mice and rats; Seligman, 1975) was viable, then surely a cognitive account of human helplessness should be more viable.

The first studies of learned helplessness in humans were simply attempts to demonstrate learning impairment following experience with uncontrollable events (for a review of these early studies, see Wortman & Brehm, 1975). Some of these studies were methodologically flawed, or unsuccessful in demonstrating the predicted impairment; however, a number were successful (e.g., Hiroto & Seligman, 1975). Most studies borrowed the triadic design from the animal research. The controllable events were typically loud noises or shocks, escapable by pushing a button, or solvable concept identification problems. The uncontrollable events were inescapable noises or shocks, or unsolvable concept identification problems.

These early demonstrations were followed by two distinct lines of work. In the first, researchers interested in the application of the phenomenon accepted it and its explanation, usually uncritically, and used it as the basis for their discussions of an incredible variety of significant failures of human adaptation. Best known is its use as a model of depression (e.g., Seligman, 1974; *Journal of Abnormal Psychology,* 1978). However, learned helplessness was also implicated in drug use (Berglas & Jones, 1978), heart attacks (Krantz, Glass & Snyder, 1974), failure in school (Dweck & Reppucci, 1973), sex differences

(Dweck & Bush, 1976), aggression (Geen, 1978), and IQ (Smith & Seligman, 1980). At this writing, the number of articles applying helplessness to human ills runs in the hundreds.

There are several possible reasons why future historians of psychology will be better equipped than present psychologists to understand the popularity of help-lessness theory. The possible reasons include: helplessness theory's basis in learning theory struck a responsive chord among psychologists interested in the relationship between the animal experimentation and the needs of people and society; the contribution of helplessness theory's optimism, borne from appar-ently ready solutions to helplessness (i.e., exposure to contingencies); the theo-ry's simplicity, straight-forward and testable predictions, made it stand in flatter-ing contrast to the muddier theories usually proposed to account for failures of adaptation; and learned helplessness theory linked experimental psychology, the past as represented by learning theory and the future as represented by cognitive theory, to a wide range of more applied areas of psychology. Learned help-lessness theory was and is of considerable interest to social, clinical, and devel-opmental psychologists, who attempt to understand complex human behavior and the ways it can go awry.

At the same time that the applications of helplessness occurred, another line of work was being conducted. A number of researchers and theorists were interested in the helplessness phenomenon itself, and their attempts to study it in detail raised serious questions about the validity of learned helplessness in peo-ple. A catalogue of anomalies accrued in the research literature; some of them were enumerated by Abramson et al. (1978), Miller and Norman (1979), and Wortman and Brehm (1975). Among the claimed anomalies were:

1. The motivational deficit described in the animal literature was not always present in humans. Although helpless subjects did not learn quickly, it was not because they failed to initiate responses. Indeed, the typical human helplessness experiment required a great deal of cooperation and instrumental responding, such as following complex instructions.

2. Some studies failed to replicate helplessness, and some found a facilitating effect of uncontrollable events; following unsolvable problems, subjects some-times did better than comparison groups.

3. Laboratory-produced helplessness sometimes generalized beyond the spe-cific pretreatment situation, and sometimes did not. For instance, for some subjects, changing the experimental room, between the pretreatment and test task was found, to wipe out helplessness effects.

4. Norms relating how other people had performed and information about the nature of the task affected the helplessness obtained.

5. A belief in response-outcome independence did not necessarily produce helplessness. Indeed, some writers argued that subjects did not always learn that responses and outcomes were independent (Peterson, 1978).

6. Competing explanations, such as expectation incongruency (Douglas & Anisman, 1975), superstitious responding (Peterson, 1978), and egotism (Frankel & Snyder, 1978), were proposed and supported by data.

In short, the simple explanation of helplessness effects (i.e., uncontrollable events → expectancy of response-outcome independence → interference with learning) was not an account of the human laboratory helplessness. In contrast to the criticisms of helplessness theory applied to animals, which took the model to task for being too cognitive, the criticisms of the theory applied to people charged that the theory was not cognitive enough! The critics of helplessness theory applied to people called for a more complex and sophisticated account (e.g., Wortman & Brehm, 1975). Most of these authors, in keeping with current trends within social psychology, suggested an attributional reinterpretation of the phenomenon.

THE REFORMULATION

In response to the anomalies, Abramson et al. (1978) proposed a reformulation of learned helplessness. According to Abramson et al. (1978), more than an expectation of response-outcome independence was necessary to account for helplessness in the laboratory and depression outside of the laboratory. The reformulation proposed that causal attributions were critical variables. Internal attributions about negative events produce lowered self-esteem, and global and stable attributions produce generalized helplessness, across situations and time. Therefore, the reformulated model assumes that although the consequences of doing so may be maladaptive, people act rationally, in accordance with their attributions. The "man as scientist" metaphor (Kelley, 1973; Kelly, 1955) of attribution theory is embodied in the learned helplessness reformulation. Such rationality is open to criticism, these criticisms are discussed as they apply to the reformulation.

The reformulation accounted for most of the laboratory anomalies noted earlier (see Abramson et al., 1978), and Miller & Seligman, 1980, for detailed discussion of this point), as well as for several problems involved in applying helplessness theory to depression. In passing, it is noted that if revisions in a laboratory model of psychopathology, undertaken to improve the fit to laboratory data, also clarify the psychopathology modelled, more confidence is justified in the fit of the model to the pathology. This criterion for modelling may be added to the more obvious ones of similar symptoms, causes, physiology, cures, and prevention, discussed by Abramson and Seligman (1977).

One example of how the reformulation made the helplessness theory a better explanation of depression has to do with bad events and depression. ("Negative life events" are found to be jargon; therefore, hereafter they are called "bad events.'') Relationships have been demonstrated between bad events and depression (Brown & Harris, 1978; Paykel, 1974); however, they are not as robust as the original helplessness theory suggested. The reformulated model explains these weak relationships by saying that they do not reflect individual differences in attributions about the causes of the bad events. Indeed, Semmel, Peterson, Abramson, Metalsky, and Seligman (1980) demonstrated that the bad event/depression link is increased if attributions are taken into account.

A second example of how the reformulated model allows better sense to be made of what is known about depression is the depressive paradox (Abramson & Sackeim, 1977; Janoff-Bulman, 1979; Peterson, 1979; Peterson, Schwartz, & Seligman, 1981). Depressives tend to blame themselves about events over which they feel no control; this is quite awkward for the original learned helplessness theory to explain. However, it is quite easily accommodated by the reformulated helplessness theory, which recognizes the difference between internal attributions (self-blame) and expectations of response-outcome independence (helplessness).

ATTRIBUTIONAL STYLE

The investigations of the reformulation by our research group have focused largely on individual differences in the tendencies to make internal, stable, and global attributions. Although the reformulation was not presented exclusively in terms of individual differences, such a strategy seemed necessary in order to explain why some people become helpless following an experience with uncontrollable events and others do not. A reasonable assumption is that people have a characteristic attributional style or a tendency to make similar sorts of attributions about a variety of events. Theoretically, a depressive attributional style is one that habitually attributes bad events to internal, stable, and global causes. Such an assumption does not minimize the role of situational evidence in determining what attributions people make; the vast social psychological literature documents the importance of such evidence (e.g. Harvey, Ickes, & Kidd, 1976). For instance, bad experiences are on the whole attributed to external causes, while good experiences are on the whole attributed to internal causes (e.g. Peterson, 1980; Weiner, 1974). One tends to explain one's own behavior by external determinants; while one tends to explain the behavior of others by internal, dispositional determinants (e.g. Jones & Nisbett, 1971; Monson & Snyder, 1977), and so on. Given the constraints of situational evidence, our interest is in explaining why, in the same situation, people may differ in their helplessness and depression reactions. It is assumed, then, all other determinants of attributions being equal, that people have explanatory styles that are applied to the events they encounter.

This assumption is in keeping with other cognitive accounts of individual differences, such as theories of cognitive style (Goldstein & Blackman, 1978), personal constructs (Kelley, 1955), locus of control (Rotter, 1966), negative schemata (Beck, 1976), and so on. Put simply: It is assumed that people react to events in accordance with their interpretaions; these interpretations are jointly determined by the events themselves, and by the biases that people impose on the events.

The frequent debates about whether personality characteristics operate across situations usually do not focus on cognitive traits, such as attributional style. Indeed, in light of evidence demonstrating that they have considerable cross-situational consistency, some critics make an explicit exception for cognitive traits (W. Mischel, 1968). Our assumption, by holding that the critical differences are attributional (i.e., pertain to the causal inferences made by people), differs from other cognitive accounts of individual differences. In contrast, other accounts, focus on structural characteristics of cognition (Scott, Osgood, & Peterson, 1979), on naive epistemologies other than causal ones (Kruglanski, 1980), and so on.

The research undertaken by our group has had several thrusts, which are now explained. First, we were interested in whether there exists an attributional style descriptive of depression. To this end, attributional style in several populations, including depressed individuals, was assessed. It was hoped that a specific attributional style would be found that: (a) characterized depressives as opposed to nondepressives; (b) characterized different kinds of depressives; (c) varied with severity of the depressive symptoms; and (d) did not characterize other psychopathologies. Second, there was interest in determining if the depressive attributional style caused depression. This question was attacked in two ways; one strategy used causal modelling techniques to predict later depression from earlier attributional style, the second strategy used laboratory experiments to make the same inferences.

THE MEASUREMENT OF ATTRIBUTIONAL STYLE

Because the existence of attributional style was postulated, the first problem was how it should be measured. A difficulty arose immediately: Are all causal attributions accessible to a person's awareness? When Heider (1958) first described causal attributions, he made it clear—in branding his endeavor the study of naive psychology—that he was talking about a person's thoughts as they could be communicated to others. Other authors have taken issue with this, preferring instead to regard such cognitive constructs as tacit. The best known of such critics are Langer (1978) and Nisbett and Wilson (1977).

Attributions are regarded as hypothetical constructs (MacCorquodale & Meehl, 1948) akin to constructs such as hunger and expectation. This means that attributions are not defined (and exhausted) by introspective evidence; otherwise, they would be intervening variables. Rather, a variety of kinds of evidence bear on whether or not an attribution is present—introspection, betting behavior, voluntary action, and others—and a subjective report is neither necessary nor sufficient. A deaf mute boxer who: can report no attribution, but bets his life savings that he will win; trains 16 hours per day; increases the distance he runs each day during training; and measures his lung capacity weekly can be said, with some confidence, to attribute his victory to wind, endurance, and other skill-effort factors. Therefore, to ask whether attributions are conscious or unconscious is to make a category mistake (Ryle, 1949). Attributions are not the sort of entity that can be either conscious or unconscious; rather, evidence about conscious experience bears on whether they are in play, just as does evidence about behavior. However, the attribution is no more the conscious experience than the subjective report of hunger is hunger. The introspection counts toward the belief that hunger is in play, just as do the number of hours of deprivation, the activity of the hypothalamus, the amount of adulteration of food that will be tolerated; the introspection is neither necessary nor sufficient. The phenomenological view of attribution, which holds the introspection is necessary and sufficient for the attribution, is making the same serious error for cognition that Skinner makes in the realm of behavior—that intervening variables, or constructs whose meaning is exhausted by operational definition[1] of input-output relations, are useful forms of scientific explanation.

Thus the dilemma becomes not whether attributions are conscious, but what can best be ascertained about the attributions by talking to an individual, and what other characteristics can best be ascertained by means other than talking. Two extremes exist for ascertaining attributions. One is simply to ask people in rather abstract terms about them; their reports bear on their attributions. The other is to observe people. One can observe people in situations in which what they do is ipso facto evidence that a given (tacit) attribution has been held. This latter strategy was followed by the experiments leading up to the reformulation of the learned helplessness model, and has been followed in new tests of the reformulation. People are put in laboratory-manipulated situations in which the alteration of an attribution could be inferred with some confidence, and changes in overt behavior observed.

The first sense of ascertaining attributions involves asking people about their own attributions, and then seeing if attributions assessed in this manner bear

---

[1]We are not against operational definitions or well-definedness of terms in mapping how a concept is instantiated in a particular experiment. The concept that underlies the particular operations from experiment to experiment, however, cannot be operationalized by necessary and sufficient conditions in hypothetical construct sceince.

reasonable relationships to other things these people do. Recent research along this line and the second line is reported. This research was designed to see if, and where, the two senses of assessing attributions converge.

THE ATTRIBUTIONAL STYLE QUESTIONNAIRE

In the research to be reported attributional style was measured with a paper-and-pencil instrument called the "Attributional Style Questionaire" (ASQ). Several considerations led to its format. Questions were needed that would measure the degree to which subjects used attributions falling along the dimensions of internality, stability, and globality, as defined by the reformulated learned helplessness mode. Constraining subjects by producing them with possible attributions (e.g., ability, effort, task difficulty, luck, and so on), had to be avoided for two reasons: First, there is no guarantee that an attribution regarded by an attribution theorist as, for example, unstable is so regarded by all subjects; some may believe that low effort is a stable characteristic of the individual (laziness), others may perceive it as unstable (sloughing off). Second, Falbo and Beck (1979) have shown that the attributions assumed by Weiner (1974) (ability, effort, task difficulty, and luck) to exhaust the internal-external and stable-unstable dimensions, neither occur preponderantly in free-responding nor cluster as expected when they do occur.

On the other hand, Ross' (1977) observation that the coding of causal attributions into abstract categories depends more on the (theoreticaly irrelevant) grammatical form of the attribution than on its actual meaning, argues against the use of completely open-ended questions. The report by Elig and Frieze (1979) also contends that open-ended attributional measures are not as reliable as fixed-format procedures. However, in some research (e.g., Peterson, 1980), high reliability in the coding of open-ended causal responses have been reported.

A reasonable compromise was employed between closed and open-ended questions in the assessment of attributional style. For each of 12 (six good and six bad) hypothetical events involving themselves, subjects were asked to generate a cause. They were then asked to rate their provided cause along 7-point scales that corresponded to the internality, stability, and globality dimensions. This format does not constrain or create the causal attributions, but it does allow for simple and objective quantification. Further, this format allows the researcher to content analyze the chosen attributions whenever it is desired.

The questionnaire (ASQ) is group administered; the following directions appear on the first page of the booklet:

> Please try to vividly imagine yourself in the situations that follow. If such a situation happened to you, what would you feel would have caused it? While events may have many have many causes, we want you to pick only one—the major cause

if this event happened to you. Please write this cause in the blank provided after each event. Next we want you to answer some questions about the cause.

Twelve different hypothetical events follow these instructions. Half are good events (e.g., "you do a project which is highly praised"); while half are bad events (e.g., "you meet a friend who acts hostilely toward you"). The wording of the various attributional dimension rating scale questions reflects the specific event to be explained. However, in general, the subject is asked to circle a number from 1 to 7 for scales anchored by: (a) totally due to other people or circumstances totally due to me; (b) will never again be present/will always be present; (c) influences just this particular situation/influences all situations in my life. These questions pertain to the cause, and operationalize the externality-internality, unstability-stability, and specificity-globality dimensions.

The rating scales associated with each event are scored in the directions of increasing internality, stability, and globality. Composite scores are created simply by totaling the appropriate items and dividing the sum by the number of items, in the composite. The practice has been to compute internality, stability, and globality scores separately for good and for bad events; thus, each of these six subscales consists of six items. Further the subscales are combined (internal plus stable plus global) for good events by totaling them; the same is done for the bad events. Table 6.1, presents the means, standard deviations, and incorrelatins of the six subscales, based on a sample of 130 undergraduate (50 males, 80 females) enrolled in an abnormal psychology course at the State University of New York at Stony Brook. The scale reliabilities, estimated by Cronbach's (1951) coefficient alpha, are also present. As can be seen, the scale reliabilities mostly exceed the scale intercorrelations; however, the values are still relatively low. Greater reliability is achieved when the good and bad subscales, respectively, are combined; this yields an alpha of .75 for the good composite and .72 for the bad composite. In light of this increased reliability, unless the researcher is interested in the individual dimensions, it is recommended that the composite scales be used.

Also of note in Table 6.1 is the fact that for the positive events, the individual attributional dimensions are intercorrelated at a level much nearer that of their reliabilities than are the dimensions for negative events. Thus, the present instrument did not discriminate among these dimensions for positive events to the degree that it did for negative events. Why should this be the case? Perhaps people make fewer discriminations among good events. They may not spend as much time ruminating over good events as they do over bad events; therefore, they may attend less to the causes of good events and are less articulate (cf. Scott, Osgood, & Peterson, 1979) in rating them (cf. Langer, 1978; Peirce, 1955; Ryle, 1949).

One hundred of the subjects who provided the above data also completed the attributional style questionnaire five weeks later. Table 6.2 summarizes the test-

TABLE 6.1
Intercorrelations of the ASQ Subscale

Subscale	1	2	3	4	5	6	7	8
Positive events								
1. internality	(.50)							
2. stability	.62*	(.58)						
3. globality	.36*	.59*	(.44)					
4. composite	—	—	—	(.75)				
Negative events								
5. internality	.11	.01	−.03	—	(.46)			
6. stability	−.17	−.07	.03	—	.18*	(.59)		
7. globality	−.15	.04	.24*	—	.28*	.45*	(.69)	
8. composite	—	—	—	—	—	—	—	(.72)
mean	5.28	5.36	5.13	—	4.30	4.16	3.89	
s.d.	.79	.68	.80	—	.84	.71	1.07	

Note: Figures in parentheses are reliabilities, estimated by Cronbach's (1951) coefficient alpha.
*$p < .05$

retest correlations of the attributional dimensions and the composites. As had been hoped, the correlations are respectably high, because the scores are hypothesized to reflect a "style." It is worth observing that not all measures of cognitive style proved to be so reliable, either internally or across time (Goldstein & Blackman, 1978; Streufert & Streufert, 1978); therefore, this finding is underscored.

TABLE 6.2
Test-Retest Correlations of the ASQ

Subscale	r
Positive events	
internaiity	.58*
stability	.65*
globality	.59*
composite	.70*
Negative events	
internality	.64*
stability	.69*
globality	.57*
composite	.64*

*$p < .001$

THE RELATIONSHIP OF ATTRIBUTIONAL STYLE TO DEPRESSION

Among the first studies that followed the reformulation were several that correlated individual differences in the attributional style with depressive symptoms. Seligman et al. (1979) reported a study using undergraduates at the University of Pennsylvania. These students completed the ASQ and two measures of depressive symptoms: The Beck Depression Inventory (BDI; Beck, Ward, Mendelson, Mock, & Erbaugh, 1961) and the Multiple Affect Adjective Checklist (MAACL; Zuckerman & Lubin, 1965). The BDI is an often used and well validated self-report questionnaire measuring the severity of 21 different symptoms of depression (see Beck, 1967, and Bumberry, Oliver, & McClure, 1978, for validity evidence, both in clinical and undergraduate samples). The MAACL asks subjects to circle various adjectives characterizing their mood; depression, anxiety, and hostility scores are derived from this instrument.

Seligman et al. (1979) found, as predicted by the reformulated model, that an attributional style in which bad events were attributed to internal, stable, and global causes was correlated with the BDI and the MAACL, both for the individual dimensions and for the composite. To a lesser degree, the opposite style for good events was correlated with the BDI. Although this preliminary study was an important one, it left several important questions unanswered. First, would the correlation between attributional style and depressive symptoms obtain for more severe depression? Second, is the attributional style particularly characteristic of depression, as suggested by the reformulation, or is it a more general characteristic of psychopathology?

In order to answer both of these questions, a second study was undertaken by our research group (Raps, Peterson, Reinhard, Abramson, & Seligman, 1982). The second study administered the ASQ to unipolar depressed patients hospitalized in a Veterans' Administration Medical Center. Two nondepressed groups of patients also completed the ASQ, schizophrenics and surgical patients. Both comparison groups controlled for the effects of hospitalization per se (because other research suggests that hospitalization can result in helplessness and depression; Raps, Peterson, Jonas, & Seligman, 1982); in addition, the schizophrenic group assessed whether the "depressive" attributional style is specific to depression.

Table 6.3 summarizes the means of the attributional dimensions and composites for each of the three patient groups. As can be seen, the predictions of the reformulated learned helplessness model were strongly supported; depressed patients were more likely than surgical and schizophrenic patients to attribute bad events to internal, stable, and global causes. As with the student study, although to a lesser degree, the opposite style for good events was also associated with depression. For the most part, the schizophrenic patients rated their provided causes similarly to the surgical patients; when differences occurred, they were in

TABLE 6.3
Attributional Style Means—Patients

Group	Style for Bad Events				Style for Good Events			
	INT	STA	GLO	COMP	INT	STA	GLO	COMP
Unipolar								
Depressives (n=30)								
mean	4.90	4.89	4.84	4.88	4.93	4.90	5.10	4.98
s.d.	1.12	1.16	1.29	2.92	1.33	1.39	1.41	3.81
Surgical patients (n=64)								
mean	4.30	4.06	3.65	4.00	5.49	5.53	5.31	5.44
s.d.	1.18	.90	1.37	2.73	.83	.81	1.16	2.21
Schizophrenics (n=15)								
mean	3.51	4.01	4.00	3.87	5.67	5.57	5.27	5.50
s.d.	1.18	1.01	1.19	2.26	1.19	1.02	1.16	3.02
p depressives vs. surgical patients	.001	.001	.002	.001	.017	.008	ns	.03
p depressives vs. schizophrenics	.001	.016	.069	.001	.07	.10	ns	.17
p surgical patients vs.	.002	ns	ns	ns	ns	ns	ns	ns

Note: Abbreviations are as follows: INT=internality, STA=stability, GLO=globality, and COMP =composite. The higher the number the more internal, stable, or global the score. Comparisons between groups were made with *t*-tests; *p* levels are for two-tailed tests.

a direction away from the depressives. Thus, it can be concluded that the insidious attributional style is not generally associated with psychopathology. Further, it can be concluded that clinically depressed patients have an attributional style like that of mildly depressed students; thus, support is given to the idea that, at least cognitively, mild and severe depression may be continous. Although no single study, or pair of studies, will decide the issue of continuity, once the ground rules are established, it is an issue with an empirical answer. In order to find the answer, it is suggested that the controversy be moved from the arm chair or the couch to an explicit empirical domain.

Do children with depressive symptoms have this insidious attributional style? Answering this question is a conceptual replication of the previous discussion, however, because certain theorists doubt the very existence of childhood depression (e.g., Lefkowitz & Burton, 1978), is also of interest in its own right.

The advent of behavioral and cognitive formulations of depression, emphasizing overt manifestations, reopened the issue of childhood depression (e.g., Schuldenbrandt & Raskin, 1977). Children display many of the symptoms, that are called depressive in adults. These symptoms are dismissed by some as transient development by-products, or signs of inner turmoil; one of the things to be tested was the duration of these symptoms. Depending on the degree that the symptoms: cohere with each other, as they do in adults; are associated with similar attributional style, are caused by similar attribultional style; and have similar cure and prevention, they are considered depressive symptoms; it is concluded that there is an entitiy of childhood depression.

The study of children begins to provide some evidence about the origins of attributional style. The learned helplessness model has been silent on the source of attributional styles; however, attributional literature suggests that such styles might arise in at least two ways (Kelley, 1973). First, as the result of experiences that suggest the same obvious kind of cause; people eventually come to apply that attribution to events a priori (Peterson, 1980). Second, the style may be learned abstractly as a maxim for living. With close analysis, distinctions between these two ways of acquiring attributional tendencies break down; even inductive learning must be grounded in abstract beliefs about which causes are relevant (Ajzen, 1977).

Parents are, of course, a reasonable source of attributional style; a child may hear its parents habitually explaining events in a certain way and come to do the same. Peterson recently witnessed a father and his young son at a basketball game. In the first half of the game, the son watched with wide eyes as his father attributed every call against the Celtics to the "stinking referees"; in the second half, the son did the same thing, as his father nodded his agreement. The son had come to "understand" the causal structure of basketball (Berger & Luckmann, 1966). Of course, it is understood that Julius Erving was a much more robust cause of the Celtic ills than were the referees.

The first attempt to assess attributional style in children with the adult ASQ failed, because the younger children in the pilot samples had trouble using the rating scales for stability and globality. Therefore, it was necessary to retreat from the strategy of compromising between open and closed-format questionnaires; instead, the children were given a closed-format instrument, which they were able to understand and complete satisfactorily.

In the questionnaire (CASQ), the children were given a series of hypothetical events; for each event they chose between two possible causes. The response alternatives varied one of the attributional dimensions; the other two remained constant. For example, in this item:

You get an A on a math test.
(a) I'm smart.
(b) I'm smart at math.

Alternative (a) is a global attribution; alternative (b) is a specific attribution. Internality and stability are held constant. This questionnaire has 48 items—

eight items for each of the six attributional subscales (internality, stability, and globality for good events versus bad events). Table 6.4 summarizes the intercorrelations and internal reliabilities of these subscales for the sample described. As can be seen, although they tend to exceed the scale intercorrelations, the reliabilities are more modest than for the adult scale. The composite scales for good and bad events improved the reliabilities to .66 and .50, respectively at Time 1, and .73 and .54 at Time 2.

Ninety-six children in grades 3 through 6 (in two Philadelphia elementary schools) completed the questionnaires at two different times, separated by an interval of six months. Table 6.5 summarizes the test-retest correlations, which were substantial. It was concluded that even for children, there are stable attributional tendencies. The children also completed a self-report depression inventory created by Kovacs and Beck (1977) and modelled after the BDI. At both admin-

TABLE 6.4
Intercorrelations of Attributional Style Dimensions Children (CASQ)

Subscale	1	2	3	4	5	6	7	8
Time 1								
Positive Events								
1. internality	(.32)							
2. stability	.26*	(.55)						
3. globality	.33*	.41*	(.40)					
4. composite	—	—	—	(.66)				
Negative events								
5. internality	−.22*	−.45*	−.14	—	(.43)			
6. stability	−.22*	−.15	−.02	—	.18	(.42)		
7. globality	−.01	−.02	−.27*	—	−.02	.27*	(.31)	
8. composite	—	—	—	—	—	—	—	(.50)
Time 2								
Positive events								
1. internality	(.43)							
2. stability	.25*	(.54)						
3. globality	.35*	.57*	(.55)					
4. composite	—	—	—	(.73)				
Negative events								
5. internality	−.24*	−.41*	−.14	—	(.56)			
6. stability	−.13	−.23*	−.16*	—	.25*	(.13)		
7. globality	−.20	.03	.03	—	.05	.23*	(.39)	
8. composite	—	—	—	—	—	—	—	(.54)

Note: Figures in parentheses are reliabilities, estimated by Cronbach's (1951) coefficient alpha.
*p < .05

TABLE 6.5
Correlations Between Attributional Style
and Depression—Children (CASQ)

Subscale	Correlation with CDI	
	Time 1	*Time 2*
Positive events		
internality	−.34*	−.31**
stability	−.47*	−.54***
globality	−.35*	−.39***
composite	−.53*	−.54***
Negative events		
internality	.45*	.28**
stability	.31*	.26*
globality	.21*	.26*
composite	.51*	.40***

*p < .05
**p < .01
***p < .001

istrations, the Children's Depression Inventory (CDI) correlated with the attributional subscales and composites as predicted by the reformulation; these correlations were observed both for the good and for the bad events.

More detailed analysis of the data revealed: (a) that girls were more depressed than boys ($p <.05$) at both administrations; and (b) that there was no tendency for depressive symptoms to change with age. These findings indicate that the greater incidence of depression among adult females (e.g. Radloff, 1975) occurs as early as nine years of age (cf. Dweck & Bush, 1976). Depressive symptoms in children are not "transitory developmental by-products"; They are highly stable, and do not disappear with age. The mothers of 47 of these children and the fathers of 36 completed the BDI and the ASQ, and returned them to the researchers. The child measures were averaged for the two administrations, and correlations with those of the parents were computed. Briefly: (a) mother's attributional style for bad events correlated with her child's attributional style for bad events (.39) and with her child's depressive symptoms (.42); (b) mother's depressive symptoms correlated with her child's depressive symptoms (.37); (c) father's attributional style and depression were not related to scores of his spouse or their children. The intercorrelations of the mother and child composite measures are presented in Table 6.6. More detailed analysis suggested that the bulk of the relationships among the composite attributional measures resulted from the contributions of the internality and globality subscales.

It is speculated the cognitions of the depressive (Beck, 1967) may be embedded within an interpersonal vicious circle. The depressions of mother and child may maintain each other, particularly when each has the depressive attributional style. If so, then the currently popular individual therapies used with depressives (e.g., Beck, Rush, Shaw, & Emery, 1979) might be supplemented with family therapy; this has been done with other disorders in which family interaction contributes. Most generally, the results suggest that the depressed child is apt to be found in a family in which the mother is also depressed, and vice-versa. Depressed mothers not only hurt themselves but their children as well. The fact that fathers' depression and attributional style were not associated with those of their wives or children may be due to a characteristic of the modern family; fathers spend less time with their children than do mothers.

Implicit in the reformulation is the notion that changes in attributional style should accompany successful therapy for depression (Seligman, 1981). Indeed, an important aspect of the currently popular cognitive therapy for depression (Beck et al., 1979) is an emphasis on changing the depressive's worldview, particularly the way in which the causes of an event are construed. To date, as a consequence of therapy, changes in attributional style have not been documented; however, there is some case history evidence regarding such changes. Nine transcripts of segments of therapy sessions with depressed patients were blindly coded for depressive attributional style, by members of our research

TABLE 6.6
Intercorrelations of Depression and Attribution Style—
Mother and Child

Measure	1	2	3	4	5	6
Mother						
1. ASQ composite positive events	(.65)					
2. ASQ composite—negative events	$-.12$	(.79)				
3. depression (BDI)	$-.34^*$	$.60^{***}$	(.92)			
Child						
4. CASQ composite—positive events	.08	$-.07$	$-.03$	(.82)		
5. CASQ composite—negative events	$-.09$	$.39^{**}$	.27	$-.26$	(.76)	
6. depression (CDI)	$-.27$	$.42^{**}$	$.37^{**}$	$-.48^{***}$	$.49^{***}$	(.84)

Note: Figures in parentheses, on diagonal, are reliabilities, estimated by Cronbach's (1951) coefficient alpha.

$^*p < .05$
$^{**}p < .01$
$^{***}p < .001$

group. The transcripts were then rank-ordered by how bad the attributional style was. It was then revealed that the coded transcripts did not belong to nine different patients, but rather in the course of therapy to three different points of only three patients. Thus, it was possible to test the prediction that as improvement occurred, the patients would be less likely to explain bad events in terms of internal, stable, and global causes (thus more likely to employ external, unstable, and specific attributions).

The transcripts were edited excerpts from psychodynamic therapy sessions (under the supervision of Mardi Horowitz) with three depressed women, all of whom had recently experienced a traumatic loss, such as the death of a parent or spouse. Three transcripts from each patient were available, from the beginning, middle, and end of therapy. Each transcript was approximately four to five double-spaced typed pages in length, and was edited to: protect the confidentiality of the patient; to remove nonattributional clues about severity of depression, and when in therapy the session occurred; and the fact that each transcript was paired with the transcripts of two other patients.

All phrases involving a specific bad event, for which a causal attribution was made, were extracted from each transcript. In all, 78 such event-attribution units were obtained; an average of 9.2 per transcript, with a range from 5 to 21. These units were then randomized and presented to four judges, who using the three dimensions from the ASQ (i.e., the 1 to 7 scales measuring internality, stability, and globality) independently rated each cause.

Product-movement correlations between the ratings by all pairs of judges were computed, as well as for a composite attributional score. The reliabilities were quite high, indicating that the judges could agree about the designation of a given attribution. For each of the nine transcripts, mean scores for each of the dimensions and composite were formed. (The individual dimensions ordered the transcripts in much the same way as did the composite.) For all three patients (all of whom, it turned out, improved over therapy), the attributions changed in the course of therapy. As hypothesized by the reformulation, the changes were away from internal, stable, and global cuases toward external, unstable, and specific causes. In addition, severity of depression across patients seemed roughly related to insidiousness of the attribution style.

The procedures used here were conservative ones; coding was totally blind, relation to depression was blind, and the exact nature of the transcripts was not known to the group while they were coded. Further, therapy was conducted by a therapist, not particularly sympathetic to our position. Indeed, because his theoretical preference is to look beyond the manifest content of patients' attributions he presented the transcripts as a challenge. The very small sample makes this "evidence" highly tentative; however, this study may be added to the others as supportive of the idea that an insidious attributional style is associated with depression. Such an association was demonstrated with college students, depressed in-patients, and patients in analysis. Further, the findings suggest that the insidious attributional style is a relatively stable characteristic, that style for positive events is essentially independent of style for negative events, and that there is a correspondence between the styles of mothers and their children.

ATTRIBUTIONAL STYLE AS A CAUSE OF DEPRESSION

Several longitudinal studies of the development of depressive symptoms with individuals' initial attributional style as the risk factor are described. This is followed by a description of several laboratory studies that examine the consequences of helplessness induction for subjects with different attributional styles. Both sets of studies test whether or not attributional style contributes causally to depression.

The first study (Semmel et al., 1980) investigated both attributional style as a risk factor in the development of depressive symptoms and the role of subsequent bad events. None of the correlational studies described earlier assessed whether or not actual bad events correlated with depressive symptoms, however, this is critical to the reformulated model. The model does not claim that the insidious attributional style in and of itself is sufficient for depression to develop; rather, a bad event processed through the insidious attributional style is needed. This hypothesis was investigated using a sample of college students at the State University of New York at Stony Brook; it replicated a pilot study done at the University of Pennsylvania.

Early in the semester 119 students in an abnormal psychology course had their attributional style assessed (with the ASQ) along with their depressive symptoms (with the short form of the BDI; [Beck & Beck, 1972]). An intervening event also occurred—the midterm examination. According to the reformulation, depressive changes should most likely occur among those students who possess both a prexisting insidious attributional style and who in their own eyes, "fail" on the midterm. Failure on the midterm was determined by asking the students if they were satisfied or dissatisfied with the grade they had received.

The students were devided according to whether they reported being satisfied ($n = 43$) or dissatisfied ($n = 76$) with their midterm grade. It is important to note that the two groups did not differ with regard to initial attributional style, nor initial depression and grade aspirations (which were also assessed early in the semester). However, the two groups, of course, differed in the actual grades they received, which means that their satisfaction reflected somewhat uniform standards. The satisfied students averaged in the B/B+ range; those in the dissatisfied group scored in the C range. Overall, the two groups did not differ with regard to depression, neither immediately following the return of the midterm, nor four weeks later; meaning that a bad event in and of itself was not sufficient for depresive symptoms to develop. Nor was the insidious attributional style alone sufficient to bring about depressive symptoms. Among students satisfied with the grade, no relationship was found between attributional style and depressive symptoms (see Table 6.7). If attributional style, per se, were a cause of depression, those students who succeed, but who have an insidious style, should become more depressed than those who succeed but have a nondepressed style.

In contrast, when attributional style scores were correlated with ensuing depressive symptoms for the dissatisfied group, statistically significant correlations were found (see Table 6.7). For these students, a prior attributional style in which bad events are attributed to internal, stable, and global causes correlates with depressive symptoms one week and four weeks following the midterm; the insidious style for good events (external, unstable, specific) correlated with depressive symptoms four weeks following the midterm. Thus, both the insidious attributional style and dissatisfaction with grade were necessary for later depressive symptoms; these results support the reformulation. A depressive attributional style puts a person at risk for later depressive symptoms, but only when a bad event ensues. Neither the life event nor the style alone leads to depressive symptoms. The correlational studies are clarified: Overall correlations between attributional style and depression presumably result because part of the sample has experiences recent bad events. The results were more pronounced four weeks after the bad event than immediately after the event; this implies that the depressive symptoms were not transient disappointment or bad mood.

A second longitudinal study used the children described earlier. The attributional style and depression of the 96 children were measured two times separated by an interval of 6 months. Causal modelling was employed to evaluate the hypothesis that attributional style is a "risk factor" for depression. It is possible to decide questions of causal priority among nonmanipulated variables by using a longitudinal design and cross-lagged panel correlational analyses (Campbell, 1963; Campbell & Stanley, 1963; Kenny, 1973, 1975, 1979). The correlations

TABLE 6.7
Correlations between Attributional Style and
Depression—Midterm Examination Study

Correlation	Dissatisfied Students	Satisfied Students
One Week After Exam		
positive composite with BDI	−.05	.04
negative composite with BDI	.25*	.04
Four Weeks After Exam		
positive composite with BDI	−.24*	.18
negative composite with BDI	.28*	−.06

$^{*}p < .05$

TABLE 6.8
Cross-Lagged Correlations Between Attributional Style (CASQ)
Composites and CDI Scores—Children

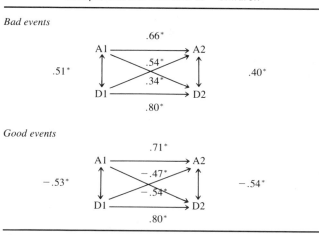

Note: A1 and A2 are attributions scores at Times 1 and 2, respectively;
D1 and D2 are depression scores at Times 1 and 2, respectively.
*p < .001

between attributional style and depression across time were computed. Because causes work forward in time, differences between the correlations of attributions at Time 1 and depression at Time 2 versus depression at Time 1 and attributions at Time 2 suggest causal priority. (For examples of recent uses of this inferential technique, see Kahle & Berman, 1979, and Knight, Roff, Barnett, & Moss, 1979). Because of the modest reliabilities of the attributional subscales, only the composites were used. Table 6.8 summarizes the relevant correlations. It can be seen that the correlation between attributional style for bad events at Time 1 and depression at Time 2 exceed the correlation betwen depressive symptoms at Time 1 and attributional style at Time 2 (*p < .02*). This supports the prediction of the insidious attributional style about good events; the cross-lagged correlations were essentially the same (−.47, −.54), implying no causal priority. Golin, Sweeney, and Shaeffer (1981) have found similar results for adults.

These findings support the reformulated helplessness model, however, a shortcoming should be mentioned. Depression, as operationalized here, was more stable across six months than attributional style. The learned helplessness model suggests that attributional style is more characteristic of a person than is depression, which is sometimes a consequence of attributional style. Accordingly, the stability of depression should be lower than the stability of attributional style. One possibility is that the lower reliabilities of attributional style accounts for the discrepancy (the reliabilities of the CDI at the two administrations were .86, and .80, respectively, estimated by Cronbach's [1951] coefficient alpha), because the reliability of a measure puts an upper limit on its stability. Another possibility is that attributional style is not a particularly stable individual difference, or that it may be more stable (and more predictive of depression) in some individuals than in others (Abramson & Martin, 1980).

Several pilot laboratory investigations of the reformulation are discussed. A number of studies, reviewed by Abramson et al. (1978), Miller and Norman (1979), and Roth (1980), have shown that following helplessness induction, situational manipulations of attributions determine the nature and extent of deficits. Such studies are, of course, compatible with the reformulated model, and in fact, they led to it; however, they do not speak to the role of attributional style in helplessness and depression. In other words, do the attributions which people habitually make their dispositional characteristics, affect helplessness deficits?

To answer this question, the authors are in the process of doing several studies, all having essentially the same design: Subjects are divided on the basis of their scores on the ASQ, they are given helplessness induction, and then a test task. Performance on the test task is predicted to be jointly determined by the pretreatment and attributional style. Such a design constitutes a strong and direct test of the reformulation. The strength of the test stems from the fact that individual differences in attributional style are predicted to operate in a situationally constrained setting (i.e., a laboratory helplessness experiment). The learned helplessness model does not claim that dispositional attributional style will always override situational determinants of attributions, so attention must be paid to whether or not the situational constraints were weak enough to allow attributional style to do its dirty work.

Following helplessness induction, each of the three attributional dimensions have a specifically predicted property: (a) people with an internal attributional style for bad events will show self-esteem deficits; (b) people with a stable attributional style for bad events will show deficits across time; and (c) people with a global attributional style for bad events will show deficits across situations.

We have not yet investigated prediction (a) in the laboratory; however, (b) and (c) have been addressed in pilot work. In one experiment, 96 subjects designated as stable or unstable (on the basis of a median split on this dimension of the ASQ) were given one of three pretreatments (escapable noise, inescapable noise, no pretreatment control) and then were tested to terminate noise on a hand shuttle-box, either immediately after the pretreatment or after a delay of three days (see Hiroto & Seligman, 1975, for a description of this apparatus). It was predicted that only the stable subjects would show helplessness three days later, but that both stable and unstable subjects would show helplessness on the immediate test.

Table 6.9 summarizes the results for two dependent measures: number of successful escapes and mean latency of responses. For both measures, the same

TABLE 6.9
Shuttlebox Performance—Stability Study

Condition	Stable Subjects		Unstable Subjects	
	# Successes	Mean Latency (Seconds)	# Successes	Mean Latency (Seconds)
Immediate Test				
escapable	18.38	1.90	18.00	1.99
inescapable	9.00	3.63	5.75	4.18
control	15.75	2.68	15.88	2.38
Delayed Test (3 days later)				
escapable	18.38	2.07	18.25	2.25
inescapable	6.25	4.16	10.75	3.09
control	13.62	2.99	10.75	3.33

results occurred: inescapable groups, except for the unstable subjects at three days, did worse in the task than the escapable and control groups. This is exactly what was predicted, and it was obtained even when the subjects' internality and globality scores (from the ASQ) were used as covariates in the appropriate analyses of variance.

In the second experiment, 144 subjects designated as global or specific (again by a median split on this dimension of the ASQ) were given one of the three pretreatments and then tested on a task which was either similar or dissimilar to the pretreatment task. The similar task was the hand shuttlebox (both the pretreatment task and the shuttlebox involved escaping noise); the dissimilar task was a series of 20 anagrams (see Hiroto & Seligman, 1975). The prediction was that global subjects would show deficits following inescapable noise on both the similar and dissimilar test tasks; specific subjects would show deficits only on the similar test task. The results of this study are in Table 6.10. Again, two dependent measures were recorded for each task; each showed the same pattern of results that were predicted by the reformulation. Inescapable subjects did badly at the test task in all conditions, except for specific subjects with a dissimilar test, even when internality and stability scores were used as covariates.

These two studies provide support for the reformulated model, however, they are pilot work. Additional work, in which the sample size of the studies is increased, and the parameters varied so that attributional style has more "room" to operate, will be done.

Nevertheless, there is reason to be optimistic about the hypothesis that attributional style "causes" later depressive symptoms and helplessness. The longitudinal studies and the laboratory experiments provide converging evidence that a person's habitual attributional tendencies processing uncontrollable, bad events

TABLE 6.10
Globality Study

Condition	Global Subjects		Specific Subjects	
	# Successes	Mean Latency (Seconds)	# Successes	Mean Latency (Seconds)
Similar Task				
escapable	15.67	2.62	18.00	2.03
inescapable	12.75	3.22	12.58	3.17
control	14.58	2.71	13.83	2.82
Dissimilar Task				
escapable	18.18	17.85	17.27	22.15
inescapable	14.91	39.42	18.08	19.53
control	17.67	23.47	17.58	22.58

produce depressive deficits. To a considerable degree, the reformulation has been supported by the research undertaken to date. In the last section of this chapter, some doubts about the reformulation are presented. Current controversies in the social psychological literature on attribution theory are the point of departure; and these suggest potentially fertile directions for future helplessness research.

CONCLUSION: SUMMARY, CRITIQUE, AND NEW DIRECTIONS

The empirical work described addressed two main questions. Does an insidious attributional style characterize depression? Does this style cause depression? Other questions addressed included: (a) Are mild and severe depression continuous? (b) Is childhood depression a viable concept? (c) What are the origins of attributional style? (d) Does attributional style as assessed by questioning a person relate to behavior?

The authors are now in a position to offer some answers to these questions: A tendency to attribute bad events to internal, stable, and global causes is associated with depressive symptoms. All of the studies point to this conclusion. Some people have remarked: "Of course this attributional style characterizes depression—it is a symptom of depression." In a certain sense, such a reduction of our research to the trivially obvious is flattering. However, the fact remains, that such a symptom of depression is not listed in any diagnostic manual. In addition, nondepressed people have this alleged symptom; these are the individuals who, as predicted, are at risk for depression when bad events strike.

Brief answers to the subsidiary questions addressed in the recent research may also be provided. First, there is no evidence in the studies that shows mild depression and severe unipolar depression to be anything but different in degree. Still, it is recognized that much more extensive study of clinical populations is needed, and we are turning our attention to such investigations. Second, childhood depression seems to be a meaningful concept; because it is not transient, it has the same symptoms as adult depression, and it has the same cognitive risk factors. Third, attributional style in children appears to derive, at least in part, from mothers. Fine-grained study of mother-child interaction is recommended, in order to discover how it is transmitted; the ultimate goal is to immunize children against depressogenic parents. Fourth, there appears to be considerable use to assessing attributional style by talking to a person. The Attributional Style Questionnaire taps introspection about causes, and suggests that a person's causal inferences about the world are not entirely tacit; if they were, none of the relationships found would be easily interpretable. In contrast to the vast social psychological literature documenting discrepancies between what a person says and what a person does (Wicker, 1969), research suggests that sensibly asked questions are a fertile source of predictions about how a person will act.

There are several worries about the lines of research and theorizing undertaken. First, the "man as scientist" metaphor: such a model usually ignores motivational constructs (although not always; cf. Heider, 1958). People hold certain attributions, not because they are motivated to do so, but because—granted their premises—it is rational to do so (Nisbett & Ross, 1980). This notion contrasts starkly to psychoanalytic conceptions of depression that hold depressives to be motivated to maintain their depression. At the present time, there is insufficient evidence to decide if the attributional style shown by depression is at all motivated.

Another criticism of the "man as scientist" metaphor has to do with the "rationality" it assumes (Nisbett & Ross, 1980). The learned helplessness model assumes that people operate logically with their attributional premises; however, a great deal of recent research has demonstrated that normative models of information processing are sometimes inaccurate descriptions of what people actually do (e.g. Kahneman & Tversky, 1973; Nisbett & Ross, 1980; Ross, 1977; Slovic & Lichtenstein, 1971). Future work should be directed at uncovering the heuristic bases of depressives' judgments, perhaps taking as a point of departure Beck's (1976) errors of logic. Some theorists have argued that the so-called causal attributions made by people are not technically causes but rather justifications (Buss, 1978; Harre & Secord, 1971; T. Mischel, 1964). Answers beginning with "because" need not refer to prior causes, but intead to goals that rationalize the action in question. The upshot of this point is that the attributional style of depressives may be forward looking, and not backward looking, as implied by the reformulation. If you are hit by lightning and survive, the fact that the cause of your bodily injuries is unstable, external, and specific is of no consolation, if you have to face a year's worth of complicated surgery and convalescence. Attributional style in depression is probably related not just to prior causes, but also to future consequences.

Related to this point is a question raised by Wortman and Dintzer (1978) and Janoff-Bulman (1979) in their critiques of the reformulation. They doubted whether the three attributional dimensions studied so far exhaust the critical cognitive precursors of depression, and suggested that attributions of controllability were also crucial. According to Janoff-Bulman (1979), only if the internal attribution is about character will the attribution be depressive. In contrast, internal attributions about behavior are antidepressive. According to Janoff-Bulman (1979), people are powerless to change their character, but they can modify and control their behavior.

To test this proposal, a sample of 87 undergraduates were asked to complete an expanded version of the ASQ along with the BDI (Peterson, Schwartz, & Seligman, 1981). The modification of the ASQ asked the subjects to quantify the control they perceived over each of the events. The authors then blindly content analyzed the attributions they provided as external, internal-behavioral, or internal-characterological. Briefly, the findings supported Janoff-Bulman (1979). Only characterological attributions were associated with depressive symptoms; both external and behavioral attributions were rated as more uncontrollable than behavioral attributions. However, it was also found that characterological attributions were rated as more stable and more global than were behavioral attributions. In short, the factor of control could be reduced to the factors of stability and globality, or vice versa. Thus, although a large number of characteristics of depressive attributional style could be proposed, in all likelihood, many of them would be redundant. For the time being, although recognizing that other names could be attached to them, the authors will stay with the dimensions of internality, stability, and globality. Other orthogonal dimensions might indeed exist, however, researchers must demonstrate not just the conceptual distinctiveness of additional dimensions, but also their empirical distinctiveness.

A final issue, which should worry helplessness theorists, had to do with the maladaptiveness of helplessness and depression. Because of the way helplessness experiments are set up and because the test tasks are solvable, a belief in noncontingency between responses and outcomes, and the holding of the insidious attributional style, are usually maladaptive. However, other views of depression see it as adaptive: a means of taking stock when surrounded by brick walls; a signal to disengage from fruitless pursuits (Klinger, 1975); and a message that one's commerce with the world is not all right (Rippere, 1976). All failures of adaptation are not the fault of the individual; often it is the world which is responsible for the "problem," the "maladaptive" cognitions of the victim.

In summation, a good deal was gained by the reformulation of the learned helplessness model. It better explained the facts of helplessness and depression.

However, something was also lost—the "learning" part of the original model. The old model, coming out of the animal learning tradition, specified precisely the environmental contingencies that brought about helplessness. The new model, with its emphasis on the person's cognition is less straight forward; the transduction from environmental contingency to expectation is modified by other cognitions, such as attributional style. Such a loss may be necessary, at least for now; however, the final recommendation is that future researchers attempt to understand how attributional style is acquired. It is hoped that this conference provide the impetus for such an attempt.

ACKNOWLEDGMENTS

The research reported here was supported by PHS MH 19604 to M. Seligman. We would like to acknowledge the help and advice of our colleagues, especially the members of the Helplessness Seminar at the University of Pennsylvania.

REFERENCES

Abramson, L. Y., & Martin, O. (1980). *Depression and the causal inference process.* Unpublished manuscript, State University of New York at Stony Brook.

Abramson, L. Y., & Sackeim, H. A. (1977). A paradox in depression: Uncontrollability and self-blame. *Psychological Bulletin, 84,* 839–851.

Abramson, L. Y., & Seligman, M. E. P. (1977). Modeling psychopathology in the laboratory: History and rationale. In J. D. Maser & M. E. P. Seligman (Eds.), *Psychopathology: Experimental models.* San Francisco, CA: Freeman.

Abramson, L. Y., Seligman, M. E. P., & Teasdale, J. D. (1978). Learned helplessness in humans: Critique and reformulation. *Journal of Abnormal Psychology, 87,* 49–74.

Ajzen, I. (1977). Intuitive theories of events and the effects of baserate information on prediction. *Journal of Personality and Social Psychology, 35,* 303–314.

Alloy, L. B., & Seligman, M. E. P. (1979). The cognitive component of learned helplessness and depression. In G. H. Bower (Ed.), *The psychology of learning and motivation* (Vol. 13). New York: Academic Press.

Beck, A. T. (1967). *Depression: Clinical, experimental, and theoretical aspects.* New York: Hoeber.

Beck, A. T. (1976). *Cognitive therapy and the emotional disorders.* New York: International Universities Press.

Beck, A. T., & Beck, R. W. (1972). Screening depressed patients in family practice: A rapid technic. *Postgraduate Medicine, 52,* 81–85.

Beck, A. T., Rush, A. J., Shaw, B. F., & Emery, G. (1979). *Cognitive therapy of depression.* New York: Guilford.

Beck, A. T., Ward, C. H., Mendelson, M., Mock, J., & Erbaugh, J. (1961). An inventory for measuring depression. *Archives of General Psychiatry, 4,* 561–571.

Berger, P. L., & Luckmann, T. (1966). *The social construction of reality.* Garden City, NY: Doubleday.

Berglas, S., & Jones, E. E. (1978). Drug choice as a self-handicapping strategy in response to noncontingent success. *Journal of Personality, 36,* 405–417.

Brown, G. W., & Harris, T. (1978). *Social origins of depression: A study of psychiatric disorder in women*. New York: Free Press.

Bumberry, W., Oliver, J. M., & McClure, J. N. (1978). Validation of the Beck Depression Inventory in a university population using psychiatric estimate as the criterion. *Journal of Consulting and Clinical Psychology, 46,* 150–155.

Buss, A. R. (1978). Causes and reasons in attribution theory: A conceptual critique. *Journal of Personality and Social Psychology, 36,* 1311–1321.

Campbell, D. T. (1963). From descripton to experimentation: Interpreting trends as quasi-experiments. In C. W. Harris (Ed.), *Problems in measuring change*. Madison: University of Wisconsin Press.

Campbell, D. T., & Stanley, J. C. (1963). Experimental and quasi-experimental designs for research on teaching. In N. L. Gage (Ed.), *Handbook of research on teaching*. Chicago: Rand McNally, 1963.

Cronbach, L. J. (1951). Coefficient alpha and the internal structure of tests. *Psychometrika, 16,* 297–334.

Douglas, D., & Anisman, H. (1975). Helplessness or expectation incongruency: Effects of aversive stimulation on subsequent performance. *Journal of Experimental Psychology: Human Perception and Performance, 1,* 411–417.

Dweck, C. S., & Bush, E. S. (1976). Sex differences in learned helplessness: 1. Differential debilitation with peer and adult evaluators. *Developmental Psychology, 12,* 147–156.

Dweck, C. S., & Reppucci, N. D. (1973). Learned helplessness and reinforcement responsibility in children. *Journal of Personality and Social Psychology, 25,* 109–116.

Elig, T. W., & Frieze, I. H. (1979). Measuring causal attributions for success and failure. *Journal of Personality and Social Psychology, 37,* 621–634.

Falbo, T., & Beck, R. C. (1979). Naive psychology and the attributional model of achievement. *Journal of Personality, 47,* 185–195.

Frankel, A., & Snyder, M. L. (1978). Poor performance following unsolvable problems: Learned helplessness or egotism? *Journal of Personality and Social Psychology, 36,* 1415–1423.

Geen, R. G. (1978). Effects of attack and uncontrollable noise on aggression. *Journal of Research in Personality, 12,* 15–29.

Goldstein, K. M., & Blackman, S. (1978). *Cognitive style: Five approaches and research*. New York: Wiley.

Golin, S., Sweeney, P. D., & Shaeffer, D. E. (1981). The causality of causal attributions in depression: A cross-lagged panel correlational analysis. *Journal of Abnormal Personality, 90,* 14–22.

Harre, R. M., & Secord, P. F. (1971). *The explanation of social behaviour*. Oxford: Basil Blackwell.

Harvey, J. H., Ickes, W. J., & Kidd, R. F. (1976). *New directions in attribution research* (Vol. 1). Hillsdale, NJ: Lawrence Erlbaum Associates.

Heider, F. (1958). *The psychology of interpersonal relations*. New York: Wiley.

Hiroto, D. S., & Seligman, M. E. P. (1975). Generality of learned helplessness in man. *Journal of Personality and Social Psychology, 31,* 311–327.

Janoff-Bulman, R. (1979). Characterological versus behavioral self-blame: Inquiries into depression and rape. *Journal of Personality and Social Psychology, 37,* 1798–1809.

Jones, E. E., & Nisbett, R. E. (1971). *The actor and the observer: Divergent perceptions of the causes of behavior*. New York: General Learning Press.

Journal of Abnormal Psychology, (1978). 87(1).

Kahle, L. R., & Berman, J. J. (1979). Attitudes cause behaviors: A cross-lagged panel analysis. *Journal of Personality and Social Psychology, 37,* 315–321.

Kahneman, D., & Tversky, A. (1973). On the psychology of prediction. *Psychological Review, 80,* 237–251.

Kelley, H. H. (1973). The processes of causal attribution. *American Psychologist, 28,* 107–128.

Kelly, G. A. (1955). *The psychology of personal constructs.* New York: Norton.

Kenny, D. A. (1973). Cross-lagged and synchronous common factors in panel data. In A. S. Goldberger & O. D. Duncan (Eds.), *Structural equation models in the social sciences.* New York: Seminar, 1973.

Kenny, D. A. (1975). Cross-lagged panel correlation: A test for spuriousness. *Psychological Bulletin, 82,* 887–903.

Kenny, D. A. (1979). *Correlation and Causality.* New York: Wiley.

Klinger, E. (1975). Consequences of commitment to and disengagement from incentives. *Psychological Review, 82,* 1–25.

Knight, R. A., Roff, J. D., Barnett, J., & Moss, J. L. (1979). Concurrent and predictive validity of thought disorder and affectivity: A 22-year follow-up of acute schizophrenics. *Journal of Abnormal Psychology, 88,* 1–12.

Kovacs, M., & Beck, A. T. (1977). An empirical-clinical approach toward a definition of childhood depression. In J. G. Schulterbrandt & A. Raskin (eds.), *Depression in Children.* New York: Raven, 1977.

Krantz, D. S., Glass, D. C., & Snyder, M. L. (1974). Helplessness, stress level and the coronary-prone behavior pattern. *Journal of Experimental Social Psychology, 10,* 284–300.

Kruglanski, A. W. (1980). Lay epistemo-logic—Process and contents: Another look at attribution theory. *Psychological Review, 87,* 70–87.

Langer, E. J. (1978). Rethinking the role of thought in social interaction. In J. H. Harvey, W. J. Ickes, & R. F. Kidd (Eds.), *New directions in attribution research* (Vol. 2). Hillsdale, NJ: Lawrence Erlbaum Associates.

Lefkowitz, M. M., & Burton, N. (1978). Childhood depression: A critique of the concept. *Psychological Bulletin, 85,* 716–726.

MacCorquodale, K., & Meehl, P. E. (1948). On a distinction between hypothetical constructs and intervening variables. *Psychological Review, 55,* 95–107.

Maier, S. F., & Jackson, R. L (1979). Learned helplessness: All of us were right (and wrong): Inescapable shock has multiple effects. In G. H. Bower (Ed.), *The psychology of learning and motivation* (Vol. 13). New York: Academic Press.

Maier, S. F., & Seligman, M. E. P. (1976). Learned helplessness: Theory and evidence. *Journal of Experimental Psychology: General, 105,* 3–46.

Maier, S. F., Seligman, M. E. P., & Solomon, R. L. (1969). Pavlovian fear conditioning and learned helplessness. In B. A. Campbell & R. A. Church (Eds.), *Punishment and aversive behavior.* New York: Appleton-Century-Crofts.

Miller, I. W., & Norman, W. H. (1979). Learned helplessness in humans: A review and attribution theory model. *Psychological Bulletin, 86,* 93–119.

Miller, S. M., & Seligman, M. E. P. (1980). *The attributional reformulation of helplessness: Recent evidence.* Unpublished manuscript, University of Pennsylvania.

Mischel, T. (1964). Personal constructs, rules, and the logic of clinical activity. *Psychological Review, 71,* 180–192.

Mischel, W. (1968). *Personality and assessment.* New York: Wiley.

Monson, T. C., & Snyder, M. (1977). Actors, observers, and the attribution process: Toward a reconceptualization. *Journal of Experimental Social Psychology, 13,* 89–111.

Neisser, U. (1967). *Cognitive Psychology.* New York: Appleton-Century-Crofts.

Nisbett, R., Ross, L. (1980). *Human inference: Strategies and shortcomings of social judgment.* Englewood Cliffs, NJ: Prentice-Hall.

Nisbett, R., & Wilson, T. D. (1977). Telling more than we can know: Verval reports on mental processes. *Psychological Review, 84,* 231–259.

Overmier, J. B., & Seligman, M. E. P. (1967). Effects of inescapable shock upon subsequent escape and avoidance learning. *Journal of Comparative and Physiological Psychology, 63,* 23–33.

Paykel, E. S. (1974). Recent life events and clinical depression. In E. K. E. Gunderson & R. D. Rahe (Eds.), *Life stress and illness.* Springfield, IL: Thomas.

Peirce, C. S. (1955). Philosophical writings of Peirce (J. Buchler, Ed.). New York: Dover.

Peterson, C. (1978). Learned helplessness following insoluble problems: Learned helplessness or altered hypothesis pool? *Journal of Experimental Social Psychology, 14,* 53–68.

Peterson, C. (1979). Uncontrollability and self-blame in depression: Investigation of the paradox in a college population. *Journal of Abnormal Psychology, 88,* 620–624.

Peterson, C. (1980). Attribution in the sportspages: An archival investigation of the covariation hypothesis. *Social Psychology Quarterly, 43,* 136–140.

Peterson, C., Schwartz, S. M., & Seligman, M. E. P. (1981). Self-blame and depressive symptoms. *Journal of Personality and Social Psychology, 41,* 253–259.

Radloff, L. S. (1975). Sex differences in depression: The effects of occupation and marital status. *Sex Roles, 3,* 249–265.

Raps, C. S., Peterson, C., Jonas, M., & Seligman, M. E. P. (1982). Patient behavior in hospitals: Helplessness reactance or both? *Journal of Personality and Social Psychology, 42,* 1036–1041.

Raps, C. S., Peterson, C., Reinhard, K. E., Abramson, L. Y., & Seligmen, M. E. P. (1982). Attributional style among depressed patients. *Journal of Abnormal Psychology, 92,* 102–108.

Rippere, V. (1976). Review of Seligman's Helplessness. *Behavior Research and Therapy, 15,* 207–209.

Ross, L. (1977). The intuitive psychologist and his shortcomings: Distortions in the attribution process. In L. Berkowitz (Ed.), *Advances in Experimental Social Psychology* (Vol. 10). New York: Academic Press.

Roth, S. (1980). A revised model of learned helplessness in humans. *Journal of Personality, 48,* 103–133.

Rotter, J. B. (1966). Generalized expectancies for internal versus external control of reinforcement. *Psychological Monographs, 80*(1, Whole No. 609).

Ryle, G. (1949). *The concept of mind.* London: Hutchinson, 1949.

Schuldenbrandt, J. G., & Raskin, A. (1977). *Depression in children.* New York: Raven.

Scott, W. A., Osgood, D. W., & Peterson, C. (1979). *Cognitive structure.* Washington, DC: Winston.

Seligman, M. E. P. (1974). Depression and learned helplessness. In R. J. Friedman & M. M. Katz (Eds.), *The psychology of depression: Contemporary theory and research.* Washington, DC: Winston.

Seligman, M. E. P. (1975). *Helplessness: On depression, development, and death.* San Francisco: Freeman, 1975.

Seligman, M. E. P. (1981). A learned helplessness point of view. In L. P. Rehm (Ed.) *Behavior Therapy for Depression: Present Status and Future Directions.* New York: Academic Press.

Seligman, M. E. P., Abramson, L. Y., Semmel, A., & von Baeyer, C. (1979). Depressive attributional style. *Journal of Abnormal Psychology, 88,* 242–247.

Seligman, M. E. P., & Maier, S. F. (1967). Failure to escape traumatic shock. *Journal of Experimental Psychology, 74,* 1–9.

Seligman, M. E. P., Maier, S. F., & Soloman, R. L. (1971). Unpredictable and uncontrollable aversive events. In F. R. Brush (Ed.), *Aversive conditioning and learning.* New York: Academic Press.

Seligman, M. E. P., Weiss, J., Weinraub, M., & Shulman, A. (1980). The Seligman-Weiss debate. *Behavior Research and Therapy, 18,* 459–512.

Semmel, A., Peterson, C., Abramson, L. Y., Metalsky, G. L., & Seligman, M. E. P. (1980). *Predicting depressive symptoms from attributional style and failure.* Unpublished manuscript, University of Pennsylvania.

Slovic, P., & Lichtenstein, S. (1971). Comparison of Bayesian and regression approaches to the study of human information processing in judgment. *Organizational Behavior and Human Performance, 6,* 649–744.

Smith, R., & Seligman, M. E. P. (1980). *Black and lower class children are more vulnerable to impairment of problem solving following helplessness.* Unpublished manuscript, University of Pennsylvania.

Streufert, S., & Streufert, S. C. (1978). *Behavior in the complex environment.* Washington, DC: Winston.

Weiner, B. (1974). *Achievement motivation and attribution theory.* Morristown, NJ: General Learning Press.

Wicker, A. W. (1969). Attitudes versus actions: The relationship of verbal and overt behavioral responses to attitudinal objects. *Journal of Social Issues, 25,* 41–78.

Wortman, C. B., & Brehm, J. W. (1975). Response to uncontrollable outcomes: An integration of reactance theory and the learned helplessness model. In L. Berkowitz (Ed.), *Advances in experimental social psychology* (Volume 8). New York: Academic Press.

Wortman, C. B., & Dintzer, L. (1978). Is an attributional analysis of the learned helplessness phenomenon viable? A critique of the Abramson-Seligman-Teasdale reformulation. *Journal of Abnormal Psychology, 87,* 75–90.

Zuckerman, M., & Lubin, P. (1965). *Manual for the Multiple Affect Adjective Check List.* San Diego: Educational and Industrial Testing Service.

7 Feeling versus Being Helpless: Metacognitive Mediation of Failure-Induced Performance Deficits

Julius Kuhl
Max-Planck-Institute for Psychological Research
Munich

Some years ago, a newspaper printed an article about a gang of burglars who robbed a warehouse and locked the two night watchmen in the trunks of two cars. One of the men survived by breathing air from the spare tire. The next morning he was able to attract the attention of some people passing by the car. The other man had suffocated before the trunk was opened (cf. Atkinson, 1964, p. 74). If one could have observed the less fortunate man shortly before his death, one might have noticed that he did not try at all to find a solution to his problem. If the man could have been asked why he did not try, he might have attributed his lack of motivation to the hopelessness of his situation, he did not expect to be able to control the situation, so he gave up. Motivational psychologists would be delighted with this pattern of observations. They would conclude that the unfortunate man's behavior was perfectly consistent with an expectancy-value theory of motivation, however, this insight would not have been of much help to the poor man in the trunk.

This little story may illustrate some of the problems involved in cognitive theories of action, in general, and the cognitive theory of learned helplessness, in particular. In most studies, empirical tests of hypotheses regarding cognitive mediators of behavior are based on correlational evidence. On the one hand, there is some measure of the assumed cognitive mediator, such as causal attribution, self-efficacy, or belief in the uncontrollability of outcomes (cf. Bandura, 1977; Roth & Kubal, 1975; Weiner, Frieze, Kukla, Reed, Rest & Rosenbaum, 1971). On the other hand, there is some index of the behavior psychologists are interested in, for instance, risk taking, behavioral change, or performance, respectively. Of course, it is known that one may not draw causal inferences from correlational evidence, but more often than not it is done, especially when correlational data is all that is available.

To return to the unfortunate man in the trunk: Is it true that he does not find the solution because he does not try? Is it true that he does not try because he feels helpless? Or could the causal chain work just in the opposite direction? Could it be that the man, in spite of initially trying very hard, actually was helpless right from the beginning? In this case, the primary problem would be a functional helplessness, that is, the man may have been so overwhelmed by the dangerous situation that he could not think clearly. Motivational helplessness, that is, giving up because of feeling helpless, may have developed as a result of functional helplessness, rather than being its cause. Thus, one may ask whether the man felt helpless as a result of being helpless or whether he became helpless as a result of feeling helpless.

LEARNED HELPLESSNESS

Consider the typical laboratory experiment on learned helplessness. Subjects who have been exposed to repeated uncontrollable failure on some training task typically show impaired performance on a subsequent test task, compared to a control group that was allowed to succeed on the training task, or did not work on that task. The performance deficits in the failure group have been observed even when the test task was totally different from the training problem (e.g., Hiroto & Seligman, 1975). Seligman and his associates have attributed impaired performance following helplessness training to an expectational deficit. According to this theory, subjects develop a belief in the uncontrollability of outcomes that results in a motivational deficit. Deteriorated performance is considered a direct consequence of reduced motivation.

An alternative explanation of helplessness phenomena is presented. This alternative is consistent with what is known from theory and research in achievement motivation. Unfortunately, this body of research within the literature on learned helplessness has been neglected; although the two research traditions are based on very similar experimental paradigms. It has been theoretically expected and empirically demonstrated that repeated exposure to uncontrollable failure is associated with an increase rather than with a decrease in the need for achievement (Atkinson, 1958; McClelland, Clark, Roby & Atkinson, 1949). This phenomenon has been called *the motivational effect of failure* (Atkinson & Birch, 1974). In their discussion of an experiment on learned helplessness, Miller & Seligman (1975, p. 236) report an observation that is consistent with that effect, however, they do not emphasize the fact that it runs counter to what should be expected on the basis of their theory of helplessness. The subjects from the failure group seemed to try hard when confronted with the test task and later, when they noticed how poor they were performing, gave up. There is reason to believe that the need for or the personal value of achieving success does not decrease following failure. But what about the assumed expectational deficit?

Do subjects transfer reduced expectancy of control from the training task to the test task? The theory of learned helplessness is based on the assumption that people generalize their experiences extensively (Seligman, 1975). The author would like to emphasize the discriminative abilities of human subjects. Mischel (1968; 1973) has collected a great amount of evidence suggesting that human subjects may discriminate precisely, even between seemingly similar situations. An extensive study was conducted on the degree to which cognitive variables generalize across various situations. Among all the parameters included in the study (for instance, expectancy, causal attribution, personal standards, perceived value of success), expectancy variables turned out to be the most specific (Kuhl, 1977). Analyses of the data based on Rasch's stochastic measurement model (Rasch, 1960), revealed that concepts of one's own ability to control outcomes typically were not transferred from one task to another.

If neither the value nor the expectancy of succeeding at the *test* task is reduced, as a result of failing on the training task, it is difficult to account for the observed performance deficits on the basis of expectancy-value theory alone. This theory may explain what people intend to do; however, it has to be extended, in order to explain the degree to which they actually accomplish their goals. Discrepancies between motivation and performance have been attributed to detrimental effects of overmotivation. This explanation actually begs the question: What are the cognitive processes that intervene between the intention to achieve a goal and the performance of the activities necessary to reach that goal? The expectancy-value theory should be extended by a third factor, which the author calls *action-control*. This factor presumably controls the extent to which an intended action is actually performed.

Among the various cognitive processes controlled by that factor, selective attention presumably plays a major role. Specifically, it is assumed that performance should be facilitated when attention is focused on action-related information. Conversely, when attention focuses on state-related information, the performance of an intended action should be impaired. The degree of state-orientation may mediate failure-induced performance deficits. Subjects may be preoccupied, focusing on the state created by the failure experience, trying, for instance, to explain why they failed or trying to analyze their own emotional state. One advantage of this interpretation of helplessness effects is that it explains the generalization of performance deficits. This is done without making unnecessary assumptions regarding a transfer of perceptions of uncontrollability to tasks that are perceived as totally different from the task one has failed to accomplish. If performance deficits are attributable to deteriorated cognitive functioning, as a result of interfering state-related cognitions, they can transfer to any kind of behavior, even to activities that are not achievement-related. A person who is preoccupied with analyzing his or her state may show impaired performance on any type of test, burn the dinner, or behave awkwardly toward his or her friends. The theory of action-control is consistent with an attentional theory of anxiety (Wine, 1971) as well as with Diener & Dweck's (1978) empirical analysis of helplessness effects. In this study, children who showed impaired performance following helplessness training were more preoccupied with, what the author calls, *state-oriented* thinking than children whose performance did not deteriorate.

ACTION-CONTROL

Before the results from two experiments testing some of the assumptions are presented, an attempt is made to specify, in greater detail than earlier theories, the nature of the cognitions, which presumably interfere with performance, and the functional significance of those cognitions. Action-control at first, was not thought of as a means to explain helplessness effects; originally, the construct was proposed to explain why people sometimes do what they intend to do and why they sometimes fail to behave according to their intentions. Naturally, action-control should be a function of personality and situational variables. A questionnaire was constructed to assess individual differences in action-control (Kuhl, 1985). The validity of this questionnaire could be demonstrated in a recent study (Kuhl, 1982). Sixth graders (48) from a German school were asked to rate to what extent they intended to engage in various activities such as playing in a ballgame, watching TV, or reading a book, after school. The next day, subjects were asked how much time they had actually spent doing those activities. Correlations between reported degree of commitment and reported time spent were computed separately for each activity within two groups, classified as state-oriented or action-oriented, according to the median of the action-control scale. Figure 7.1 illustrates the results of this study. If the action-control scale is a valid measure of a person's tendency to behave according to his or her intentions, there should be a greater correlation between intention and behavior within the action-oriented group than within the state-oriented group. This was actually the case for 11 out of 13 free-choice activities. The study also included a situational variable affecting action-control. The list of activities also described nine forced-choice activities, which are usually carried out under social pressure in that age group. When the performance of an activity is mainly externally controlled, congruence between intention and performance should not require a strong degree of action-control; the results were also in line with this prediction. Correlations between degree of intention and actual performance for the nine externally controlled or routine activities, such as brushing one's teeth or doing one's homework, did not differ consistently between action and state-oriented subjects.

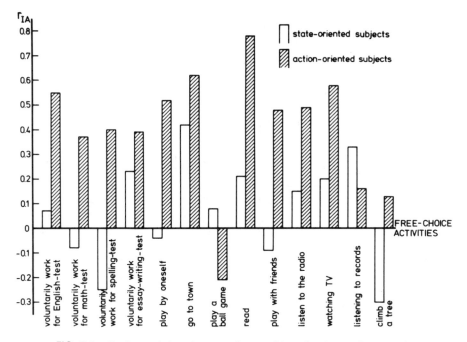

FIG. 7.1. Rank correlations between degree of intentional commitment and reported time spent for 13 free-choice afterschool activities, computed separately within subjects groups classified as state-oriented or action-oriented.

What is the theoretical status of action control? How does it affect behavior? Some possible answers to those questions are outlined in Fig. 7.2. Action-control is thought of in terms of a metacognitive process aiming at the performance of an intended action. This process is classified as metacognitive for two reasons: first, it presumably organizes and controls cognitive operations, such as selective attention and the amount and content of information processed, in a way that maximizes the congruence between intention and performance; second, action-control presumably relies heavily on knowledge about the effectiveness of various cognitive operations for achieving that objective. The degree of action-control aroused in a particular situation may vary between the two extremes called state-orientation and action-orientation.

What could be a definitional basis for describing an organism as action-oriented rather than state-oriented? The author would like to define the organism as action-oriented when it successively or simultaneously attends to all of the following elements: the present state; some future state; a discrepancy between the two states; and action alternatives that may help transform the present into the

222

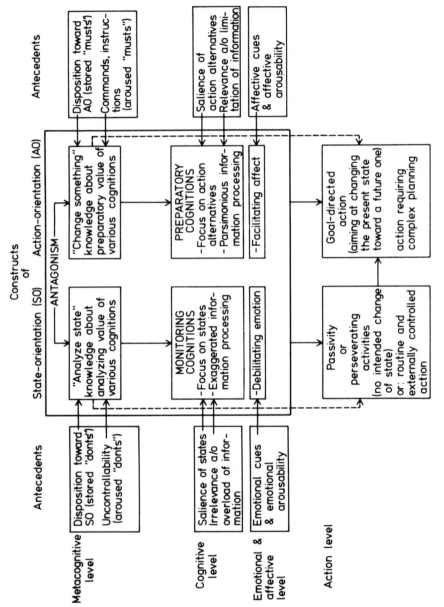

FIG. 7.2.   A metacognitive model of action-control.

intended future state. If one of those elements is missing, the organism is said to be state-oriented.

Figure 7.2 outlines the theory of action-control. On the metacognitive level, the theory assumes an antagonism between state-orientation and action-orientation. State-orientation is conceptualized as a metacognitive tendency controlling cognitive operations that facilitate the analysis of some past, present, or future state. Action-orientation is considered a metacognitive tendency that instigates cognitive operations that, in turn, facilitate the arousal of goal-directed action tendencies. Action-oriented cognitions may focus on expectancy, or value-related information regarding the usefulness of various action alternatives. Examples for state-oriented activities may be: ruminating about possible causes of the present state, such as after a series of successive failures; or attending to one's own emotional state. State-oriented cognitions are considered not to instigate any action tendency. They may even actively inhibit action tendencies, or block the expression of action tendencies, as a result of the assumed partial incompatibility between state and action-orientation. As the amount of state-oriented cognitions aroused, increases, the probability that the person performs some intended action decreases. Specifically, it is assumed that an action which requires complex preparatory planning cannot be performed when the organism is state-oriented, because part of the attentional capacity needed is used for state-oriented processes. Routine activities or activities that are under strong environmental control may be performed even when the organism is mildly state-oriented.

Among the assumed mediators of action-control described on the cognitive level of the model (see Fig. 7.2), selective attention may be the most effective one. Presumably, the metacognitive tendency toward action-orientation arouses a tendency to selectively attend to stimuli that are relevant for the performance of an intended action; whereas, state-orientation should be mediated by attention focused on state-related information. Ach (1910) regarded selective attention as the most important determinant of what he called the *efficiency of the will.* Unfortunately, his early phenomenological analysis of the process intervening between intention and performance—a process which he simply called *the will*—was ignored in later theories of motivation. The main reason for this may be Lewin's (1935) criticism of the concept of volition and his attempt to replace the problem of volition by the problem of motivation (cf. Kuhl, 1984b).

Besides selective attention, a second factor may mediate between intention and performance. State-orientation may be associated with a greater amount of information processed than is necessary for performing an action; action-orientation may be mediated by a strategy aiming at the most parsimonious processing of action-related information. Also, the two antagonistic metacognitive processes are considered to be associated with two opposing feelings. State-orientation should be associated with emotions that interfere with the instigation of action tendencies. Pribram (1971) uses the word *e-motion* literally, referring to a process that takes the organism ''out of motion.'' Conversely, the feelings associated with action-orientation may be called *affects*. Ach (1910) used this term when referring to facilitating effects of the feelings aroused following an unexpected failure outcome. As one can see from Fig. 7.2, the extent to which each of the three assumed factors (selective attention, parsimony of information processing, and emotional or affective feelings) mediates between the metacognitive and the behavioral level should depend on respective antecedent conditions (the salience of action vs. state-related cues, the amount of relevant or irrelevant information available, and the arousability of debilitating or facilitating feelings within the person).

It would be beyond the scope of the present contribution to report the empirical evidence related to various aspects of the model (see Kuhl, 1985, for a detailed summary). The results of two studies conducted to test selected aspects of the model are summarized. In one study (see Fig. 7.3), the mediating role of selective attention could be demonstrated (Kuhl, 1983, p. 269). Attention to task-relevant or task-irrelevant stimuli was assessed by a method based on memory recall. The results indicated that action-oriented subjects recalled significantly less task-irrelevant stimuli than did state-oriented subjects. However, when the task was made uncontrollable the results were reversed. In an uncontrollable condition, action-oriented subjects appeared to pay less attention to task-relevant stimuli than state-oriented subjects. This pattern of results is consistent with the assumption of a metacognitive strategy aiming at the maintenance of action-control. In order to stay active, the organism should selectively attend to action-related stimuli, and stop attending to them when the situation becomes uncontrollable. The latter strategy facilitates a change to another—controllable—activity.

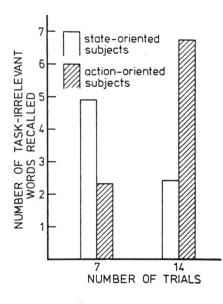

FIG. 7.3.   Number of task-irrelevant words recalled in two experimental conditions (7 vs. 14 trials) and two groups of subjects (action vs. state-oriented Ss)

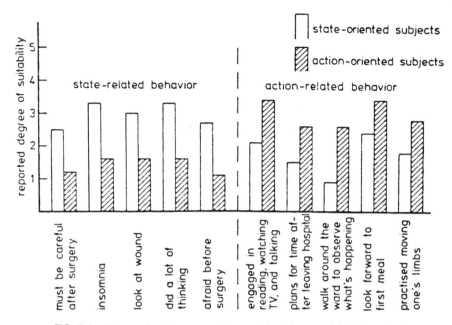

FIG. 7.4.   Degree of endorsement of 5 state-related items and 5 action-related items for two groups of subjects.

The second study (see Fig. 7.4) revealed some correlates of action-orienta-tion, related to all three intervening processes postulated in the model (Kuhl, 1984a). Subjects who had undergone a hernia operation were selected from three German hospitals. Two days after their operation, they were administered the action-control scale and several other scales. State-oriented subjects rated the intensity of their pain, as expected, significantly higher, and requested double the amount of analgesics than was requested by action-oriented subjects. The postulated debilitating effect of greater emotionalism in state-oriented indi-viduals was also indicated. State-oriented subjects reported to have less fre-quently left the room to see what was going on in the ward, and they reported to have fewer plans for the time after leaving the hospital than was the case for action-oriented subjects. Also, state-oriented subjects more frequently reported to have been engaged in thinking about their situation and to have looked at their incision than was reported by the action-oriented subjects.

ACTION-CONTROL AND LEARNED HELPLESSNESS

Note that the model expects that the amount of action or state-orientation aroused on the metacognitive level should be a function of an interaction between a personal disposition toward action or state-orientation, situational determinants, such as uncontrollability of outcomes, and commands or instructions, exerting some pressure on the person to initiate some action (Fig. 7.2). In the present context the controllability factor is of special interest. Recently (Kuhl, 1981), I proposed a three-factor theory of learned helplessness that summarizes the theoretical points already made in this discussion. The three-factor model is based on a dynamic theory of achievement motivation (Atkinson & Birch, 1974; Kuhl & Blankenship, 1979a, 1979b). According to this model, repeated exposure to uncontrollable outcomes first increases a (metacognitive) tendency toward action-orientation that is replaced by a tendency toward state-orientation when a perception of uncontrollability has developed (cf. Fig. 7.5, a & b). State-orientation may interfere with optimal cognitive functioning, especially when the task is complex enough to demand full attention. The two lower curves in Fig. 7.5 describe the assumed changes in motivation during helplessness training.

In contrast to traditional helplessness theory (Abramson, Seligman & Teasdale, 1978; Seligman, 1975), a distinction is made between motivation for the training task and motivation regarding the test task. This distinction has to be made in situations in which subjects discriminate regarding the type of abilities involved, between training and test task. The lower curve (Fig. 7.5, e, f), referring to the subject's motivation to work on the training problem, predicts heightened motivation during the first phase of helplessness training and below baseline motivation when outcomes are considered uncontrollable. This curve represents Wortman and Brehm's (1975) extension of the theory of helplessness, including an initial phase of reaction. Increased motivation as an initial response to failure is consistent with various developments within the theory of achievement motivation (Atkinson & Feather, 1966; Kukla, 1972; Meyer, 1973), as well as with earlier theories of motivation (Ach, 1937; Hillgruber, 1912).

When training and test tasks are not perceived to be a function of similar factors, motivation to engage in the test task is assumed to be inversely related to the inclination to persist on the original problem. As long as the person is still strongly motivated to overcome the difficulties on the training problem, motivation to switch to a different task should be low. However, as soon as the motivation to persist on the original problem ceases, an increase in the motivation to demonstrate one's ability on a different task is expected. This prediction is based on the assumed substitutional relation between various achievement-related tasks. If the need for achievement cannot be satisfied on one task, a tendency to demonstrate one's ability on some substitute task should be aroused. The traditional theory of helplessness represents a special case of the three-factor model. When training and test tasks are identical or similar, the lowest curve in Fig. 7.5 is sufficient to explain performance deficits, following prolonged exposure to uncontrollable outcomes.

In two recent experiments, an attempt was made to discriminate between the two theoretical explanations, which are at stake. In the first study, 36 subjects were randomly assigned to one of six groups. The six groups resulted from

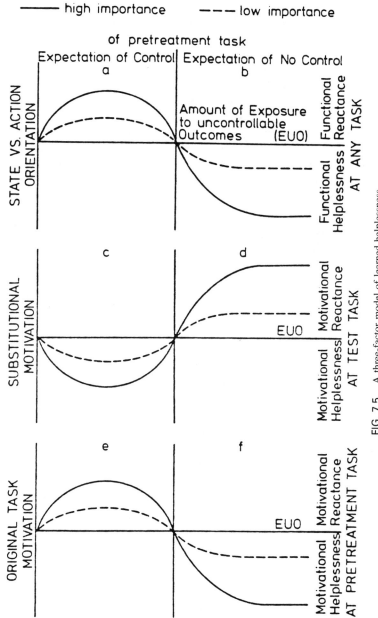

FIG. 7.5. A three-factor model of learned helplessness.

227

crossing two types of pretreatment with three types of intervention following pretreatment. The two pretreatment conditions were incontingent failure feedback at a Levine-discrimination task, and a control condition in which subjects merely "had a look at the tasks." The intervention conditions were (a) induction of state-orientation; (b) induction of action-orientation; and (c) no-intervention control. At the beginning of the experiment, subjects were introduced to both tasks that were to be used in the experiment. Following the training phase, induction of state-orientation was attempted by allotting the subjects 5 minutes to write an essay about the present situation and about the reasons for their performance.

Induction of action-orientation was attempted by having the subjects read a story about a little child with eating problems. During the test phase, a standard concentration test ("d2-test" Brickenkamp, 1962) was used. In this test, the subject has to mark all the letters d having two apostrophes, from a random sequence of d's and p's having 0, 1, or 2 apostrophes, above and/or below the letter. Before and after pretreatment subjects responded to four scales assessing expectancy of success and perceived controllability regarding both the training and the test task.

In order to check the extent to which expectancy and controllability beliefs had been transferred from the training to the test task, the two measures were compared between the failure and the no-failure groups. There were no reliable differences in expectancy of success or in perceived controllability, regarding either task, prior to the training phase. Significant differences were found following training between the failure groups and the no-failure groups both in expectancy and in controllability ratings (Fig. 7.6), regarding the training task. However, a similar difference was not found, on the posttraining measures of expectancy or controllability regarding the test task. The results based on expectancy ratings are shown in Fig. 7.6. The results indicate that neither reduced expectancy of success nor the reduced perception of controllability has been transferred from the training to the test task. Also, no evidence was found suggesting a motivational deficit regarding the test task. To the contrary, subjects in the failure conditions reported significantly greater importance to performing well on the test task than control subjects. Further, subjects from the failure condition which included an induction of state-orientation, reported significantly greater effort expenditure on the test task than did control subjects. Obviously, these results are more in line with the three-factor theory than with traditional helplessness theory emphasizing motivational deficits.

An analysis of performance data from the test task revealed a significant main effect of failure induction. As can be seen from Fig. 7.7, the number of symbols checked was significantly lower in the failure groups. Planned comparisons of performance scores, between each failure group and the no-failure-no-intervention control group, showed that only the failure group that was instructed to engage in a state-oriented activity displayed a significant performance deficit.

The fact that performance deficits were most dramatic in the state-oriented failure group supports the alternative explanation proposed by the three-factor model.

However, the induction of action-orientation does not seem to have been successful. Although subjects in that condition did not have significant performance deficits compared to the control group, they did not show the expected

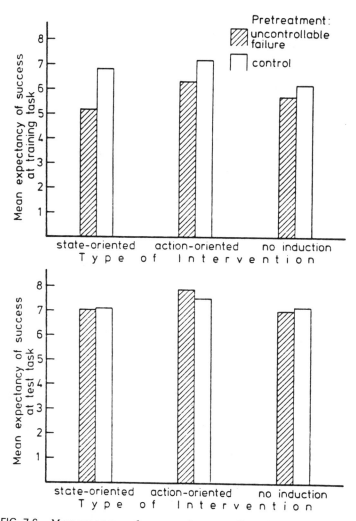

FIG. 7.6.   Mean expectancy of success ratings, regarding training and test task, obtained following pretreatment as a function of type of intervention (SO = state-oriented, AO = action-oriented, C = no intervention) and type of pretreatment (S = unsolvable task, C = "just looking at the tasks").

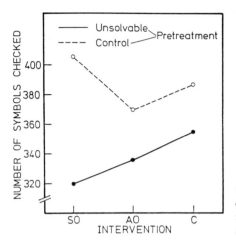

FIG. 7.7. Performance (number of symbols checked) at the test task as a function of pretreatment and intervention. (SO = state-orientation; AO = action-orientation; C = no intervention).

reversal of performance deficits compared to the state-oriented failure-group. The reason for this may be that, in order to prevent state-orientation, it may not be sufficient to distract attention from the failure experience by having the subjects read a nonachievement related story. A second experiment was designed to study the effects of another procedure, aimed at the induction of action-orientation.

Three groups were run in this experiment. Besides the usual no-failure control group, there were two failure groups. In one of them, subjects were instructed, prior to the training phase, to explicitly state the hypothesis they were testing. The other group received the usual instructions suggesting implicit hypothesis testing. The experiment also included a measure of the assumed personality determinant of generalized helplessness effects. Each group was split in two subgroups, according to the median of the scores on the action control scale. It was hypothesized that performance deficits should be most pronounced in the state-oriented failure group involving implicit testing of hypotheses. A reversal of this helplessness effect was expected in the state-oriented failure group that was instructed to explicitly state their hypothesis on each trial. Explicit hypothesis testing was expected to prevent state-cognitions from occurring; it should help subjects maintain a systematic problem-solving approach, which should prevent them from engaging in state-oriented thinking. For action-oriented subjects, no such difference between explicit and implicit hypothesis testing was expected. Instead, action-oriented subjects were expected to show facilitation of performance compared to baseline performance.

The results (Fig. 7.8) were in line with most of the predictions; state-oriented subjects from the condition involving implicit testing performed significantly worse than state-oriented subjects from the condition involving explicit testing. Within the control group, action-oriented subjects performed significantly better than state-oriented subjects. Therefore, baseline performance was not computed from this control group, but rather from control groups taken from two other experiments. In those experiments, within the control groups there was no difference in performance between state-oriented and action-oriented subjects. Compared to this baseline, state-oriented subjects, who had stated their hypotheses, explicitly showed a significant facilitation effect; the performance deficit found in state-oriented subjects from the implicit-testing condition approached statistical significance.

Analysis of expectancy and controllability ratings obtained after training, revealed that those performance effects cannot be attributed to respective changes regarding expectancy of success or perceived controllability (Fig. 7.9). Although the two measures regarding the training task dropped in the two failure groups, no such drop was found in ratings of expectancy and controllability of the test task. Also, performance deficits cannot be attributed to a motivational deficit; there were no significant differences between the groups with regard to perceived importance of good performance or reported effort expenditure at the test task.

In summary, these experiments suggest that performance deficits following failure were not associated with a belief in uncontrollability, generalized from the training task to the test task; in other words, people did not seem to become helpless on the test task because they felt helpless when they began working on that task. Subjects' reports did not indicate any motivational deficit regarding the test task that might have resulted from a generalized belief in a loss of control. Thus, researchers are faced with a problem that cannot be solved on the basis of an expectancy-value theory of motivation. Performance deficits were obtained

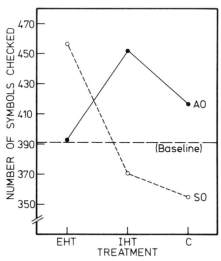

FIG. 7.8.   Performance (number of symbols checked) as a function of disposition for action-orientation (AO), state-orientation (SO), and type of pretreatment (EHT = explicit hypothesis testing and incontingent failure; IHT = implicit hypothesis testing and incontingent failure; C = no-failure control).

without respective deficits regarding expectancy or value of a good performance. An attempt has been made to formulate a theory of action-control that proposes an extension of expectancy-value theory. According to this extended theory, a discrepancy between motivation and performance is expected when the subject is state-oriented. The experiments show that significant performance deficits could be found only when there was reason to believe that subjects were state-oriented,

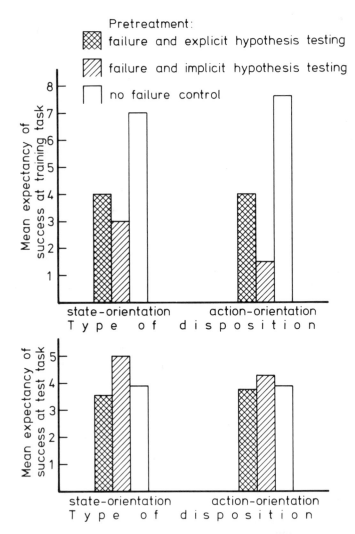

FIG. 7.9.   Mean expectancy-of-success ratings regarding training and test task obtained following pretreatment as a function of pretreatment (EHT = incontingent failure and explicit hypothesis testing; IHT = incontingent failure and implicit hypothesis testing (= no-failure control) and state vs. action-orientation (SO vs. AO).

either as a result of experimental induction of or as a result of a disposition toward state-orientation.

These results have important implications for applied purposes. Take, for instance, underachievement or depression. To the extent that such disturbances are attributable to functional helplessness, rather than to a motivational deficit, an attributional intervention may not be the most effective strategy. An underachieving child or a depressive person may show impaired performance in a variety of situations because he or she is too much concerned with explaining the problem. An attributional therapy that reinforces this state-oriented attitude toward the problem may even aggravate the disorder. An alternative approach may focus on helping the client shift his or her attention away from the possible causes of the problem, which may never be found with absolute certainty. Instead the client should be encouraged to think about possible ways of changing the situation; giving up unattainable goals and focusing on new attainable goals. The client may learn that thinking about change is more helpful than ruminating about the present state and its causes.

One final remark regarding the fruitfulness of the helplessness paradigm. The demonstration of the transfer of performance deficits following failure across considerably different tasks is of great theoretical significance. It calls attention to a problem that has almost been forgotten since the time of Ach's analysis of the "efficiency of the will." It may appear ironic that the transfer of helplessness effects has not been discovered within the mainstream of traditional research on achievement motivation. The discovery of generalized performance deficits following failure is a very important one, even though, or maybe because, the proposed theoretical explanation may not be sufficient. The authors of the revised theory of helplessness (Abramson et al., 1978) are aware of the fact that helplessness phenomena cannot be fully explained on the basis of traditional theories of motivation; they do not attempt to remedy this problem. This author does not believe that the theory of action-control answers all the open questions; it raises many questions to be answered in the future. This may, at least, prevent researchers from getting caught in the present state of motivation theory, dominated by expectancy-value conceptions. The remedy that is suggested to prevent researchers from turning "state-oriented" is: Think of alternatives to the traditional state of the theory that suggests that people are helpless because they feel helpless, it may be that they feel helpless because they are helpless.

REFERENCES

Abramson, L. Y., Seligman, M. E. P., & Teasdale, J. D. (1978). Learned helplessness in humans: Critique and reformulation. *Journal of Abnormal Psychology, 87,* 49–74.

Ach, N. (1910). *Über den Willensakt und das Temperament.* Leipzig: Quelle und Meyer.

Ach, N. (1937). Zur neueren Willenslehre. In *Bericht über den 15 Kongreß der Deutschen Gesellschaft für Psychologie in Jena, 1936* (pp. 125–156). Jena: Fischer.

Atkinson, J. W. (Ed.). (1958). *Motives in fantasy, action, and society.* Princeton, NJ: Van Nostrand.

Atkinson, J. W. (1964). *An introduction to motivation*. Princeton, NJ: Van Nostrand.
Atkinson, J. W., & Birch, D. (1974). The dynamics of achievement-oriented activity. In J. W. Atkinson & J. O. Raynor (Eds.), *Motivation and achievement* (pp. 271–326). Washington, DC: Winston.
Atkinson, J. W., & Feather, N. T. (1966). *A theory of achievement motivation*. New York: Wiley.
Bandura, A. (1977). Self-efficacy: Toward a unifying theory of behavioral change. *Psychological Review, 84*, 191–215.
Brickenkamp, R. (1962). *Test d-2*. Göttingen, FRG: Hogrefe.
Diener, C. I., & Dweck, C. S. (1978). Analysis of learned helplessness: Continuous changes in performance, strategy and achievement cognitions following failure. *Journal of Personality and Social Psychology, 36*, 451–462.
Hillgruber, A. (1912). Fortlaufende Arbeit und Willensbetätigung. *Untersuchungen zur Psychologie und Philosophie, 1*(6).
Hiroto, D. S., & Seligman, M. E. P. (1975). Generality of learned helplessness in man. *Journal of Personality and Social Psychology, 21*, 311–327.
Kuhl, J. (1977). *Meß- und prozeßtheoretische Analysen einiger Person und Situationsparameter der Leistungsmotivation*. Bonn: Bouvier.
Kuhl, J. (1981). Motivational and functional helplessness: The moderating effect of state versus action orientation. *Journal of Personality and Social Psychology, 40*, 155–170.
Kuhl, J. (1982). Handlungskontrolle als metakognitiver vermittler zwischen Intention und Handeln: Freizeitaktivitäten bei hauptschülern. *Zeitschrift für Entwicklungspsychologie und Pädagogische Psychologie, 14*, 141–148.
Kuhl, J. (1983). *Motivation, Konflikt und Handlungskontrolle*. Heidelberg: Springer.
Kuhl, J. (1984a). Motivationstheoretische Aspekte der Depressionsgenese: Der Einfluß der Lageorientierung auf Schmerzempfinden, Medikamentenkonsum und Handlungskontrolle. In W. Wolfersdorf, R. Straub, & H. G. Hole (Eds.), *Der depressive Kranke der psychiatrischen linik: Theorie und praxis der diagnostik und therapie*. Regensburg, FRG: Roderer.
Kuhl, J. (1984b). Volitional aspects of achievement motivation and learned helplessness: Toward a comprehensive theory of action control. In B. A. Maher (Ed.), *Progress in Experimental Personality Research* (Vol. 13, pp. 99–171). New York: Academic Press.
Kuhl, J. (1985). Volitional mediators of cognition-behavior consistency: Self-regulatory processes and action vs. state orientation. In J. Kuhl & J. Beckmann (Eds.), *Action control: From cognition to behavior*. New York: Springer-Verlag.
Kuhl, J., & Blankenship, V. (1979). Behavioral change in a constant environment: Shift to more difficult tasks with constant probability of success. *Journal of Personality and Social Psychology, 37*, 549–561.
Kuhl, J., & Blankenship, V. (1979). The dynamic theory of achievement motivation: From episodic to dynamic thinking. *Psychological Review, 86*, 141–151.
Kukla, A. (1972). Foundations of an attributional theory of performance. *Psychological Review, 79*, 454–470.
Lewin, K. (1935). *A dynamic theory of personality*. New York: McGraw-Hill.
McClelland, D. C., Clark, R. A., Roby, T. B., & Atkinson, J. W. (1949). The projective expression of needs: 4. The effect of need for achievement on thematic apperception. *Journal of Experimental Psychology, 39*, 242–255.
Meyer, W. U. (1973). *Leistungsmotiv und Ursachenerklärung von Erfolg und Mißerfolg*. Stuttgart, FRG: Klett, 1973.
Miller, W. R., & Seligman, M. E. P. (1975). Depression and learned helplessness in man. *Journal of Abnormal Psychology, 84*, 228–238.
Mischel, W. (1968). *Personality and assessment*. New York: Wiley.
Mischel, W. (1973). Toward a cognitive social learning reconceptualization of personality. *Psychological Review, 80*, 252–283.
Pribram, K. H. (1971). *Languages of the brain*. Englewood Cliffs, NJ: Prentice-Hall.

Rasch, G. (1960). *Probalistic models for some intelligence and attainment tests.* Kopenhagen: Nielson & Lydicke.

Roth, S., & Kubal, L. (1975). Effects of noncontingent reinforcement on tasks of differing importance: Facilitation and learned helplessness. *Journal of Personality and Social Psychology, 32,* 680–691.

Seligman, M. E. P. (1975). *Helplessness: On depression, development, and death.* San Francisco: Freeman.

Weiner, B., Frieze, H. J., Kukla, A., Reed, L., Rest, S., & Rosenbaum, R. M. (1971). *Perceiving the causes of success and failure.* New York: General Learning Press.

Wine, J. (1971). Test anxiety and direction of attention. *Psychological Bulletin, 76,* 92–104.

Wortmann, C. B., & Brehm, J. W. (1975). Responses to uncontrollable outcomes: An integration of reactance theory and the learned helplessness model. In L. Berkowitz (Ed.), *Advances in experimental social psychology* (Vol. 8, pp. 277–336). New York: Academic Press.

III UNDERSTANDING AND LEARNING

In this section, learning refers to the acquisition of new knowledge, understanding conceptual relationships, and problem solving. The chapters by Chi, Glaser and Pellegrino, and Greeno and Riley stem from an information processing perspective that is frequently represented in terms of computer analogies. The results of theoretical and empirical work in this field have suggested that two types of knowledge are necessary for understanding: factual and procedural knowledge appropriate to a particular content domain in which an individual must solve problems and take action, and metacognitive knowledge concerning how to direct and organize cognitive activities. Metacognitive knowledge was discussed earlier by Brown, Flavell, and Kluwe.

Chi's discussion is directly related to the chapters in the first section of this volume. Chi demonstrates the relevance of domain-related knowledge to developmental research concerning cognitive abilities, especially metamemory skills. Using the notion of production rules, Chi provides a framework for distinguishing among declarative and procedural "domain knowledge," "strategic knowledge," and "metacognitive knowledge," which includes procedural and declarative components as well. Chi discusses metamemory within this framework, and points out that the use of the prefix "meta" may cause confusion. In addition, she notes that before we can expect insights about metacognitive development, we require greater knowledge about the development of cognitive strategies.

The chapter by Robert Glaser and James Pellegrino provides a comprehensive analysis of inductive thinking. They describe a research project designed to allow a thorough analysis of the abilities that are central to inductive thinking.

Glaser and Pellegrino's results show that subjects who differ with regard to the success of their inductive inferences may be distinguished according to three features: management of memory load, knowledge of task constraints, and the accuracy of their knowledge representation. These results are used to formulate guidelines that may be useful for adapting instruction to the cognitive abilities of the learner, and for improving those cognitive abilities.

The development of a taxonomy of different types of learning is a central concern of the chapter by Greeno and Riley. They address two concerns: the extent to which metacognitive knowledge is conscious, and the relationship between metacognitive knowledge and planning knowledge. Of particular interest is the distinction between explicit and implicit understanding and how this distinction relates to verbal reports concerning one's own thinking. The experimental procedures used with children often reveal that they have an implicit, although not verbalizable understanding of the problems they are given. Understanding, according to Greeno and Riley, entails the elaboration of an appropriate internal representation of a problem (what they call a problem schema) and the deployment of actions adequate for solving the problem (action schema). In this sense, understanding is an analogue to knowledge as addressed earlier by Brown and Kluwe. Greeno and Riley provide empirical results that illustrate the function of an appropriate internal representation to problem solutions.

8

Representing Knowledge and Metaknowledge: Implications for Interpreting Metamemory Research

Michelene T. H. Chi
Learning Research and Development Center
University of Pittsburgh

Children's memory development has traditionally been interpreted in terms of the development of control processes or strategies. However, experimental results that purport to show strategic deficiencies in young children often require implicit or explicit assumptions about the nature of a child's knowledge base. If careful consideration of the knowledge base is made, it becomes clear that such results may be due to an inadequate knowledge representation that may not permit the application of a mature strategy. This alternative interpretation would point to the importance of examining the knowledge base in determining memory performance.

In order to discuss knowledge organization, a representational framework is needed. Procedural knowledge (general strategies and domain-specific procedures) may be represented as production rules, declarative knowledge may be embodied in a node-link network. Such a representation is useful not only for explaining some of the well known developmental phenomena, but can also be extended to represent metaknowledge. This extension leads to a taxonomy of various types of metaknowledge.

By using such a representation and classification of metaknowledge, metamemory research can be examined. Such an analysis shows that some metamemory research may not tap metaknowledge at all, or that it may not discriminate between knowledge and metaknowledge. In any case, it is clear that before progress is made in this area, the concepts of metacognition and metaknowledge need to be defined and examined more closely.

This chapter is composed of four parts. The first section briefly describes why a knowledge emphasis is important in cognitive developmental psychology. The second section postulates a representational framework for the discussion of various forms of knowledge: declarative, procedural, strategic, and meta-knowledge. Within the framework proposed, the third section evaluates the term metamemory and related research. The final section concludes with a general discussion.

KNOWLEDGE APPROACH TO MEMORY DEVELOPMENT

Within the last decade, there has been a trend in both cognitive psychology and artificial intelligence research toward exploring the knowledge that must be possessed by an individual and/or an intelligent system. The new theory of artificial intelligence sees an intelligent system as one that can use and express different forms of knowledge. The change in focus, from programming a system with powerful search heuristics to programming a system to possess a large quantity of organized knowledge, was necessitated by the parallel findings in cognitive psychology concerning humans' dependence on a large and well struc-tured knowledge base. For example, a chess master's expertise derives not from his powerful search heuristics, but rather from the large storage of meaningful patterns in long-term memory. This large storage of patterns is manifested when the chess master is able to reproduce a board position after viewing it for only 5 seconds (Chase & Simon, 1973). A computer with powerful search heuristics has yet to match the chess master's capabilities in finding good moves; however, the greater the amount of knowledge that is programmed into the computer, the closer is its approximation to a human player. (For a more extensive review and discussion, see Chi, Glaser, & Rees, 1982.)

At about the same time, the idea that knowledge may be a fundamental source of developmental differences in memory was entertained by Brown (1975), Chi (1976), Huttenlocher and Burke (1976), and others. To appreciate the distinction of this outlook, one has to understand, up to that point in time, the theoretical orientation of developmental psychology. One could say that developmental psychology in the late 1960's was influenced predominantly by Piaget's theory, and attempts in the American literature were characterized by the question of stages and transition between stages. The research focused not only on norming when a child enters each stage, but also on showing how the stage theory is really transitory. For example, it was discovered that children of younger ages are really capable if one provides hints, such as attending to the "relevant"cues, of doing tasks at a more sophisticated level, as exemplified by the influential thesis of Rochel Gelman (1969).

Evidence for Strategy

The onset of the Atkinson and Shiffrin (1968) process model of memory, caused American developmental psychologists to wonder whether or not the child is inferior in the control processes used to manipulate information. These control processes are usually called strategies. Rehearsal, labeling, elaboration, and categorization are a few of the strategies that have been identified. Hence, research in the first half of the decade of the 1970's was aimed at demonstrating the limitations of young children in their use of control processes; in fact, the demonstration was quite simple, straightforward, and clear. In general, young children (around the age of 5) were found not to use strategies; the appearance of active use of strategies was found to develop with age. Finally, even at times when the routine of the strategy is available (such as knowing how to repeat a string of items), the strategy does not necessarily mediate performance.

The importance of strategic deficiencies was further confirmed when it was shown that the lack of a strategy hinders performance, and the possession of a strategy facilitates performance. For example, the amount of recall has been shown to correlate directly with the amount of rehearsal. If six and seven-year-old nonrehearsers were induced to rehearse, their recall would be elevated to the level of children who normally rehearsed (Keeney, Cannizzo, & Flavell, 1967).

Hence, because most developmentalists implicitly assume that there is a "sufficiency criterion" involved, particularly for simple tasks, there has been no need to bring in the knowledge base as a potential source for age differences. For example, for digit recall, as in a digit span task, the assumption is that being able to identify the digits by name is a sufficient criterion for maximal performance in that task. This assumption is usually made as a result of generalization from adult research. In the adult research, one generally assumes that individual differences are minimal, and that all adults have approximately the same knowledge about digits; therefore, performance in tasks requiring digits can and should only reflect other processing differences. However, this implicit assumption simply cannot be made in developmental research. The following example should illustrate the point.

A common task used in developmental research to assess memory performance is free recall. Typically, approximately 20 items are presented to the child to free recall. These 20 items fall into four or five taxonomic categories, such as Furniture, Clothing, Animals, etc. One common performance measure is the amount of recall. For children of around age 5, the amount of recall is usually around four items; for older children, it can vary from 9–12 items, depending on the age. Eleven-year-olds typically remember at most, eight items (Tenney, 1975).

The interpretation of the performance difference between age groups is that younger children do not apply efficient organizational strategies. How is such an interpretation substantiated? By looking at the recall output (that is, the pattern of response sequence), one can seek some measure of organization, such as the amount of clustering, subjective organization, chunking, or whatever. Typically, younger children exhibit less organization in their recall output than older children (Moely, 1977). Their organization also tends not to be consistent from trial to trial. The lack of an orderly and consistent output is interpreted to mean that young children do not impose an organization on the material to be recalled.

Inadequate use of organizational processes can also be shown to occur during the encoding of the stimulus material, independent of a recall task (Ornstein & Corsale, 1979). To do so, one typically assesses the degree to which children can sort the presented items into their taxonomic categories prior to recall. The typical findings mirror those found in the organization of the recall output. That is, again, younger children's sorting is less reliable, more random, and shows a weaker organization; they tend not to put items into the taxonomic categories that they belong in, and so on.

However, such differences in organization are seldom attributed to a knowledge-based problem (although currently, investigators such as Ornstein & Corsale, 1979, and Lange, 1978, are orienting toward a knowledge interpretation). Because the child, when asked to do so, can easily identify the categories to which these items belong, the investigator generally assumes that these items and their membership in the taxonomic categories are known to the child. For example, the child may be asked explicitly to put all the animals together, and he or she will generally be able to do so. Alternatively, a child can produce a set of "core" members when a category label, such as "animal," is presented (Nelson, 1974).

The foregoing analysis illustrates why the interpretation preferred by developmentalists is dictated by the observation of the child's inadequate use of retrieval, or encoding strategies, to facilitate recall. Primarily, this is because such inadequate strategy usage is accompanied by a seemingly adequate knowledge base. However, using the given example, it is asserted that, to be able to recognize that cats and dogs are both animals does not require the same knowledge structure as to be able to group them together without prompting. Figure 8.1 shows two tree structures, depicting how that knowledge can be represented. In the first case, members of the taxonomic categories are represented in the way they are envisioned by the adult experimenter: a hierarchy with class members associated with their superordinate nodes. In the other case, each instance of the category simply has attached to it a set of features, one of which is the nature of the item. For example, cat is seen as an animal, just as cat is also known as having four legs, being furry, and so on. But somehow, the data base is not organized so that cats and dogs are embedded under the superordinate Animal node. Such a structure would produce exactly the results obtained: Children do not spontaneously organize the items according to the taxonomic categories, but will organize the items when prompted; this is because they can recognize that a cat is an animal and a dog is an animal. Therefore, the interpretation presented is that the developmental findings reflect, in part, the organization of knowledge, rather than strictly the application and use of strategies. A test of this interpretation would be to first ask each individual child to produce his or her "core" category members, and then to ask each child to sort or recall them. Presumably, these "core" members would be represented as a group, and organization during input and output should be facilitated by the existing cohesive structure in memory. Some

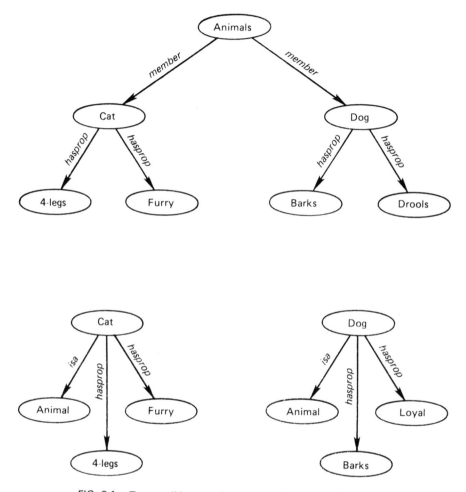

FIG. 8.1.   Two possible semantic structures for concepts in memory.

evidence of this interaction of the structure of semantic memory and organization is provided in Chi (1985).

There are additional reasons for taking a knowledge approach. The most blatant one is that there are times when age differences in memory performance are not accompanied by strategy differences, suggesting that some other sources, such as knowledge, must have produced the difference. One kind of evidence is provided by the study of Huttenlocher and Burke (1976); they specifically presented the stimulus items in a memory span task so as to induce grouping. They reasoned that because adults grouped digits in three's, children might benefit from such grouping; therefore, to facilitate encoding, they presented the digit string in groups of three. They found that children between the ages of 4 and 11, all benefited from such grouping; however, differences were still maintained across the age groups, suggesting that it is not a simple matter of a difference in the use of grouping strategy.

A similar type of evidence can be found in training studies. That is, if training in the use of strategies is provided for children of both age groups, both groups will improve their performance so that the initial age difference is still maintained (e.g., Storm, 1978). A third kind of evidence concerns studies where very young children (in the 2–4 age range) are tested; it is assumed that children in this age range do not actively use strategies (Myers & Perlmutter, 1978), yet their memory recall does improve with age. Although each of these three kinds of evidence may be subjected to alternate interpretation, taken as a whole, they suggest that age differences in memory performance are not always accompanied by observable strategy differences. Instead, an alternative source of development, knowledge, must at times be taken into consideration. (For an extensive review of this interpretation, see Chi & Ceci, in press).

Evidence for Knowledge

Beyond the studies cited, there is actually direct support for the notion that knowledge may be an important component of memory development. One way to test this hypothesis is to seek evidence where age differences are minimized because knowledge differences are reduced. Two related experiments illustrate that approach. Dempster (1978) showed that when one controls for stimulus familiarity in a memory span task, by using consonant letter strings that have little structural similarity to English, age differences disappear between first and sixth graders. Similarly, Boswell (1974) manipulated the letter strings for a span task with very brief exposure durations, and found that the further away the letter strings were in their approximation to English, the more reduced the age differences were (between the second graders and adults).

Another set of studies also implicated the role of knowledge in affecting children's performance. Richman, Nida and Pittman (1976) found that in a repeated free recall learning task, older children generally learned more rapidly than younger children. However, when words were used so that the meaningfulness values were held constant across grades, between-grade learning differences were minimal. Holding the meaningfulness constant implies that there were no knowledge differences; therefore, age differences in learning performance were minimized. Similarly, when the amount of semantic knowledge children had of words in a cued recall task was controlled, no differences in recall scores were observed between 7 and 12-year-olds (Ceci & Howe, 1978). Both of these studies further point to the importance of having the appropriate semantic knowledge related to the words used in the experiment. To a large extent, the existence of the relevant knowledge determined whether or not age differences were found.

To further assess the importance of the role that knowledge plays in children's memory performance, one could presumably find situations where children actually have more domain knowledge than adults. If domain knowledge is an important source of development, perhaps a reversal of the age trend could be obtained. Precisely this manipulation was used by Chi (1978) in comparing the recall of chess positions by 10-year-old children who had greater chess knowledge than adults. A cross-over effect was obtained; the children could recall a greater number of chess pieces than adults, yet at the same time, they could recall fewer digits than the adults. The interpretation is that the results reflect the children's greater knowledge of chess, but more limited knowledge of digits, as compared to the adults. This finding has been replicated in other laboratories. For example, using words from the Battig and Montague norms for adults, and a children-generated list of cartoon names and games for children, the same cross-over effect in recall was obtained by Lindberg (1980). The results suggest that having domain-related knowledge can actually overcome children's limitation in the use of strategies.

This section began by questioning whether the role of strategy usage is all-encompassing in determining age differences in memory and cognitive performance. Evidence for the possibility of another source of development—knowledge—was proposed, by citing studies whose findings cannot be accounted for by postulating an improvement in the use of strategies. Finally, more recent evidence was provided which points directly to the importance of the role that knowledge plays, and further, shows that the often observed traditional age trend (performance improvement with age) can sometimes be reduced, eliminated, or even reversed. This suggests that to completely understand age effects, one must necessarily examine the knowledge differences between age groups. In the next section, what it means to have more knowledge, that is, to have the relevant knowledge that is organized and accessible, is examined more microscopically.

A FRAMEWORK FOR REPRESENTING KNOWLEDGE

In the previous section, the terms strategy and knowledge were loosely defined and used dichotomously. The purpose of this section is to elaborate and describe, in one possible way, the different forms that knowledge can take, as well as how the concept of metaknowledge applies. The author borrows heavily from the work of Anderson (1976), Greeno (1978), and Norman and Rumelhart (1975); however, any deviations and modifications of their work are the results of intuition and preconceived biases, suitable for explaining developmental findings.

Domain Knowledge

Domain knowledge can take two forms: declarative; and procedural. Declarative knowledge is factual in nature, such as knowing about animals, knowing about number facts, and knowing about bicycles. For example, knowing that a dog is an animal is declarative knowledge. Furthermore, declarative knowledge can be distinguished from procedural knowledge by the way it is represented. Declarative knowledge can be represented in terms of a semantic propositional network, where a concept (such as a dog) may be represented as a node, and links specify the relationships among the nodes. Hence, the proposition that "a dog is an animal" could be represented by two nodes, with an *isa* link between them (see Fig. 8.2). A child may also know that a dog has four legs, and so on; these pieces of information can simply be represented as additional related nodes linked to the "dog" node. The degree of complexity of the semantic network should correspond to the amount, elaborateness, and organization of a child's declarative knowledge (see Chi & Koeske, 1983).

Procedural knowledge is knowledge about how to do things. For example, knowing how to ride a bicycle, or knowing how to do multiplication, would be

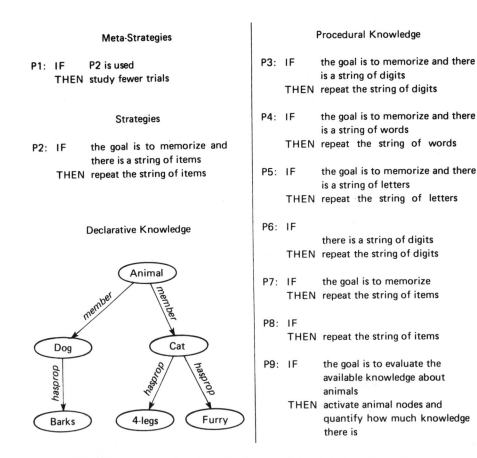

Meta-Strategies

P1: IF   P2 is used
     THEN study fewer trials

Strategies

P2: IF   the goal is to memorize and
           there is a string of items
     THEN repeat the string of items

Declarative Knowledge

Procedural Knowledge

P3: IF   the goal is to memorize and there
           is a string of digits
     THEN repeat the string of digits

P4: IF   the goal is to memorize and there
           is a string of words
     THEN repeat the string of words

P5: IF   the goal is to memorize and there
           is a string of letters
     THEN repeat the string of letters

P6: IF
           there is a string of digits
     THEN repeat the string of digits

P7: IF   the goal is to memorize
     THEN repeat the string of items

P8: IF
     THEN repeat the string of items

P9: IF   the goal is to evaluate the
           available knowledge about
           animals
     THEN activate animal nodes and
           quantify how much knowledge
           there is

FIG. 8.2.   Representations for declarative, procedural, strategic, and meta-strategic knowledge.

considered procedural knowledge. Furthermore, procedural knowledge can be represented as a set of production rules, which are condition-action pairs (Newell, 1973). The condition of a production rule specifies a feature or set of features that must match either the content of working memory (such as stimulus inputs that are stored there temporarily) or the structure of the activated portion of the semantic network. Hence, in a way, the condition side of a production rule takes as argument the structure of the declarative knowledge, and the action side constitutes procedures that either modify or add to the semantic structure, or manipulate an external environment. For example, Fig. 8.2 lists several different productions (P3, P4, P5) that may be analogous to the procedures of rehearsing a set of digits or a string of words.

Although there is an active debate concerning whether or not there should be a distinction in representation between declarative and procedural knowledge (see Anderson, 1976; Winograd, 1975), for developmental purposes, it is useful to make a fundamental distinction between the two. Procedural knowledge and declarative knowledge are also often considered to be domain-specific because they generally refer to a domain specific knowledge. For example, declarative knowledge can also be general world knowledge; in some sense, all knowledge is classifiable into some type of domain. However, a more important distinction, although still rather arbitrary, is the difference between procedural knowledge and strategies.

Strategies

Strategies, as the concept is used in developmental research, seem to have a special status; they have the property of being general and global, rather than domain-specific. To capture that property, here a strategy is defined simply as a general procedure, in the sense of application to several domains. P2 in Fig. 8.2 is an example of a strategy. In this representation, a strategy has four properties, some of which have been implicitly assumed in the literature. First, and most important, a strategy is general and domain-independent. In the example provided by P2, that production should be used whether the "items" are digits, words, or letters. Second, a strategy as do all procedures, has a *goal*. Third, a strategy as do all procedures, can have several components; that is, the action of "repeat" can itself be a call to other procedures. The final property of strategies, as distinct from procedural knowledge, is that the total number of strategies in memory must be finite, and in fact, should be relatively small. That is, the total number of rules, such as P2, should be fewer than the total number of rules, such as P3–P9. This last property is an implicit assumption made by most researchers (see Hayes, 1985), and necessarily underlies the philosophy of training studies. If one wishes to distinguish between procedural knowledge and strategies the finiteness assumption is also necessary.

The operational definition given to strategies, has three implications. The first is that strategies do have many of the properties of procedural knowledge; basically, they are represented in the same way, as production rules. Second, because the difficulty of separating general from domain-specific declarative knowledge has already been discussed, strategy is clearly artificially distinct from procedural knowledge, in the sense that it is defined to be general rather than domain-specific. For the time being, however, because it is possible to artificially segregate the two, the distinction might serve a useful purpose. Finally, even with the simplistic and global representation described one can already begin to offer explanations for a variety of developmental phenomena in the context of this representation. One common and most serious finding is that for the purpose of generalization, strategy training has been unsuccessful. Belmont and Butterfield (1977) have reviewed a number of training studies and found only a few to have succeeded in obtaining generalization from one task situation to another. It is conjectured that one possible reason for the failure to transfer, is that perhaps what was taught was a procedure, and not a strategy; that is, a domain-specific procedure, such as P3 or P4, may have been taught, and what was required to generalize would be a production rule, such as P2 (see Fig. 8.2).

Another common finding is that younger children can often learn to use a strategy, but unless explicitly told to use it, will not apply the strategy. This can be interpreted to mean that perhaps during instruction the appropriate goal was not properly encoded. That is, with the goal missing (in the case of P6), a child will not know that the rehearsal procedure should be activated, when the task instruction to memorize is presented. (This is one possible interpretation for production deficiency.)

A third common finding is that whenever an instructional approach is used to teach or induce the use of strategies, older children often will learn and adopt it more readily than younger children. One possible explanation for this finding, according to the framework used, is that the older child may already have a number of specific versions of a production (corresponding to different domains, such as P3, P4, and P5) available in memory, so that acquisition of the general form of a strategy production (P2) would be easier. For example, the older child may already know how to repeat a string of words, a string of letters, etc., when he or she sees one. Therefore, it is easier to acquire a new production because he or she already has in store all the other approximations to the final general form of the production. Although how a learning mechanism operates has not been postulated, one can clearly accept the proposition that a new production can be learned faster and easier if there are others like it already in memory. For example, one mechanism that comes to mind, is learning by analogy (Rumelhart & Norman, 1980), another mechanism is generalization (Anderson, Kline, & Beasley, 1978).

Hence, the foregoing interpretation, although speculative, suggests that with a concrete representation of what different forms of knowledge look like, one may begin to understand developmental performance.

Metaknowledge

What is metaknowledge in the context of the present representational framework? The term meta can be used in two ways; the straightforward way is to interpret meta as a reference to cognition. Thus, metaknowledge is knowledge of cognition or memory. In this sense, one could substitute the word meta by the word cognition; therefore, metaknowledge is cognitive knowledge, and meta-memory would be memory knowledge. A more complex interpretation is to consider the term meta as a reference to second-order knowledge. Thus, it is somewhat analogous to the concept of second-order function, as in second-order derivatives in calculus. With this conception, because there are several forms of knowledge, there necessarily must be several varieties of metaknowledge. An examination of what representation the different varieties of second-order knowledge might take, as well as the more direct and simplistic view of metaknowledge, follows. Knowing the precise representation should elucidate the possible acquisition processes that develop with age and learning.

Meta-declarative Knowledge.   There might be meta-declarative knowledge, for instance, that would be knowing what I know about animals. How would one represent meta-declarative knowledge? There are two ways. One way is to treat the term meta as a reference to cognitive knowledge; meta-declarative knowledge would be factual knowledge about cognition, much like factual knowledge about any other domain, such as animals. Hence, I could have stored in memory that I am a chess expert, and therefore I know a great deal about chess; similarly, that I am a cognitive psychologist and I know a great deal about cognition and memory. In both cases, these are prestored declarative knowledge; the latter example illustrates metaknowledge only in the sense that the content of the knowledge is about cognition.

Alternatively, if the necessary knowledge about cognition, or any other domain, is not there, then a procedure is needed to assess what and how much one knows about a domain (whether the domain is cognition or animals). In this sense, the term meta refers to second-order knowledge, or a function. In representation, meta-declarative knowledge would be the same thing as a procedure or a strategy; it would be a rule that takes as inputs (the arguments) the declarative knowledge, and produces some action on the inputs, such as some kind of evaluation. Hence, theoretically, meta-declarative knowledge would take the same form as either procedural knowledge or strategies. What appears to be awareness of one's declarative knowledge may be nothing more than an activation of the declarative knowledge in the context of the experimenter's or self-inquiry. For example, if the experimenter asks me if I know about animals, or how much I know about animals, that would constitute meta-questions. To answer the first type of question one needs to search or activate the relevant nodes in semantic network, and answer when the available structure is activated.

If the question requires an evaluation of how much knowledge, then in addition, some kind of assessment of quantity has to be made. The complexity of the processes needed to answer meta-declarative type of questions depends on whether or not the question addresses a prestored declarative knowledge, or if a procedure is needed to assess existing declarative knowledge about cognition.

To recapitulate, according to the formulation, the kind of knowledge used for answering meta-type questions depends entirely on the questions the experimenter posed, and whether or not the specific answer is already prestored as a proposition. Thus, if the experimenter asked "What do you know about animals?" the child can answer simply by activating the animal nodes, and assuming that the activated portion of the semantic network is the content of working memory, give a core-dump of the contents of a working memory. Likewise, if the experimenter asks "Are you a good chess player?" the response may also be a prestored proposition—a simple declarative statement that can be retrieved. But if the experimenter asks, "How much do you know about animals?" it may require not only the activation of the animal nodes, but also some evaluation and quantification of the activated portion of the semantic network. In Figure 8.2 P9 may be an example of such a procedure. For developmental interests, the question boils down to whether or not children possess the additional evaluation function, such as P9; the answer is probably not. They probably acquire them with development, in the same manner that other complex procedures are acquired, including quantification processes.

In sum, it has been proposed that meta-declarative knowledge can be of two kinds. First, what is often meant by metaknowledge (or knowledge about cognition) may be nothing more than prestored declarative knowledge. For example, knowing what task and strategy variables influence memory performance may be the same kind of knowledge as knowing what climate an animal prefers to live in. They are both declarative knowledge; it is only meta when one is discussing cognitive knowledge. The second kind of metaknowledge uses the term meta in the sense of a function or second-order operation. A function or a procedure is used when an evaluation or any other form of action is taken on the existing declarative knowledge. Therefore, in order to answer a question about some content domain, whether it is memory or animals, an evaluation procedure is needed; this usually occurs if a response does not already exist in memory.

Meta-strategies.   What about meta-strategies? Meta-strategies would be like knowing that my rehearsal production is efficient. Again, there are two ways to represent meta-strategic knowledge. One way is direct prestored declarative knowledge. For example, to answer the question "Do you remember better than your friends?" (Kreutzer, Leonard, & Flavell, 1975) may consist of nothing more than retrieval of past encodings of those remembering events. In other words, every time a situation arises in which my memory is pitted against my friends' memories, I might encode, on a relative scale, how good my remembering skills are. In this sense, the term meta is used only to refer to knowledge about strategies or activities of remembering.

Alternatively, one can also view meta-strategic knowledge as second-order operations. In this case, meta-strategy would be a rule that evalutes another rule. Meta-strategies would take the entire strategy production as inputs and output some evaluation of the production (see P1, in Fig. 8.2). For instance, meta-strategies may be needed to answer the same question: "Do you remember better than your friends?" if the answer to such a question is not already prestored. In which case the response requires an assessment of what kind of remembering strategies are available to oneself, and how well those strategies facilitate remembering. The assessment is quite complex, requiring two evaluations: one at the level of the output of each individual memory strategy; the other at the level of the sum of all the available strategies for remembering.

Hence, in the present conceptualization, meta-strategic knowledge can take two forms: a simple interpretation is that it is declarative knowledge about procedures of remembering; a complex interpretation is that it is a rule evaluating another rule. In the latter sense, meta-strategies are distinctly different from strategies, and may be conceived of as having special status (Chi, 1981). However, because meta-strategies can themselves be represented as production rules, they are not different in form or quality from other production rules, such as strategies and procedural knowledge. Hence, there is agreement with Flavell's (1979) assumption that "metacognitive knowledge and metacognitive experiences differ from other kinds only in their content and function, not in their form or quality" (p. 906).

Meta-procedural Knowledge.   Meta-procedural knowledge would be very much the same as meta-strategies, with the exception that the inputs to the meta rules would be procedural knowledge rather than general strategies; they both take the same form. Meta-procedural knowledge would be rules that evaluate other domain-specific rules. For example, the processes of predicting how well one can come up with a good chess move could be considered meta-procedural knowledge; whereas, the processes of assessing how well one can rehearse could be considered meta-strategy.

Summary and Discussion

The proposition of this section is that if there are different forms of knowledge (declarative, procedural, and strategic), then there must necessarily be different types of metaknowledge (such as meta-declarative, meta-procedural, and meta-strategic). Possible representations for these different types of metaknowledge were discussed. Of the three types, meta-strategy and meta-procedural knowledge take a slightly different representation from the other knowledge: It is a rule of a rule.

It is suggested that the term meta can be used in two contexts. In one sense, the term meta may refer only to knowledge that is cognitive in nature; meta-declarative knowledge would refer to declarative knowledge about memory facts. Meta-strategic knowledge would refer to declarative knowledge about memory processes, much like what Flavell and Wellman (1977) refer to as knowledge about strategy variables. In another sense, the term meta may refer to second-order knowledge. In this case, meta-declarative knowledge would be a procedure that takes as input declarative knowledge, and the action would be an evaluation or some kind of assessment. Similarly, meta-strategic knowledge would be a rule that takes as input another rule, and output some appropriate evaluation or action.

Postulating the different possible representations of metaknowledge is useful, not only for the purpose of understanding which category of knowledge a given meta-phenomenon might fit, but also, it will help to understand how the mechanism for learning and acquisition of that knowledge might develop. In the next section, the different varieties of meta-phenomena are discussed, and the category of metaknowledge each fits is explored.

So far, the different types of knowledge, which refers to information that is stored and can be retrieved from memory, have been discussed. In this context, processes are the execution of a sequence of procedures, which may be production rules of any of the varieties that have been mentioned—procedural knowledge, strategic knowledge, or meta-strategies. Beyond these rules, there should be a set of executive rules, controlling the entire system's on going activities (whether the system is a child, a program, or an adult). Executive rules are analogous to an interpreter that determines the sequence of processes to be executed (Newell & Simon, 1972). A variety of processes, such as monitoring one's own state of processing and allocating ongoing attention, has now been given a new status of meta-processes. Evidence that shows that these meta-processes also develop with age, is now accumulating. Why these executive processes have been given a new name, other than the possibility that they control memory processes, is unclear. This is discussed later, in greater detail.

METAMEMORY RESEARCH

In this section, selected aspects of metamemory research in the literature, and how they can be conceived in the theoretical framework proposed in the second section of this paper, are summarized. It is difficult to integrate the large varieties of this research, therefore, only a small sample is discussed: namely, meta-knowledge of person variables; sensitivity; monitoring, and checking. This is a somewhat random selection, simply because it is nearly impossible to be exhaustive for a paper of this length. The selected examples serve to illustrate the complexity and fuzziness of some of the metamemory research.

Metaknowledge of Person Variables

Flavell (1979) and Flavell and Wellman (1977) have proposed at least three categories of metaknowledge that one can acquire about one's ability to memorize. One of them, known as knowledge of person variables, is a person's knowledge about intrinsic and stable characteristics about him or herself and others. For example, a child's knowing that he or she "can learn things better by listening than by reading," or that one of his or her friends is "more socially sensitive than another," (Flavell, 1979, p. 907), would be considered knowledge of person variables. This knowledge is meta because it concerns knowledge about one's cognitive functions, such as memorization. Younger children have been shown to possess less accurate metaknowledge of person variables than older children. One such demonstration is to show that children are unrealistic when it comes to estimating their own memory performance, such as in digit span task, or other types of serial recall tasks. For example, comparing a child's prediction of how many digits he or she can recall with how many he or she can actually recall, shows that young children are less accurate than older children in their estimation (Flavell, Friedrichs, & Hoyt, 1970; Yussen & Levy, 1975).

According to the conceptual framework used, the examples of meta-knowledge of person variables illustrate the two kinds of meta-declarative knowledge discussed in the previous section. In the one case, asking a child whether he or she can learn better by listening than by reading could be considered declarative knowledge, that is meta only in so far as it refers to cognitive abilities. It is very much like one's knowledge about any other domain, such as the eyes and how they see, and the nose and how it smells. Similarly, Johnson and Wellman's (1982) research on what the child knows about the brain, is also declarative knowledge of this variety. The reason it is classified as meta is because it is about cognition; however, the form of the knowledge is no different than one's knowledge of the eyes or any other domain of knowledge, such as animals.

The knowledge of person variables is declarative because, as Flavell and Wellman (1977) have already noted, a large proportion of this person variable knowledge is acquired through experience. The child could have encoded from perceptions of past experiences whether he or she is better at listening than reading. For example, after the first encounter of this kind, the child may decide that he or she is relatively better at listening than reading (let's say 3 on a 5 point scale). The next occurrence of such an event could either reaffirm the initial impression or change the evaluation so that now the child thinks he or she is considerably better at listening than at reading (let's say the rating has changed from a 3 to a 4). The mechanism that allows a child to decide what he or she can learn better by listening than by reading could be the retrieval of this single proposition, encoded as a result of past experiences in which listening and reading outcomes were compared. In this sense, whether or not an age effect is manifested probably depends on a number of factors, such as: (a) the total amount of experiences of this kind; (b) whether or not greater amounts of experience would produce a more accurate and robust assessment; and (c) the consistency of the early encounters. For example, if a minimal amount of experience is sufficient to produce a robust assessment, then a stable knowledge of person variables could probably be reached early in life; consequently no age effects will be observed. Likewise, if the first few encounters are relatively consistent, that factor may also lead to the establishment of an early stable assessment. All these factors, prior to the event when the meta-question was asked, may contribute toward the mechanism by which a decision is made and prestored.

Hence, from this analysis, the interpretation of the results from such studies depends on how knowledge of person variables was derived by the child from past experiences. The multitude of factors affecting that decision (prior to answering the meta-question) may contribute to the mixed age effects obtained in the literature, regarding why some aspects of metaknowledge are available to a young child and others are not.

A second way of deciding if one could learn better by listening than by reading, if such knowledge was not prestored and known, would be to evaluate and compare the outcome of reading and listening processes, and then decide which one is more optimal. This strategy of responding would require several meta-strategic rules, such as evaluating the outcome of comprehension processes or the amount of comprehension in listening versus reading, as well as the complexities of decoding in listening and reading. Such a decision requires more processing than a retrieval of a stored proposition. It reflects meta-declarative knowledge of the second kind; a procedure or several procedures are needed to evaluate either declarative knowledge or other procedural or strategic knowledge. In sum, it is proposed that to answer a simple meta-question, such as the one posed about listening and reading, either a simple retrieval of previously encoded proposition can occur, or a complex set of decision processes can occur. In the former case, the process of retrieval itself may be simple; however, the processes leading to the formation of the prestored decision may be quite complex. In the latter case, the decision processes themselves are complex. In either case, the complexity may contribute to the mixed results concerning age changes in metaknowledge of person variables.

One aspect of metaknowledge of person variables that shows a clear developmental trend, is the memory estimation paradigm. Because of the potentially complex decisions required of the task, the interpretation from these results— younger children have poorer metaknowledge—may be premature. It is conceivable that the developmental trend reflects the same kind of difficulties that younger children encounter in any complex task. There may not be any uniqueness to the "meta-ness" of the task, nor to the interpretation of the results. Consider the processes involved in making a decision of the kind usually requested in an estimation task. Young children are presented with a stimulus array of n items. After a brief exposure, they are asked to predict how many of the n items they think they can recall in correct serial order. There are at least two ways to answer such a question. One way is again the simple direct retrieval method, which relies on past experiences; that is, if you remember that you usually recall four digits, then you report four. Even though this explanation has been dismissed by findings that show that young children, in view of obvious failures, will not change their outlandish answers (Yussen & Levy, 1975), one could argue that temporary short-term feedback does not provide convincing or sufficient evidence to the child; and moreover, probably can not be encoded and integrated with existing knowledge in memory.

The second method requires an evaluation of the recall procedures. One technique is to do an immediate simulation (i.e., self-testing), then report the number of items recalled in the simulation. If immediate simulation is the mechanism by which subjects derive an answer, then because recall per se is affected by familiarity with the stimulus material, presumably, subjects' estimation should somehow be affected by familiarity with the stimulus material. A study was conducted in which this mechanism of estimation had to be used, rather than the one dependent on past experiences; because the task was such that no prior recall experiences could have been possible. The task was to ask subjects to estimate, after viewing it for 5 seconds, the number of pieces on the chess board that they thought they could reconstruct (Chi, 1978). This task was particularly suitable for the present purposes because, presumably, the chess players had never had experience memorizing chess board positions before (unless they had played blindfolded chess). A second task was also administered. From intuition, this task seemed more complicated, and responses to the task do not seem to be susceptible to the processes of an immediate simulation. The task required the subjects to estimate how many trials of viewing they expected they would need in order to perfectly reconstruct the board position. Hence, it was hypothesized that the first task, pieces estimation, is susceptible to a simulation strategy, but not a direct memory retrieval strategy; the second task, trials estimation, is susceptible to neither a simulation nor a direct retrieval strategy.

The subjects were 18 adults of varying skill levels. Their chess abilities were determined by the amount of time it took each one to complete a task called the Knight's Tour (Chase & Simon, 1973). The 18 subjects were then ranked according to their Knight's Tour times; the six fastest subjects were classified as Good; the six slowest were classified as Poor. Prediction accuracies (determined by the differences between predictions and actual recall) for two types of board positions (middle and end games) for both tasks are shown in Fig. 8.3. Middle games have 23 pieces and end games have 15 (Chi, 1978). In general (ignoring for the moment the dotted lines in Figure 3a), there was increased accuracy of prediction with skill for both tasks. This suggests that in general, the amount of domain-specific declarative and procedural knowledge facilitated estimation performance. To extrapolate, this suggests that, when younger children are less

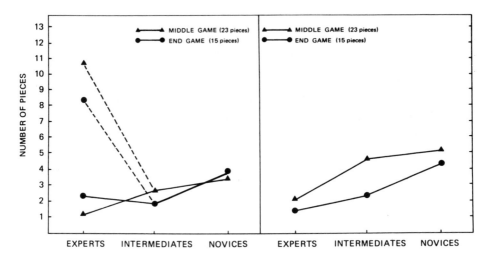

FIG. 8.3.   Prediction accuracies as a function of skill, determined by taking the absolute differences between predictions and actual recall, for pieces and trials estimation tasks.

accurate in an estimation task, in some sense it may reflect their limited knowledge of the stimulus domain. Because the exact processes used in an estimation task are unknown, one cannot rule out the influence of domain knowledge.

The increased prediction accuracy did not, however, reach significance for the pieces estimation task. This probably was due to the small sample size; three subjects' data—the dotted lines—had to be excluded. However, the increased accuracy of the trials estimation task was highly significant. The greater effect of skill, in what was presumed to be the more complex task (trials estimation), even when age is not considered, points to the complex interaction of skill with task difficulty.

The possibility that direct memory retrieval of past experiences can determine one's estimation decision was suggested by the peculiar data of the three expert subjects (the dotted lines in Fig. 8.3a). Having been overly confident that they could recall all the pieces on the chess board, they were extremely outlandish in their predictions. Responses on a questionnaire indicated that they were the only three subjects who had played blindfolded chess. It is possible that they were misled by their blindfolded chess playing ability, assuming that it must indicate a superior memory ability. That is, in playing blindfolded chess, one probably has to memorize the sequence of moves, that can easily be reconstructed by a good chess player. Such memories require different demands than remembering the exact location of each individual chess piece. In the former case the three expert subjects' superior memory probably misled them into assuming that their memory skill is also superior in the latter case, resulting in overly confident predictions. This particular finding also shows that, in the estimation of their memory abilities, young adults much like young children, can be extremely unrealistic.

In sum, it is suggested that knowledge about person variables, which presumably is tapped by an estimation task, may be no different in form from other types of declarative knowledge, such as one's chess playing abilities, or one's driving abilities. It is meta only in the sense that it is about cognition. As an illustration, in the study described, the questionnaire asked subjects some factual questions (such as: At what age did you start playing chess?), and some questions requiring them to assess their chess playing abilities (such as: Are you a good, mediocre, or poor player? How often do you beat your opponents?). The results show that subjects of different skill groups were quite accurate at rating their chess playing abilities: the Good players rated themselves 4.5 on a 5 point scale; the Mediocre players rated themselves 3.7; and the Poor players rated themselves 2.5. Furthermore, they were only slightly less accurate about the frequency with which they beat their opponents; the Good players thought they beat their opponents between 50–75% of the time, so did the Mediocre players; the Poor players said that they only beat their opponents about 50% of the time. Finally, the Good players claimed that they started playing chess at an earlier age (8.3 years) than the Mediocre players (11.0 years) and the Poor players (12.3 years), on the basis of their skills, this seems logical. In general, in these types of questions, which required the retrieval of past perceptions, there were no skill differences. Because these questions are not about cognition, they are not meta in nature.

On the other hand, knowledge about persons variables, as exemplified by an estimation task, may be meta when it requires an evaluation of existing declarative as well as procedural knowledge. The chess results show that when such processing is required, even when age is not manipulated, skill differences can be exhibited. These results indicate that interpretations of studies where age is manipulated require caution.

In this study, no skill differences were obtained in the subjects' abilities to assess their own chess playing abilities and yet some differences in their actual abilities to estimate their memorizing abilities were obtained. This occurred even though such a pattern of results should not have been obtained for a homogeneous age group—adults; they should have been as accurate in estimating their memorizing abilities as they were in estimating their chess playing abilities. However, such results can be interpreted by assuming that a simple memory retrieval of past experiences was used to assess one's chess playing abilities; a complex set of decsion processes was used to assess one's memorizing abilities in chess (because even if the subjects have had the experience of playing blindfolded chess, they should not have had experience memorizing locations of chess pieces). The more complex the decision processes were (comparing pieces to trials estimation), the more pronounced the effects of experience and skill. Thus, many factors can influence such decision processes, including familiarity with the stimulus domain and complexity of the task. Furthermore, such results also suggest that the estimation paradigm need not reflect knowledge and processes that have any special status, such as being meta; however, such tasks may reflect the complexities of this type of decision process.

Sensitivity

Sensitivity, according to Flavell (1978), is the awareness that certain situations require intentional memory-related behavior and that other situations do not. For example, a child may be aware that he or she needs to prepare for effective future recall, and therefore, should deliberately engage in preparation activities. The most relevant data are those showing that the young child does not realize that when an explicit request is made to memorize a set of items for future recall, it implies that he or she should engage in some kind of activity, such as rehearsal. This is taken to mean that the young child has not acquired "the metamnemonic knowledge that the memorization instruction is a tacit invitation to be planful and goal-directed" (Flavell, 1978).

In the conceptual framework used, the behavior exhibited by the young child can be interpreted by postulating that he or she has not acquired the mature memory strategies (such as for rehearsal (P2)), where the goal of remembering is attached to the strategy. The interpretation is that a young child has in memory, only production rules that approximate the final mature rules (such as P6), but not the mature rules themselves (such as P2). Therefore, the overt request to memorize is not a sufficient cue to trigger the strategic rule P2 and other similar rules. One way to test the hypothesis is to teach children strategic rules that incorporate the goals (of remembering), and then retest them in the same meta questioning situation.

In a sense, the lack of sensitivity on the part of the young child is not different from Flavell's (1970) original notion of production deficiency, which denoted the child's inadequate use of strategies to facilitate remembering. The explanation offered is also applicable to the phenomenon of production deficiency. Therefore, even though sensitivity is given a special meta status, the interpretation would strip it of its meta status; in other words, in the present conceptualization, sensitivity refers to the incompleteness of the strategic rules. This is one possible interpretation. Sensitivity, therefore, need not be meta in either sense of the word: whether it refers to cognitive knowledge or to second-order operations. Sensitivity may reflect only a deficit in existing cognitive rules.

Monitoring and Checking

Monitoring, another form of metamemory, is knowledge of the current state of one's memory. Monitoring may be viewed as an on going activity that occurs in conjunction with the main activity. For example, memory monitoring (Flavell, 1978) would be the processes of checking oneself for the degree of memorization. Such metaknowledge has been shown to be influential in a child's memory behavior. It is reasoned that retrieval efforts should reflect the degree to which one can assess one's current state of knowledge. Presumably, if a child can assess in advance that he or she does not know an item, then the child should prolong the use of effective retrieval or study strategies; if the assessment is that he or she does know it, then retrieval or study activities should terminate. A variety of empirical findings of this particular phenomenon have shown that younger children (such as kindergarteners) are less accurate at sensing when they have studied a set of items well enough for recall (Flavell, Friedrichs, & Hoyt, 1970). Another study showed that third graders appropriately allocated their study efforts on the basis of their estimates of which items they knew and which they did not; whereas, first graders did not make such "intelligent" choices (Masur, McIntyre & Flavell, 1973). These results are important; they show that attention allocation may be inappropriate in the younger child because the younger child is not aware of which of the to-be-learned items require more attention and effort.

However, there may be a number of reasons for the young child's inability to allocate attention or studying efforts appropriately. These reasons need not be related to a child's knowledge of studying efforts per se, instead they may be related to the child's ability to judge the difficulty of the to-be-learned items. One interpretation of such results is that younger children have more trouble judging the difficulty of an item, and thus are less accurate at predicting how well learned the items are, or which ones need more attention. The younger children's difficulty may stem from less developed knowledge of the stimulus items.

The distinction between relevant domain knowledge and what Flavell and Wellman (1977) referred to as knowledge of task variables (one of which is stimulus items) needs to be clarified. Knowledge of task variables (such as stimulus items) implied that sometimes subjects are aware that a more familiar type of stimulus item would be easier to learn than less familiar items (Kreutzer et al., 1975). This is knowledge of stimulus *variables*. What is proposed is that stimulus knowledge per se, affects a person's judgment of the difficulty of a stimulus item, and therefore, distorts his or her ability to allocate appropriate amounts of studying efforts. A study that has been conducted concerning adult expert and novice physicists illustrates the point (Chi, Glaser & Rees, 1982). In this study, six expert and six novice physicists were asked to judge (by rating) the difficulty of a set of physics problems. In general, the experts were more accurate than the novices at judging the difficulty of the problems. The more important finding, however, is the basis with which such judgments were made (see Table 8.1). The experts based their judgments on either the underlying physics principle governing the solution to the problem, or the physics components entailed in the problem (the first two categories in Table 8.1). The novices, however, based their decisions predominantly on superficial features of the problems (the third and fourth categories in Table 8.1). In fact, they are often reasons

TABLE 8.1
Proportion of Response Types

	Novices	Experts
Abstract Principle	9%	30%
"straightforward application of Newton's Second Law"		
"collision problem, use Conservation of Momentum"		
"no friction, no dissipative forces, just apply Energy Conservation"		
Problem Characteristics	33%	35%
"frictionless, problem is simplified"		
"massless spring simplifies problem"		
"pulley introduces difficulty"		
Nonphysics Related Characteristics	40%	28%
"problem is difficult to visualize"		
"easy calculations but hard to understand"		
"many factors to consider, make problem difficult"		
Nonproblem related Characteristics	18%	7%
"never did problems like this"		
"numbers instead of symbols"		
"must consider units"		
"diagram distracting"		

that have nothing to do with physics at all, and should not have any influence on the difficulty of the problems. Therefore, it is suggested that when a subject (whether a child or a novice adult) is either inaccurate at judging the difficulty of a problem, or uses inappropriate reasons for his or her judgments, it follows that he or she will have more difficulty judging how well prepared he or she is, either at memorizing an item or solving a problem. Therefore younger children's inability to accurately monitor their current state of knowledge (such as preparedness for recall), as well as their inadequate allocation of attention, is attributed to an inadequacy in part of their domain knowledge related to the stimulus items, rather than strictly underdeveloped monitoring processes.

Checking, a related notion to monitoring, is the activity of checking whether the outcome of one's problem solving attempts is correct. Even though older children and adults tend to be more accurate at monitoring and checking, Baker and Brown (1984) have already argued that monitoring may not be an age related phenomenon. One concrete example can illustrate what might produce checking in some individuals and not in others. Again, the explanation centers on the presence of relevant domain knowledge. The example concerns checking the solution to a physics problem at the end of the problem solving processes. The study, conducted by Andrew Judkis in our laboratory, was concerned with another matter. The task consisted of the presentation of a physics problem, one cue at a time, to two physics professors (the experts) and two A students (the novices). The question of interest was to see how well they could anticipate the final form of a problem, starting with partial cues, and how many cues were required by each skill group to reach that decision. At the end of the presentation of the entire problem statement, the subjects were required to solve the problem. By mistake, the numerical value for one of the known variables in the problem was too large, so that the actual numerical solution was unusually small. At the end of the solution, both experts noticed the discrepancy (in the sense that the answer was smaller than they would expect). One of them, apparently confident of his calculation, merely noted the discrepancy. The other, however, double checked and noticed the unusually large value for the given, and only then was convinced that his answer was right. On the other hand, the one novice who was able to solve the problem actually commented that he thought the answer should be and was fairly large.

One possible interpretation for such results is that over years of experience, the experts have acquired schemata of problem types, and one of the slots of a schema is potential values of the solution. Hence, when a value does not correspond to the range dictated in the schema, it signals to him that he should double-check. According to this interpretation, checking is totally an outcome of the presence of the relevant domain knowledge in memory, and not a meta-strategy that some individuals have and others do not. Of course when age differences were found, this explanation would be offered as an extrapolation to developmental results. The fact that expertise and experience are often the relevant factors has also been suggested by Brown and DeLoache (1978).

Summary and Discussion

This section reviewed a very small sample of metamemory research within the framework of understanding: (a) how the phenomena under study are considered meta; (b) how the phenomena fit in with the theoretical conception of meta-knowledge proposed in the prior section; and (c) how labelling it meta facilitates the understanding of its acquisition. The general conclusion is that calling a variety of phenomena meta sometimes adds confusion to the overall picture. Often, all the term meta implies is a reference to the fact that the domain being discussed is cognition. Therefore, in discussing knowledge about task variables and person variables, it is more elucidating to simply refer to them as such, so that one can easily see the analogy to other types of similar knowledge (knowledge about animals, knowledge about the nose and the ears). If one understands how knowledge about the nose is acquired, then similarly, one should postulate the same mechanism for the acquisition of metaknowledge about person or task variables.

Because a clear conception of metaknowledge of person variables has not been forwarded, the tasks designed to tap this knowledge may be misleading. For example, the often used memory span estimation task may be influenced by a variety of factors, making it difficult to: interpret the results; to tease apart the aspects of the task that are meta, the aspects that are simply memory retrieval, and the aspects that are complex decision processes that a child would not normally possess, much like their lack of other complex processes.

Sensitivity, a new notion in metamemory, is postulated to be somewhat related to the older notion of production deficiency. It is assumed here that the same mechanism involved in general strategy learning would explain their acquisition.

Finally, it was suggested that monitoring, checking, and other types of executive control processes, need not have any special status and need not be called meta. It is not surprising that younger children may have deficiencies in these types of processes, as they do in many other types of processes. These processes deserve some attention in developmental studies; however, other than the fact that executive processes control other memory and cognitive processes, why they need to be studied under the topic of meta is unclear. It was shown that executive processes are quite complex, and may be influenced by experience and learning; therefore, their acquisition may not be any different from the acquisition of other types of complex processes.

GENERAL DISCUSSION

This paper began by documenting the trend in cognitive developmental research from centering on the child's use and acquisition of strategies to focusing on the child's acquisition of knowledge. Because strategies are also one form of knowledge, it is important to understand their distinction. A distinction was made by specifying how knowledge (both declarative and procedural) and strategies can be represented. Using this representation to serve as a conceptual framework, metaknowledge is seen as either knowledge about factual events of cognition, or knowledge about strategies and/or procedures. Of these, only the latter, knowledge about strategies and procedures, because they are comparable to second-order knowledge, may be seriously considered as having the special status of meta; that is, they are rules about rules. In the last section, some of the current research concerning metamemory and metacognition was discussed. In particular, it was suggested that some metamemory research need not be called meta, other results may actually be artifacts of other types of knowledge. In order to untangle the somewhat mixed, irregular, and unclear results, a clearer conceptual framework is obviously needed to guide future empirical studies.

With a possible representational framework of what some of these meta-phenomena might be, there appears to be less mystery about the concept of metacognition. For instance, it has been assumed that knowledge about one's cognitive processes (such as knowing about how much one can generally recall, knowing about what task variables are the most difficult) probably is predominantly declarative knowledge, acquired with experience. The ability to respond appropriately to the experimenter's questions probably depends on how complicated the question is, and whether the question requires a simple direct retrieval of stored information, or whether it requires one or more transformations of the stored information. The greater the amount of transformation required, probably, the more salient the age effects; presumably, younger children have not acquired the complex rules for these transformations. Sensitivity is defined as the lack of relevant goals attached to the mnemonic rules that may be used with memorizing tasks. Again, the goal is simply another component of the mnemonic rule that may be acquired with experience. Finally, monitoring is seen as an activity much analogous to the executive control processes of a system, whether it is an individual or a computer. It is believed that even a young child has a sufficiently sophisticated control structure to guide his or her processing. Some of the by products of the executive control structure (such as checking), can be explained in terms of the complexity and structure of the domain-specific declarative knowledge base. It was conjectured that the reason that children may not, for example, check their solution as readily as adults, reflects not so much deficits in their control or monitoring processes, but rather, the lack of a relevant schema in the declarative knowledge base to tell them that the answer was inappropriate.

The initial impetus for examining meta-phenomena was for the purpose of explaining why children do not spontaneously use effective strategies in a memorizing situation. It had occurred to Flavell (1971) that perhaps children are not aware that they need to use strategies. If "the child is not aware of his own limitations as a learner or the complexity of the task at hand, then he can hardly be expected to take preventive actions," in order to maximize performance (Baker & Brown, 1984). To make this statement more concrete, in the digit span task discussed earlier, this would imply that because the younger child is less accurate at estimating his or her own digit span, it must mean that the child is not aware of his or her own limitation. Therefore, the child is less likely to use a strategy, such as rehearsal, to help remember. This would explain why young children are so unintentional in their use of strategies; they do not realize that they need them.

The research on this topic as a whole, however, has shown little relation between memory and metamemory performance. It is believed that one reason is that a precise definition of what metamemory and metaknowledge are has not been forwarded. An attempt has been made to argue that: (a) a variety of meta-type tasks are really not meta, (that is the tasks do not necessarily capture knowledge about cognition or memory) therefore, one would not expect performance on those tasks to correlate with memory performance; (b) metaknowledge is not unlike knowledge of any other domain, and it is conceivable that knowledge of cognition and knowledge of noncognitive domains develop simultaneously and independently, so that one need not bear on the other; and (c) the only kind of processes that must have some relation to cognition are those that evaluate other strategies or rules. Now the problem is how meta-rules are acquired. In a sense, the question of development has been pushed back one step: How are meta-strategies or meta-rules learned and acquired with development? Because even the initial question of how rules are learned in the first place cannot be answered, will it not be more difficult to understand how meta-rules are learned? The outlook is promising, however. If researchers worry more seriously about the precise definitions and differentiations between cognition and metacognition, they may advance the understanding of rule acquisition in general. The purpose of this paper was to take one step in that direction.

ACKNOWLEDGMENTS

Preparation of this manuscript was supported in part by funds provided by the Learning Research and Development Center, University of Pittsburgh, which is funded in part by the National Institute of Education (NIE). The opinions expressed do not necessarily reflect the position or policy of NIE, and no official endorsement should be inferred. The author is also grateful for funds provided by the Spencer Foundation in support of this research. The paper benefited from critical comments provided by Carl Johnson and Catherine Sophian. (A translated version of this paper was published in German, in F. E. Weinert & R. Kluwe (Eds.), *Metakognition, Motivation und Lernen*. Stuttgart West Germany: Kohlhammer.)

REFERENCES

Anderson, J. R. (1976). *Language, memory and thought*. Hillsdale, NJ: Lawrence Erlbaum Associates.

Anderson, J. R., Kline, P. J., Beasley, C. M. Jr. (1978). *A general learning theory and its application to schema abstraction*. ONR Technical Report.

Atkinson, R. C., & Shiffrin, R. M. (1968). Human memory: A proposed system and its control processes. In K. W. Spence & J. T. Spence (Eds.), *The psychology of hearing and motivation: Advances in research and theory* (Vol. 2). New York: Academic Press.

Baker, L., & Brown, A. L. (1984). Metacognitive skills of reading. In D. Pearson (Ed.), *A Handbook of reading research*. New York: Longman.

Belmont, J. M., & Butterfield, E. C. (1977). The instructional approach to developmental cognitive research. In R. V. Kail & J. W. Hagen (Eds.), *Perspectives on the development of memory and cognition*. Hillsdale, NJ: Lawrence Erlbaum Associates.

Boswell, S. L. (1974). *The development of verbal and spatial organization for materials presented tachistoscopically*. Unpublished doctoral dissertation, University of Colorado.

Brown, A. L. (1975). The development of memory: Knowing, knowing about knowing, knowing how to know. In H. W. Reese (Ed.), *Advances in child development and behavior* (Vol. 10). New York: Academic Press.

Brown, A. L., & DeLoache, J. S. (1978). Skills, plans, and self-regulation. In R. Siegler (Ed.), *Children's thinking: What develops?* Hillsdale, NJ: Lawrence Erlbaum Associates.

Ceci, S. J., & Howe, M. J. (1978). Semantic knowledge as a determinant of developmental differences in recall. *Journal of Experimental Child Psychology, 26,* 230–245.

Chase, W. G., & Simon, H. A. (1973). Perception in chess. *Cognitive Psychology, 4,* 55–81.

Chi, M. T. H. (1976). Short-term memory limitations in children: Capacity or processing deficits? *Memory & Cognition, 4,* 559–572.

Chi, M. T. H. (1978). Knowledge structures and memory development. In R. Siegler (Ed.), *Children's thinking: What develops?* Hillsdale, NJ: Lawrence Erlbaum Associates.

Chi, M. T. H. (1981). Knowledge development and memory performance. In M. Friedman, J. P. Das, & N. O'Connor (Eds.), *Intelligence and learning.* New York: Plenum Press.

Chi, M. T. H. (1985). Interactive roles of knowledge and strategies in development. In S. Chipman, J. Segal, & R. Glaser (Eds.), *Thinking and learning skills: Current research and open questions* (Vol. 2). Hillsdale, NJ: Lawrence Erlbaum Associates.

Chi, M. T. H., & Ceci, S. J. (In press). Content knowledge: It's representation and restructuring in memory development. In H. W. Reese & P. Lipsitt (Eds.), *Advances in child development and behavior* (Vol. 20). New York: Academic Press.

Chi, M. T. H., Glaser, R., & Rees, E. (1982). Expertise in problem solving. In R. Sternberg (Ed.), *Advances in the psychology of human intelligence.* Hillsdale, NJ: Lawrence Erlbaum Associates.

Chi, M. T. H., & Koeske, R. D. (1983). *Network representation and recall: A case study of a child's dinosaur knowledge. Developmental Psychology, 19,* 29–39.

Dempster, F. M. (1978). Memory span and short-term memory capacity: A developmental study. *Journal of Experimental Child Psychology, 26,* 419–431.

Flavell, J. H. (1970). Developmental studies of mediated memory. In H. W. Reese & L. P. Lipsitt (Eds.), *Advances in child development and behavior* (Vol. 5). New York: Academic Press.

Flavell, J. H. (1971). First discussant's comments: What is memory development the development of? *Human Development, 14,* 272–278.

Flavell, J. H. (1978). Metacognitive development. In J. M. Scandura & C. Brainerd (Eds.), *Structural/process theories of complex human behavior.* Alpha a.d. Rijn, The Netherlands: Sijtoff & Noordhoff.

Flavell, J. H. (1979). Metacognition and cognitive monitoring: A new area of cognitive-developmental inquiry. *American Psychologist, 34,* 906–911.

Flavell, J. H., Friedrichs, A. G., & Hoyt, J. D. (1970). Developmental changes in memorization processes. *Cognitive Psychology, 1,* 324–340.

Flavell, J. H., & Wellman, H. M. (1977). Metamemory. In R. V. Kail & J. W. Hagen (Eds.), *Perspectives on the development of memory and cognition.* Hillsdale, NJ: Lawrence Erlbaum Associates.

Gelman, R. (1969). Conservation acquisition: A problem of learning to attend to relevant attributes. *Journal of Experimental Child Psychology, 7,* 167–187.

Greeno, J. G. (1978). Natures of problem solving abilities. In W. K. Estes (Ed.), *Handbook of learning and cognitive processes* (Vol. 5). Hillsdale, NJ: Lawrence Erlbaum Associates.

Hayes, J. R. (1985). Three problems in teaching general skills. In S. Chipman, J. Segal, & R. Glaser (Eds.), *Thinking and learning skills: Current research and open questions* (Vol. 2). Hillsdale, NJ: Lawrence Erlbaum Associates.

Huttenlocher, J., & Burke, D. (1976). Why does memory span increase with age? *Cognitive Psychology, 8,* 1–31.

Johnson, C. N., & Wellman, H. M. (1982). Children's developing conceptions of the mind and brain. *Child Development, 53,* 222–234.

Keeney, T. J., Cannizzo, S. R., & Flavell, J. H. (1967). Spontaneous and induced verbal rehearsal in recall task. *Child Development, 38,* 953–966.

Kreutzer, M. A., Leonard, S. C., & Flavell, J. H. (1975). An interview study of children's knowledge about memory. *Monographs of the Society for Research in Child Development, 40* (1, Serial No. 159).

Lange, G. (1978). Organization-related processes in children's recall. In P. A. Ornstein (Ed.), *Memory development in children*. Hillsdale, NJ: Lawrence Erlbaum Associates.

Lindberg, M. A. (1980). Is knowledge base development necessary and sufficient condition for memory development? *Journal of Experimental Child Psychology, 30,* 401–410.

Masur, E. F., McIntyre, C. W., & Flavell, J. H. (1973). Developmental changes in apportionment of study time among items in a multi-trial free recall task. *Journal of Experimental Child Psychology, 15,* 237–246.

Moely, B. E. (1977). Organizational factors in the development of memory. In R. V. Kail & J. W. Hagen (Eds.), *Perspectives on the development of memory and cognition*. Hillsdale, NJ: Lawrence Erlbaum Associates.

Myers, N. A., & Perlmutter, M. (1978). Memory in the years from two to five. In P. A. Ornstein (Ed.), *Memory development in children*. Hillsdale, NJ: Lawrence Erlbaum Associates.

Nelson, K. J. (1974). Variations in children's concepts by age and category. *Child Development, 45,* 577–584.

Newell, A. (1973). Production systems: Models of control structures. In W. G. Chase (Ed.), *Visual information processing*. New York: Academic Press.

Newell, A., & Simon, H. A. (1972). *Human problem solving*. Englewood Cliffs, NJ: Prentice-Hall.

Norman, D. A., & Rumelhart, D. E. (1975). *Explorations in cognition*. San Francisco: Freeman.

Ornstein, P. A., & Corsale, K. (1979). Organizational factors in children's memory. In C. R. Puff (Ed.), *Memory organization and structure*. New York: Academic Press.

Richman, C. L., Nida, S., & Pittman, L. (1976). Effects of meaningfulness on child free recall learning. *Developmental Psychology, 12,* 460–465.

Rumelhart, D. E., & Norman, D. A. (1980). *Analogical processes in learning* (Rep. No. 8005). La Jolla, CA: Center for Human Information Processing.

Storm, C. (1978). Acquiring principles of semantic organization. *Journal of Experimental Child Psychology, 25,* 208–223.

Tenney, Y. T. (1975). The child's conception of organization and recall. *Journal of Experimental Child Psychology, 19,* 100–114.

Winograd, T. (1975). Frames and the procedural-declarative controversy. In D. G. Bobrow & A. M. Collins (Eds.), *Representation and understanding: Studies in cognitive science*. New York: Academic Press.

Yussen, S. R., & Levy, V. M. Jr. (1975). Developmental changes in predicting one's own span of short-term meory. *Journal of Experimental Child Psychology, 19,* 502–508.

9 Aptitudes for Learning and Cognitive Processes

Robert Glaser
University of Pittsburgh

James W. Pellegrino
University of California, Santa Barbara

This chapter discusses intelligence—an aspect of human performance that appears to encompass all three of the topics of this symposium: metacognition, cognitive style, and learning. In particular, we consider how intelligence, defined as aptitude for learning, can be investigated in terms of current cognitive theory. At the present time, cognitive psychologists are studying individual differences in intelligence and aptitude in terms of the structures and processes hypothesized in the study of cognition and cognitive development. The research carried out along these lines is predicated on the assumption that aptitude tests should be viewed as more than primarily predictors of achievement. Rather, such tests should assist in identifying the processes involved in intellectual competence, and further indicate how these processes can be influenced and utilized to benefit learning.

In order to contribute to this purpose, we have undertaken a research program in an attempt to identify directly the cognitive processing components of performance on tasks used to assess aptitude. The immediate goal is to analyze test tasks, develop process models of task performance, and utilize these models as a basis for individual difference analysis. The ultimate goal is to use the knowledge gained to design conditions for learning that could be adjusted to these individual characteristics, or design instruction to directly or indirectly teach the processes that facilitate learning. The objective is not to train individuals to score higher on tests of mental ability, but to directly or indirectly improve the cognitive processes that underlie successful performance, both on tests of aptitude and in instructional settings.

As a general background for this summary report of the research, four operating constraints that are important in a task-analytic effort aimed at understanding individual differences in aptitude processes are briefly mentioned. First, a particular task or set of tasks chosen for analysis should have a strong history of reliable association with an aptitude construct that is of reasonable generality; it also should have a consistent predictive validity with respect to a criterion performance of significant interest. Second, in the analysis of any particular aptitude construct, it is important to simultaneously consider the various tasks that define an aptitude factor. The analysis of multiple tasks should enable one to differentiate general and more content specific cognitive processes. Third, the analysis of a particular task must also be explicitly concerned with explicating the sources of item difficulty that provide the basis for individual variation in test performance. An understanding of individual differences in task performance must include a process theory of item difficulty. For this purpose, the processes specified as components of performance must explain individual item characteristics, individual subject performance as a function of ability and developmental level, and the interaction of the two. A fourth constraint is dictated by the goal of developing a theory of individual differences in aptitude processes that can be translated into instructional investigation. The empirical and theoretical results of any particular analysis of the cognitive components of a task should be evaluated by asking whether such results suggest testable instructional hypotheses. Such internal tests of the task-analytic effort can be sobering indications that a research program has yet to achieve a sufficiently useful level of analysis. As this chapter indicates, we are at the beginning of an ambitious research program that attempts to comply with the previous constraints.

THE RELEVANCE OF RULE INDUCTION

Research that our group and others have conducted on a class of tasks that is presumed to assess a psychological capacity for rule induction and is commonly found on tests of aptitude and intelligence is now discussed. This set of intercorrelated tasks involves several task forms such as classification, series extrapolation, analogy, and matrix tasks. These task forms simultaneously vary along content dimensions that include letters, numbers, words, and geometric figures as shown in Fig. 9.1, which shows series completion and analogy problems. Spearman (1923) considered such tasks as measures of g, and viewed them as an index of the capacity to engage in intellectual processes that he referred to as the "eduction" of relations and correlates. Thurstone and Thurstone (1941) treated these tasks as representative of a primary mental ability called Induction (I), and suggested that, as a second-order factor, rule induction might be identical with Spearman's g. In more recent hierarchical aptitude models, such tasks have been treated as measures of gf or fluid analytic ability (Brody & Brody, 1976). It seems clear that such rule induction tasks assess basic reasoning abilities comprising a robust aptitude construct that has relevance for a larger domain of

SERIES COMPLETION PROBLEMS

Number Series
   32 11 33 15 34 19 35 _ _ _ _
   72 43 90 71 47 85 70 51 80 _ _ _ _

Letter Series
   c d c d c d _ _ _ _
   j k q r k l r s l m s _ _ _ _

ANALOGY PROBLEMS

Verbal (A:B : : C:D')
   Sugar : Sweet : : Lemon :
            Yellow   Sour   Fruit   Squeeze   Tea
   Abate : Decline : : Wax :
            Increase   Improve   Blemish   Polish   Wane

Numerical (A:B : : C:D : : E:F')
   7:21 : :   5:15 : :   4:
   15:19 : :   8:12 : :   9:
   10:40 : :   6:36 : :   5:
   28:21 : : 24:18 : : 20:

Geometric

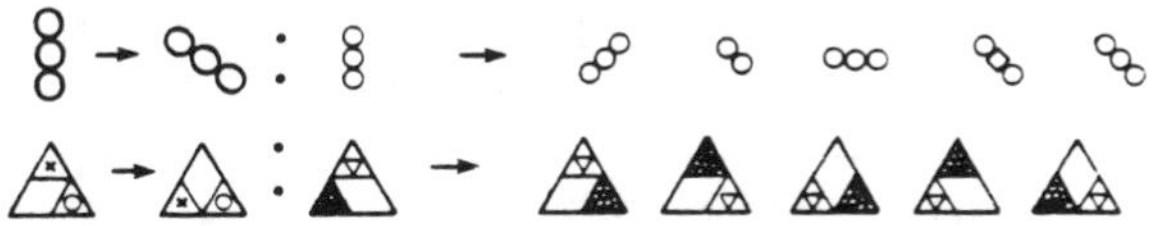

FIG. 9.1.   Task forms associated with rule induction.

human performance. It has been argued that rule induction processes are similar to those demanded in concept formation, and that they are related to a major form of human problem solving that results in the acquisition of knowledge.

Our tentative view of such inductive reasoning tasks is that they sample the way in which an individual makes use of existing knowledge to solve problems where the solution depends on an analysis of the underlying relations (or conceptual similarity) among a set of problem elements. Within important limitations, performance on these tasks has consistently correlated with academic achievement; individual differences in the capacity to engage in such analyses appear to have direct implications for commonly required classroom learning processes.

A number of research findings on various inductive reasoning test tasks are now described. This research is presented in the form of succinct descriptions and conclusions, with little of the experimental detail and caveats found in various reports of research (see references cited at the end of the chapter).

Series Completion Problems

Series completion items, as shown in Fig. 9.1, are found at several developmental levels on many standardized aptitude tests. Such items may be represented as letter series, number series, picture series, or geometric figure series problems. In all cases, the task structure is the same: elements comprising the series are ordered according to some specific interitem relationship; and the individual's task is to extract the basic relationships and generate, predict, or select the next item(s) in the series. The acquisition of serial pattern concepts has an extensive history of psychological investigation. Of particular interest in this discussion is Simon and Kotovsky's (1963) and Kotovsky & Simon's (1973) work on the analysis of letter series problems of the type developed by Thurstone and Thurstone for their Primary Mental Abilities test battery. Simon and Kotovsky developed a computer simulation model to represent the component processes necessary for solution.

One important aspect of the analysis of this task is the distinction between the declarative knowledge and the procedural knowledge or processes necessary for the task. The declarative knowledge base for such letter series problems is limited to knowledge of alphabetic order and to relational concepts, such as identity (same letter), next (the next letter), and backwards-next (or reverse ordering). Obviously, letter series problems do not involve an extensive declarative knowledge component, and it would not be expected that individual differences would arise from declarative knowledge deficiencies.

Given that the appropriate declarative knowledge is available, the completion of any letter series problem requires a set of basic procedures that are hierarchically organized. In the Simon and Kotovsky (1963) simulation model, there are two basic routines: a pattern generator and a sequence generator. The first of these routines, pattern generation, can be broken down into three processes: (a) detection of the interletter relations for the given problem elements, (b) use of the relational information to extract the period length of the pattern within the problem, and (c) generation of a pattern description or rule involving both the relations and the periodic structure of the problem. This rule, specifying the pattern description, serves as input to the sequence generator, which applies it to the current state of the problem and then extrapolates the pattern to generate the additional elements required for problem solution. Differences in item difficulty and potential individual differences in problem solution can result from the application of any or all of these specific processes.

Concerning sources of task difficulty, a number of systematic properties of the individual items determine the difficulty of a problem. One aspect of the probability of error is the type of relation involved. Identity relations are easier to detect than next relations, which, in turn, are easier than backwards-next relationships. The difference in difficulty between extrapolating identity and next relationships also varies as a function of the position of the relationship within a period.

These sources of error are readily explainable if one considers the requirements of working memory. Identity relationships do not place demands on working memory, whereas successive nonidentity relationships involve accumulating placekeepers. The longer the period length, the greater the memory demands of a problem, and the greater the likelihood that working memory limits may be reached. For example, the letter and number series problems in Fig. 9.1 differ in both period length and pattern complexity. Thus the overall pattern description that constitutes a problem is related to problem difficulty. The length of the pattern description, which is a function of period length, the types of relationships involved, and the resulting working memory requirements, are highly correlated with problem errors. These errors can arise from performance inadequacies, which differ among individuals in relation detection, discovery of the periodic structure, completion of a pattern description, or in the extrapolation process.

Consider instructional experimentation based on this model. It has been demonstrated that Simon and Kotovsky's (1963) model of serial completion items provides a reasonable account of performance in this task; their simulation of human protocols provides a partial validation of the model. Given a concern with the criterion of instructional tractability, another way in which such models can be validated can be considered. If the processes embodied in a simulation model are similar to those used by humans, then individuals whose performance represents a low or intermediate level of task competency might be trained in these processes. However, if the processes specified by the model are incompatible with human cognitive structures, then there will either be difficulty in training these processes, or they will have no positive, and perhaps a negative, influence on performance.

In an attempt to provide such an instructional test, a study was conducted that involved direct and independent training in discovery of relations and discovery of periodicity with a sample of children, from grades 1 through 6 (Holzman,

Glaser, & Pellegrino, 1976). Both the training group and a control group were given a pre and posttest set of letter series problems, identical in rule structure, but initialized at different points in the alphabet. The results showed a significant gain in performance for the training group. In particular, the training group showed a percentage reduction in errors, over twice the number shown by the control group (32% vs. 13%). Furthermore, the training group showed significantly greater gains on problems based on more difficult patterns, whereas the control group remained the same or reduced errors only on the easier items. Thus, the training appropriately functioned where it was most needed—that is, when individuals encountered more difficult relations and problems. The qualitative difference between control and experimental conditions also suggests that explicit training on the identified component processes may have provided an information management strategy that facilitated pattern description and extrapolation.

Related instructional studies conducted on series completion performance showed an interaction between type of training and performance level. Sheer practice on the test items was sufficient to produce significant gains in performance at some levels of initial competence, however, at lower levels of initial ability, explicit process training was more effective than practice. The source of this interaction needs to be more precisely determined by explicit analysis of the process differences among individuals that define different levels of task competence and intellectual development.

Analogical Reasoning Problems

We now present another task form presumed to assess the capability for inductive reasoning. Of the many tasks that are assumed to assess this capability, the analogy problem is the most pervasive. Over the entire course of the testing movement, analogy items, as shown in Fig. 9.1, have constituted a significant portion of intelligence tests. Sternberg (1977a, 1977b) has provided a detailed review and discussion of the importance of analogical reasoning within the field of differential psychology. The centrality of this type of reasoning in the concept and measurement of intelligence can be found in the writings of such individuals as Spearman (1923) and Raven (1938).

In the past few years, Spearman's theory has been expanded and refined in the more precise, experimentally founded theory presented by Sternberg. Sternberg has proposed and tested a theory of analogical reasoning that specifies several processes intended to apply across all analogical reasoning tasks. In Sternberg's analyses, emphasis is placed on developing general models of analogy solution and specifying individual differences, in terms of latency parameters, for the various processes involved. However, the qualitative characteristics of these processes remain largely unspecified, and there is still no adequate understanding of how the processes are executed, what information or content must be processed, or how such information contributes to differences in item difficulty and performance errors.

In the analysis of individual differences in analogy solution, we have attempted to specify the components of task performance that differentiate between levels of aptitude and how these components interact with differences in item structure or content. A general overview of the work is reported in the remainder of this paper. For this purpose, and at the expense of oversimplification, we infer from this work three interrelated elements that appear to differentiate high- and low-skill individuals in analogical reasoning test tasks. These elements are the management of memory load, procedural knowledge of task constraints, and organization of an appropriate conceptual knowledge base. We discuss each with reference to relevant studies of figural, verbal, and numerical analogy tasks, and then suggest implications for improving these skills.

Figural Analogies (Memory Load)

We first investigated figural analogies (see Fig. 9.1) because the type of item features in these problems seemed easier to analyze (see Mulholland, Pellegrino, & Glaser, 1980). In contrast to the symbolic aspects of verbal and numerical analogies, the information necessary for item solution is externally represented in the physical problem array. The specific aspects of item content are the figural elements that are used to construct the separate analogy terms, and the spatial and logical transformations that are applied to the elements to construct overall rules. The elements that comprise the terms are easily perceived plane geometric figures—lines, circles, triangles, and quadrilaterals. The basic transformations include: removing or adding elements; rotating, reflecting, and displacing elements; size changes; and variations in element shading.

A simplified model (see Fig. 9.2) of the relationship between item content and processing assumes an initial phase of pattern comparison and decomposition process that yields units of information, representing the individual elements of a pair of analogy terms. The complexity of such a process is a function of the number of elements that must be isolated. The second stage of processing is transformation analysis and rule generation. This phase of processing attempts to determine the transformations that specify the rule for changing the A stimulus into the B stimulus. The complexity of identifying and ordering a set of transformations is a direct function of the number of transformations required in an item.

Each operation associated with pattern decomposition and transformation analysis of an A-B pair of terms yields a unit of information that is stored in working memory, and each element-transformation proposition requires an individual placekeeper or slot in working memory (e.g., Rumelhart, 1977; Simon & Kotovsky, 1963). As a consequence of this, the largest single source of error is multiple transformation of single elements. In this type of problem, the intermediate results of the C-D rule generation inference process must be retained in

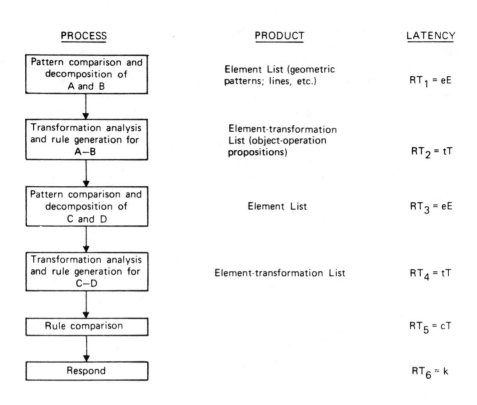

PROCESS	PRODUCT	LATENCY
Pattern comparison and decomposition of A and B	Element List (geometric patterns; lines, etc.)	$RT_1 = eE$
Transformation analysis and rule generation for A–B	Element-transformation List (object-operation propositions)	$RT_2 = tT$
Pattern comparison and decomposition of C and D	Element List	$RT_3 = eE$
Transformation analysis and rule generation for C–D	Element-transformation List	$RT_4 = tT$
Rule comparison		$RT_5 = cT$
Respond		$RT_6 = k$

$$RT_{total} = xE + yT + k$$

FIG. 9.2. Simplified process model for figural analogy verification task.

memory and the entire transformation sequence inferred before the appropriateness of the D terms can be judged. Thus, due to such additional demands on working memory, it is possible for some of the original element-transformation information to be lost or degraded.

To be somewhat more specific on this matter, consider that the time to identify and order a set of transformations appears to be a function of the number of elements and transformations that comprise an item; the probability of error of an item should increase as a function of the number of cognitive operations required to identify elements and the transformations applied to them. These general assumptions were tested in the Mulholland, et al. (1980) experiment, where figural analogies in a reaction time verification task were presented to university undergraduates. The analogies were generated from six types of elements and six types of transformations that frequently occur on items found on aptitude tests. The elements were easily perceived geometric figures. The transformations included: rotation, reflection, size increase and decrease, doubling and halving elements, and identity (no transformation). The number and type of elements and transformations were systematically varied in the construction of items, as shown in the examples of true and false items in Fig. 9.3.

Performance on these experimental items correlated highly ($r = .69$) with scores on a figural analogy test, used as a subtest of a standardized test of cognitive abilities. Individual latencies for solving the experimental items differed as a function of item structure in a systematic and reliable manner. Fig. 9.4 shows the latency data for various item types (i.e., combinations of number of elements and transformations). The data are consistent with the assumption that individuals decompose the terms of an analogy task in serial fashion; that is, they isolate and identify the elements one by one, and with each additional element, there is an increment in time. The processing time of transformations also represents a similar serial and additional processing mode.

As the effects of element and transformation requirements combine, that is, as item complexity increases, there begins to be a problem of mental bookkeeping. Each operation performed in decomposing the terms of an analogy and determining the individual transformations yields units of information that take up space in memory. As more partial information is accumulated and entered into memory, one may begin to approach the limits of working memory: Processing time and processing effort may have to be partially diverted to updating and maintaining the accumulated contents of memory. The assumption of an increasing memory load in complex items suggests that it is a potential source of performance errors. This is supported by the error data shown in Fig. 9.5, which shows that errors increased as a function of the number of transformations and increased most rapidly when several different transformations had to be performed on a single element. The latter result suggests that, in items of this type, a special cognitive demand is retaining and operating on the intermediate products of transformation in memory. Thus, in the processing of such figural analogies, young children and less proficient solvers appear to be particularly inefficient in these aspects of performance (Pellegrino & Glaser, 1982).

As described earlier, the memory load influence on performance has been verified by empirical studies of other test item forms (such as series extrapolation problems), where individual letter series problems, which theoretically involve several placekeepers in working memory, show the highest error rates (e.g., Holzman, Glaser, & Pellegrino, 1976; Kotovsky & Simon, 1973). A similar set of processing and working memory assumptions may also be applicable to performance differences across items on figural matrix problems, such as those in the Raven's Progressive Matrices Test (see Hunt's, 1974, analysis of this task). In all the work of this kind, the strategies that individuals use to manage memory load, and the extent to which different individuals, in order to reduce memory load, represent figural elements in memory in different ways, has not been carefully studied.

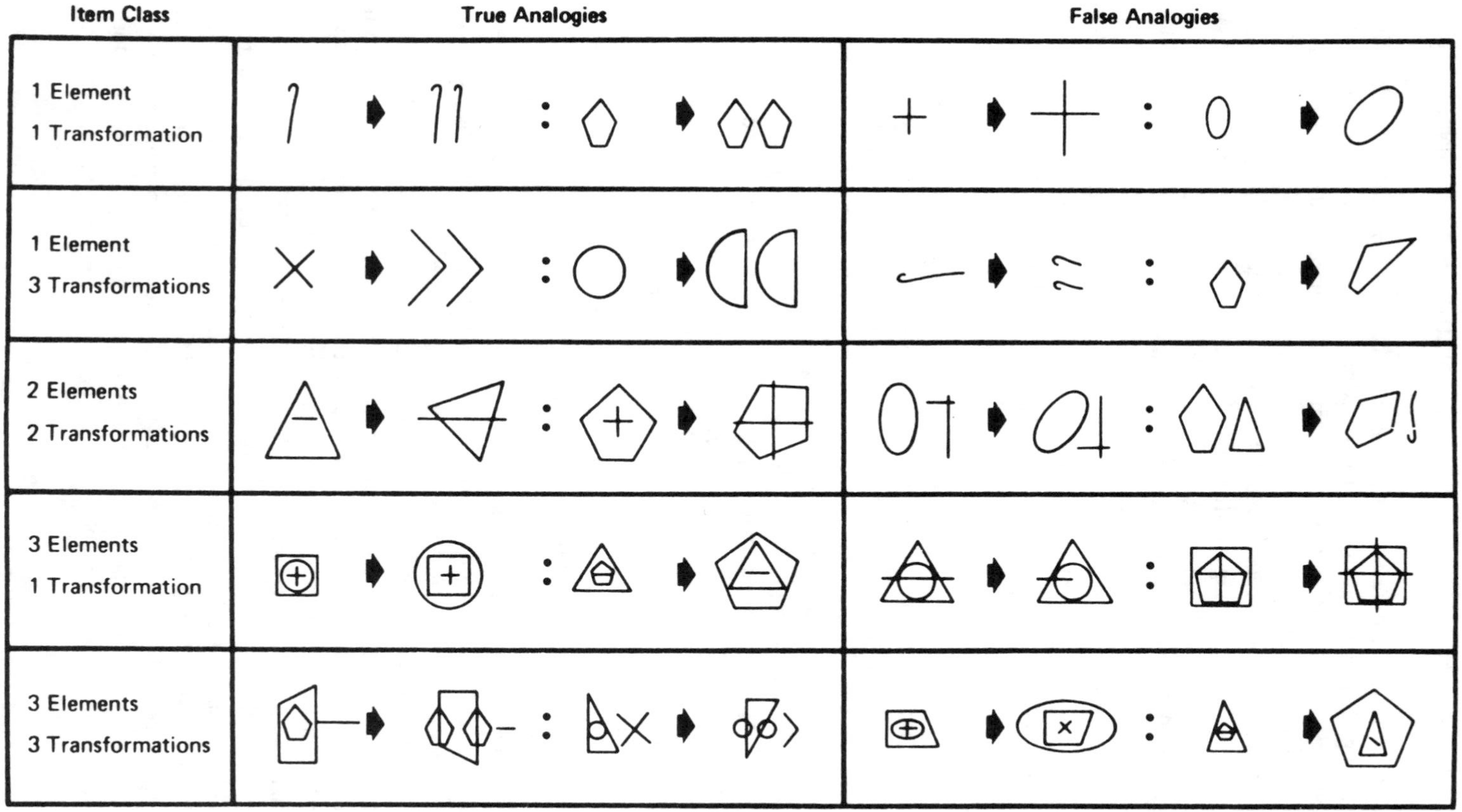

FIG. 9.3. Examples of true and false geometric analogies used for the verification task.

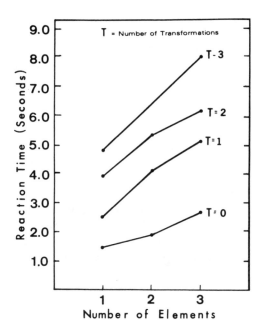

FIG. 9.4. Mean reaction times for true analogies as a function of the number of elements and transformations.

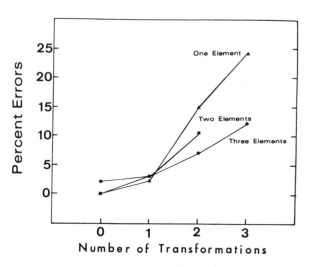

FIG. 9.5. Mean errors for true analogies as a function of the number of elements and transformations.

Verbal Analogies (Procedural Constraints)

The notion of differential procedural task constraints for high and low aptitude individuals has been developed in studies of verbal analogy test tasks. On the basis of an extensive protocol analysis study of multiple choice verbal analogy items, Heller (1979) has proposed a general model of analogical reasoning performance that attempts to describe the information processing differences between individuals of varying skill, in terms of behaviors that conform to or violate analogy task constraints. Effective problem solution is characterized as a series of steps directed toward the satisfaction of specific goals, and the more constraints a solver is aware of, the more highly constrained will be the goals pursued.

By considering the "syntax" or rules for interpreting the structure of analogy items, solution protocols can be examined to determine whether or not they include behaviors that violate task constraints. When this is done, three categories of solutions emerge: analogical, nonanalogical, and "buggy" solutions. Solutions that contain no violations of task constraints are categorized as *analogical*. These analogical solutions are characterized by: (a) consistent attention to the relations contained in two allowable word pairs, and (b) consistent attention to the match between these pairs of relations.

Solutions that contain major violations of task constraints throughout a solution episode are categorized as *nonanalogical*. Nonanalogical solutions are characterized by: (a) attention only to relations between illegal pairs of elements; and/or (b) consistent attention to the match between inappropriately selected pairs of relations in two word pairs; and/or (c) a consistent disregard for the match between relations contained in two word pairs.

In the category called *"buggy"* solutions, some solution behavior violates task constraints, however, most is analogical. (The term "buggy" is borrowed from the computer programming notion of program "bugs," corresponding essentially to analogical procedures with subroutines that misfire under certain conditions, or analogical procedures with missing or faulty subroutines that manifest themselves under certain conditions.) "Buggy" analogical solutions contained both of the types of behavior described for analogical and nonanalogical solutions. Sample solution protocols for analogical and nonanalogical types are shown in Table 9.1 (Heller, 1979).

Analogical Solutions. When the performance of individuals who did solve items analogically is examined, a major distinction among analogical solutions is apparent in the development of the solvers' understanding of the analogical rule in an item, solutions can be "conceptually driven" or "interactive." In the conceptually driven solutions (Protocol 1 in Table 9.1), the solver's initial understanding of the A-B rule drives evaluation of the optional completion terms and is sufficient for discrimination among the options. However, in interactive solutions (protocol 2), the A-B relation is either initially inaccessible, or does not permit identification of a unique completion term from the option set; therefore with reference to C-D relations, the rule is identified or modified. Because they involve increasingly detailed specification of the analogical rule and/or consideration of alternative conceptualizations of the rule, interactive solutions require more extensive processing than conceptually driven solutions.

Individual differences in analogical reasoning ability appear to correspond to the differential availability or utilization of these additional processes. Low-ability solvers show an increased reliance upon conceptually driven solutions. That is, when low-ability individuals use the analogical solution procedure, they tend, more often than high-ability solvers, to evoke a sequence of processes corresponding to initial identification of the analogical rule; however, they do not subsequently modify that rule. Although low-ability solvers are also capable of solving items interactively, they do so less often than higher ability solvers. On more difficult items, which are less likely to be solvable in the conceptually driven mode, low-ability solvers exhibit performance that violates task constraints. This observation is further apparent in the examination of nonanalogical solutions.

Nonanalogical Solutions.   Three types of nonanalogical solutions were identified: One type (Protocol 3) represents solutions in which no attempt was made to identify the A-B relation—attention was paid only to the presence or absence of C-D' relations. (D' indicates a multiple choice response.) A second type (Protocol 4) represents solutions in which an attempt was made to identify both A-B and C-D' relations, but no apparent attempts were made to determine whether any two relations matched. A third type (Protocol 5) represents solutions in which all four analogy terms were considered, but attention was paid to the interrelations among three or four terms rather than to the match between two distinct relations within element pairs.

By definition, all three types of nonanalogical solutions include, a violation of the central constraints of the analogy task—essentially that behavior should be directed toward identifying two distinct relations that are analogous or matching. However, to different extents, the three conform with task constraints and individual differences were reflected in the ability to solve analogies in accordance with task constraints. Nonanalogical solutions by the low-ability solvers were primarily of the types where no attempt is made to identify the A-B relation or to refer to two distinct relations. Higher ability solvers, on the other hand, considered all four terms in most of their nonanalogical solutions and attended to two allowable relations.

In general, this research suggests that skilled analogy solvers are characterized by more knowledge of task constraints, and by the ability to develop an understanding of the analogical rule in response to the item stem, the relationships involved, and the response options. Conversely, less skilled solvers

TABLE 9.1
Sample Solution Protocols (from Heller 1979)

Analogy Elements Presented		*Solver's Response*

Analogical Solution: Protocol 1
Conceptually driven; one option matches initial specifications

TEA:COFFEE::BREAD:		Tea is to coffee as bread is to . . . rolls because tea and coffee, they're both drinks, and they're about the same thing, just two different names for two different drinks, and a bread and a roll would be about the same—two different names for the same thing.
MILK	(Reject)	That doesn't fit, it's a drink.
BUTTER	(Reject)	Butter is something you put on bread, that doesn't fit.
ROLLS	(Accept)	That's good.
JAM	(Reject)	It's like butter, something you put on bread. It wouldn't fit because you don't put coffee on tea or in tea.

Analogical Solution: Protocol 2
Interactive; initial failure to identify A-B relation—analogical rule identified during option verification

ABATE:DECLINE::WAX:		This is a good one, Oh Christ, I don't know—I can't say anything yet because I don't know what "abate" means.
POLISH	(Accept)	Well, wax and polish mean almost—well they're very close, and maybe abate and decline are very close. I don't know, I'm just gonna put true.
INCREASE	(Reject)	I just don't know.
WANE	(Reject)	To me, decline seems to have something to do with abate, even though I don't know what it means, but wane doesn't have anything to do with wax.
IMPROVE	(Reject)	I was thinking, maybe abate means "to decline" because wax may mean "to improve." And like before, it means "to polish." I like polish better, though.

Non-Analogical Solution: Protocol 3
Consideration of C-D′ relations only

LINE:RULER::CIRCLE:		Ball. Because a ball is a circle, it's round.
ROUND	(Accept)	Yeah, a circle is round.
DRAW	(Accept)	No, because draw can't be a circle. Oh! Yes, it could be because you draw a circle.
RADIUS	(Accept)	Radius is the numbers in the circle, that's good.
COMPASS	(Accept)	Compass you use to go around—like you put your pencil and it's a circle.

TABLE 9.1 (*Continued*)

Analogy Elements Presented	Solver's Response
(Which of these do you think best completes the analogy?)	Round, because a circle is round.

Non-Analogical Solution: Protocol 4
Identification of A-B and C-D' relations; no relational comparison

TELL:LISTEN::GIVE:		Take. If you tell something, they're like taking it in. If you give something, they take it.
PRESENT	(Accept)	Tell is to listen as give is to present? Yeah, I'd go with that! You give presents?
LOSE	(Reject)	No. Most people find something, they ain't gonna give it back.
GET	(Accept)	Yeah. If you get something, somebody gave it to you.
HAVE	(Accept)	When they give it to you, you have it. Yeah.
(Which of these do you think is best?)		Present. Because you give presents.

Non-Analogical Solution: Protocol 5
Consideration of A-B-C-D interrelations only

SUBJECT:CITIZEN::KING:	King—king—queen.
(Could you explain how you got that?)	Well, subject to citizen—like the king is married to a queen so I figured king and queen. They stay together.
(What about subject and citizen made you think you'd need something that went with a king?)	Well, citizen is a person and is like a subject. So I figured that king and queen ought to fit into it. Same as subject and citizen. If I hear you talking about a subject, then it's probably the queen.
RULE (Accept)	This one is a good one here because you're describing the rules. The king and rule is almost like the citizens and rule and I think that, I guess this is a pretty good one. It's kinda hard.
(Could you explain a little bit more what subject has to do with citizen and king has to do with rule?)	Well, the subject is a type of one thing and a citizen is like a person. So the king is a man who's higher and the rule is—the king rules the citizen.
KNIGHT (Reject)	I don't think so. Because knight—I can't really say why.
(What is a knight?)	A knight is a man that guards the king. That's all I can really say.

(*Continued*)

TABLE 9.1 (*Continued*)

Analogy Elements Presented	Solver's Response
PRESIDENT (Accept)	This one's all right. President—king's almost the same thing, and both of them are citizens and they're subjects.
(What do you mean "They are subjects?)	Well, it's something—subject to something—I can't explain. King and president are citizens and they're subjects to another person—they're the subject of what other people are talking about.
KINGDOM (Accept)	This one's all right because the kingdom's where the king lives. I guess it's all right—I can't go against it.
(You said that president, kingdom, and rule are possible. Which of those three do you like the best?)	President. I like the king and the president because they're almost the same persons, they both rule in different places.
(And how do they connect with subject and citizen?)	Because they're both citizens and are subject to a person.

proceed analogically when they can easily identify an analogical rule, but if that rule is initially inaccessible, or no C-D′ relation can be found to match the initially specified rule, they violate task constraints of appropriate analogical syntax.

Numerical Analogies (Knowledge Base Influences)

Thus far in the discussion, the issue of the declarative or conceptual knowledge base necessary for solving analogies, has essentially been ignored. The discussion now turns to the work on numerical analogies, where the influence of knowledge structure on solutions has been the focus of several studies (Corsale & Gitomer, 1979; Pellegrino, Chi, & Majetic, 1978). Although such knowledge is relatively circumscribed for problems using numbers in the typical range of 0–1000, it is, nevertheless, variable across individuals, depending on their background and experiences, and differentially affects performance. The study by Corsale and Gitomer (1979) attempted to characterize the nature of the differences in the knowledge bases of high- and low-ability individuals, and then to indicate how these knowledge differences influence subjects' problem solution strategies. Two kinds of data were collected: an initial set that was used to characterize the knowledge representations of the elementary school children participating in the study, and a second set of protocol data taken from their problem solutions.

Two tasks were designed to tap the representations of the children's knowledge of numerical relationships. The first task was a grouping task; the children were given a matrix of numbers from 0–32, and were asked to select groups of numbers that went together, and then to justify their groupings. On the basis of these justifications, the kinds of groups that the children made were classified into four types: (a) abstract concepts, representing mathematically based group-ings with superordinate labels, such as the set of primes and multiplicative or exponential relationships; (b) operational concepts, which involved the stringing together of numbers into number sentences; (c) nonmathematical concepts, which were idiosyncratic groupings, or groups based on orthographic sim-ilarities; and (d) digit based groupings, involving numbers that shared common digits, the set of single digit numbers, etc. In the second knowledge representa-tion task, children were presented with 20 pairs of numbers and were asked to state as many relationships as they could for each pair.

Data from the grouping task and the pairs task were reduced by means of a factor analysis. Three factor scores were derived for each child. The first factor was readily interpretable as an estimate of the degree of abstractness found in the children's groupings and pair relationships. The second was a nonmathematical factor, seeming to estimate the number of groupings and relations generated. The third factor represented a preference factor, in which operational or computation-based groups and relations were preferred or were more salient than abstract groupings. Multiple regression analyses on these factor scores, using analogy test performance as the criterion variable, indicated that the degree of ab-stractness in number knowledge is a significant predictor of success in analogical problem solving.

Having demonstrated that the form of knowledge representation is an influen-tial variable, Corsale and Gitomer (1979) examined the interactions of knowl-edge representation and strategy usage for children of different abilities. The highest and the lowest scorers on the standardized analogy test were selected and engaged individually in a session of oral problem solving. Analysis of these protocols indicates that knowledge representation drives solution strategies by defining the limits of the problem domain. Thus, high-ability individuals, who have clear, high level number concepts that are abstract in nature, limit their analogical hypotheses to a few plausible mathematical relationships. In contrast, low-ability children have lower order number concepts, and their analogical solutions indicate that they do not solve analogies with systematic, mathe-matically based rules.

There were two categories of errors in analogy solution; these are listed in Table 9.2. The first, mathematical errors, were of two types: (a) computation errors; and (b) digit errors, in which the subject treated a number not as a total number concept, but as a set of isolated digits (e.g., "64 and 16 go together because they both have a 6 in them"). The second category of errors, analogical ones, contained a variety of types: (a) nonrestrictive errors, where the rela-tionship between the numbers in a pair was not specific enough to allow dis-tinguishing among the options; (b) series errors, where analogy problems were

TABLE 9.2
Errors in Numerical Analogy Solution

Mathematical Errors
  1. Computation errors
  2. Digit errors

Analogical Errors
  1. Non-restrictive errors
  2. Series errors
  3. Single pair errors
  4. AC-BD errors
  5. Non-analogical computation errors
  6. Errors where an individual applied the correct rule, but in the wrong direction

---

turned into series problems; (c) single pair errors, where the subject adopted a rule to apply to E that was true only of AB or CD, but not both; (d) AC-BD errors, where children looked for relationships across pairs rather than within pairs; (e) nonanalogical computation errors, where computations were analogically inappropriate; and (f) errors where an individual applied the correct rule, but in the wrong direction.

Low-ability children committed more analogically inappropriate computation, nonrestrictive, and digit errors. The kinds of errors they made indicated that they do not restrict their hypotheses concerning an analogical rule to mathematical concepts (as noted by the digit errors), or to analogical concepts (as noted by analogically inappropriate computation). Apparently, low-skill subjects have more diffuse, less structured knowledge representations of number, and this is manifested in the kinds of errors they make.

Based on evidence of the less structured knowledge of low-skill children, the lack of solution power can be seen particularly on the probability of success in the interactive solution procedure. As previously indicated, this occurs in the course of solving an analogy, when an individual does not initially infer the AB relationship and uses a backward inference strategy when presented with the CD pair. Both low- and high-skilled individuals use an interactive strategy with equal frequency; however, its successful use is significantly higher in high-aptitude individuals.

The parallel between knowledge representation and solution strategy can also be seen in errors of the high-ability individuals. Analogies were turned into series problems more frequently by highly skilled children. This is a sophisticated kind of error that involves the detection of mathematical relationships across pairs and that follows a constraint rule. In general, the errors made by skilled individuals show that the knowledge representation data, which indicated constrained mathematical concepts for these individuals, parallels their use of that knowledge. When they could not detect a rule, high-ability children would "give up" and not select a multiple choice answer, whereas low-ability children would select an answer—usually a wrong one—and justify it post-hoc. High-ability children operate within both mathematical and analogical constraints in order to achieve an analogically correct answer. They know when they are wrong and give up rather than choose an answer that they know is wrong. Not only do low-ability children choose the wrong answer rather than give up, but the protocol evidence suggests that they justify their choices on nonanalogical and/or nonmathematical grounds.

Considering both the knowledge representation data and the protocol data, the study by Corsale and Gitomer (1979) suggests that the high-scoring individuals on the number analogies aptitude test task have a greater degree of abstract mathematical knowledge and show a greater salience of abstract over operational concepts. This knowledge correlates with and predicts analogy performance. High-ability subjects use their knowledge of abstract number relationships to constrain the domain of permissible operations; this knowledge base determines the appropriate use of strategies. In contrast, low-skill children, often engaged in analogically inappropriate computation and nonrestrictive errors. They apparently have not developed the highly constrained organizational structure of knowledge that would provide them with constrained rules of operation.

IMPLICATIONS

As is apparent from the work reported here, researchers are in the early stages of the effort to understand and assess the nature and instructability of (learning the) skills that comprise aptitude for learning. Nonetheless, our findings thus far (and only their flavor has been described in this paper) permit some speculation. Three interrelated factors emerge that appear to differentiate high- and low-skill individuals. First, the management of memory differs, as is reflected by speed of performance and handling of demands on working memory. Second, individuals show differences in their knowledge of the constraints of problem-solving procedures—what we have called the syntax of analogical problem solving. Effective problem solution is characterized by problem-solving steps that satisfy goals determined by problem constraints: The more constraints the solver is aware of, the more highly constrained will be the goals pursued. Faced with a difficult problem, a skilled individual generates subgoals that enable a return to higher level goals. For the low-skill individual, solution difficulty results in violations of problem-solving constraints, the imposition of procedural bugs, and the inability to recover higher level goals when subgoals need to be pursued. Third, the structure of the declarative-conceptual knowledge base and the level of representation of this knowledge differ as a function of ability. High-skill individuals employ conceptual forms of knowledge that constrain their induction of relations; low-skill individuals encode their knowledge at more concrete surface levels, as is manifested by their limited inferential power.

What are the implications of these findings from the experimental analysis of prototypical test tasks for a conception of academic learning skills? Of the three differentiating aspects mentioned, the memory management component might suggest some sort of processing facility and process training, such as the employment of rehearsal and organizational strategies of the kind studied in memory experiments. The other two components, however, which are concerned with knowledge representation and problem-solving procedures, suggest a different emphasis.

An emphasis on memory management leads one to consider influencing *mental processing skills,* such as better methods for searching memory and elaborating connections, which would facilitate storage and retrieval. For example, an individual could be taught to see fewer single elements and more wholistic features in figural analogy problems. In contrast, an emphasis on the knowledge base and its representation, and an emphasis on the knowledge of problem-solving constraints suggest that one consider a *knowledge strategy.* In a knowledge strategy, progress is seen in terms of improving the ways a knowledge base is recognized and manipulated. When highly skilled individuals learn something new or undertake a new problem of induction, they engage a highly organized structure of appropriate facts and relationships, and associated procedures and goal constraints. Skilled individuals are skilled because of their knowledge of both the content involved in a problem and the procedural constraints of a particular problem form, such as inductive or analogical reasoning. These two kinds of knowledge interact so that procedural constraints are exercised in the content knowledge base; the knowledge base enables procedural goals to be attained.

This analysis leads to the suggestion that the improvement of the skills of learning will take place through the exercise and development of procedural (problem-solving) knowledge, in the context of specific knowledge domains. The suggestion is that learning skills are developed when one teaches more than mechanisms of recall and recognition for a body of knowledge. Learning skill is acquired as the content and concepts of a knowledge domain are attained in learning situations that constrain that knowledge in the service of certain purposes and goals. The goals are defined by uses of that knowledge in procedural schemes, such as those required in analogical reasoning and inductive inference.

At this point, it is difficult to say how this facility could actually be taught. One might teach more of the knowledge base and its high level concepts, or one might teach procedural knowledge, such as planning ahead and recognizing when procedural constraints are violated. Teaching either separately would probably be unsuccessful, because each kind of knowledge facilitates the development of the other. Such learning skills are probably developed through graded sequences of experience that combine conceptual and procedural knowledge. (This is what must take place when a good instructor develops a series of examples that stimulate thinking.) Eventually, procedural schema for various problem forms, such as analogical reasoning, might be abstracted from a variety of knowledge bases, so that a generalized form of procedural knowledge can transfer and be generally applied to new events.

Finally, there is the problem of diagnosing the weaknesses in individuals who are unskilled in academic learning. When this is done, one generally finds that their knowledge base is not rich and that their skill in maintaining directed use of knowledge is not developed. Perhaps a reasonable tactic is to identify, in an individual, some attained knowledge base where instruction can begin. Knowledge developed in the course of an individual's prior cultural experience can provide knowledge representations and goal-directed behavior that can be exploited. As a result of prior experiences, these exist in varying degrees in individuals, and they can be transferred to domains of related knowledge that approximate more and more closely the formal abstractions and procedural requirements necessary for school learning.

FURTHER RESEARCH

As indicated earlier in this paper, the work reported is just a beginning, and further research needs to be done before theory and practice in the measurement and training of aptitudes for learning can be significantly influenced. In our laboratory, currently, research is contemplated to further understanding of analogical reasoning problems. In work on figural analogies, there are plans to study how the figures presented are encoded and represented, prior to the subsequent processes of pattern comparison, transformation, and rule comparison. The analyses of verbal analogies reported in this paper are essentially concerned with the syntactic rules of the task. New research will consider the interaction between syntactic constraints of the problem and the semantics of word meanings and word relationships. The work on numerical analogy problems suggests a similar investigation of mutual influence between conceptual knowledge of numbers and the operation of procedural knowledge of task constraints. The results of the numerical analogy study also suggest a training experiment in which children learn certain levels of number knowledge, and the influence of these levels upon problem solution is observed.

ACKNOWLEDGMENTS

Preparation of this paper was supported by funds provided by the Learning Research and Development Center, University of Pittsburgh, which is supported in part by the National Institute of Education, U.S. Department of Health, Education, and Welfare.

REFERENCES

Brody, E. B., & Brody, N. (1976). *Intelligence: Nature, determinants, and consequences.* New York: Academic Press.

Corsale, K., & Gitomer, D. (1979). *Developmental and individual differences in mathematical aptitude.* Paper presented at the meeting of the Psychonomic Society, Phoenix, AZ, November.

Heller, J. T. (1979). *Cognitive processing in verbal analogy solution.* Unpublished doctoral dissertation, University of Pittsburgh.

Holzman, T. G., Glaser, R., & Pellegrino, J. W. (1976). Process training derived from a computer simulation theory. *Memory & Cognition, 4,* 349–356.

Hunt, E. (1974). Quote the Raven? Nevermore! In L. W. Gregg (Ed.), *Knowledge and cognition.* Potomac, MD: Lawrence Erlbaum Associates.

Kotovsky, K., & Simon, H. A. (1973). Empirical tests of a theory of human acquisition of concepts for sequential events. *Cognitive Psychology, 4,* 399–424.

Mulholland, T. M., Pellegrino, J. W., & Glaser, R. (1980). Components of geometric analogy solution. *Cognitive Psychology, 12,* 252–284.

Pellegrino, J. W., Chi, M. T. H., & Majetic, D. (1978). *Ability differences and the processing of quantitative information.* Paper presented at the meeting of the Psychonomic Society, San Antonio, TX, November.

Pellegrino, J. W., & Glaser, R. (1982). Analyzing aptitudes for learning. In R. Glaser (Ed.), *Advances in instructional psychology* (Vol. 2). Hillsdale, NJ: Lawrence Erlbaum Associates.

Raven, J. C. (1938). *Progressive matrices: A perceptual test of intelligence, 1938, individual form.* London: Lewis.

Rumelhart, D. E. (1977). *Introduction to human information processing.* New York: Wiley.

Simon, H. A., & Kotovsky, K. (1963). Human acquisition of concepts for sequential patterns. *Psychological Review, 70,* 534–546.

Spearman, C. (1923). *The nature of intelligence and the principles of cognition.* London: Macmillan.

Sternberg, R. J. (1977a). Component processes in analogical reasoning. *Psychological Review, 84,* 353–378.

Sternberg, R. J. (1977b). *Intelligence, information processing, and analogical reasoning: The componential analysis of human abilities.* Hillsdale, NJ: Lawrence Erlbaum Associates.

Thurstone, L. L., & Thurstone, T. C. (1941). *Factora studies of intelligence.* Chicago: University of Chicago Press.

10 Processes and Development of Understanding

James G. Greeno
Mary S. Riley
University of Pittsburgh

This chapter has two main sections. In the first section some general remarks about processes of understanding are presented. In these remarks two general issues that are important to metacognitive and attributional processes, as well as to understanding, are addressed. The first issue is whether metacognitive knowledge, attributions, or understanding necessarily involves awareness. The second issue is the relationship between various forms of metacognitive knowledge, in particular, between knowledge that is involved in evaluating cognitive procedures and knowledge that is involved in planning and other strategic aspects of performance.

In the second section the results of some empirical and theoretical research regarding the development of children's skill in solving a class of problems are presented. These findings indicate that the major component that develops is ability to understand the problems that are presented.

PROCESSES OF UNDERSTANDING

The ideas presented have been developed in the context of studies of cognitive processes relevant to school mathematics. Specific analyses in this program have been presented in previous reports (Greeno, 1978; 1980a; 1980b) and further analyses are forthcoming.

In studying various phenomena involving understanding in mathematics, it has become clear that the term "understanding" does not have a single referent. Several quite different things are referred to when one speaks of understanding; discussion is helped if these different referents are explicitly identified.

TABLE 10.1
Forms of Understanding

I. *Theoretical: Related to General Principles*

A. Explicit: Expressible in Language, Including Explanation
    Example: Physics Experts (Chi, this volume)
B. Implicit
    1. Evaluation of Performance
        Examples: Geometry Proof Checking
                  Watch a Puppet Count (Mierkiewicz & Siegler, Note 2)
                  Adjust Counting Procedure (Gelman & Gallistel, 1978)
    2. Analogical Use of Structure
        a. Mapping of Procedures
            Example: Subtraction with Numerals and Blocks (Resnick, 1982)
        b. Transfer
            Example: Learn Procedures in Relation to a Schema
                     (Wertheimer, 1945; Anderson, Greeno, Kline, & Neves, 1987)
        c. Solving Problems of Application
            Examples: Word Problems in Algebra (Paige & Simon, 1966)
                      Word Problems in Arithmetic
C. Conformity

II. *Intrinsic Structure of Performance*

A. Knowledge for Planning
    Examples: Abstract Planning Space (Newell & Simon, 1972)
              Hierarchically Organized Actions (Sacerdoti, 1977)
B. Integrated Performance
    Example: Independence from Visual Cues in Algebra (Davis, Jockusch, &
             McKnight, 1978)

One question of particular concern is understanding in the context of cognitive procedures. This question of understanding a procedure is whether the person performs with some understanding or whether performance is rote and mechanical. Table 10.1, organized in two main categories, lists several forms of understanding that involve procedures. The forms of understanding that are called theoretical involve some general principle or structure that is related to the procedure; the forms that are called intrinsic involve factors that are included in the procedure itself.

Theoretical Understanding

Many cognitive procedures, at least to some extent, are based on general principles. Many of the capabilities that are referred to as understanding relate to an individual's knowledge of such principles. For example, preschool children can count small sets of objects correctly. It is theoretically and educationally important to consider whether this ability reflects more than the cognitive procedure of counting. That is: Do preschool children understand principles of number and quantity, such as the principle of cardinality and one-to-one correspondence? (cf. Gelman & Gallistel, 1978). To address such questions, hypotheses about the nature of understanding and about tasks for which children's performance would provide evidence of the extent of their understanding, are needed.

Explicit Knowledge.   One form in which a person might understand a principle is to know how to state the principle in a language and to explain the consequences of the principle to the procedure. This criterion of understanding is often met by adult experts, such as the advanced physicists studied by Chi (chapter 8, this volume). When individuals can state relevant principles and explain why they are relevant, clearly, they are aware of the principles they understand. On the other hand, one often attributes understanding, both to adults and children, when individuals cannot state principles explicitly in a theoretical language. This indicates that the criterion of explicit linguistic knowledge of the principle, at least in some circumstances, is stronger than one wants to adopt. If understanding is attributed to someone who is not able to state the principle, that person may be unaware of the principle.

Conformity.   Frequently, a lack of understanding is attributed to someone whose performance does not conform to a principle. For example, if a child were to perform a counting procedure with a set of objects, but then could not answer the question, "How many are there?" one would probably conclude that the child did not understand the principle of cardinality. When individuals' performance does conform to a principle, it is possible that they understand the principle, and that their understanding does not include awareness of the principle. However, the attribution of understanding, simply on the basis of correct performance, seems rather gratuitous, and would probably make it difficult to maintain a coherent theoretical distinction between merely knowing a procedure and understanding the procedure. It can be concluded that the criterion of a procedure's conforming to a principle is not sufficient for attributing understanding of the principle.

Implicit Understanding.   The criterion of conformity is too weak; however, the criterion of explicit linguistic knowledge is too strong for attributing understanding of a principle. The question that arises is whether or not there are definite criteria that are stronger than conformity, but weaker than explicit knowledge. We propose two such criteria; each criterion has a reasonable basis in theory and the scientific literature. One of the criteria is an ability to evaluate examples of performance according to the principle—that is, to judge whether or not specific examples are consistent with the principle. Uhe other criterion is use of the principle to identify structural properties shared between procedures in different domains, or to solve problems in a domain different from the one in which the procedure was initially acquired.

Evaluation of Performance.   There are two domains in which knowledge of a concept is tested by determining whether or not an individual can correctly distinguish between positive and negative examples of the concept. One is in traditional laboratory studies of concept attainment (e.g., Bruner, Goodnow & Austin, 1956), where subjects have the task of inducing a concept from information about examples that are or are not members of a category, and demonstrate that they have acquired the concept by correctly sorting a set of examples. A second domain is in computational linguistics, where a knowledge of the syntax of a language is represented by a recognition machine that successfully parses sentences of the language, but fails to parse strings that are not well formed sentences.

In procedural domains, one kind of understanding of a principle can be tested by presenting examples of performance, and testing whether or not an individual correctly discriminates between examples that are or are not consistent with the principle. For example, in one current research project, Magone and Greeno (Greeno, 1983) used the task of proof checking to test students' understanding of the principle of deductive consequence. It was found that students, who have become quite competent in constructing proofs, often fail to detect errors in proofs that are shown to them, especially when the errors involve an insufficient basis in previous assertions for a step in the proof. There was also success in instructing some students in a method of proof checking, designed to improve their understanding of deductive consequence.

Counting by preschool children is another domain where understanding has been tested by evaluation of examples. Mierkiewicz and Siegler (1980) recently conducted a study in which children are shown a puppet counting a set of objects. The puppet sometimes makes errors that violate general principles, such as the principle of one-to-one correspondence. Children who identify these errors indicate their knowledge of the relevant principle, especially when they also give sound explanations supporting their evaluative judgements.

Ability to evaluate procedures is also tested when children are required to adjust their method of counting. Gelman and Gallistel (1978) asked children to count a set of objects; designated one of the objects and said, "Make this the *n*," where *n* varied from one trial to the next. To accomplish this task correctly, a child must devise a new procedure for counting, different from the preferred method in which objects are counted in regular order from one end to the other. Children adjust their counting procedures in various ways, only some of which conform to general principles of counting. For example, if the designated object is given a numeral that is smaller than it ordinarily would have, when the number is to be used, some children will skip to it, and not return to include the skipped objects in the count. This violates the principle of one-to-one correspondence and results in an assignment of an incorrect cardinal number to the set. However, many children adjust their counting procedures in ways that conform to the general principles of counting. A reasonable inference is that, at least by some of the children, a process of choice is included in the adjustment. Children who choose adjustments that conform to the general principles perform an evaluation of alternative procedural components; those who choose correct procedures indicate that they understand the principles on which the choice is based.

Analogical Use of Structure. A problem is encountered in some domain, and the person has not previously learned how to solve that problem. There are problems in another domain, however, for which the person knows a solution procedure; and a principle underlying that procedure applies to both of the domains. If the procedure in the known domain can be used in solving the new problem, or can be used to facilitate learning of a new problem-solving procedure, then the basis of that transfer, or new learning, can reasonably be inferred to be understanding of the principle that is shared by the procedures in the two domains.

Instructional Mapping of Procedures. An example of the understanding of a principle in learning of a procedure is in research conducted by Resnick (1982). Resnick has developed an instructional method for teaching children a correct procedure for subtraction of multidigit whole numbers. The method uses place-value blocks: small cubes correspond to units, bars (10 long) that correspond to tens; and flat shapes (10 by 10) that correspond to hundreds.

Resnick identified children whose performance on subtraction problems was incorrect in a systematic way, which is interpreted as indicating that the child lacks understanding of some significant arithmetic principle. The procedure with blocks was designed in a way that makes some important contraints quite salient. For example, the procedure with blocks involves taking blocks away from a set that is present; if the number to take away is greater than the number that is present, there obviously is an impediment to performance. The procedure with blocks requires that the child know a correspondence between the representations of numbers with numerals on paper and with blocks.

When the procedure with blocks had been learned, Resnick instructed the child in a set of correspondences between procedures with the blocks and with numerals on paper. Each time a change is made in the problem with blocks, a corresponding change must be made in the numeral-paper representation. For example, when a child trades a ten-block for ten unit-blocks, there are two steps (removing one ten-block and bringing in ten units); each of these steps corresponds to a change that must be made in the numerals (crossing out the tens-numeral, replacing it with the next-smaller numeral, and inserting a ''one'' next to the units-numeral). When the child had learned to perform subtraction in the blocks and numerals simultaneously, Resnick gradually removed the blocks from the procedure, so that the child performed subtraction correctly with just numerals.

Used in this way, the blocks provide a basis for some children acquiring correct procedures for subtraction. There is suggestive evidence that this is accomplished through acquisition of general principles of arithmetic that are abstract enough to be applied both to numerals and to blocks. For example, one child was asked how the procedure that had been learned differed from the one the child had used previously. The child answered, "Before, I just took the numbers apart. Now, I leave them together, and take them apart too." This provides evidence that the general principle shared across the two domains was understood by the child.

Transfer.   Ability to transfer procedures to novel problems provides relatively strong evidence that a person understands general principles in the solution (e.g., Gagne, 1966; Katona, 1940; Wertheimer, 1945/1959). Wertheimer's best known example is the problem of calculating the area of a parallelogram. Wertheimer argued that the procedure of calculating, using the formula $A = b \times h$, could be mechanical or could involve understanding. He characterized understanding as including appreciation of spatial relations that involve the way a parallelogram can be transformed into a rectangle. He described children's performance on various transfer tasks, as evidence of their understanding.

In a recent analysis of meaningful learning, Greeno (1983) has developed an hypothesis about the cognitive process involved in learning that can be transfered to novel problem situations. According to this analysis, transfer is enabled by a schema that can be used to represent the structure of problems in the domain where a procedure is learned, as well as in the domain of transfer. Simulations of learning were programmed to clarify the difference between meaningful learning, with procedures embedded in a schema, and more mechanical learning, in which procedures are associated with specific stimulus conditions of a problem situation. The learning that was simulated involved geometry problems in which line segments are related to one another as parts of larger units. If a learner acquires proof procedures that are embedded in a schema of part-whole relationships, then those procedures can be used in another domain, such as adjacent angles, where the objects can also be organized in terms of part-whole relationships. The simulation provides an explanation of transfer to a problem of proving the congruence of vertical angles, discussed by Wertheimer (1945/1959).

Problems of Application.   A third kind of indication of understanding is ability to solve problems of application, as when algebra formulas can be used to solve word problems. Paige and Simon (1966) found that a variety of processes involved in understanding problems led to different representations, some of which enabled subjects to detect inconsistencies in information in problem statements. Mayer and Greeno (1972), and Egan and Greeno (1973) studied different methods of instructing subjects about the binomial formula for calculating probabilities of outcomes in random experiments. They found that more meaningful instruction led to better performance in application problems, as well as in more frequent detections of inconsistent or insufficient information in problem statements.

Another example of problem solving mapping between a verbal and mathematical domain is in story problems that are solved by primary grade children, using simple addition and subtraction of numbers. Research based on problems in this domain is discussed in the second part of this chapter.

Intrinsic Understanding

Most frequently when one speaks of understanding a procedure or solution of a problem, one refers to a relationship to some general principle. However, one can also speak of understanding of a less general kind, involving apprehension of the intrinsic structure of a problem solution or a problem-solving procedure. Greeno (1977) has proposed that understanding a problem solution is analogous to understanding a sentence, where understanding consists of constructing a representation that includes relations among the ideas that are mentioned in the sentence. In this sense, understanding a problem solution or problem-solving procedure would consist of constructing a representation of the solution or procedure, including meaningful relations among the various steps of the solution or the various cocomponents of the procedure. Understanding of this kind may be analogous to metacognitive knowledge, consisting of strategies for performance (Brown, chapter 3, this volume; Kluwe, chapter 2, this volume).

Two forms of intrinsic understanding can be distinguished. The first form is an aspect of strategic knowledge, involving knowledge for planning solutions of specific problems. The second form, which may or may not be a consequence of the first, consists of integrated knowledge that enables a person to perform a task in a smooth, coherent manner.

Knowledge for Planning.   Understanding of a sequence of things often includes realizing the way in which subsets of the things fit together in groups. In language, understanding of a sentence includes realizing the sets of words that fit together in phrases. In the solution of a problem, understanding includes realizing the sets of problem steps that fit together in meaningful units. It seems reasonable to classify the "phrases" of a problem solution as sets of steps that are related to a single major goal of the problem, or that are the details of a single global action. Newell and Simon (1972) used the term "episode" to refer to such units. If a person understands another's solution for a problem, then the episodes in the solution should be apparent, and the understanding should include the subgoals that motivated the activity in episodes, as Brown, Collins, and Harris

(1978) observed. Similarly, if a person's own solution of a problem is accomplished with understanding, then the various steps should be organized in a meaningful way, with individual steps performed in relation to subgoals that determine an organization of episodes in the solution.

Knowledge of the kind required for this kind of understanding has been characterized as knowledge for planning. Newell and Simon (1972) hypothesized that planning requires a representation of the problem that distinguishes between essential and inessential problem features. A plan is constructed as a sequence of subgoals that involve essential features; execution of the plan requires accomplishing these subgoals, including working out details corresponding to inessential features of the solution. A similar idea was developed by Sacerdoti (1977), who hypothesized that knowledge required for planning consists of information about global actions. These global actions correspond to sets of more elementary actions that can be performed directly in the problem environment. Organized problem solving occurs when an individual constructs a sequence of global actions that can lead to the main problem goal, and then, in turn, works out the details of each of the global actions.

Knowledge used in planning is metacognitive, in the sense that it is about cognitive procedures. In order to plan one's own problem-solving activity, or to understand the plans involved in another's problem solutions, a person requires knowledge about the individual procedural components in a solution that shows how the components are grouped into episodes and related to subgoals. This metacognitive knowledge does not necessarily include explicit representation of general principles, nor is it necessarily accompanied by any self-conscious processes that would constitute awareness of the cognitive organization that it determines.

Integrated Performance.   A kind of understanding is often attributed to someone who has become highly skilled in a task. For example, a musical performer, after studying and practicing it, may say that he or she understands a piece; whereas, initially the piece could be played successfully, but without a sense that it is understood. It seems reasonable to hypothesize that the understanding that results from practice includes appreciation of relationships within the piece that were not appreciated initially. There relationships might well be provided by a structure of knowledge involving global actions or subgoals like those involved in planning.

One consequence of developing higher order cognitive units, needed to organize problem solving in a skilled way, has been noted by Davis, Jockusch, and McKnight (1978). This consequence, observed in students as they became more skilled in algebra, was that their performance became less dependent on the explicit intermediate results that they wrote out as they solved problems. Davis et al. referred to performance in early stages of practice as visually modulated sequences, in which intermediate results are written and used as cues for continuation of the performance. They hypothesized that practiced students have acquired general schematic action structures that enable them to direct their performance without using the visual cues provided by written intermediate results. This kind of general schema might also be responsible for the ability to perform planfully, and therefore would constitute understanding, in the same way that understanding may be attributed to a person with knowledge for planning.

DEVELOPMENT OF ABILITY TO UNDERSTAND

In this section some empirical findings regarding development of skill in problem solving are presented. There is evidence that in the specific tasks studied, the main developmental component that accounts for older children's better performance is acquisition of improved ability to understand problems.

The problems studied involve children's knowledge of numbers and arithmetic. The understanding that is required is one of the forms of implicit theoretical understanding, discussed earlier. Specifically, these problems require mapping from a problem domain, described in some text, to the domain of arithmetic or counting. Relationships described in the problem text must be understood, and problem-solving procedures are chosen on the basis of the understanding that is achieved.

Theoretical Framework and Issues

The framework used in this discussion is sketched in Fig. 10.1. Important components of this analysis were contributed by Joan Heller (see Riley, Greeno & Heller, 1983). The terms *Problem Schemata* and *Action Schemata,* shown in brackets, refer to knowledge that the problem solver is required to have stored in order to perform the tasks. Problem schemata are general conceptual structures that are used in representing the information in problem texts. These are structures like those hypothesized in recent analyses of language understanding (e.g., Norman & Rumelhart, 1975; Schank & Abelson, 1977). Action schemata are general procedural structures that function as plans for problem-solving activity. These are knowledge structures, like those hypothesized in recent analyses of knowledge for problem solving, involving knowledge about actions at different levels of generality (e.g. Brown & Burton, 1978; Sacerdoti, 1977).

It is hypothesized that the process of solving a problem involves three main processes, which do not necessarily occur in a strict sequence. One process is comprehension of the text, resulting in a representation of the concepts and relationships that are described. A second process, using the information in the problem representation, is selection of an appropriate set of problem-solving

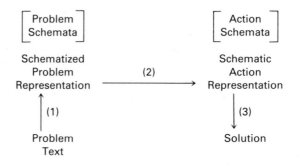

FIG. 10.1. Framework of a model of problem understanding and solution. Arrows represent processes of (1) comprehension, (2) mapping from conceptual relations to quantitative procedures, and (3) execution of procedures.

procedures. Finally, the procedures that have been chosen are executed to obtain the problem solution.

This framework suggests alternative hypotheses about possible sources of developmental improvement in problem-solving skill. If it is decided that some task requires a specific kind of action schema, the older children perform better on that task than younger children, one might conclude that the older children have acquired that schema that younger children lack. This kind of inference was typical in Piaget's work.

However, another possibility is that younger children have the relevant action schema for solving a problem, but that schema is not activated by the situation in which the problem is presented. In principle, failure of activation could occur for any of three reasons: first, linguistic processes needed to translate text into a semantic representation could be lacking; second, connections between the problem representation and action schemata might be lacking; and third, the required problem schemata might be lacking. Evidence is presented that seems to rule out the hypothesis that children lack the action schemata needed for the problems studied. We currently favor a hypothesis that combines the first and third alternative possibilities; that is, the knowledge that children acquire in becoming skillful in simple arithmetic word problems includes procedures and general conceptual knowledge that enables them to represent problem information successfully.

The conclusion that we reach in our analysis puts us squarely in the middle of a current issue in the literature of cognitive development. On the basis of failures in various tasks, Piaget and his associates concluded that children lack understanding of some very important concepts: conservation of number; class inclusion; seriation; and so on. Evidence for these failures came from performance that is inconsistent with the general concepts. For example, when a child sees two sets with the same number of objects and says one set has more, that performance is inconsistent with the concept of number conservation. On the other side, numerous investigators have shown that children will show performance that is consistent with thise principles in other circumstances. For example, Gelman and Gallistel (1978) provided evidence that preschool children understand principles of number, and Trabasso, Isen, Dolecki, McLanahan, Riley, and Tucker (1978) summarized evidence that children, under appropriate circumstances, show that they understand the principle of class inclusion.

Our conclusion concurs with recent investigators that the standard Piagetian conclusion of structural deficiency is too simple; yet another instance is added, in which an action schema that was thought to be lacking in young children has to be present for them to perform as they do in a modified task. However, we also conclude that the difference between younger and older children is more profound than simply acquiring the meanings of a few linguistic terms. The most plausible hypothesis, regarding the problems analyzed, is that younger children have the general procedures needed to solve the problems, but they lack ability to coherently represent problem information. The ability to construct those representations constitutes a set of important conceptual advances that older children have achieved.

Evidence for Action Schemata

Consider the following example: "Joan has $8 and Sue has $11. How many more dollars does Sue have than Joan?" The answer is found by subtracting 8 from 11, but because quantities must be identified and the decision to subtract numbers requires understanding of quantitative relationships, a more complicated procedure is needed.

Figure 10.2 shows one procedure for solving problems that involve the comparative question, "How many more?" In thinking about this procedure, it is convenient to think of a child using some blocks to work out the solution. However, a similar procedure also may be used when blocks are not used, in which case the operations involving sets refer to mental representations of quantities.

Apply the procedure in Fig. 10.2 to the example as follows: X and Y are Sue's and Joan's dollars, respectively; $N1$ is 11, $N2$ is 8. In the first two steps, representations of these sets are formed; with blocks, two piles would be made; 11 in one pile and 8 in the other. The third step involves identifying a subset of X that has the same number of blocks as Y; in the description of the procedure this subset is called Z. Physically, a child might form pairs of blocks, with one block from X corresponding to each block in Y. In any case, Step 3 of the procedure depends on the idea of one-to-one correspondence. In Step 4, the complement of Z in X is formed and brought into attention. In working with blocks, the set W would just be the blocks remaining, after Z was formed. Step 4 depends on the

---

Compare X, More, Y
  (X has N1, Y has N2)

---

1. Makeset: X, N1
2. Makeset: Y, N2
3. Make Match: Z in X match Y
   a. Form subset of X equal to Y (one-to-one correspondence)
   b. Z = matching subset
4. Make Remain: W in X from Z
   a. Separate X: Z and remainder (class inclusion)
   b. W = remainder
5. Count W

FIG. 10.2.   Procedure for Answering, "How many more?"

idea of class inclusion. Finally, the answer to the question is obtained by counting the number of blocks in *W*.

This problem is interesting, partly because it is quite difficult for children. Table 10.2 shows data collected by Riley as part of a study of the development of children's ability to solve simple arithmetic word problems. Most of the kindergarten children were 6 years old, most of the first grade students were 7 years old, and so on. The first two columns show data for problems asking, "How many more in one set than another?" The next two ask, "How many less or fewer in one set than another?" The problems in the last two columns gave a quantity, and a number that was lost or taken away, and asked, "How many resulted?" An example of the last kind involving money would be: "Sue had $11 and spent $8. How many does she have now?" The columns marked "Without Blocks," show data when the children were simply given the problems orally. The columns marked "With Blocks," show data when children were given the same problems, but where there were small wooden blocks that the children could use to represent the numbers in the problems. Note that questions of "How many more?" or "How many less?" pose significant difficulty for children as old as 8 years; however, other problems solved by subtraction are quite easy for children, before they enter first grade.

Why are problems involving comparison so difficult for younger children? It is tempting to conclude that they lack the cognitive procedures required to find the answer. In Riley et al's (1983) analysis, processing requires formation of subsets, one of which is formed by putting its members in one-to-one correspondence with members of another set. A conclusion that these processes are not yet in the repertoire of young children would be consistent with Piaget's (1952) well known findings regarding class inclusion and conservation of number.

This interpretation, however, is contradicted by data collected by Hudson (1980), who presented problems of the kind shown in Fig. 10.3 to 12 nursery school, 24 kindergarten, and 28 first grade children. Two different questions

TABLE 10.2
Proportions of Correct Solution

School Grade	How Many More?		How Many Less?		How Many Now?	
	Without Blocks	With Blocks	Without Blocks	With Blocks	Without Blocks	With Blocks
K	.13	.17	.13	.04	.61	1.00
1	.33	.28	.17	.22	1.00	1.00
2	.65	.85	.65	.75	1.00	1.00
3	1.00	1.00	1.00	1.00	1.00	1.00

were asked. One question was the usual comparative question, in this case, "How many more birds than worms are there?" The other question was an alternative that Hudson devised: "Suppose the birds all race over and each one tries to get a worm? How many birds won't get a worm?" The results were striking; they are shown in Table 10.3. Hudson gave different questions of each type, and the proportions indicated are for children who gave six or more responses of the same kind. Correct responses were the set differences—for example, one more bird than worms, or one bird won't get a worm. The most frequent incorrect response was the number in the larger set—for example, "How many more birds than worms?" "Five"; or "Five birds." Another frequent error was to give both set sizes, for example: "Five and 4," or "Five birds and 4 worms." Very few of the nursery school or kindergarten children answered the "How many more?" questions by giving the difference between the sets. However, nearly all the children of all three ages answered the "How many won't get?" questions correctly.

Hudson's results clearly contradict the hypothesis that young children lack a procedure for finding a set difference. To answer "Won't get" questions, children carried out a procedure essentially like the one in Fig. 10.2; forming the correspondence of sets indicated in Step 3, and then counting the remaining subset of the larger set. Many of the children did this overtly, pointing with their fingers, either in counting equal subsets or in forming pairs of objects from the two sets. Because children clearly have this procedure in their repertoire, one must look elsewhere for an explanation of their difficulty with the "How many more?" questions.

An alternative interpretation of young children's difficulty is that they have not yet acquired procedures for representing the information in the "How many more?" problem, including the meaning of the question; that is, they do not yet have the schema for comparison needed to form representations that include comparative relationships between quantities. If it is assumed that the restatement of the question enables children to activate procedures for forming corresponding sets and counting the remainder without forming an intermediate sche-

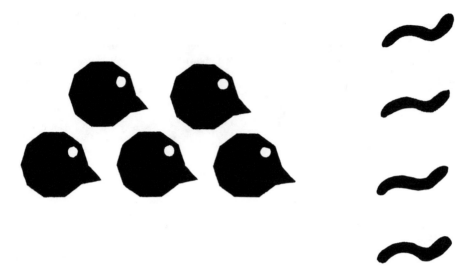

FIG. 10.3.   Example Problem From Hudson's Experiment

matized representation of the problem information, this interpretation is consistent with Hudson's findings. In Fig. 10.1, this would involve a process going directly from problem text to schematic action representation—an arrow diagonally from the lower left to the upper right of the diagram. This seems a reasonable hypothesis about the effect of Hudson's form of the question. The remark that birds will race over and each will try to get a worm, communicates a strong suggestion about forming corresponding sets; the question How many won't get a worm? focuses directly on the complement of the set formed by correspondence.

Analysis of Developmental States

We propose a hypothesis that the main form of growth in problem-solving skills consists of processes of understanding. However, a hypothesis that older children solve problems more successfully because they understand better does not

TABLE 10.3
Proportions of Children with Consistent Correct Responses

Grade	How Many More?	How Many Won't Get?
Nursery School	.17	.83
Kindergarten	.25	.96
First	.64	1.00

answer the question of developmental change adequately; it merely identifies a domain in which to look for an answer. An adequate answer requires an analysis of the ability to understand problems, as well as an analysis of the changes that result in the cognitive abilities that are required in order for understanding to occur. In this section the results of an empirical developmental study of skill in solving arithmetic word problems are presented, and some theoretical conclusions about the states through which children develop as they acquire stronger ability to understand these problems, are described.

Empirical Analysis. An empirical study was conducted by Riley, in order to provide a reasonably thorough descriptive account of children's performance on a variety of problem-solving tasks. The problems were selected on the basis of an analysis by Heller and Greeno (see Greeno, 1980a; Riley, Greeno & Heller, 1983) of a set of semantic schemata that forms a sufficient basis for understanding the variety of arithmetic word problems that are solved by addition or subtraction. The three general categories of problems are called Change, Combine, and Compare. In a Change problem, there is a quantity that is either increased or decreased by some event. For example: "Kurt had $11 dollars and he gave $8 to John. How many dollars does Kurt have now?" In the second kind of problem, called Combine, there are two quantities; neither quantity is changed; the problem solver must think of the combination of the quantities. For example, "There are five boys and six girls. How many children are there?" Finally, in Compare problems there also are two quantities that do not change; the problem solver must think of the difference between them. For example: "There are 5 girls and 2 boys. How many more girls are there than boys?" The problem types are listed in Table 10.4.

In Riley's experiment, all three kinds of problems were presented to children. A further difference among problems also was used, as shown in each kind of

TABLE 10.4
Kinds of Problems

Change				Compare	
Direction	*Unknown*			*Direction*	*Unknown*
1) Increase,	Result			1) More,	Difference
2) Decrease,	Result			2) Less,	Difference
3) Increase,	Change			3) More,	Compared
4) Decrease,	Change			4) Less,	Compared
5) Increase,	Start			5) More,	Referent
6) Decrease,	Start			6) Less,	Referent
		Combine, Unknown			
		1) Combination			
		2) Subset			

problem—Change, Compare, and Combine—there are three items of information. Different problems can be formed by varying the items of information given, and by varying the item to be found by the problem solver. In Change problems, the three items are the starting quantity, the amount of the change, and the resulting quantity. Any of these can be found if the other two are given, therefore, there are three different cases: the unknown quantity can be the start; the change; the final result. Furthermore, the change can either be a decrease or an increase; therefore, there are six kinds of Change problems. A similar set of variations exists for Compare problems, where the direction of difference may be more or less; the unknown quantity may be the amount of difference (How many more? or How many less?), the quantity used as the referent (that is, in "A has 5 less than B," B is the referent that A is compared to); or the quantity that is being compared. In Combine problems there are fewer semantic categories—the unknown is either the combined quantity or one of the subsets.

In her study, Riley used all these kinds of problems, including subsets of the Combine category that varied in the order of presenting the information; this resulted in a total of 18 problems. Eighty-one children were interviewed; 23 from kindergarten, 18 from first grade, and 20 each from the second and third grades. Each child was interviewed twice. In the first session, the 18 problems were presented orally; the child was asked to give an answer and write an arithmetic expression for the problem. In the second session the same problems were presented; the child was asked to repeat each problem and then solve it using some wooden blocks.

Only a few summary findings from Riley's experiment are presented. Table 10.5 shows average performance for children of different ages on the problems in the three general semantic categories. First, as one would expect, older children performed better on these problems than younger children. Second, the three categories of problems were not equally difficult. The Compare problems were harder, on the average, than the Combine or Change problems.

A reasonable hypothesis is that there are conceptual schemata corresponding to these three problem types—a schema of quantitative change, a schema of combination, and a schema of comparison. It might be tempting to speculate that these three schemata emerge at different times in cognitive development. For

TABLE 10.5
Proportion Correct by Grade and Problem Type

Grade	Change	Combine	Compare
K	.48	.42	.11
1	.66	.60	.21
2	.89	.83	.62
3	.90	.95	.88

TABLE 10.6
Proportion Correct by Unknown
Quantity

| | Unknown | | |
Type	1	2	3
Change	.95	.77	.53
Combine	.96	.57	
Compare	.52	.52	.33

example, at a certain age, a specific child might have the schemata of change and combination, but not the schema of comparison. However, data given in Table 10.6 show that such a view would be too simple. Table 10.6 shows average performance for problems of the same general category, differing in the items of information that were unknown. The data show that the different problems of each semantic type differed in difficulty. For example, children had no difficulty with change problems if the problem gave the start and change amounts and asked for the result. If the result and change were given, with the starting quantity unknown, most of the younger children had difficulty. The remaining case, with the start and result given, was intermediate. These findings show that one must consider specific features of problems in an effort to understand the problem-solving skills of children at different ages.

Another result involves the difference between performance with and without blocks as aids for solving the problems, shown in Table 10.7. On the average, use of the blocks facilitated solution of problems, especially for the youngest children. The facilitating effect of having objects available for representing aspects of the problems is not surprising, and should be taken into account in developing a theoretical analysis of the development of problem-solving skill.

Theoretical Analysis.   The framework used in this analysis was discussed earlier. Recall that two main components of knowledge are postulated: schemata

TABLE 10.7
Proportion Correct by Problem-Solving
Situation

Grade	Without Blocks	With Blocks
K	.26	.41
1	.50	.49
2	.72	.84
3	.91	.95

for representing problems, and schematic representations of actions for planning problem solutions.

It is assumed that there are three schemata used in understanding simple arithmetic story problems: a schema for Change problems; a schema for Combine problems; and a schema for Compare problems. Fig. 10.4 is a diagram of the structure that is hypothesized as the schematic representation of one of the forms of the Change type of problem; a problem involving a decrease in a quantity, with the result unknown. The problem might be, "Joe had 8 rabbits; 5 ran away; how many rabbits does Joe have now?" The model developed to simulate understanding of such problems builds the first component, labeled (1) in Fig. 10.4, when it receives "Joe had 8 rabbits." Then when a sentence such as "Five ran away." is received, it infers that the problem is about a change, and constructs the nodes labeled (2) in Fig. 10.4. Finally, when the question "How many now?" is received, the structure is completed by constructing the nodes labeled (3) in Fig. 10.4.

In the analysis of developmental change that was worked out by Riley et al. (1983), different stages of skill are represented by different abilities, for representing problems and performing actions. Different schemata are required to represent the three problem types. Change problems include start, change, and result quantities as in Figure 10.4. Combine problems require representations involving three quantities, two of which are parts of the third quantity, the whole. For Compare problems, a schema was hypothesized that includes a difference between two quantities, one of which is identified as the referent and the other as the comparison quantity.

The action schemata hypothesized include the following: (MAKESET X N), which takes a number and creates a set of objects with that number in it, called X;

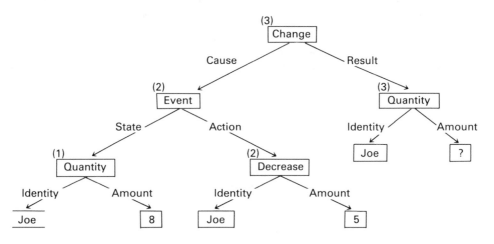

FIG. 10.4.   Schematized Representation of a Problem

(PUTIN *X N*), which adds a number of things to an existing set; (TAKEOUT *X N*) which removes a number of things from an existing set; and (COUNT X), which determines the number of objects in a set. Fig. 10.5 shows a problem-solving plan for the problem whose representation is shown in Fig. 10.4. The problem-solving system assembles this plan from the action schemata, when the representation in Fig. 10.4 has been formed. In addition to the schemata mentioned, the repertoire of action schemata includes structures, such as those mentioned in Fig. 10.2; (MATCH *Y* in *X*) and (SEPARATE *X: Z* and remainder).

In Riley's analysis of developmental states, different stages of skill are represented by different schemata for representing problems. Children with more problem-solving skill are assumed to have an ability to represent problems more completely; that is, they have more detailed schemata for representing relationships among quantities. Their representational skills also include capabilities for representing some items of information internally, rather than depending on external realizations of quantities in the form of sets of objects.

Riley's analyses were based on systematic patterns of performance that she observed in her developmental study. Within each set of problems—those involving Change, Combine, and Compare problems—she was able to identify two or three graded subsets of problems. The easiest subset was a group of problems that were solved correctly by nearly all the children, including the kindergarten children. A second subset of problems was solved correctly by some, but not all of the children; in one case there were two intermediate subsets. For many of the problems in which errors occurred, children tended to give characteristic errors—that is, a particular incorrect response occurred with quite a high frequency.

An example is in Table 10.8 which presents data from children's performance, when they had blocks available to aid in solving the problems; the numbers given as errors are illustrative. Different children solved these problems with different numbers; therefore, a characteristic error indicates the kind of answer given. For example, in problem 3, the specific number that was given, whatever that number was, was the final result.

When blocks were available, nearly all the children solved problems 1, 2 and 4 correctly. One problem, number 3, was of intermediate difficulty, and problems 5 and 6 were the most difficult. Children who made errors on problem 3 usually said ''8'' (giving the final result rather than the amount of change); ''5''

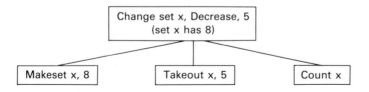

FIG. 10.5.   Schematic Plan for Problem Solution

TABLE 10.8
Patterns of Performance on Change Problems

Example Problems	Levels of Performance		
	1	2	3
Result unknown			
1. Joe had 3 marbles.			
He found 5 more marbles.			
How many marbles did Joe have then?	+	+	+
2. Joe had 8 marbles.			
He lost 5 marbles.			
How many marbles did Joe have then?	+	+	+
Change unknown			
3. Joe had 3 marbles.			
He found some more marbles.			
Then Joe had 8 marbles.			
How many marbles did Joe find?	"8"	+	+
4. Joe had 8 marbles.			
He lost some marbles.			
Then he had 3 marbles.			
How many marbles did Joe lose?	+	+	+
Start unknown			
5. Joe had some marbles.			
He found 5 more marbles.			
Then he had 8 marbles.			
How many marbles did Joe have to begin with?	"5"	"5"	+
6. Joe had some marbles.			
He lost 5 marbles.			
Then he had 3 marbles.			
How many marbles did Joe have to begin with?	NA	NA	+

was a characteristic error for problem 5 (giving the amount of change instead of the starting amount). The characteristic error in problem 6 was to remain silent, looking puzzled.

Riley developed hypotheses in the form of models that represent skill at different levels. The theoretical goal was to simulate the different levels of children's performance on these problems. That is, she developed hypotheses about the kinds of information-processing components needed to explain the different patterns of children's performance on the various problems. The models differ in the ways in which quantitative information is represented.

Riley developed three models for different levels of performance on the Change problems. In the simplest model, the only problem schema for representing quantitative information, identifies an object (e.g., Joe's rabbits) with a quantitative value. Action schemata that are used include: MAKESET; PUTIN; TAKEOUT; and COUNT. This model is sufficient to solve the first two problems correctly. A starting set is created, and then either increased by PUTIN or decreased by TAKEOUT. When the question is asked, the resulting state is created and counted.

The main difference between Riley's models for Level 1 and Level 2 is that at Level 2 it is assumed that additional information is represented internally. This model can construct representations using the schema for change problems, shown in Fig. 10.4, where a mental record is kept of the structural role of each item of information. This additional structural information enables the model to give the correct answer to Problem 3. The external actions with blocks are the same on the first and third problems—first making a set of 3 and then increasing the set to 8 (either with PUTIN or with MAKESET). The Level 1 model, without a record of the structural information, cannot distinguish these two situations; however the Level 2 model identifies the set of 8 as the result, and remembers that initially that set had 3; therefore, it is able to infer (or remember) the amount of the increase correctly.

Notice in Table 10.8 that although Problem 3 was answered incorrectly by children at the lowest level of performance, typically, Problem 4 was solved correctly by all children; this probably was fortuitous. When a set is made initially and then reduced (in this case to 3) the removed set of blocks is still available for inspection. Thus, children were able to give the correct answer to Problem 4, even if they did not keep a memory record of the structural relationships.

Finally, Riley's Level 3 model employs a schema for combination of quantities shown in Fig. 10.6, and constructs plans using the following action schemata: (MAKESET X ?), which constructs a representation of an unknown quantity; (JOIN S T U), which forms a superset by putting two subsets together; and (SEPARATE U S T), which forms two subsets from a superset. Riley hypothesized that problems with the start unknown are understood by a kind of translation into concepts of set combination. Consistent with this idea is the fact that the

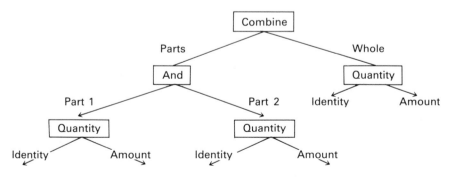

FIG. 10.6.   Schema for Combination of Quantities

difficulty of problems 5 and 6 was very similar to the difficulty of Combine problems with subsets unknown, for each group of children that Riley observed.

Riley also developed models of levels of performance on the Combine and Compare problems, in which different levels of skill are simulated with representational components analogous to those described for the Change problems. At the lowest level, Riley assumed that the child's representations of problems are limited to the external displays of blocks; at an intermediate level some relevant additional information is represented internally; and at the most advanced level there are features represented internally that direct the understanding and actions in a top-down manner.

A test of these models was obtained by determining how many of the children in the experiment performed in one of the ways consistent with a model. Table 10.9 shows the proportions of children in the various age groups whose performance was consistent with each of the modes at each age level. The data are from performance when blocks were available. Performance without blocks involves retention in memory, which produces additional complications. The columns labeled 3a for Change and Compare problems indicate children whose performance exceeded Level 2, but included an error on a problem that would be performed correctly by a child who had Level 3 knowledge. Keep in mind that the models were developed after inspection of the data for patterns of systematic performance. Even so, it is encouraging that explainable patterns could be found

TABLE 10.9
Proportions of Patterns Consistent with Models

	Level	Grade			
		K	1	2	3
Change	1	.35	.39	0	0
Problems	2	.39	.17	.10	.05
	3a	.13	.17	.30	.15
	3b	.09	.22	.60	.80
	Residual	.04	.05	0	0
Combine	1	.52	.28	.05	0
Problems	2	.22	.28	.05	0
	3	.17	.22	.85	.95
	Residual	.09	.22	.05	.05
Compare	1	.48	0	0	0
Problems	2	.22	.67	.10	0
	3a	.04	.11	.45	.45
	3b	0	.05	.20	.55
	Residual	.26	.17	.25	0

that showed this degree of consistency with the children's performance on these problems.

CONCLUSIONS

Uniqueness cannot be claimed for the models developed in these analyses. Indeed, there are some redundant features in the models; somewhat simpler accounts could be given to explain the observed improvements in skill. Even so, we are quite confident that the children's improvement in skill in these problems involves something along the lines of these models. The more skillful models have their skill because they understand problems better. That is, their representations of problems include the relevant features of the problem more completely, and in ways that lead to choice of appropriate problem-solving actions.

In the final section the results of Hudson's (1980) and Riley's developmental studies in relation to the ideas about understanding, presented earlier, are discussed.

In the tasks studied by Hudson and Riley, solutions for problems are obtained by procedures for making quantitative inferences. In analyses presented here procedures have been characterized as counting operations; however, similar analyses would result if more advanced arithmetic operations, such as addition and subtraction of numbers, we were considered. The problems that children are asked to solve are presented verbally, or with pictures. Thus, in order to choose an appropriate problem-solving procedure, the child is required to make some kind of translation from the verbal or verbal/pictorial presentation. There is evidence that this translation is the major source of difficulty encountered by young children for these problems, and that the major developmental changes that enables older children to perform successfully is acquisition of procedures of understanding that construct representations of problem situations.

Strong evidence for the importance of understanding is provided by Hudson's findings, which show that a change in the wording of problems greatly facilitates young children's ability to solve them. Similar findings have been obtained for other problem domains. For example, Markman (1979) has shown that use of a class term, rather than a collection term (e.g., "forest" rather than "trees") greatly facilitates children's performance on class-inclusion problems. It may be that in many domains, young children have acquired general procedures for making inferences before they have been thought to do so, and, because of undeveloped skills in understanding, perform weakly on cognitive tasks.

In our analysis of the understanding process that children acquire, based largely on Riley's developmental study, we hypothesized that older children have procedures for constructing general representations of quantitative relationships. These schematized representations mediate between problem texts and problem-solving procedures. They represent general structural features of problem situations; therefore, the ability to form these representations constitutes an important aspect of understanding, referred to as implicit theoretical understanding.

Regarding young children's difficulty with problems, we conclude from Hudson's results and similar findings that children probably have acquired procedures that conform to general principles, such as one-to-one correspondence. However, procedural conformity is different from stronger forms of understanding. The question whether children have acquired something like implicit theoretical understanding of a concept, such as one-to-one correspondence, is not answered by showing that they have a procedure that is consistent with that concept. In general, the question *whether* a child understands some general principle is probably not well formed. Instead, we expect that a detailed analysis of just what cognitive processes and structures a child has, usually will benecessary for an adequate assessment. In other words, we analysis of *what* and *how* a child understands is preferable to arguments about *whether* understanding has been achieved.

ACKNOWLEDGMENTS

The research reported herein was supported by the Learning Research and Development Center, supported in part by funds from the National Institute of Education (NIE), United States Department of Health, Education, and Welfare. The opinions expressed do not necessarily reflect the position or policy of NIE, and no official endorsement should be inferred.

We are grateful to Tom Hudson for discussions and helpful criticisms of this chapter.

REFERENCES

Brown, J. S., & Burton, R. R. (1978). Diagnostic models for procedural bugs in basic mathematical skills. *Cognitive Science, 2,* 155–192.

Brown, J. S., Collins, A., & Harris, G. (1978). Artificial intelligence and learning strategies. In H. F. O'Neil (Ed.), *Learning strategies.* New York: Academic Press.

Bruner, J. S., Goodnow, J. J., & Austin, G. A. (1956). *A study of thinking.* New York: Wiley, 1956.

Davis, R. B., Jockusch, E., & McKnight, C. (1978). Cognitive processes in learning algebra. *Journal of Children's Mathematical Behavior, 2,* 5–320.

Egan, D. E., & Greeno, J. G. (1973). Acquiring cognitive structure by discovery and rule learning. *Journal of Educational Psychology, 64,* 85–97.

Gagné, R. M. (1966). Human problem solving: Internal and external events. In B. Kleinmuntz (Ed.), *Problem solving: Research, method, and theory.* New York: Wiley.

Gelman, R., & Gallistel, C. R. (1978). *The child's understanding of number.* Cambridge, MA: Harvard University Press.

Greeno, J. G. (1977). Process of understanding in problem solving. In N. J. Castellan, D. B.

Pisoni, & G. R. Potts (Eds.), *Cognitive theory* (Vol. 2). Hillsdale, NJ: Lawrence Erlbaum Associates.

Greeno, J. G. (1978). A study of problem solving. In R. Glaser (Ed.), *Advances in instructional psychology* (Vol. 1). Hillsdale, NJ: Lawrence Erlbaum Associates.

Greeno, J. G. (1980a). Analysis of understanding in problem solving. In R. H. Kluwe & H. Spada (Eds.), *Developmental models of thinking*. New York: Academic Press.

Greeno, J. G. (July 1980b). *Forms of understanding in mathematical problem solving*. Paper presented at the meeting of the 22nd International Congress of Psychology, Leipzig.

Greeno, J. G. (1983). Forms of understanding in mathematical problem solving. In S. G. Paris, C.-M. Olson, & H. W. Stevenson (Eds.), *Learning and motivation in the classroom*. Hillsdale, NJ: Lawrence Erlbaum Associates.

Hudson, T. (1980). Young children's difficulty with "How many more than . . . are there?" questions (Doctoral dissertation. Indiana University). *Dissertation Abstracts International, 41,* 01.

Katona, G. (1940). *Organizing and memorizing*. New York: Columbia University Press.

Markman, E. M. (1979). Classes and collections: Conceptual organizations and numerical abilities. *Cognitive Psychology, 11,* 395–411.

Mayer, R. E., & Greeno, J. G. (1972). Structural differences between learning outcomes produced by different instructional methods. *Journal of Educational Psychology, 63,* 165–173.

Mierkiewicz, D. B., & Siegler, R. S. (August 1980). *Preschoolers' abilities to recognize counting errors*. Paper presented at the meeting of the Fourth International Conference for the Psychology of Mathematics Education, Berkeley, California.

Newell, A., & Simon, H. A. (1972). *Human problem solving*. Engelwood Cliffs, NJ: Prentice-Hall.

Norman, D. A., & Rumelhart, D. E. (1975). *Explorations in cognition*. San Francisco: W. H. Freeman.

Paige, J. M., & Simon, H. A. (1966). Cognitive processes in solving algebra word problems. In B. Kleinmuntz (Ed.), *Problem solving: Research, method, and theory*. New York: Wiley.

Piaget, J. (1952). *The child's conception of number*. London: Routledge & Kegan Paul.

Resnick, L. B. (1982). Syntax and semantics in learning to subtract. In G. Carpenter, J. Moser, & T. Romberg (Eds.), *Addition and subtraction: Developmental perspective*. Hillsdale, NJ: Lawrence Erlbaum Associates.

Riley, M. S., Greeno, J. G., & Heller, J. I. (1983). Development of word problem solving ability. In H. P. Ginsburg (Ed.), *Development of mathematical thinking*. New York: Academic Press.

Sacerdoti, E. D. (1977). *A structure for plans and behavior*. New York: Elsevier-North Holland.

Schank, R. C., & Abelson, R. P. (1977). *Scripts, plans, goals, and understanding: An inquiry into human knowledge structures*. Hillsdale, NJ: Lawrence Erlbaum Associates.

Trabasso, T., Isen, A. M., Dolecki, P., McLanahan, A. G., Riley, C. A., & Tucker, T. (1978). How do children solve class-inclusion problems? In R. S. Siegler (Ed.), *Children's thinking: What develops?* Hillsdale, NJ: Lawrence Erlbaum Associates.

Wertheimer, M. (1945). *Productive thinking*. New York: Harper & Row. (Enlarged edition, 1959)

Author Index

Duncker, K., 55, *62*
Dweck, C. S., 146, 153, 155–57, 172, *181,*
187, 188, 200, *212,* 220, *234*

E

Ebbinghaus, H., 2, *14*
Egan, D. E., 294, *314*
Elig, T. W., 193, *212*
Eller, S. J., 151, 162, *184*
Elliot-Faust, D., 9, *15*
Emery, G., 201, *211*
Emswiller, T., 157, *181*
Erbaugh, J., 146, *181,* 196, *211*
Ericsson, K. A., 69, 72–78, *111*
Ermshaus, W., 148, 154, *182*
Ernst, G. W., 83, *111*
Eysenck, H. J., 3, *14*

F

Fabricius, W. V., 11, *14*
Falbo, T., 162, 165, *181,* 193, *212*
Farris, E., 146, 157, *181*
Feather, N. T., 156, *181,* 226, *234*
Feldman, N., 40, *64*n
Feltovich, 86
Fencil-Morse, E., 151, 162, *182*
Ferrara, R. A., 73, 87, 101, 107, 109, *110,*
111, 118, 125, 134, 135, *139*
Ferretti, R. P., 129, *138*
Feuerstein, R., 102, *111,* 118, 135, 136, *139*
Fitch, G., 146, 148, 155, *181*
Flanagan, J. C., 75, *111*
Flavell, J. H., 9, *14,* 17–18, 21, 23, 24, *29,*
31, 32, 36, 37, *62, 63,* 66, 68, 69, 72,
73, 75, 77, 88, *111, 112, 113,* 118–20,
127, 129, 131, 132, *139,* 241, 250–53,
258, 259, 263, *265, 266*
Flores, C. F., 82, *112*
Foote, K., 42, *63*
Ford, L. H., 45, *61*
Forgy, C., 83, *113*
Forrest-Pressley, D., 9, *15*
Foxman, P. N., 76, *111*
Frankel, A., 151, 162, *181, 184,* 189, *212*
French, L. A., 101, 102, 108, *110*
Friedrichs, A. G., 31, 37, *62,* 66, 69, *111,*
118, 120, 127, 131, *139,* 253, 259, *265*

Friedrichsen, G., 34, 35, *63*
Frieze, H. J., 217, *235*
Frieze, I. H., 193, *212*
Fromkin, V. A., 96, *112*

G

Gagné, R. M., 76, *112,* 294, *314*
Gallistel, C. R., 290, 292, 299, *314*
Gardner, E., 69, 71, 88, *112,* 120, *139*
Gardner, W. P., 85, *114*
Geen, R. G., 188, *212*
Gelman, R., 89, *112,* 240, *265,* 290, 292,
299, *314*n
Gerbasi, K. C., 149, 185
Gholson, B., 39, *64*
Gilliard, D., 156, *181*
Gilmor, T. M., 149, *181*
Gitomer, D., 282, 283, 285, *288*
Glaser, R., 4, 5, 10, *14,* 78, 86, *114,* 238,
240, 259, *265,* 271–75, *288*
Glass, D. C., 187, *213*
Gleitman, H., 71, 95, 106, *112*
Gleitman, L. R., 95, *112*
Goldin, S. E., 42, *62,* 83, 86, *112*
Goldstein, K. M., 191, 195, *212*
Golin, S., 205, *212*
Goodnow, J. J., 292, *314*
Green, F. L., 24, *29,* 88, *111*
Greene, P. H., 82, *112*
Greenfield, P. M., 102, 108, *111*
Greeno, J. G., 5, 10, 49, 79, *112,* 238, 245,
265, 289, 292, 294, 295, 297, 300, 303–
5, 307–12, *314, 315*
Griffith, M., 151, *181*
Guilford, J. P., 4, *14*

H

Hacker, W., 6, *14*
Hagen, J. W., 11, *14*
Halasz, F. G., 80, 81, *113*
Hale, G. A., 42, *62*
Halisch, F., 148, 154, *182*
Hammen, C. L., 152, *182*
Hanel, J., 155, *183*
Hanusa, B. H., 151, *182*
Harre, R. M., 209, *212*
Harris, G., 295, *314*

Subject Index

DATE DUE

AUG 1 6 1999			